JOURNEY TO HONOR
BY JAMES G. BUCK

"Journey to Honor," by James G. Buck. ISBN 978-1-60264-209-6 (soft) 978-1-60264-210-2 (hard).

Published 2008 by Virtualbookworm.com Publishing Inc., P.O. Box 9949, College Station, TX 77842, US. ©2008, James G. Buck. All rights reserved. No part of this publication may be reproduced, stored in a retrieval system, or transmitted in any form or by any means, electronic, mechanical, recording or otherwise, without the prior written permission of James G. Buck.

Manufactured in the United States of America.

To Daddy Buck and Dad – Better late than never.

Foreword

They say that truth is stranger than fiction. What they don't say, or at least I have not heard them say it, is that fiction can sometimes get closer to a greater truth than a bare recitation of facts. In his novel of the Twenty-third New Jersey Infantry regiment, a unit from Burlington County, New Jersey, enlisted in 1862 for a nine month service stint in the Civil War, Jim Buck has taken on the task of telling that greater truth. And he succeeds admirably in doing it.

Unlike many novelists, Jim has done a prodigious amount of historical research to uncover that truth, traveling back and forth across the country and digging deep into a trove of primary sources. I can personally attest to the diligence of his work. The vividly written story of Josiah Crispin and his fellow soldiers of the "Yahoos" of the Twenty-third is the result.

Buck's gripping minute by minute account of the furious combat that swirled around Salem Church in May, 1863 as the Yahoos and the First New Jersey Brigade closed with General Cadmus Wilcox's Alabamans, is as close to being there and experiencing Civil War combat as one can get. The horrific aftermath of that fight and the entry into the story of Lieutenant Rufus Jones, a Confederate officer whose sense of honor and compassion link him forever after with a dying Yankee enlisted man, is the stuff of real life drama rendered through the vehicle of fiction. The continuing saga of Lieutenant Jones, a remarkable man in his own right, carries forward the narrative that began in Burlington County, through the horror of Salem Church, to the end of the war.

Joseph G. Bilby
Wall Township, NJ
June 8, 2008

JAMES G. BUCK

Joe Bilby is the author of numerous books about the Civil War and over 250 articles on New Jersey military history and outdoor subjects. Joe is a columnist for The Civil War News, the New Jersey Sportsmen's News and contributing editor for Military Images Magazine. He has appeared on the History Channel's Civil War Journal and the Discovery Channel's Discovery Magazine as an expert consultant on the Civil War and 19th century firearms.

Acknowledgements

Some of my earliest memories of my father, James G Buck Sr, are about him trying to type a transcript of the Josiah Crispin diary in the mid 1950s. I believe my grandfather, Watson Buck, bought the diary at an estate sale and gave it to Dad. Dad finished a partial transcription but never proceeded further with the project. The diary was largely forgotten until I found the old typed pages while going through his papers in December 2006.

Prior to that time, my writing had been limited to research papers about Washington State Legislative activities. I wondered if I had the self discipline to write a historic novel that would do justice to the events in the diary. I decided I did. I started in March of '07. In addition to the diary, Dad left me Pvt. Joshua Kimble's original copy of the *History of the Reunion Society of the 23rd New Jersey Volunteers* and nearly 100 first edition Civil War books. These sources provided valuable primary source documents relating to the events Crispin wrote about.

I live in Washington State which is a long way from a Civil War battlefield. It did not take long to realize I needed to walk in Crispin's shoes. I had to follow the route he traveled or I would be unable to accurately represent what he saw. That meant a trip to Maryland and Virginia. My wife, Donna, and I made that journey in June of 2007. We traveled from Camp Cadwallader in Beverly, New Jersey to Frederick, Maryland, to Fredericksburg and back by the closest roads we could find to those Crispin described. It is only right that Donna be the first to be mentioned in this acknowledgement. This book would not have been possible without her computer skills, creativity in finding sources, assistance with maps, and her support for the project.

We encountered America's best on our journey. The first was D. P. Newton, the curator and owner of The Camp White Oak Church Museum. We arrived at the museum near Falmouth unannounced. I showed D.P. the diary and he softly drawled, "Well, the 23rd New

JAMES G. BUCK

Jersey's camp was over by that swimming pool" as he pointed to the site across the White Oak Road. D.P. provided valuable information and help for the book. I am proud to count him as my friend.

Historians Don Pfanz, Francis A. O'Reilly and the staff at the Chatham Manor and the National Park Headquarters in Fredericksburg deserve many thanks for the help and encouragement they provided.

The story was nearing completion in September '07 when I decided it might be a courtesy to let someone in New Jersey know what I was doing. I contacted Joe Bilby at the New Jersey Civil War Heritage Association. Joe encouraged me to delve deeper into the history of the regiment. He suggested sources that provided little known details about the regiment. This account would not be what it is without Joe's advice and encouragement.

I followed up on Joe's sources in January of '08. What I found required a rewrite of the book. My goal is to tell Crispin's story while providing the most accurate history available. Crispin recorded the events he saw, but he did not know why many of the things he recorded occurred. Only our historical perspective explains what was unfolding around him. Joe suggested where I might find some of those details.

Many very kind people helped with clues to the perspective. Doug Oxenhorn and Maureen O'Rourke at the New Jersey Historical Society in Newark helped me find Henry Ryerson's eye-witness accounts of the Battle of Fredericksburg. The staff of the New Jersey State Archives in Trenton deserves my thanks for tolerating the neophyte researcher who jumped in the air when he recognized the authentic casualty list from the Battle of Salem Church in their files. The staff at the Burlington County Historical Society were equally patient when I found Burd Grubb's explanation for the disappearance of the 23rd Regiment's records.

Arthur House and his staff at the National Archives and Records Administration also deserve a lot of credit. They patiently coached me, a very inexperienced researcher, through a maze of details over the Internet, and did so with ease and generosity.

Several others deserve to be recognized. Forrester L. Taylor's great grand daughter, Melanie Taylor, provided independent confirmation that corroborated many entries in Crispin's diary. Judy Olson, whose *Pemberton, An Historic Look At a Village on the Rancocas*, gives a heart-wrenching account of the effect the war had on Captain Augustus Grobler and his men from Pemberton. Thanks to Bruce Serak and Betsy Carpenter for their help in letting Burlington County people know about this effort to tell Crispin's and the 23rd's story.

Finally, I have to acknowledge my friend and a true friend of the 23rd New Jersey, Russ Dodge. Russ has spent years creating a virtual cemetery for the Yahoos. To date, he has found and recorded over 600 Yahoo graves. Russ provides a valuable resource for all who want to know about the Burlington County Regiment. You can find his site at http://www.findagrave.com/cgi-bin/fg.cgi?page=vcsr&GSvcid=114 .

August 18, 1862 - Drumthwacket Mansion, Trenton, New Jersey

"So, it's settled then," said Governor Charles Olden as he gazed at a glowing spark in the late summer night's sky from the porch of his mansion.

"Yes, we can avoid a draft if we can get 10,478 men to volunteer. With your permission, I will sign General Order Number 4 in the morning and distribute it to the counties and the newspapers," said General Robert Stockton, Adjutant General of the New Jersey Militia. "You seem pensive tonight, Charlie. What's bothering you?"

The Governor continued to stare up at the sky. "See that star that looks like a spark? That's the Tuttle Comet, Bob. They say those things are omens. They foretell war, famine, pestilence and death."

"You believe those tales?"

"I don't know what to believe. What I do believe is the casualty figures I have to look at every morning, men dying of wounds, men losing arms and legs, men dying of God knows what else. For Christ's sake, Jimmy Simpson's whole damned regiment got captured last month at Gaines Mill."

"We already have more men in the field than any other state our size. I want to preserve the Union and get this war over as much as anyone, but I hate sending more of our boys into this fight. You're the General, how long is this going to take?"

Stockton gazed up at the comet for a few seconds and sighed. "I don't know how to answer you, Charlie. It should have been over by now, but McClellan came out of the Peninsula Campaign with an army almost half the size he started with. The disease and battle losses have been frightful. These new cannons and rifled muskets are much more deadly than anything I ever fought with."

"Will the 300,000 men the President called for be enough to get the job done? Can it be done in nine months?"

"I think one decisive battle will end the Rebellion. Most people think that if we send an overwhelming force against the Rebels, beat them and move on into Richmond, it will be all over. Phil Kearney has

1

our New Jersey Brigade whipped into shape. I know we can count on him to get the job done."

"I hope so," said Olden. He gazed at the comet for a long time. War, famine, death and pestilence had already arrived in Virginia. He hoped those plagues would not visit New Jersey and the rest of the Union.

August 26, 1862 - Moorestown, New Jersey

"I do not approve of you going off to war," said Paul Crispin quietly. "It is a violation of your Quaker peace testimony. You could face expulsion from the Society of Friends."

Josiah Crispin sighed. "Father, I don't want to argue. We have talked about this over and over. This war has been thrust upon us. This country is worth protecting. We wouldn't be able to have a Peace Testimony without the freedom we enjoy here."

Paul was clearly uncomfortable. His faith taught him to avoid divisions within the family. This was a serious division.

Josiah continued, "It is pretty easy to maintain a peace testimony when we haven't had a war here for generations."

Paul frowned. "The Longwood Meeting will be held soon. There is talk of disowning members who join the war."

"I think that is unreasonable. It is pointless to have a faith that abhors slavery and not support efforts to end it. The Rebels started this war. They are doing terrible things to Quakers down south. Some of the stories of their behavior are downright barbaric."

Paul gave up. "I am not going to talk you out of this, am I?"

"No, father, I have no wish to make you angry. I am not being disrespectful. I believe the Union must be preserved and slavery abolished. We must make war to end war."

"If you must go, then we have some things to do. There is a meeting tonight. I will go with you to learn as much as we can. I bought this book for you." He handed Josiah a small paperback book called *The Soldier's Handbook*.

He continued, "I want you to read it, so you know what you are getting into. I expect you to act like a gentleman and be the God-fearing man I raised you to be. No drinking, no women, no gambling and no swearing. You will have enough to explain when you meet your maker without falling into bad habits and sin."

Josiah drew a breath. It was obvious his father did not approve of his actions. The book also made it plain he was prepared to let Josiah go. Many of their neighbors had already left for the Army, and some were Quakers. All of the points they discussed had been discussed a hundred times before.

In the end, it came down to a consensus that each individual should be governed by his or her conscience, and not some external authority. Josiah accepted the book. He opened it and started to read.

The hall in Moorestown was noisy. Hundreds of men and a few ladies were gathered to hear about the troop levy and the possibility of a draft.

The people agreed to form an organization to support the volunteers, and elected Henry Warrick as President. Lloyd Hunt was appointed secretary, and they got down to the business at hand.

Warrick read Governor Olden's proclamation declaring a draft, and then read General Order Number 4. The order announced that no draft would take place if the regiments could be filled with volunteers. The order required 728 men to be raised from Burlington County. That was almost enough for a full regiment. Quotas were required for each township. Moorestown's was thirty. That quota was already full, but other companies with openings were being raised all over the county. Captain George Brown's American Blues from Mount Holly was full and marching to Beverly in the morning. Word was that Captain Burnett's Mount Holly Company and Captain McCabe's company from Crosswicks still had openings.

Josiah Crispin looked at his father, Paul. "Looks like I'll have to go to Mount Holly. The Beverly and Burlington Companies are already full."

Paul nodded in doleful agreement. "If you must go, the people at the court house will tell you where they are gathering."

"I can use that $75 bounty, Dad, and I will make $13 a month. I could put some money away."

"I know," said Paul, "but you could also get hurt like Eldridge over there." Josie looked over at the Lieutenant. The officer was home on leave after being severely wounded in the right arm. Eldridge smiled as he accepted a beautiful sword from Warwick with his left hand. There was noisy applause for the hometown hero.

Then Warwick read a resolution that stated the feelings of many people in the county.

Part of the resolution stated: "Resolved, that sympathizers at home with the enemy, are as deep in guilt as the traitors who are in open Rebellion; and that discipline of the law should rigidly visit all overt acts and spoken or written words of treachery; and that all virtuous women, honest men, and innocent children, should unite in putting the traitors under the ban of contempt." The resolution was adopted.

Burlington County had its share of Southern sympathizers who supported secession. They were called Copperheads, and they bristled at the resolution. Bitter friction between them and the Unionist groups was growing every day.

August 31, 1862 - Moorestown, New Jersey

It promised to get hotter and more humid before the end of the day, but for now it was clear and cool. Men all over New Jersey were rising for their last morning at home for nine months. Thousands were heading to assembly areas to join the army.

Josiah was among them. His whole family, along with neighbors Sam Ashbridge, and Charlie and Martha Witcraft, gathered to see him off. Hannah, Josiah's stepmother, was subdued. The gravity of the situation weighed on her.

Josiah's younger brothers, Sam and Frank, were marching around like soldiers. Two-year-old sister Sarah was fussing in her crib on the stoop of the little Crispin farmhouse near Moorestown.

Paul held out his hand, noticing Josiah hadn't grown into his hands and feet yet. He wondered if he would see the boy grow into a man. "I guess it's time for you to go, son, if you want to get a ride to Mount Holly."

Josiah shook hands with Sam and Charlie. There wasn't much to say. The past days had been an endless stream of advice about steering clear of loose women and booze and lectures about the virtues of behaving oneself like a gentleman, along with a strict admonition not to be a hero.

Martha gave him a hug and a peck on the cheek.

Hannah gave him a hug. "Be careful, son, we want you back safe and sound."

"I will. The enlistment is only for nine months, so I'll be back before you know it. They say the nine-month regiments will do garrison duty to free up the army, and the 3-year regiments will do the fighting. I'll be safe and back in time to help with next summer's crops," he said with a grin. "You just take good care of the little ones."

Hannah was a good stepmother. Paul had married her after Josiah's mother, also named Hannah, had died in 1848. Her death had devastated Josiah, his older sister Mary and brother Randy. The already close sibling relationship was drawn still closer by the death. It had been a stressful adjustment to have a new woman in the house, but

Hannah had been kind and kept a good house. Life was easier after the wedding, and when the younger brothers and sister came along, the family was remade whole.

"You boys give Josiah a hug, he has to go," said Paul. Sammy and Frank came over and threw their arms around him.

"Bring me back a Reb sword, Josie," cried Frank. "Me too, Josie, me too," cried Sammy. Paul looked pained. He wasn't sure how to reconcile the war play with his peace testimony.

"I'll do it. Now you two behave yourselves, and help Dad and Randy with the chores."

"Yes, Josie," And they were off around the house, arguing over who was going to be the Reb and who was going to be the Yank. Soon the sound of clashing stick swords could be heard out by the barn.

Mary Crispin walked out of the house with a small package in her hand. "I have a gift for you, Josie."

Josiah looked at her carefully. They had been inseparable since their mother's death, and he knew they were both going to cry when he left. "What is it?"

"You will have to open it and see," she said as she handed it to him.

"Why, it's a diary."

"I thought you might like to write about what you see every day, so you can tell us about it when you get back. Make sure write to us, too. We are going to miss you." She hugged him, both had tears in their eyes.

Hannah came down the steps with baby Sarah. Josiah kissed them and shook hands with Paul again. He walked down the lane to the road. John and Sam Ashbridge and Sam Witcraft tagged along, showing more than a little hero worship. Seventeen-year-old Mary Witcraft waved from the Witcraft farmhouse. Josiah grinned and waved back.

Late in the afternoon, Josiah found a place to stay. The air was still, hot and heavy with humidity. Thunder echoed in the distance. He spent a restless first night away from home. In the morning, he would look for a company.

September 1, 1862 - Mount Holly, New Jersey

Crispin spent the morning reading his *Soldier's Handbook* and watching the companies drill. He noticed friends marching in McCabe's Company. Edwin Lloyd, George Hullings, Joe Conover, Elwood Goodenough and George Howard were all schoolmates. He knew George Sharp and John Sweesley from Moorestown.

He remembered the advice from the *Soldier's Handbook* to look for a company or regiment that rejected "hard cases" and men with vicious habits. With friends from Moorestown, Marlton and Westhampton already in the company, it looked like a good place to serve.

He walked over to them while they were eating lunch. They interrupted their meal and crowded around him. Ed Lloyd looked surprised. "Why, Josie Crispin, what are you doing here?"

"Hello, fellas," he grinned. "I came to sign up."

The men traded glances and started talking at once. The chatter boiled down to, "Josie, this is a big step for a Quaker. It violates the peace testimony. Are you sure? What's Paul say about this?"

They quieted down and Josie replied, "Paul doesn't like it much, but we talked it over and he said it was my decision. I think saving the Union is important, so I am willing to volunteer. I see some of the other boys from our meeting here."

Lloyd smiled as he answered for them. "Yes, this is a very nice group. They are decent men. If you are going to volunteer, it might as well be with friends. I'll take you to Captain McCabe."

Sharp watched them walk toward McCabe, laughing about some inside joke. The two lanky teenagers looked like overgrown puppies. They were obviously best friends. He wondered out loud, "Josie Crispin in the Army? Well, I'll be damned."

That afternoon, Josie signed up to join H Company. Per the Governor's instructions, he received his first month's pay, $13, and a $2 bonus. By the end of the day he was learning to soldier in a field behind the Burlington County Jail.

It was good they had a dry place to sleep. Thunder and lightning passed through the humid South Jersey air most of that night. It was the same storm front that rained on the Battle of Chantilly a hundred eighty miles to the south.

September 4, 1862 - Mount Holly, New Jersey

"The New Jersey Mirror" hit the streets early, and the county went into shocked mourning. General Phil Kearney was dead. The Rebs had killed him in a thunderstorm at the Battle of Chantilly on September 1st. There was a collective feeling of stunned disbelief. The General was a strict disciplinarian, but his men knew they could always count on him to bring them through a fight. He was a larger than life figure that some considered invincible.

In addition to his loss, the county started to see the casualty lists from a second battle at Manassas. The Jersey Brigade had been in the thick of the fight and was still counting its killed, wounded and missing when the paper went to press.

———————

McCabe and Burnett were ready to march to Beverly, but received word to wait at Mount Holly until the 8th. There were almost 3,000 troops converging on Camp Cadwalader, and there was no place to put them all. The camp was so full that Captain Brown's American Blues were billeted at a farmhouse a half mile below Beverly.

Burlington County exceeded its levy of 748 men, so Governor Olden agreed to let the county form a full regiment of 1,000 men.

McCabe's Company was designated H Company. Since McCabe had taken the lead in recruiting the company, the men elected him, 1st Lieutenant David Root, and 2nd Lieutenant James Carter as the officers. Governor Olden approved their commissions.

H Company fielded 102 enlisted men. They elected their sergeants and corporals. The men elected John Sweesley as Section Sergeant, because he was known in the community as a fair man. Reuben Hartman, a construction foreman, was chosen as the 1st Sergeant. His reputation for running a tight job site insured his election.

September 13, 1862 - Camp Cadwalader, Beverly, New Jersey

Brigadier General G. M. Robeson gazed across Camp Cadwalader's parade ground. The camp was set up on a flat piece of farmland on the Beverly – Mount Holly Turnpike. General Robeson was Camp Cadwalader's commanding officer.

It was hard to believe everything that had happened in two short weeks. The volunteers began to arrive at camps around the state at the end of August, and by September 3rd, ten thousand were on the march. When the numbers were counted from all of the camps, Major General Stockton was pleased to inform Governor Olden and the President that the entire New Jersey quota had been filled without having to draft a single man.

The last month had been a whirlwind of activity. The President's call for reinforcements on August 4th had been a logistical challenge for the camp, as well as the entire Army. The General had been given less than three weeks to prepare Cadwalader to receive the volunteers for three entire regiments. His problems were not his alone. The North was not prepared to supply and maintain 300,000 troops on three weeks' notice.

His orders were to support the regimental commanders in organizing and training the infantry regiments. By September 3rd, almost 3,000 men had arrived in camp. Contingents from other South Jersey communities joined those from Burlington County. That meant many mouths to feed. It also meant providing shelter, organization and training time. The wagons bringing military equipment and food from the Camden and Amboy railroad station to the camp had run almost nonstop.

The last companies marched into camp on the 8th. They were the H and I Companies of the 23rd New Jersey. They were five days behind on medical examinations and drawing their equipment. They were also five days behind on the training they would need to be effective fighting units.

The regiment started with over 1,000 men. The surgeons gave each man a medical examination. Some were found unfit, and that pared the number down to 955 enlisted men and 39 officers.

Each regiment had ten companies of about 100 men. Each company was commanded by a Captain. The men were divided into two platoons. The Captain commanded the 1st Platoon, and the 1st Lieutenant commanded the 2nd. Platoons were divided into two sections, each of which was led by a sergeant. Each section had two squads, and each of these was supervised by a corporal. The 1st Sergeant, known as the "Top Sergeant," was the conduit from the officers to the ranks and back for the day-to-day operation of the company.

Volunteer companies were permitted to elect their officers and non-commissioned officers. The officers were then permitted to elect the regimental officers. This could cause trouble, because the election did not take a person's military experience or leadership ability into account.

Robeson's experience in the Mexican War told him the 23rd was somewhat of a problem. The officers elected by the men had no military experience and were having a difficult time learning their drill, let alone teaching it to their soldiers. They elected John Cox Colonel. He seemed to be more of a politician than a commander. In the few days since his arrival, Robeson noticed he was overbearing and tended to like his drink.

George Brown, a dentist from Mount Holly, was elected Lieutenant Colonel, and Alfred Thompson, who also had no military experience, as major. They both appeared overwhelmed by their responsibilities.

The days since September 3rd had been filled with organizing the companies and getting them equipped. Each man was supposed to receive a blue blouse, two flannel shirts, one pair of pants, two pair of flannel underdrawers, an overcoat, two pairs of wool socks, one pair of shoes, a fatigue cap, one wool blanket and one rubber blanket, a knapsack, a haversack, half a shelter tent, a canteen and mess kit. The enlisted men were each supposed to draw a "stand of arms" that included a musket, cartridge box and bayonet. Not counting personal gear, the whole kit weighed about 60 pounds. Unfortunately, Uncle Sam was short on muskets, canteens and shelter halves.

The late summer days were spent instructing the new recruits in military life and teaching them the "school of the soldier." This was supposed to consist of facing movements, position of attention, manual of arms, and the basics of marching. They were still mostly farm boys and artisans, but they were beginning to understand what it meant to soldier. Fortunately, they were a far cry from the volunteers in 1776 that needed hay and straw tied to their feet so they could tell left from right. Drilling without muskets was awkward for all involved. Performing the manual of arms and the musket loading drill was impossible.

The 23rd could not move to the front until it was mustered into federal service. That was supposed to happen on September 3rd. There were so many new units being formed in the North that there were not enough officers to muster all of the regiments. Finally, Captain William Royal of the 5th U.S. Cavalry had arrived last night. This morning Robeson watched as he supervised mustering the 23rd into the Army. Each man's name was recorded, and the officers signed their Loyalty Oaths.

In the afternoon, Colonel Cox and his staff paraded the troops in an albeit awkward display of marching prowess, and Captain Royal administered the Oath of Allegiance. As the ceremony was concluding, a bald eagle circled the parade ground as if to add a blessing to the oaths taken to preserve the Union and pledge allegiance to the flag. It was a proud occasion for all concerned.

Robeson knew the news from the war was not good. Pope's forces were mauled at the Second Battle of Bull Run at the end of August, and the Army had fled, more than retreated, into the fortifications at Washington. His friend, Brigadier General George Taylor, and 331 Jersey men from the Jersey Brigade had been lost at Bull Run Bridge. Another friend, Phil Kearney, was killed at Chantilly. Many of the wounded would not be rejoining the ranks. The Army was in turmoil after the defeat. Pope had been relieved, and McClellan was frantically trying to reorganize the dispirited forces. Jeb Stuart's Cavalry had raided as far east as Alexandria and even threatened to attack Washington across the Chain Bridge. Lee and the Army of Northern Virginia crossed the Potomac near Berlin on the 4th of September. McClellan and the Army of the Potomac were moving toward Frederick to protect Washington and Baltimore. It was still an open question whether Maryland would secede and join the Confederacy. The war was going badly. There was no question in Robeson's mind that this new regiment was going to see action. It was only a matter of time. Robeson hoped they would measure up.

———— —— ————

That evening, the men had some free time. Crispin, Lloyd, Hullings, Sharp, Conover, Goodenough, and Howard were lounging on the parade ground's grass. They were joined by Cornelius Terhune, a scarecrow of a man from Monmouth County.

"Well, this life doesn't seem to be too bad. We get three squares a day and a roof, and we're getting paid," said Sharp. "All we have to do is march around."

"You think we did the right thing electing McCabe and the officers?" questioned Elwood.

"McCabe seems all right," said Sharp as he swatted a mosquito. "Don't think much of Cox, though. Seems like all he can do is yell."

The others nodded. Crispin said, "We've only been here a few days and we have a lot to learn. All this saluting and marching and right face, left face, about face gets confusing."

"Cox says he wants to take the regiment into action as soon as he can. Hell, we don't even have guns yet," complained Terhune.

"Before we signed up, I heard we was supposed to just be garrison soldiers, Corn." said Sharp. "We were to watch the forts while the regular army and the 3-year boys fought the war." The others nodded in agreement.

"I know," said Terhune, "but that Cox is hot to make a name for himself. I hear he's trying get orders for the regiment to join the New Jersey Brigade and march us out of here right away."

"I heard the Governor won't let us leave the state until the Army sends us guns. He's afraid they will just use us for laborers," added Lloyd.

Crispin thought for minute. "I'm worried. After that fight at Manassas last week, I am afraid the Army's going to need a whole lot more men. I hope we do garrison duty, but …"

"Did you see Cox when we were drilling this afternoon?" asked Elwood. "He looked like he was drunk, swears a lot, too. He was chewing out one of the Lieutenants, and I think the Colonel made the mistake. Didn't seem right."

"Elwood, we are in the Army now. We are privates. A lot of things don't seem right, but we volunteered, and we have nine months before we are free," grinned Crispin.

September 26, 1862 – Philadelphia, Pennsylvania

The regiment formed at Camp Cadwalader early in the morning, carrying the muskets they had been issued the day before. They marched out the gate, and crossed the Camden and Amboy tracks into Beverly. They paraded down Broad Street to the docks. The steamboats "New York" and "Washington" were waiting. By 10 AM they were on the riverboats for the trip down the Delaware River to Philadelphia. A cheering throng of well-wishers saw them off, but these men were going to war, and many of the cheers were accompanied by tears.

Reports were just coming in about a great battle near Sharpsburg in Maryland. McClellan had finally won a battle for the Union, but it was a bittersweet victory. The cost had been appalling. Rumors said nearly 25,000 men had been killed or wounded. Little was known about how the New Jersey Brigade had fared.

Lee was back in Northern Virginia - still a threat to the North. The well-wishers had good cause to be worried about their men.

Robeson watched them go, and he was worried, too. The troops and officers had barely mastered the school of the soldier and company drills, let alone battalion and regimental maneuvers. The officers and NCOs were unskilled at marching and did not understand their responsibilities. They had been issued their muskets the day before, and those were obsolete, broken-down 1842 flintlocks that had been converted to fire with percussion caps. They had never fired a shot, were unskilled with the bayonet and had never been on guard. They needed to know more than fifty bugle and drum commands to function in the field, and they had practiced less than half. They still had no canteens. He hoped they wouldn't see combat soon. In their current condition, they were nothing but cannon fodder.

The boats made a good start, but before long the steam engine on one broke down and another had to be found to finish the trip. What should have been a routine seventeen-mile ferry ride to the Washington

Street Wharf took seven hours. The unit made it to Philadelphia around 5 PM. They formed into companies, marched up Washington Street and made a left turn onto Otsego Street.

Fifty yards to the south, the patriotic citizens of Philadelphia were waiting for them. Families and friends of the regiment had been invited to a "sendoff" at the Cooper Volunteer Refreshment Saloon, and Colonel Cox was not about to disappoint them. Cox assembled his troops and called them to attention. "Men, the good people of Philadelphia have put together a good-bye feast for you. I expect you to be gentleman and make the regiment proud. We will assemble in four hours and march to the railway station. Be ready to march at 9 o'clock. Enjoy yourselves and say your good-byes. We won't be back until June. Stack your arms and follow your officers."

The officers commanded, "STACK ARMS."

Crispin looked at his Squad Leader, Corporal Rue. "What's stack arms mean?"

Rue looked around and pointed to a group of men who were arranging their guns in a pyramid. "That's stack arms," said Rue smugly.

Sharp watched as the Colonel entered the door. He glanced around the squad and said, "Every time Cox opens his mouth, I get mad."

"Keep your tongue, George," Sergeant Sweesley said. "I can't have you disrespecting officers."

"I know, damn it, but the man has no idea what he's doing. The way he has treated us is terrible. If he leads us into a fight, he's going be the first one shot, and it'll be by his own men."

Sweesley growled, "I ain't going to tolerate that kind of talk, George. You stop it right now. That's an order."

Sharp stared at Sweesley for a time. "I'll stop, but you know I am right."

Sweesley returned his gaze and said nothing. Sharp was right, and he wasn't the first man Sweesley had heard say the same thing.

The women of the Southwark neighborhood had awakened one morning in April 1861 to find lines of troops waiting for a train at the Philadelphia, Wilmington and Baltimore Railroad depot at Washington Avenue and Broad Street. It didn't take long for the women to start handing out coffee. It also didn't take long to figure out there were going to be a lot more troops coming. A patriotic fervor gripped Philadelphia; the people wanted to do something to show their appreciation for the sacrifice these men were making to preserve the Union. Soon, an association was formed. The owners of the cooper shop had suspended their barrel-making operations because of the war, and they offered the building to the association. So was born the Cooper Shop Volunteer Refreshment Saloon, and almost every unit that passed through Philadelphia on its way to the war stopped for a visit. The saloon was a two-story brick building about thirty-two feet wide and one hundred fifty feet long. A tall brick chimney rose from the back of the building. Off to one side was a covered area where troops could wash up before eating. Above it all flew a giant stars and stripes on a stout flagpole.

The officers marched the troops into the building in single file. There was seating for over a thousand men in the giant room, and it was immaculate. As the men entered the building, they saw six giant tables. On the left side of the room were two that were one hundred feet long. To the right of them were three more tables that stretched the length of the room. There was a table for the officers to the right of the entrance, and another side table for soldiers to the left. In the back of the room was a huge fireplace with a brick and iron oven. It had a boiler that could make one hundred gallons of coffee an hour, and another for boiling hams and vegetables. Gleaming cooking utensils covered the back wall. Each table was covered with a pressed white linen tablecloth, on which were arranged white stoneware plates and mugs, cutlery and all the things necessary for serving a proper meal. Bouquets of fresh flowers were set as centerpieces.

No one had to coax hungry young soldiers to go to a party after three weeks of Camp Cadwalader food. The wonderful smell of boiled ham and cabbage wafted out the door and down the cobblestone street. Almost a thousand men started salivating in unison. As they took their seats at the tables, the ladies of Philadelphia served them boiled ham, corned beef, bologna sausage, fresh bread, butter, vegetables, cheese, milk, tea and coffee. All ate their fill.

"Have you ever seen such a sight" said Rue. The saloon was festooned with flags, red, white and blue bunting, and patriotic banners and garlands of evergreens. The Philadelphia hosts and hostesses beamed as they served the new soldiers the hearty feast.

"Never in my life," munched Crispin. "This will be something to tell everyone back home about."

Colonel Cox and the officers were joined by Bill Cooper and Walter Mellon of the Refreshment Saloon Committee. "Colonel Cox," smiled Cooper, "Welcome to the Refreshment Saloon, and thanks to the 23rd for its service to the Union."

"Mr. Cooper, Mr. Mellon, we should be thanking you for this wonderful meal," said the colonel. "This is such a beautiful setting, and the food is so good. How can you do this for all of us?"

"We have a grand community that donates all the food and labor. It's the least we can do for you," said Cooper.

"It is amazing to see how organized this is, and everything is so clean."

"Yes, sir, the ladies of the committee have put it all together themselves. Mrs. Cooper, Grace Nickles, Sarah Ewing and many others work at it every day. We've fed almost every regiment that's come through the city. You know they all take the trains from here to Baltimore and Washington."

"How many can you feed in a day?" asked Major Thompson.

"The most we have fed in a single day is about three thousand," was greeted by smiles and appreciation from all the officers. "Dr. Nebinger is here, if any of your men need medical attention."

Surgeon Cook looked up from his plate, "You even have a doctor here?"

"Yes, sir," smiled Mellon. "We have plans for a hospital, and there's talk of a soldiers' home." The officers and men visited for almost an hour; the time passed quickly. By unspoken agreement, all avoided talking about the news from the war.

Before anyone knew it, it was 9 o'clock. The regiment formed and Colonel Cox called the members of the Refreshment Saloon to the street. He made a short speech. "I can speak for all the men when I say how grateful we are for this meal. The patriotic people of Philadelphia will always have our gratitude and thanks. Three cheers for the Cooper Volunteer Refreshment Saloon." While the men were cheering, Cox shook hands with Mellon and Cooper as the regiment marched off to the depot.

The only transport available was boxcars, so the 23rd New Jersey Volunteers loaded up and headed south like freight on the Philadelphia, Wilmington and Baltimore Railroad. Most of the troops had never been on a train, let alone more than twenty miles from home, thus the trip through southeast Pennsylvania was quite an experience. The power and speed of the steam engine fascinated them. The puffing engine, the whistle and click-click, click-click of the wheels on the tracks was mesmerizing. They were traveling faster than a horse could run, at twenty-five miles an hour. They had managed to cram 1,000 troops and their equipment into or on seventeen cars.

Darkness obscured the scenery as they rolled through Delaware. The train reached Wilmington late in the evening. Hundreds of

Wilmington's citizens were gathered by torchlight along the tracks to wish the boys well, but the showstopper was half a dozen ten-year-old girls who stepped out on the platform and sang the Star Spangled Banner for the soldiers. The people cheered at the troops, and the troops hurrahed back to them. The train arrived at the Susquehanna River around 1 AM. The river was too deep and broad to bridge at Port Deposit in 1862, so the regiment crossed on the PWBRR steam ferry *Maryland.* The *Maryland* had two decks. The upper deck could carry twenty-one rail cars, while the lower deck was reserved for passengers, freight and baggage. They picked up another engine on the south shore and resumed their trip to Baltimore.

September 27, 1862 - Baltimore, Maryland

The train arrived at the PWBRR station in Baltimore between 5 and 6 in the morning. Daylight revealed a station full of wounded troops returning from Antietam. Orderlies were carrying them on stretchers from the train, loading them into wagons and taking them to hospitals all around Baltimore. This was another thing the boys had never seen before. Many of the wounded were missing limbs; some more than one. Bloody bandages were everywhere. The bodies of those who had not survived the trip were covered with coats and blankets on one side of the platform. The boys had never seen nor smelled the results of war, and it sobered every one of them.

At 6:30 they marched to the Union Relief Association for breakfast. The URA was Baltimore's counterpart to the Cooper Street Refreshment Saloon, and was much appreciated. The troops formed up at 7:30 AM and marched to the side of the Baltimore and Ohio Railroad. There, they boarded passenger cars for Washington.

The chugging steam locomotive had lulled most of the troops on the train to sleep. Edwin Lloyd was gazing out the window as the train started over a bridge when he saw the first sentries. He nudged Josiah. "Josie, look at that. There are guards on the bridge."

A few minutes later they saw another group of guards with two cannons guarding another bridge. By now, everyone in the car was up and looking out the doors.

"Lieutenant Root, Sir? There are troops along the railroad."

Root nodded his head and looked out the door. "Boys, we are getting closer to the South, and things have happened around here."

"Are there any Rebs here? Are we going to be in a fight?" Just then the train passed two new earth revetments with cannons pointing down a road. Now everybody was all ears.

People in the car quieted to hear what Root was saying. "We don't have to worry about Reb troops around here. There is a whole army between us and them, but there are a lot of Rebel sympathizers and there has been trouble here. Last summer, before the Battle at Bull Run when President Lincoln called up the troops, a group of Rebel partisans burned bridges and tore up some tracks to keep our reinforcements from using the line to get to Washington."

"Regiments had to take that ferry boat you rode last night from Port Deposit to Annapolis, and then march to Washington. Then they crossed the Potomac and took the hills around Alexandria and the Chain Bridge. Our troops got there before the Rebs, but it was a close thing. Until they did, the government was in range of Confederate cannons."

"How come the bridges are painted white?"

"The railroad did that to make it harder set them on fire. They are painted with many coats of whitewash."

All conversation stopped as the train broke out of a woods. The troops gazed out the door in silence. Thousands of workers were clearing the forest and burning piles of trees as far as could be seen on both sides of the track. The clearing stretched almost two miles toward the capitol. Thousands more laborers were building huge earth fortifications on hills around the city. Revetments of compacted earth twelve to eighteen feet thick could be seen. Each was surrounded by a dry moat and an abatis of sharpened poles. Artillery of all shapes and sizes was everywhere.

"Those must be the forts we are going to garrison," shouted Terhune above the noise of the train.

Fort Lincoln could be seen off to the right, with Fort Saratoga and Fort Bunker Hill stretching of to the West. Others dominated the hilltops in both directions, commanding roads, railroads, shipping lanes and river fords. A garrison flag, a giant set of U.S. colors, flew from each. In the distance was the skyline of Washington, and the unfinished white marble Capitol dome dominated the skyline. The dome seemed to reach to the clouds. It was the tallest building any of them had ever seen. The boys were getting excited. They had spent a little time in Philadelphia and traveled through Wilmington and Baltimore, but now they were going to the Capitol.

The regiment arrived in Washington at 2 PM. As they pulled into the station, another train full of wounded was being unloaded. More wounded from Antietam were arriving every hour. They got off the train and lined up for dinner at a place called The Soldier's Retreat. Dinner was a big disappointment when compared to the sumptuous meal they were served at the Cooper Shop. It consisted of some kind of warm swill made out of greasy bacon fat and decayed vegetables left over from meals served to other soldiers several days before. They ate little and, in keeping with the name of the establishment, retreated.

Following dinner, they marched to East Capitol Hill, where they pitched camp on the grounds overlooking the Anacostia River. They had a brief chance to look around as the sun set. To the south was the broad Potomac. The wreck of a large bridge was nearby, only the pilings remained. The famous Long Bridge was upstream from the wreckage. It was built on timber pilings with planks for a roadbed and stout timber railings on the sides. It was not very high above the water. It stretched off across the river toward Fort Jackson. They could see the defensive fortification built just to protect it from the enemy.

The Long Bridge was an invaluable asset to the Union Army. Security around it was tight. Sentries monitored every move anyone made, and many batteries of artillery covered all the approaches. At least four guardhouses were located at each end, and tents marked the quarters of the sentries. Anybody crossing was subject to search and intense questioning as the White House was three miles away. There would be no spies, infiltrators or enemies allowed on the bridge. The bridge was too weak to handle locomotives and trains, but it could handle single rail cars. Rails had been laid on it. They watched as a team of horses pulling a freight car started off toward Fort Jackson on the Alexandria side. An engine was waiting there to move the cars to their destination. Telegraph poles lining both sides of the bridge were festooned with wires. This was the main telegraph communications hub between the Army in Virginia and Washington. Beyond the wire to the West lay the Blue Ridge in the late September haze. Somewhere over there was the Army, and so many bloody battlefields.

September 29, 1862 – Washington, D. C.

The 23rd awoke to a busy day of improving their camp. When they completed improving their camp, they proceeded to police and level a parade field on which they could drill. The officers supervised the sergeants; the sergeants supervised the men. By 3:30 in the afternoon, all were ready for battalion drill. Everyone returned to their tents to get ready. At 4 PM, the drummers sounded assembly and the regiment formed ranks. Much to everyone's surprise, Colonel Cox was not there to command the drill. After a few minutes, Lieutenant Colonel Brown sent Captain Parmentier to get him.

The men could not hear what the Captain said, but something was wrong. Soon Captains Smith and Carr joined First Sergeant Herbert and Sergeant Moore at the Colonel's tent. Some dispute was developing. Within seconds, Cox came out of the tent in a drunken rage. He was swearing and yelling at the top of his lungs. He struck the captains and sergeants with the flat of his sword and staggered back into his tent. Brown and the other officers were embarrassed. It took a few minutes to gather their wits. In the end, Brown held battalion drill without Cox.

After the drill, the men had the evening to themselves until "call to quarters." They cooked their suppers and muttered about Cox. Later, they wandered toward the Capitol and the Mall to see the sights. Josiah, Ed Lloyd, George Hullings and Joe Conover joined the crowd. Crispin acted as the tour guide. He was well read and knowledgeable about the city. Washington was fast becoming the most fortified city in the world. Artillery and cavalry units jammed the streets, and ambulances and supply wagons bustled in every conceivable direction.

A runaway team of mules careened past them, out of control. "I think I know that driver," said Lloyd. "I think he's from our headquarters." Panic-stricken people fled like chickens from a farmer's dog, desperate to get out of the way.

They continued west to the United States Capitol and wondered at the mammoth size of the unfinished building. Work had been halted when the war started, but President Lincoln just ordered the work to start again. He said working to preserve the Union should go hand in hand with working to build the nation's capitol. The dome was uncompleted. They could see it was being built very strong to support the huge cast bronze statue of "Freedom" that was to adorn its top. The statute was so big, it had to be cast in nine pieces. It would not be assembled until it was put together on the peak. The building seemed to reach to the sky. The derrick used to lift the construction materials dwarfed anything they had ever seen.

Next they wandered south to the Washington Memorial. Already, the building was huge. The engineers said it would rise 550 feet. It was going to be the tallest building in the world when it was done, but not a stone had been had been laid since 1856. The impending war and government financial difficulties stalled the project. The boys would have liked to look at the fifteen-foot thick walls at the base, but they could not get to it. A huge cattle corral surrounded that end of the mall. It was the beef depot for the Army of the Potomac. Thousands of cattle were assembled here before being driven over the Long Bridge to hungry units in the field. The boys left the corral and started towards the White House. A train of wagons carrying feed for the cattle blocked their way for a few minutes. They gazed at the beautiful mansion, and then the young soldiers returned to their camp at dusk. Others did not. Some caroused around the town all night.

———————

Regimental Quartermaster Lieutenant Abel Nichols had pulled some strings and gotten authorization to get four wagons for the regiment. Each was pulled by a team of four mules. Nichols and Quartermaster Sergeant Ed Dobbins got a detail and headed for the remount facility to pick up the mules and bring back the wagons. However, the mules at the remount facility were wild. Breaking them entailed throwing a rope around their necks, dragging them out of the corral and hanging on until they stopped bucking. After much pandemonium, the 16 animals were harnessed and hitched to the wagons. Dobbins was trying to bring them back to East Capitol Hill when his team started running away. He had a wild ride through the streets of Washington until the team came to rest against a porch. They got back to camp about dark. Dobbins was a nervous wreck.

———————

While the boys were touring the city, three captains and two non-commissioned officers were visiting a member of the Inspector General's staff.

"Let me get this straight," said the officer. "Colonel Cox was drunk at 4 in the afternoon, and struck you with his saber?"

The five men were standing at attention. Parmentier said, "Yes sir."

The IG paused. "Gentlemen, I am not questioning your integrity, but did others see this happen?"

"Yes sir, the regiment was forming and most of the men saw what happened," said Parmentier quietly. The other four nodded in agreement.

The officer was silent for a long time. "Gentlemen, this is a serious court martial offense. It is at least drunk and disorderly while on duty, and conduct unbecoming an officer and a gentleman. Are you sure you want to press these charges? Because once you do, there will be no turning back. It means court martial for the Colonel, and if he is found innocent, you are done in the Army. You may be done anyway."

Parmentier didn't squirm. "Sir, it happened, it's not right. My men's lives are at stake, and I cannot deny it and look them in the eye. I am willing to press charges, and I believe these men are too."

The IG looked at each man, and each nodded his head in agreement.

"I will have to name you as witnesses. Do you agree?"

Each mumbled their agreement.

"Was anyone else involved?"

The men looked pained and glanced at each other. "Yes, sir," said Parmentier. "Doctor Cook was also drunk, but he didn't do anything."

"I can't very well charge the Colonel and not the doctor if both were drunk on duty."

"Sir, Doc Cook has been a good regimental surgeon so far. Isn't there anything you can do to help him out of this scrape?"

"That will be up to the Court Martial, Captain. They can take extenuating circumstances into account. I am not sure what extenuates drunk at 4 o'clock in the afternoon of a duty day. I will draw up the charges, but you are walking a thin line here, gentlemen. If any of you treats Colonel Cox or Surgeon Cook with the least disrespect, you could find yourselves up on charges, too."

The five men indicated they understood. They signed their statements, and the IG dismissed them. Then he sat down to draw up the charges.

Somewhere to the southwest, Robert E. Lee was rebuilding the Army of Northern Virginia. His command was recruiting new soldiers and rounding up stragglers. Rest, food, shoes and fresh clothing were making the Confederates a threat again. They were disciplined, battle-hardened and committed to their cause.

To the West, the Army of the Potomac was licking its wounds near Sharpsburg. McClellan started the battle with over 70,000 men and lost more than 12,000 men, a staggering one out of six. He was working hard to reorganize and re-equip his army and give his units some rest. Rumor was, the two armies had lost almost 25,000 men killed, wounded or missing, and the battle only lasted one day.

New Jersey had fielded a full brigade of almost 3,200 infantry early in the war. It was one of the few brigades that contained men from just one state, and was the 1st Brigade of Brigadier General William T. H. Brooks' 1st Division of the 6th Corps. Colonel Alfred Torbert was the Brigade Commander. Normally a brigade had four regiments, but the strength of this unit had been steadily whittled down during the last year. It suffered terribly during June's Peninsula Campaign when it lost over 1,000 men and 30 officers at Gaines Mill and Malvern Hill. Fortunately, over 400 men from the 4th regiment who were captured by the Rebels were paroled and rejoined the brigade. At the end of August it lost 339 killed, wounded or missing, along with its Brigade Commander, Brigadier General Taylor, at the Manassas Bridge. Three weeks later, it was back in action near Sharpsburg. Attacking through Crampton's Gap at South Mountain, it lost another 40 killed and 132 wounded.

These losses, combined with deaths and disabilities caused by wounds and disease, left just a little over 1,000 men present for duty. The brigade needed a new regiment to bring it back up to strength. Orders went out to move the 23rd to Frederick, Maryland as soon as possible.

Many Union Army units were facing similar manpower problems. Disease and combat losses, coupled with the near rebellion by some Union Army units after President Lincoln's announcement of the Emancipation Proclamation on September 22nd, made it essential for the Army to start consolidating its forces. McClellan might be slow and cautious, but there was no doubt in his mind that he was going to need a lot more troops the next time he met Lee, and he didn't think that would be too far in the future.

September 30, 1862 - Washington, D. C.

A dispatch rider arrived at Regimental headquarters early in the day with orders. The Regimental Duty Officer aroused a number of very grumpy men, including a very grumpy colonel. Their orders were to strike camp, march back to the railroad station within the hour and board a waiting train for Frederick, Maryland.

Colonel Cox had a hangover and was in a foul mood. He had been out until the early hours of the morning, and had way too much to drink. Command of the regiment was not all it was cracked up to be. He was up all hours of the day and night. His officers had trouble getting the troops to do what they were told, and other officers were beginning to talk about the unit. He had already had to report six desertions in less than two weeks, and now he had orders to move, and his troops were all over Washington. His own men were threatening to shoot him in the back if he led them into battle. The company commanders knew they couldn't account for all of their men, so sergeants were sent to comb the streets for troops who had been out all night. Eventually, the regiment was ready to return to the station with no one missing movement. That was no small accomplishment. Fortunately, no trains were available.

Cox was dissatisfied with the muskets the regiment had been issued before leaving Beverly. He made such a fuss about it that someone had got around to sending an officer from the Ordnance Department to inspect them. To no one's surprise, the horrified officer took one look at the weapons and condemned the lot on the spot. Shortly after the inspection, a wagon delivered the regiment's long-awaited canteens.

Late in the afternoon, the regiment was ordered to the Washington Arsenal to get newer muskets. It was a 3-mile march to the arsenal and, of course, a 3-mile return trip. Colonel Brown and the Captains tried to convince Cox to leave the heavy packs at the camp under guard, but Cox would have none of it. He was still smarting from his confrontation the night before. They carried their full packs and gear both ways in the Indian summer heat. Confidence in the colonel further deteriorated.

The proceedings at the arsenal went a long way toward soothing the troops. They exchanged their old muskets for newer 1842 .69 caliber smoothbores.* The .69 caliber round ball could be loaded with three smaller buckshot balls. The combination was called "buck and ball", and was quite deadly at close range. The troops were ecstatic to

*This is an interesting dilemma. All agree the muskets issued to the 23rd at Beverly were substandard. A letter in the NJ Mirror dated November 6 says "they were not worth breaking up." That letter goes on to say the regiment marched to the arsenal "to change our guns for better ones." Crispin's diary says: "We have new and effective guns. We leave our old ones." An October 9 New Jersey Mirror article says, "The next day they were supplied with Enfield muskets and at 11 o'clock at night they started for Frederick." The dilemma occurs because page 626 of Bilby/Coble's *Remember, You are Jerseymen* shows the New Jersey Quarterly Ordnance Reports for the 23rd. The reports say the Regiment was armed with 900 "smoothbore muskets altered to percussion" on September 25, 1862. These were old .69 caliber flintlocks that had been modifed to accommodate percussion caps. Quarterly reports for Fourth Quarter 1862 and First Quarter 1863 say the regiment was armed with a combination of 1842 smoothbore and altered .69 caliber muskets. I find it difficult to believe two US Army inventories did not know what firearm they were looking at, so this book assumes the Yahoos were armed with 42s. The number of muskets inventoried in the quarterly reports provide an interesting view of the unit's attrition.

get rid of their condemned old weapons.

As the regiment stood in line to receive the new muskets, they gazed around and were amazed to see the firepower being assembled at the arsenal. Long rows of artillery and caissons of all calibers were lined up. Some of the siege mortars were at least 5 feet in diameter. Giant stacks of cannon balls stretched off in all directions.

When the last man was issued his weapon, the regiment marched back to the railroad station, but the train was still not there. The troops spread their bedrolls and slept in the street.

"This isn't what I expected," complained Sharp.

"It's not what any of us expected, George," answered Sergeant Sweesley. "We are in the Army. We go where we are ordered and do what we are told."

"Well, damn it, it ain't fair. We are supposed to be garrison troops."

"I wish it were so, but it's not. The officers say we are going west to join the New Jersey Brigade."

"Those people who recruited us lied."

"Those people didn't know what they were talking about. You saw all the wounded they were bringing from Antietam. There's a war on, boy, plans change and you'd better get used to it."

"But, John, we ain't trained enough to fight yet, and that damned glory-hungry colonel is going to get us killed."

"George, you can complain all you want. If an officer hears you, he is going to make it tough for you. I have told you before, watch your mouth. It's for your own good."

October 1, 1862 - Washington, D. C.

Crispin spent a restless night on the dirt and cobblestones, and finally got up to walk around the streets of Washington. He viewed with wonder its beautiful parks and the magnificent statues. A little more sightseeing took him past the residences of several noted men, such as Benton's and Fremont's. At last darkness fell, and again the regiment slept upon the streets. Finally, late in the evening a train came to move the troops to Baltimore and then west to Frederick.

The railway system had orders to move the 23rd to Frederick, but it took almost a day to round up a train. Congress had authorized the President to seize the nation's railroad and telegraph systems in early 1862. In practice, there was no need for seizure in the North.

Cooperation was the rule--when a train was needed, it appeared. Seizure only occurred when Union forces captured a line in the South.

October 2, 1862 - Frederick, Maryland

They chugged almost all the way back to Washington Junction through the darkness and the cool fall air of early October. At the B&O yard south of Baltimore, they switched to a B&O track heading west to Frederick. The fact that a train was made available as soon as possible did not mean it would be a nice train. The boys boarded a train of bedraggled old Baltimore and Ohio freight cars with no windows or doors.

The troops resented the condition of the cars. In order for the whole regiment to fit on a single train, some men had to ride on the roofs. Partway through the journey, the rotten wood of the roofs collapsed. Fortunately, no one was hurt. The rotten old cars provided little shelter, and the continuous rush of the 25 mile per hour wind, sparks and smoke from the steam engine made travel extremely uncomfortable. They suffered through it, wrapped up in their overcoats, wool blankets and gum blankets. The cars were nothing but bedraggled old freight cars when they left Washington. When they rode into Frederick, the men had torn the rotten wood apart. They were nothing but bedraggled old flatcars. Some still had frames.

The train and the regiment pulled into B & O's Frederick Station at 2 PM. They had passed through some intimidating country with mountain gorges, swift rocky rivers and deep valleys. They crossed the new Monocasy Creek Bridge. The Rebels had blown up the old one just three weeks before. Parts of the ruined bridge were still scattered all over the banks of the stream.

They debarked from the train and marched to an encampment about one and a half miles west of the city in a cornfield. They did not have their tents with them, so they built little shelters out of cornstalks and fence rails.

The Union Army had pushed the Rebel rear guard out of Frederick and over the Cotoctin Mountains just before Antietam. A series of sharp skirmishes around the town and up the road toward Middletown had devastated the country. They marched through fields of trampled crops. Fences were torn down, trees were riddled with bullets, and some buildings were burned. The sight of wounded amputees at the railroad stations had sobered them. The devastation of the countryside sobered them even more.

General Lee had hoped to recruit troops in Maryland and convince the state to secede, but the devastation had cooled the secessionist ardor of many of the people. They weren't quite ready to, in Lee's words, "throw off the yoke of oppression" and cast their fortunes with the Confederacy.

Crispin scoured the devastated grounds hoping to find some relic he could take home. Eventually, he found an old Rebel cap and pulled off a button.

October 3, 1862 - Frederick, Maryland

The regiment had an easy day. Colonel Cox presided over what some men would call drill, and then dismissed the troops for the rest of the day. The men amused themselves as they saw fit. In the afternoon, Crispin decided to take a walk and found his way to an Army mortuary unit. He would have avoided it if he had known what it was. By the time he figured it out, it was too late. The doctors were preparing the bodies of slain soldiers for transport to their home towns for burial. Railroads would not transport decaying bodies, so they either had to be embalmed or sealed in metal containers. He saw sights that day which left an enduring and deep impression on his mind. Some of the most horrible corpses were beyond imagination. One was an officer who had been disinterred after being buried for one month. Crispin would not describe him in his diary.

October 4, 1862 – Frederick, Maryland

Army regulations prescribed the daily activities of an infantry unit. The commander sets the times for reveille depending on the month: 5 AM in May, June, July and August; 6 AM in March, April, September and October; and 6:30 during the short winter days in November, December, January and February. In camp, the commanding officer also prescribes the hours for roll calls at reveille, retreat and tattoo, along with the daily dress parade, guard mounting and training.

Unfortunately, Colonel Cox was not very familiar with the regulations, and there was no one to explain the importance of establishing the daily military routine. The lack of training and discipline observed by Robeson when the unit left Beverly was not improving.

Reveille was at the prescribed 6 AM, and roll call was taken. Any organized activity and schedule after that was pretty haphazard. After breakfast, Crispin and some of the squad members decided to go to the Monocacy and wash. After a tiresome journey of three miles they came to the creek. It was a chilly, but welcome relief to wash away the accumulated grime of the march in the early October heat. The leaves on the trees were just starting to change. Fall was starting, and the beauty of the fields and surrounding hills charmed the troops.

They stopped at a farmhouse on the way back from the creek to talk to the owner. The farmer gave them cider and apples and told them about some startling incidents connected with Jackson's invasion of the state.

They returned to camp, and another day of training was lost. Unbeknownst to them, Colonel Cox was beginning to understand his duties. Things would be changing soon.

October 5, 1862 - Frederick, Maryland

Brigadier General Gabriel Paul was reading his dispatches near Frederick, Maryland. He had been promoted to General of Volunteers just a month ago, and was still getting used to wearing stars. They had been a long time coming. Paul graduated from West Point in '34 and had fought in Mexico with distinction. After the war he fought Indians near Santa Fe, and had been in the fight at Glorieta Pass early in the war. Now he was a brigade commander in the 1st Division of the 1st Corps.

He signed off on several orders when he came to one that directed him to find the 23rd New Jersey Volunteers. He was to present the Colonel and the Surgeon with charges for a court martial and relieve the Colonel. Paul frowned. No one liked to do this type of thing, but his experience with almost 30 years in the Army told him it had to be done. He called his aide to get their horses, and they set out to find the 23rd.

After an hour of searching, the General headed southwest of Frederick and found the 23rd in a cornfield. They had no tents. They were living in shelters of fence rails thatched with corn stalks. There was no guard, there was no drill, no training schedule and almost all of the soldiers were off somewhere. Colonel Cox had already had "a few drinks" and was not in command of the regiment. Years of professional military experience went into action instinctively. A chastened Cox was relieved, charged with two court martial offences, arrested and presented with a copy of the charges in very short order. The Surgeon suffered the same treatment. As Brigadier General Paul rode away from the awful encampment, he reconsidered his opinion about serving court martial charges. He realized he could grow to like this.

Josie had spent the day exploring the area with his friends. They looked at the Rebel's abandoned camp at Prospect Hall. Then they hiked up to Fairview Pass to see where Stuart's cavalry fought Pleasanton. They were walking into camp around 5 o'clock when Lieutenant Root and Sgt Sweesley found them.

"Where in the hell have you been?" barked Sweesley as First Sergeant Hartman paced back and forth. "You men fall in and stand at attention when I am talking to you."

The boys looked sheepishly at each other and fell into a line. It wasn't a very impressive line. Sweesley called them to attention and had them dress right as Hartman glowered at them.

"We were exploring, Sarge," mumbled Conover.

"You were gone yesterday and all day today, and I have had my ass chewed royally over it. Let's all get a few things straight. You are not home on the farm, where you go and do what you like. You volunteered for the Army and gave your word you would do a good job for the Union. You are not on a picnic, and this is not a sightseeing tour. Nobody leaves this camp unless he is on orders or has a pass. Is that clear?"

A set of mumbled replies was cut off by a sharp, "IS THAT CLEAR?"

"YES, SGT SWEESLEY."

"Rue, you get these men back to their tents and get their kits cleaned up. First Sergeant Hartman will be inspecting your stuff in thirty minutes."

Thirty minutes later, the whole platoon was standing in formation. The use of inspections as a tool for discipline is well known in every army. It took an hour to look over everyone's equipment. Hartman gave a long list of shortcomings to everybody in the platoon. When he was done, they were given thirty minutes to fix their kit, and then they were inspected again. Hartman finally dismissed them near dark.

It took Dobbins and O'Niel four days to drive the mules from Washington to Frederick with the regimental wagons. The men were able to get their tents, camp chests and cooking utensils. They had just enough daylight left to abandon the cornstalk shelters and set up a respectable camp.

The troops gathered around the cook fires, had their supper and ate some of the bread they had bought earlier. It was the most expensive bread they had ever heard of. They also shared some pies and milk one of the men had bought in town.

The small talk around the fire was subdued. "Sweesley seems a little carried away with himself," said Sharp as he stared into the fire. The others started to mumble their agreement.

27

Rue broke in before they could finish. "I am afraid Sweesley is right."

"Awe, for Christ's sake, not you too, Joe?" groaned Sharp.

"Now hear me out, George. John Sweesley and me have been neighbors for a long time, and I know the man. He didn't like doing what he did, but he didn't have much choice. He is responsible for what goes on in this squad; he can get in big trouble if things don't go right. I am talking about jail type trouble." The rest of the squad was listening.

"While you were gone, the Colonel was arrested for that drunken tirade back in Washington. Doc Cook got arrested, too. Brown got all over the Captains, and they got after the Lieutenants, and they got after the Sergeants. Things have got to change around here or it's going to get real miserable. The Provost Marshals are looking for AWOLs and deserters from the whole army, and we don't want to get mixed up in any of that. You just can't go running off when you want to anymore."

"And another thing, there is a lot of work to be done around here, and when someone runs off everybody else has to pick up the slack. Fair is fair, you guys need to stick around and do your share."

Sharp nodded his head and said nothing. The rest of the boys stared into the fire. After a few minutes, Conover looked over at Josiah and asked, "What did you see over there, anyway?"

"The place is shot up pretty bad. It's all trampled. There's lots of bullet holes in the trees. The fences are all pulled down, and we saw an old apple tree with a cannon ball hole clean through it." The group around the fire murmured their amazement.

Conover looked interested. "Did you go all the way up top?"

"Yup, I saw where the Rebel batteries were planted. It was so high up they could shell the towns and villages. Our troops must have had a terrible time attacking that position. You can see a long ways up there."

"How long?"

"Well, I could see all the way to the Blue Ridge and Alleghenies off to the West and the Potomac River to the south. There sure are a lot of meadows, and corn fields everywhere you look."

Gradually, the small talk trailed off and people started to head for their tents.

Josie hadn't told them about looking toward home. He didn't say anything about staring toward New Jersey for almost an hour. He tried to will himself to see that far, but he couldn't. He didn't want them to know how homesick he was.

October 8, 1862 - Frederick, Maryland

The regiment was awakened at 5 AM with the drummers beating reveille. The rumor was that they were marching to Bakersville to join the Jersey Brigade and Brooks' First Division of the 6th Corps. Soon the rumor proved true, and there was much confusion as the troops broke camp, packed up their kit and prepared for their first march.

They marched through Frederick past a cheering crowd, with many a woman waving the stars and stripes from their front porch.

The column passed out of Frederick and turned toward Boonsboro on the National Road. The highway was started in 1806 during the Jefferson administration, and eventually reached from the Cumberland Gap in Maryland all the way to Vandalia, Illinois. It was thirty feet wide and made of crushed stone. A constant stream of Conestoga wagons and any other form of rolling stock that could be pressed into service moved thousands of settlers and their animals to the Ohio and northern Mississippi River Valleys between 1810 and 1835. After that, railroads and canal systems picked up the bulk of the traffic. Many of the inns and taverns along the way had fallen into disrepair as travelers went elsewhere. The road had seen better days.

The regiment crossed a fertile plain and started the long climb over the Cotoctin Mountains. They marched until 11:30, and then waited in a cool shady wood for the heat of the day to pass. Ambulances full of wounded passed them heading east, and army wagon trains clip-clopped by in the heat going west. They swatted horse flies and mosquitoes and kept a watchful eye out for ticks.

They were back on the road at 4 and had an easy downhill march. Evidence of the mid-September skirmishes between the retreating Rebels and advancing Union forces were all around them.

They crossed Middle Creek on a temporary bridge next to the blasted remains of the Middle Fork Bridge just after dark. Even in the darkness, they could see the blackened foundation. At 10 PM, they went into camp on a hill covered with trees.

Ed Lloyd and Josie got their shelter halves buttoned up and pitched their two-man tent. Ed was sick, but Josie slept fine.

While the regiment marched toward Boonsboro, even though he was officially under arrest, Colonel Cox rode ahead to meet his new commander at Bakersville,. His reception at headquarters was cold. He cooled his heels for a long time outside the house Colonel Torbert was using as headquarters while orderlies came and went. Brigadier General

Brooks rode up and barely acknowledged him as he walked into the house.

Ten minutes later, Cox was summoned. He and his staff walked proudly into the house, stood at attention and saluted. "Colonel Cox reporting for duty with the 23rd New Jersey Volunteers."

Colonel Torbert was standing and in pain. He had been wounded at Crampton's Gap just three weeks earlier. General Brooks was sitting in a chair off to one side.

Torbert returned Cox's salute. Torbert was West Point, Class of '55, so he knew how to handle this meeting. "Thank you, Colonel." He looked around the room at his and Cox's staffs. "Could you gentlemen please wait outside for a few minutes?"

Cox's staff and everyone except Brooks quietly left the room.

Cox was getting nervous. He knew he was in trouble, but had hoped for a friendlier reception than this. Clearly, these men already knew about the court martial. "Where are your troops?" Cox noticed he had not been told to stand at ease, so he was still standing at attention.

"Well, sir, they left Frederick this morning and I expect them here tomorrow afternoon. They will camp west of Middletown tonight, and finish the march in the morning."

"What is your strength, sir?"

"The regiment has 35 officers and 943 enlisted men, Sir."

"Excellent, Captain Grubb will arrange for your bivouac area."

"Yes sir, I will have Lieutenant Colonel Brown meet with him." He was still standing at attention. Cox wasn't much on military courtesy, but he knew he didn't dare stand at ease without permission.

There was an awkward silence for a few seconds, broken by General Brooks. "Colonel Cox, I have been informed that you were drunk on duty in Washington and struck several captains and sergeants with your sword."

Cox turned scarlet. He stammered, "Sir, I don't recall much about that day. I had a drink or two in the afternoon with friends, and…"

The General was quiet until the time grew painful. "It had been reported that you were abusive to the men when they informed you it was time for drill, and you struck them with your sword."

Cox was squirming.

"Colonel Cox, General Slocum takes a dim view of officers assaulting his men. He also tolerates no drunkenness or conduct unbecoming an officer in his command. I will not tolerate this kind of behavior from my enlisted men, and I am certainly not going to tolerate it from my officers. We have enough trouble trying to maintain discipline in this army without friction between the officers and the men."

Cox's mouth was moving, but no sound was coming out. Governor Olden would hear of this humiliation.

General Brooks continued. "General Paul relieved you of command, and you are to remain under arrest until a general court martial is convened. The Surgeon will continue his duties."*

The timeline for the Court Martial of Colonel Cox is pretty cut and dried. General Paul penned a note on 10/5/62 from the "Provincial?? Brigade" saying that he had "transmitted charges against Col John S Cox ... and found the regiment very much disorganized and was obliged to take immediate action by placing the Colonel in arrest." General Paul notes, "A copy of the charges were furnished to the accused."

Special Order 69 dated 12 October 62 appoints BG J Newton, US Vols, BG J J Bartlett, US Vols, Col S S Buck 2nd NJ Vols, Col Brown 3rd NJ Vols, Col G W Town 95th PA Vols, Col G A Cake 96th PA Vols, LTC A D Adams 96th PA Vols, members of a General Court Martial to convene at 9 AM on 13 October, 1862.

The General Court Martial convened on October 13, but did not release guilty findings until 17 October. The muster roll for Cox dated 13 SEPT TO OCT 31 shows Cox forfeited one month's pay and was reprimanded per General Order #25 dated October 17, 1862.

Crispin's diary first mentions the reading of court martial charges at a parade on October 17th and records Cox had been under arrest for two weeks. Crispin's entry says Cox "was acquitted on the grounds that he would be severely reprimanded and one month's pay deducted." That is not an acquittal. Crispin also says, "The Colonel bore it with a very decidedly cool manner" indicating Cox was annoyed with the proceedings.

A letter to the "New Jersey Mirror" from "S" dated 10/17 and published on 11/6 describes Cox striking two captains and a sergeant with his sword on what appears to be September 29th. It goes on to say Cox was fined one month's pay, severely reprimanded by General Slocum and reinstated on 10/17. Reinstated is a questionable term. Torbert's approval of Cox's resignation indicates he was ordered to appear before a board of examination. A letter from Burd Grubb to Edwin Schermerhorn on April 13, 1910 says Cox was never restored to command after the Court Martial. Crispin only mentions the Colonel resigned on November 11.

Cox was so shocked he couldn't think of anything to say.

General Brooks bellowed, "ADJUTANT."

The captain ran into the room and snapped to attention. "Yes, sir." It was obvious there were others outside the door eavesdropping. That didn't seem to bother the general. He didn't flinch.

"Have the Division duty officer arrest Colonel Cox and hold him until I say different."

The Adjutant stared at the general to the point of gawking, and the general stared back. The Adjutant shook his head and stammered, "Y-Y-Yes sir."

"Dismissed," snapped the general. The Adjutant led the stunned colonel from the room. He was held under arrest in his tent.

Torbert let out a long sigh. He had been commander of the brigade less than two months, having replaced General Taylor who died of his wounds at the end of August after the ill-fated fight at Bull Run Bridge.

He looked at Brooks and frowned. "I never like to see that, sir."

"Me either, Al, but we can't tolerate that kind of behavior. Not only that, that regiment is a mess. Gabe Paul says the men were living in lean-tos made out of fence rails and cornstalks. There was no training going on, and most of the men had wandered off. To make matters worse, the 15th New Jersey ain't much better. It would be criminal to put either regiment in a fight right now. There's damned little discipline and no training. If we put them in the line, they would either run or die before they could get off a shot. That leaves the rest of the brigade with a hole in its line and puts even more men at risk. We can't let this rest. It has to be fixed. Do you have any suggestions for a temporary commanding officer?"

"Protocol says the Lieutenant Colonel should get the job."

"Do you know Lieutenant Colonel Brown?"

Torbert shook his head, "No sir, never met him."

"We don't have a lot of time, Al. The President and the country are insisting that McClellan go after Lee and get this damned war over as fast as possible. We could march any day now. There're 1,000 men out there that could help, but they aren't ready. I need a commander that can whip them into shape, protocol be damned."

Torbert thought for a few seconds, "Yes sir. I think Ogden Ryerson would fit the bill."

"Ryerson? Is he healthy enough to do the job?" Brooks knew that Ryerson had been wounded at Gaines Mill back in June and had spent 3 weeks in a Richmond prison before being paroled.

"Sir, he rejoined the 2nd right after Crampton's Gap. One of his wounds is still open, and he is still weak from the fever. He is quite a soldier."

Brooks thought for a minute. The brigade had lost a lot of men at Crampton's Gap, and he knew Torbert had also been wounded in the battle just 3 weeks before. "Where is he?"

"Sir, he should be over at the 2nd New Jersey."

"Round him up and have him take a look at the 23rd. They need a proven leader, and if he can handle the job, he sure fits the bill."

"Yes sir. I will handle it myself."

"Al, get somebody else to do it, and you go lay down, for God's sake. You look like death warmed over."

"Yes, sir," croaked Torbert.

October 9, 1862 - near Middletown, Maryland

The drummers had beaten reveille at dawn on the 9th, and Ed, Josie and the rest of the squad packed up and made ready to march.

They marched off early. The day was already hot when they started. Humidity was so high it limited visibility. They passed the Shoemaker house, which was still being used as a way station hospital from the South Mountain and Antietam battles. It was made of brick with a field stone foundation and a front porch that extended the whole length of the front of the house. The porch was covered with wounded. Several ambulances were parked out front, and a line of soldiers were filling their canteens at the well.

The road was steep enough for the troops to have to lean into each step. It was hot, slow, sweaty work. By the time the column marched up the long, steep mountain road to Turner's Gap, the roadside was littered with sick soldiers, wool blankets, overcoats, sets of long underwear and almost anything a young soldier could throw away to lighten his load.

The march halted for a break near the South Mountain Inn, and that's where the problems started. When it was time to reform and move on, many of the troops had wandered off to look at the destruction wrought by the battle.

There was little vegetation on the hills, because most of the timber had been cut to make charcoal. Rebel and Union gun positions were visible, along with bullet and shell-riddled landscapes and buildings. Fresh graves dotted the landscape, and the stench of decaying horses and cattle made a surreal contrast to the beauty of the surrounding countryside. Clouds of vultures and crows soared over the hills. These sights, plus the large numbers of artillery shells and remains of battle-damaged equipment, proved irresistible to young minds that had never seen such a thing. It was too hot to march, but not too hot to wander around.

By the time the boys returned from the battlefield, the column was gone. While they were away, someone had gone through their packs. Josie's vest and overcoat were gone.

It was an easy two or three-mile hike from Turner's Gap down the road in the narrow winding valley to Boonesboro and Josie, Ed and Joe Conover caught up with the column around 10 AM. The regiment had stopped to wait for the heat of the day to pass. Crispin and Lloyd found a German family who fed them a lunch of tomatoes, potatoes and bread and butter with sausage.

At 4 PM the march resumed, but the stifling heat made Conover and Crispin sick. The boys fell out of the march once again and found a place to stay in Keedysville.

The bulk of the regiment wandered into the bivouac site near Bakersville late in the afternoon, in the dust and oppressive heat. Veteran soldiers who had been fighting for over a year watched a rag-tag bunch of kids set up camp next to the 4th Regiment. They moved like a mob. Any semblance of a formation was coincidental. There was no cadence, so it bore little resemblance to marching. Stragglers stretched back up the road out of sight. To top it off, they came into camp singing, "We'll Hang Jeff Davis from a Sour Apple Tree."

Torbert had ridden over to watch the regiment come in with Colonel Bill Hatch of the 4th New Jersey, along with the CO of the 2nd New Jersey, Sam Buck, and Buck's regimental Lieutenant Colonel, Henry Ogden Ryerson. For some reason, Ryerson went by his middle name, and everyone knew him as Ogden. Torbert was thinking about offering him command of the 23rd. The four men sat their horses off to the side of the road and watched the spectacle.

Every officer dreams of commanding his own unit, so this was a bittersweet moment for Ryerson. He had been shot through both thighs in June, and the wounds were still healing. He had spent three weeks in July in a Confederate POW camp, been flat on his back with fever in August, and gotten back to the 2nd New Jersey in September just after the fight at South Mountain. The look on his face right now was akin to, "What have I done to deserve this?"

Ryerson looked down at ground for a few seconds, and looked over at Torbert. "Sir, you actually want me to command those yahoos?"

"Ogden, there is no place to go but up with them. It can't get worse. Are you up to it?" The two colonels knew what was going through his mind. They tried hard not to smirk.

The moment of truth had come. Ryerson could turn down this command, and no one would probably think less of him. At the same time, there was no telling how long it would be before he would be offered another. The war could end, and he might never have another chance at a regiment of his own. Ryerson sat up in his saddle and looked Torbert in the eye. "Sir, I am up to it. I thank you for your trust in me. I will put this unit in order."

"I am sure you will, Colonel. These yahoos need a good man, and you're it," smiled Torbert.

Buck and Hatch both offered their congratulations and rode back to their units. Torbert sat with Ryerson for a few more minutes. "Henry, I am putting you in for a promotion to Colonel. Your rank needs to be equal to the other regimental commanders. Our New Jersey colonels will work with you, but some others may try to push you around. I won't stand for that."

"Thank you, sir."

"I have a problem with Colonel Cox that you need to be aware of. The Colonel is burning up the telegraph lines back to Trenton, complaining to Governor Olden that he is being treated poorly. He is one of Olden's political appointees, so this would be politically sticky if the circumstances were not so cut and dried. Major General Parker wired me about the case, and I wired the details back to him this morning. Cox is going to be held under house arrest until they decide what to do with him. General Brooks and I talked, and if Cox is still in the Army after the Court Martial, I will order him before a Board of Examination. They will force him out for incompetence, or he can resign honorably. I need you to get in there as soon as he is gone and start putting that unit in order."

"Thank you, sir. That is very helpful information. I will do my best."

"I have also had a chance to speak with Lieutenant Colonel Brown. He seems like a good man, but has no idea of how to command a regiment. Frankly, he's intimidated by the prospect. He tells me he will help you in any way he can."

Ryerson nodded again. "Sir, I hear the Regimental Surgeon is also being court-martialed."

"That's right. He was drunk along with Cox, but he has not been relieved. It seems the men like him and are going to ask the court for leniency. You will need to keep an eye on him."

"Yes, sir, I will."

"Good luck, Colonel. I will assign you as commander as soon as Cox is removed."

Ryerson saluted. "Yes, sir. Thank you. How is your wound, sir?"

Torbert looked at him and smiled. "Hurts, how about yours?"

"It doesn't hurt so much now. It still hasn't closed. I rode a horse for the first time last week, and it stiffened up very painfully. It is easier to ride now, but I am weak and don't seem to be getting stronger."

"Well, have Oakley keep an eye on it."

October 10, 1862 - Keedysville, Maryland

Crispin and Lloyd followed the road the regiment traveled from Keedysville to Bakersville. The unit was long gone. They took their time to see the sights on the way. They were out of the mountains, so they had an easy march across a landscape of farms and gentle slopes. They passed Pry's Mill, several farms and a number of field hospitals. Soon they started seeing wreckage of the Battle of Antietam.

At noon they stopped and cooked a rabbit they had killed, and finally wandered into the regimental area late in the evening, only to be met by an angry Lieutenant Carter.

Carter stood them at attention and read them riot act. By the time he was done, they were thoroughly cowed. They had no doubt that if they skipped out again, they were going to fined and maybe even put in jail.

Hartman was furious when he found out Conover and their baggage was still at Keedysville. He agreed to get them excused from drill in the morning to bring Joe and the equipment back. Corporal Rue would accompany them to make sure they didn't wander. Things were changing in the regiment. Army regulations were starting to be enforced. No one would be permitted to leave the regimental camp without a pass, and no one would fall out of a march without permission.

The assignment of Rue to baby-sit them hurt Crispin's feelings. He had not considered that skipping out was wrong, and having his Quaker integrity questioned bothered him.

Torbert was turning in for the night and trying to get a little rest. His wound was painful and he was not in a good mood. The losses his units had suffered at Crampton's Gap, and the previous battles bothered him greatly.

He lay in bed for a while and couldn't sleep. Soon, an annoying undercurrent of noise began to disturb him. It shouldn't have been there. "Taps" had sounded, and the troops were supposed to at least be quiet, if not asleep. This noise sounded like a riotous, drunken party. It sounded like hundreds of men laughing, drinking, fighting, arguing ... violating the military discipline of the camp.

"Aide," barked the Colonel.

"Yes sir," replied the Colonel's aide.

"What is that infernal God damned racket?"

"Why sir, it sounds like that new unit, the 23rd is having a party."

The poor aide could not have picked a worse thing to say to a wounded, grouchy, full Colonel, West Point graduate.

Torbert erupted, "YOU GO OVER THERE AND STOP THAT 23rd REGIMENT YAHOO NOISE!" The term Yahoo was catching on.

October 11, 1862 - Bakersville, Maryland

Crispin and Lloyd woke to the first storm of autumn. The wind was blowing steadily, and the weather was cold and threatening. They got their pass and together with Rue headed for Keedysville on the Keedysville Road. It was a four-mile trip, and it was a much easier walk than before. The weather was cooler, and the gently rolling farmland was a welcome change from the long, hot climbs in the Cotoctin and South Mountains. The previous week's activities had also improved their physical condition. After about an hour they passed the Smoketown Road, which ran south toward Sharpsburg. About a quarter mile further, they came to the Antietam Army Field Hospital on the south side of the road.*

This field hospital was the first of its kind in history, and was actually set up like three large tent cities. There were over 600 patients being cared for, and all had been wounded in the recent Battle of Antietam. These men were too badly injured to be moved by wagon to Frederick or beyond.

Major Jonathan Letterman, Medical Director for the Army of the Potomac, had been tasked by General McClellan to improve the treatment of wounded soldiers. His ambulance plan had been a success during and after Antietam, and now his hospital plan was being put to the test. Letterman left Surgeon Bernard Vanderkieft, a recently arrived Dutch doctor and surgeon in the U.S. Volunteers, in charge of the hospital.

The boys were walking by and peeked around the corner of a tent.

*Per Letterman letters.

37

An orderly standing by a bloody table saw them and invited them over.

Rue didn't think a short stop would cause any harm, so they dropped their knapsacks.

"We have a very sick man here, and we are going to have to take his leg off in a few minutes. You boys want to watch?"

They weren't too sure about this, but nodded their heads yes.

The man was lying on a stretcher. He was conscious, but not really aware the three men were there. The orderly explained that the man had shot during the battle of Sharpsburg. He had been hit by a Minnie ball in the thigh above the knee. The ball struck the bone and split in half. Half of the bullet had been removed a week ago. The other had not. Now, the leg was infected and terribly swollen, and gangrene was setting in. The leg had to come off or the patient would certainly die.

The operating table was outside, so the surgeon could have the best light. Another orderly came over and washed the leg, the table and the instruments down with cold water. A surgeon came up, glanced at the boys and looked over the leg. He wore a white apron that was covered with blood. This wasn't the first amputation he had done this morning.

"Orderly, go ahead and give him the chloroform, and not too much."

The orderly took a napkin that had been folded into a cone and used a dropper to dispense an eighth of an ounce of chloroform in the cone. He walked to the head of the bed and placed the cone just above the wounded man's nose and mouth. This allowed the man to still freely breathe, and prevented the chloroform from getting on his face and causing blisters. The man thrashed about for fifteen or twenty seconds while the drug took effect, and then passed into a deep sleep.

The surgeon quickly put a tourniquet on the thigh above the wound and tightened down. When he was sure the blood flow was stopped, he took a knife and pushed it through the muscle up the leg from the infected tissue until it hit the bone. He quickly cut diagonally upward toward the knee and rotated the cut to the opposite side of where he started. He then reversed the knife and made a second cut downward in the same way. When he was finished, he had and upper and lower flap of skin and muscle that looked like a fish's mouth.

The surgeon quickly carved the tissue away from the bone as the orderly held the healthy flesh out of the way with a piece of cloth called a two-tailed retractor. Then he used a bone saw to sever the bone. There was blood, but not as much as one would expect.

The soldier slept peacefully. Next, the surgeon took a tool that looked like a j-shaped ice pick. He found each major vein in the thigh, pulled them out and tied them off with silk thread. Finally, he stitched the two flaps together with a continuous stitch of silk thread and motioned for the chloroform to stop.

The orderly washed off the stump with cold water, removed the tourniquet, bandaged it and carried the amputated leg to the pile of limbs that was accumulating outside of the hospital. When it was all over, the man was put on a stretcher and taken to his hospital bed. The orderly brought in another bucket of cold water, rinsed out the cloth retractor, sloshed it over the table and the surgeon's instruments, splashed a little on the surgeon's hands, and they were ready for their next operation.

Crispin, Lloyd and Rue were ashen. They had never dreamed of seeing anything like that before. The whole thing had taken less than ten minutes. They mumbled a tentative thanks to the orderly and went back to the road.

"Boys seemed a bit squeamish," said the surgeon. The orderly just grinned.

It took a while for the boys to find something to talk about after viewing the amputation. At first it seemed almost indecent to speak about it. Eventually they found their tongues, and by the time they got to Keedysville they were fine.

Joe was where they left him, and still too sick to walk. They found a patrol from the provost marshal and left Joe with them, so he wouldn't be considered AWOL. There was a military post office set up, so each wrote a letter home and posted it.

They quickly gathered their baggage and headed back to Bakersville. They didn't see the orderly when they went past the hospital, but they noticed the pile of limbs outside the tent was bigger.

It was nearly 5 PM when they got back to camp. There was a fine surprise waiting for them. The 4th New Jersey had come to visit, and there were plenty of friends from home. The first words out of Ed Lloyd's mouth were, "Guess what we saw today?"

Lieutenant Colonel Brown's orderly found Surgeon Cook at his hospital tent. His assistant surgeons Bowlby, Elmer and Hetzell were there with him.

"Sir," the private began, "Colonel Brown sent me to let you know there will be a meeting of all Regimental surgeons and medical personnel at the Antietam Field Hospital over by the Smoketown Road on Monday, October 13th at 1 PM. He will join you there, Sir."

Cook told the private they would be there, and excused him. All wondered what this was all about.

October 12, 1862 - Bakersville, Maryland

The camp was in an uproar. Jeb Stuart and 1,800 hand picked Confederate cavalrymen had ridden all the way around McClellan's Army. Just hours ago, the enemy had ridden near the regiment's old camp near Frederick. The realization that the enemy had been so close to a place they had left only four days prior sobered the men.

Sweesley's squad was getting ready for their first experience at guard duty. The troops were intimidated by the duty, especially in light of the Confederate raid. Sergeants and corporals spent hours helping each man learn his general orders. "I will walk my post and quit my post only when properly relieved…" Companies were training by going on short marches to and from their guard posts, and doing so with full packs.

The guard posts stretched over a mile along one flank of the brigade. Early in the evening, the hundreds of lighted tents in the encampment provided a beautiful spectacle. Overcoats were the rule, and fires were permitted at each post. Even with a relief every two hours, it was a cold night.

There was a general feeling of disgust that Stuart had invaded the North without opposition. This was the second time he had ridden all the way around McClellan's Army. The Officer of the Day and Sergeant of the Guard took special care to make sure the newcomers stayed alert. They were not about to be caught slacking.

October 13, 1862 - Bakersville, Maryland

The Court Martial convened at 9 AM, as required by Special Order 69 of the previous day. Brigadier Generals Newton and Bartlett, along with Colonels Buck, Brown, Town, and Cake and LTC Adams sat on the court. They were busy men, and each had his own unit full of troubles to look after. They listened to five witnesses swear that Colonel John S. Cox was drunk and disorderly on duty and assaulted five men in his unit by striking them with the flat of his sword. Cox's lame defense was unconvincing. They were not sympathetic. They found him guilty and sentenced him to forfeit one month's pay and be severely reprimanded by General Slocum.

Things went a little easier for Doctor Cook. The Court received a letter signed by most of the officers of the regiment asking for leniency for the Surgeon. It read:

Headquarters
Camp near Bakersville
23rd Regt NJV October 13, 1863
Judge Advocates

Respected Sirs,

Owing to the capabilities of William Cook MD attached to the Twenty-Third Regt NJ Vols as surgeon.
We the undersigned field and line officers of the said regiment do most humbly apply to the mercy of the court in passing sentence on said Wm Cook MD in not removing him from his position in the regiment – on his oath for nonoccurrence of charges during the balance of time in which he is under the United States service.

Very Respectfully,
Most Obedient Servants

William G Winans, Adj   *George Brown, Lt Col*
Reading Newbold, Cap. D Co   *A Thompson Major*
Lieut Wm Frazer Co I   *Augustus Grobler Capt*
Capt Samuel B Smith Co F   *Francis Higgins Capt*
Lieut EW Kirkbride Co F   *Lewis Ayres Lieut*
Lieut James Budd   *Lieu Alfred Leeds*
W G Abbott, Chaplain   *Lieut L H Ashley*
Lieut D B Newbold   *Lieut Sam W Downs*
Lieut Edward Rigg   *Samuel Carr Capt Co C*
W Parmentier Capt Co K   *Henry A McCabe Capt Co H*
Asst Surg David G Hetzell MD   *Lieut D S Root*
Asst Surg Robert W Elmer
Henry Polhemus, Hosp Stew

The Court did find the doctor guilty as charged, and fined him two months' pay. They did take the wishes of the officers into account and permitted him to remain as the Regimental Surgeon.

JAMES G. BUCK

General Brooks' orderly announced that Colonel Torbert was waiting to see the General. Brooks frowned. He had known this meeting was coming as soon as General Bartlett had told him the outcome of the Cox court martial. "Send him in and you wait outside, son," said the General.

A furious Torbert marched into the tent and very formally saluted. "Colonel Torbert reporting, Sir."

"You wish to see me, Albert?"

"Yes sir. How in the hell did that court not kick that idiot Cox out of the army, sir?"

Brook sighed. He knew Torbert didn't drink and had no patience for those who over-indulged. He also knew Torbert was hoping to replace Cox with Ogden Ryerson.

"Relax, Al, and sit down," said Brooks quietly. Torbert slowly relaxed and sat in one of the General's folding chairs. "Al," said the General quietly. "All you have to do is tell Cox he can't take command of the 23rd until he passes a Board of Examination. You know he will fail."

Torbert was not convinced. Brooks could see it, and went on.

"Al, I've been in this army a long time. Cox was charged with drunk and disorderly and conduct unbecoming. That's serious, but not worthy of dismissal unless he does it again."

"But Sir, he's totally incompetent."

"You and I both know that, and that's the beauty of this thing. If he is as bad as Gabe Paul says, there will be no denying it to anyone on the board. He will never pass the examination. He can resign with an honorable discharge, or be publicly cashiered for incompetence when he fails. Do you think he wants to go back to Mount Holly with that on his record? His neighbors would never let him live it down."

"Al, I just got word that Ogden Ryerson had a relapse of the fever and is back in the hospital at Burkettsville. He couldn't take command right now, anyway. Lieutenant Colonel Brown is going to have to do the job for the time being. I want you to get a training schedule established in that regiment. Get some officers down there and start making them into soldiers."

Brooks had caught Torbert off guard about Ryerson being back in the hospital. The General was right. Lieutenant Colonel Brown had to remain in command for the time being. The brigade staff would keep him and the regiment on a tight training schedule. Torbert finally shook

42

his head in agreement. He needed to buy time for Ryerson to get back on his feet.

"Yes sir," he replied.

———————

Cox was still a Colonel, but he was not commander of the 23rd NJ. Torbert informed him that he was being ordered before a Board of Examination. Cox could not resume command of the 23rd unless he passed the Board. Torbert could not ignore the poor condition of the 23rd, and it was Cox's incompetence that had put the unit in that condition. The board would certainly fail Cox, and that would be decidedly embarrassing. Torbert gave Cox two weeks to decide to face the Board or resign with an honorable discharge. The clock started ticking.

———————

The scene at the Antietam hospital was crowded. Regimental and Brigade Commanders and their surgeons from every unit in Brooks' Division were there. The meeting was conducted by the Division Medical Director, Edwin K Taylor.

The men were seated on benches in a tent that must have been made from four hospital tents. The director started, "Thank you for coming. The purpose of our meeting today is to brief you on our medical activities here after the Battle of Antietam."

"Before I start, I want to reiterate Army of the Potomac General Order 147 and discuss Medical Director Letterman's October 4th Circular and the impact it may have on your commands. The Corps Commander ordered all regimental commanders and their surgeons to be here so there is no confusion about these new Army policies."

The audience was genuinely attentive. They knew the importance of battlefield medicine, and any opportunity to help make it better was an opportunity they wanted. Most had lost men in battle, and a few had been very happy to see a surgeon in the last twelve months.

"Let's review General Order 147 first. It was issued on August 3rd when the Army was still at Harrison's Landing. You might remember after organizing the ambulance corps, we left most of the ambulances at Fort Monroe when we returned to Washington for 2nd Manassas. The ambulances were ordered to Washington as quickly as possible to be ready for what turned out to be Antietam. Unfortunately, only about half arrived in time. Some were lost in a storm on Chesapeake Bay, and

43

more were held up by the railroad when the Rebs destroyed the B&O railroad bridge at Monocasy Creek southeast of Frederick. This caused some disorganization in implementing the general order. The ambulances that were available were allotted to the left wing of the Army and served well. Most of the wounded were removed from the field by 2 PM of the day following the fight. The wounded on the left could not be recovered as quickly, because of the lack of ambulances. Major Letterman believes this unintended side-by-side demonstration proves the Ambulance Corps concept works and is important to improving the treatment of our wounded," observed Director Taylor.

"So, I want to reiterate the order. Each Army Corps will have an ambulance corps commanded by a captain. A first lieutenant will be assigned to handle each division, with a second lieutenant for each brigade and a sergeant for each regiment. The officers and NCOs will be mounted. Good, serviceable horses will be used for the ambulances, and carts and will not be taken for any purpose without orders from the Army Corps Commander. Each regiment will receive a transport cart, a four-horse ambulance and a pair of two-horse ambulances. Each artillery battery will get a two-horse ambulance. Each ambulance will have two stretchers. Each ambulance will be attended by three privates, one of which will be the driver. Transport carts will have one private as a driver. These are attached to your unit, but still under the command of the Corps Medical Director. The detail for this ambulance corps will be made by the corps commander, and no man will be relieved from it except by orders from that headquarters. When ambulance trains are traveling on a march, there will be a medicine wagon with each train. The wagon will be staffed with two medical officers from the reserve corps of surgeons, and a hospital steward. The ambulance train of each division will be kept together and travel in front of all wagon trains. The officers connected with the corps will ride with the train to make sure no unauthorized people ride in the ambulances. When in camp, the ambulances, transport carts and members of the command will be parked at the brigade headquarters under the supervision of the commander of the ambulance corps for the brigade. The ambulances will be, and I quote from the order, 'used on requisition of the regimental medical officers, transmitted to the commander of the brigade ambulance corps, for transporting the sick to various points and procuring medical supplies, and for nothing else.'"

Director Taylor paused and gazed around the room to make sure the point was made. "Should any officer infringe upon this order regarding the uses of ambulances, he will be reported by the officer in charge to the commander of the train, all particulars being given. The officer in charge of an ambulance train will remove any article not legitimately belonging in the train, and if room cannot be found for it in the baggage wagons, he will leave it by the side of the road. Any attempt by a superior officer to prevent him from doing his duty in this or any other instance will be promptly reported to medical director of the corps, who will bring the matter to the Army Corps Commander. The Army Corps Commander will, at the earliest possible moment, place the offending officer under arrest for trial for disobedience of orders. The men detailed by the Army Corps Commander for the ambulance corps are to report to the medical director immediately. All division, brigade or regimental quartermasters having any ambulances, transport carts, ambulance horses, or harness, etcetera, in their possession will turn them in at once to the commander of the division ambulance corps, by command of Major General McClellan. Those orders are very clear, gentlemen. There will be a break for refreshments at the tables in the back. We will resume at 2 PM."

The groups adjourned to the tables and found ginger cookies and apple cider. The Medical Director obviously was trying to put a coat of sugar on the message he had just delivered. General Order 147 had just changed several thousand years of military medical history. For the first time, a modern western military was divorcing its medical assets from its field commanders. The order was greeted with mixed emotions.

General Brooks was standing with the colonels from the first brigade. Colonel Buck was commenting, "It sounds like someone didn't get the message back in August when this order came out the first time."

Torbert looked around. "That ambulance looked awful good when it came to get me last month. I think Letterman is right. We can't have freight wagons dumping their supplies to go pick up wounded any more, and we can't have the ambulances playing second fiddle to supply wagons."

Brooks nodded his head in agreement. "This war is much different then any in history. Equipment has changed so much just since the Mexican War. Down there, if we had ten thousand men on each side, it was a big battle. We had casualties, but not in numbers like we've seen in the last year. The new rifled muskets shoot further, and the Minnie balls cause much more damage when they hit. The rifled cannon are more accurate, and they shoot further, too."

"There were more casualties at Antietam in two days last month than we lost in the whole Mexican War. There haven't been armies this big fighting each other since 1814. General McClellan has given us our orders. I don't believe any of you would violate them. We need to make sure our officers and men follow them."

"Yes sir, all we need is some overeager lieutenant or sergeant trying to throw his weight around, and there could be trouble," said Torbert. "Well, let's go see what else the good doctor has for us this afternoon."

The Medical Director started his second briefing with a new letter from Major Letterman. "Gentlemen, Medical Director Letterman issued a Circular on October 4th dealing with changing the Medical Supply Table for the Army of the Potomac. Up till now, each regiment has been furnished with three months' worth of medical supplies, but there have been no wagons allocated to carry them. Some regiments have been observed throwing away these supplies, sometimes within sight of the enemy, so the wagons could be used for other purposes. The frequent and large-scale loss of these supplies has got to stop." Some officers in the room were looking guilty. Others were looking belligerent. It sounded like more meddling in their commands by outsiders.

"The Medical Director wants to stop this wastage without restricting your access to the supplies. His orders are as follows: "The following supplies will be allowed to a brigade for one month for active field service. There will be one four-horse hospital wagon, one medicine chest per regiment, and one hospital knapsack for each regimental medical officer. The wagon, chest and knapsacks will contain enough medical supplies for one month."

"The surgeon in charge of each brigade will sign for and be responsible for all of these supplies. He will issue and have the senior surgeon in each regiment sign for the medicine chest and knapsacks. The hospital wagon, with its horses, harness, etcetera, will be signed for by the ambulance quartermaster. We want to make this easy, so the brigade medical officer will informally issue the medical officers from the regiments what they need without requisitions. The brigade medical officer does have to account for the materials he issues. Brigade Medical Officers will need to fill out requisitions for replacement supplies and submit them to the Corps Medical Officer. He is responsible to see that the supplies are not wasted, and that they are there for you when you need them. Now, brigade surgeons will have the keys to the medicine chest and inspect it weekly to make sure it is full. From now on, whenever practical, one ambulance will follow in the rear of every regiment on the march. It will carry the medicine chest, knapsacks and any cases of sickness or wounds. When an ambulance cannot accompany a regiment, one knapsack will be carried by an orderly attached to the command, and the rest will remain in the hospital wagon. Arrangements have been made to provide each regiment and each brigade with one wagon exclusively for hospital purposes. It is intended that this wagon carry the medical supplies, hospital tents, hospital cooking utensils and baggage for the medical staff. I have stressed that the wagon is exclusively for medical use. Please notice the supplies are in small enough packages that in the event of 'military necessity,' they could be carried on a horse. That concludes my briefing, Gentlemen. I would like to introduce Surgeon Vanderkieft."

A young, fair-haired doctor from Holland stepped forward. "This gentleman is the officer in charge of this field hospital. It is the first of its kind, and the Medical Department is extremely proud of the job he has done here. This hospital was the equal of almost any hospital in the world within hours of its erection. The good doctor would like to give you a tour of the facilities, if your time permits."

The officers joined the tour and found nearly 600 patients in the tents. They were clean, being fed, made as comfortable as possible and having their wounds treated well. Most were still too frail to make the wagon trip back to the railhead at Frederick.

"This sure beats that hospital I was in back at Burkettsville," commented Torbert.

When the tour was over, the officers were impressed. They went back to their commands with much on their minds. The initial resentment at having their authority over the wagons and medical supplies taken away had given way to a grudging acceptance that two issues they seldom had time to worry about had been taken off their plates.

October 17, 1862 - Bakersville, Maryland

The last week had been a good week for the 23rd. Rations were plentiful, timely and of high quality. The officers and men had taken to the training schedule, and the performance in drill was already improving. The men seemed happier, but some were still smarting about not being in garrison.

47

The weather was growing cold, and frost showed for the first time. Some of the troops who had abandoned blankets and long underwear on the march from Frederick were looking for replacements. They had to pay for the equipment they lost.

The troops had a little free time every day, and Josie and Ed Lloyd used it to improve the area under their tent. They used their bayonets to dig out a remarkable collection of pumpkin-sized rocks. They claimed sleep was much more comfortable with the rocks removed.

Joe Conover got back from Keedysville on the 13th and went on sick call. Doc Cook said he had a fever and put him on bed rest for three days.

Chaplain Abbott was organizing prayer meetings, and the attendance was surprising. Many of the troops worked and drilled all day and then visited friends, read or lounged around the campfires in their free time. Crispin read *Ten Nights in a Bar Room* by Timothy Shay Arthur and passed it on to Ed, who passed it on to Elwood Goodenough. Reading material was scarce, so any book was shared throughout the unit.

————————

The 26th New Jersey arrived on Monday, but it was just passing through.

Torbert's Brigade was turning into a very intimidating force of six regiments, all from New Jersey. They were the 1st, 2nd, 3rd, 4th, 15th, and 23rd, more than 3,000 men in all.

The troops were surprised when the Regimental Adjutant read orders court-martialing Colonel Cox and Surgeon Cook at the 5 PM regimental dress parade. When all was concluded, the Adjutant announced that Cox had been severely reprimanded by General Slocum and fined one month's pay, and the doctor was fined two months' pay. Many of the men had witnessed the incident. The rumors about the episode had been rampant around the regimental campfires since the unit left Washington.

Commanders seldom include enlisted men in their dealings with misbehaving officers. To the chagrin of many of the men, the Colonel was reinstated as a Colonel. Fortunately, he was not put back in command of the regiment.

October 18, 1862 - Bakersville, Maryland

"I hear the Rebs are down at Harper's ferry again," drawled Sharp. The others in the squad looked up at him. The weather was cold and raw, and they were huddled around the campfire. Terhune was poking at it, and put another couple of sticks on to build it up.

"Who'd you hear that from, George?" asked Hullings.

"Well, everybody knows it. That New York Brigade marched off toward Hagerstown this morning, and we all heard artillery firing over there yesterday. There's got to be something going on. What do you think, Rue?"

"I couldn't tell you. Hagerstown is the opposite direction from Harper's Ferry. The Colonel does not confide in me, and I doubt he even talks to the Lieutenant," smiled Rue. The rest of the squad chuckled. They were heating their coffee and frying up some hardtack and beef slices.

Crispin was staring into the fire. "I had a nightmare last night."

Lloyd looked at him carefully. "I'll say you did. You were screaming and woke me up. What the hell was that all about?"

"I dreamed we were fighting the Rebs." Josie glanced around and saw the rest of the group was looking at him. "I was behind a barricade that screened me from their bullets. This Reb who looked like an old man was trying to shoot me. He shot at me three or four times, and I finally aimed at him and pulled my trigger. I hit him in the chest, and he fell down and just lay there groaning. The sounds he made were so pitiful, I woke up screaming."

Sharp took a sip of his coffee and flipped the piece of hardtack in his frying pan so it wouldn't burn. "Served the sum-bitch right. Quit worryin' about it."

The orderly announced, "Sir, Doctor Cook, is here and says he needs to speak with you."

"Thanks, Foster, Go ahead and show him in," said Lieutenant Colonel Brown. "Yes, Bill, what can I do for you?"

"Sir, it's Private Johnson in C Company. I think he's got galloping consumption, and I would like your permission to send him back to the hospital in Philadelphia."

Brown frowned and paused for a minute. This was not good news. "Are you sure?"

"Yes, sir. He has all the symptoms. He's wasting away and has a bloody cough. It's catchy, and I want to get him out of here before he spreads it around. With this many men in a small place, there is no telling how many will come down with it."

"All right, go ahead and send Johnson to the hospital. Should we burn his equipment?"

"It wouldn't hurt. Might not be a bad idea to burn his tent mate's, too. The Army has plenty of tents and such."

"All right, burn the kit and send him to the hospital. Thank you for coming by."

October 19, 1862 - Bakersville, Maryland

Three shapes materialized out of the early morning darkness by the guard post near the summit of the hill.

"HALT, WHO GOES THERE!" growled Crispin. The dew had set in early in the night, and it was dark and miserable and cold. So cold, that it penetrated through the long underwear, blouse, pants, overcoat, wool blanket, and the gum blanket he had wrapped around himself. Josiah was not in a very good mood. Crispin was standing in the ready position, with his loaded and primed .69 caliber musket and eighteen inch fixed bayonet pointing at the chest of the nearest shape.

The three shadows approaching him were a little slow answering. He thumbed the hammer from half cock to full cock on the musket, and the loud metallic click echoed through the darkness. Everybody in the world knew what that click meant. Crispin wasn't taking any chances. The army was still smarting from the fallout over the Rebel cavalry raid the previous week. If this was an enemy, he knew he was going to be in for a fight. If it was just another inspection by his commanders, he knew he was going to be in trouble if he handled it wrong. The three shapes froze, and a nervous voice rang out, "Sergeant of the Guard West, Lieutenant Root and the Officer of the Day."

"Advance, Sergeant of the Guard West. Lieutenant Root and Officer of the Day, stay where you are."

West moved forward a few paces, and Crispin again commanded, "Halt."

"Times!" challenged Crispin very quietly.

"Olden," countersigned West in an equally quiet voice. The sign and countersign were used to make sure an enemy could not sneak into a position by imitating a friendly member of the unit. It was spoken quietly, so bystanders could not hear it, and it was changed every time a new guard detail went on duty.

All seemed to be in order, so Crispin allowed the others to advance. Lieutenant Root walked up to him and said, "At ease, Private Crispin, what are your General Orders?"

Crispin assumed a parade rest position with the stock of the gun resting on the ground.

"Sir, my general orders are, I will guard everything within the limits of my post and quit my post only when properly relieved. I will obey my special orders and perform all my duties in a military manner. I will report violations of my special orders, emergencies, and anything not covered in my instructions to the Commander of the Relief."

"What are your special orders?"

"Sir, my only special orders are to keep watch over this post and guard the property within its limits and watch for fires."

"Very good, Crispin, we will make a soldier out of you yet. Walk your post - - - and uncock that musket, please," said West.

"Yes sir." Crispin quickly removed the percussion cap and let the hammer down. He put the piece back at half cock and put the cap back in place so it would be ready to fire.

"Good job, Crispin, "said Root.

The sergeant and the officers walked off to the next post. Crispin hoped Lloyd would be ready. He was.

———

Cook was finishing up sick call when he heard the wagons pull up in front of the hospital tent. He got up and went to the door of the tent in time to meet a 2nd Lieutenant coming through the door. The lieutenant saluted. "Sir, I am Lieutenant Smith. I am the 1st Brigade Ambulance Officer."

Doctor Cook smiled. "Lieutenant, I am glad to see you."

"Thank you, sir. It took a while to get enough ambulances here for every unit, but here are the ones you will be working with. I also brought your supply wagon."

That put a grin on Cook's face. Bowlby, Hetzell and Elmer came over and introduced themselves to Smith, and they were grinning too. Having their own supply wagon meant not having to fight with the Quartermaster every time they needed transportation. The Quartermaster Corps was not happy with the Letterman Plan. A knock down, drag-out fight over ownership of the ambulances and wagons had gone on at the highest levels in the army for weeks. Letterman's Medical Corps had won.

They walked outside to look at the wagons. Lined up in front of them were five privates and a sergeant. All wore the new insignia of the fledgling ambulance corps: green stripes on their sleeves and a green band around their hats. Smith introduced his men to the 23rd's surgeons. Sergeant Peck was their regimental ambulance sergeant. Peck showed them around the ambulances. The men walked around and around the wagons. A crowd gathered as others from the camp came to see the new equipment. They admired the horses and looked in the wagons. A few had a chance to be carried around on one of the stretchers. The ingenious device had handles that could be folded downward, so the litter could be converted into a cot. They were sturdy. Their one drawback was they were heavy--more than twenty-five pounds.

Smith made arrangements to load the regiment's three-month stock of medical supplies into one of the wagons. While Peck had the men loading the materials, Smith and Cook inventoried and signed for the medicine chest and knapsacks. The surgeons were excited about the support they were getting from the generals. Many serious shortcomings in treatment of the wounded that had dogged the army since the beginning of the war were coming to an end.

October 22, 1862 - Bakersville, Maryland

The squad had just gotten off guard duty and everybody was tired. Just as they were getting ready to turn in the drummer beat assembly, everybody formed ranks.

"Atten-hut." The unit snapped to attention. "Dress right, dress." Each man turned his head to the right and placed his left hand on his left hip. This allowed them form a straight line with a uniform spacing to the left of each sergeant. "To." The arms all dropped back to the sides and everyone turned their heads back to the front.

"Report," commanded 1st Sergeant Hartman. "First platoon present or accounted for, second platoon present or accounted for," called out the sergeants.

The 1st Sergeant did an about face and saluted Captain McCabe. "All present or accounted for, Sir."

McCabe returned the salute. "Thank you, 1st Sergeant. Company, stand at ease. Men, you may have noticed winter is coming on, and it's a little brisk in camp on the north side of this hill. We are going to pack up camp this morning and move over to the south side to get some shelter. When I dismiss you, I want you to strike your tents and pack up your kit quick as you can, and fall back into formation. We will march to the new camp in one hour. You may dismiss the company, 1st Sergeant."

Hartman saluted the Captain, faced about. "Dismissed."

Josie and Ed strolled over to their tent. They unbuttoned the shelter halves, made up their bedrolls and put their personal effects in their rucksacks. Ed glanced over at Josie with smirk. "You gonna take your rocks?" Josie gave him a good-natured elbow to the ribs.

Brown was in his headquarters tent looking over the morning reports when Winans knocked on the door. "Sir, Captain Parmentier to see you."

Brown turned. "Show him in, Lieutenant." Winans turned and motioned the K Company commander in.

Parmentier walked into the tent, stood at attention. "Captain Parmentier reporting."

"Stand at ease, Captain, what is it?"

"Sir, I have a problem, and I need your advice."

"Go on."

"Well, it's Private Hullins, sir. I received a letter from home, and his folks say he's only 15. Seems he ran away to join the regiment and lied about his age. He is a good boy, and he carries his own weight. He hasn't been any trouble, but I've heard the Army takes a dim view of this kind of thing."

Brown thought for a minute and finally said, "Yes, allowing him to stay is definitely against regulations. The other officers tell me they have dealt with situations like this several times in the brigade."

"Sir, he has done a good job. I don't want to see him get into trouble, and I am worried that if we handle this wrong he will just run away again. I haven't said anything to him. He doesn't know that I know."

Brown was thoughtful again. "Captain, Colonel Torbert has the authority to discharge him. I will speak to him about this, and let you know what we are going to do this afternoon. Dismissed"

The captain saluted. Brown returned it, and Parmentier went back to the company.

Later in the afternoon, Torbert joined Brown, Thompson and Winans as they reviewed the afternoon drill. During the drill, Parmentier was ordered to bring Hullins to the side of the parade field. Hullins stood at attention. He was visibly nervous.

"Private Hullins," said Torbert. "Your captain tells me you are a good soldier."

"Yes sir, thank you, sir."

Torbert paused a second. "How old are you, son?"

Hullins paled. "I am ... I am ..." he drew a quick breath, and tears showed in his eyes. "I am 15, sir."

Torbert looked at him kindly. "You're a good boy, and you have been a good soldier. If I gave you an order, would you carry it out?"

The boy looked uncertain; tears were streaming down his face. "Yes, sir."

Torbert said gently, "I order you to go home. You are still in the Army until you are discharged, so you know you have to follow my orders, don't you?"

"Yes sir, but I want to stay. My friends are all here," sobbed Hullins.

"I know, but Army Regulations won't allow you to stay. I have to discharge you. If I don't, I will get in trouble. Lieutenant Winans will write your orders, and the Army will give you your pay and a train ticket back to Beverly."

"William, I am proud of you. You have done a man's job. I am ordering you to go home and go to school. This country will need hard workers like you after the war. Can I count on you to obey my orders?

"Yes, sir," came the weak reply.

"Good. Your Captain will take you back to camp to get your things." Parmentier and the boy saluted and walked away.

Brown looked at Torbert. "Thank you, sir. That was well done."

Torbert merely nodded. He was thinking how good it was to spare a 15-year-old from the sights he knew this unit was going to see.

October 24, 1862 - Mercerville, Maryland

Drums beat assembly at 8:30, and the ten companies fell in. They quickly came to attention and dressed their ranks.

K Company was a little slow, as they said their last goodbyes to Billy Hullins. The officers had let him spend the night with the company. He had been well-liked, and while the men were a little surprised by the disclosure of his age, they all knew others in the regiment who weren't old enough to be there. None were more than a few months under age, so nobody was talking. All agreed two years was too much, and Hullins was too young.

Companies were lined up in two platoons, one behind the other, with each platoon having two lines or ranks. When everybody was present, this provided a shoulder-to-shoulder front twenty-four men wide. It was assumed each man took up two feet.

When the unit went into action, the second platoon could follow the first, or they could link up to form one long line of two ranks. The company front would be nearly one hundred feet wide. On the Captain's order, that front could fire a murderous burst of one hundred .69 caliber balls weighing nearly an ounce apiece. Each ball was accompanied by three smaller rounds of buckshot, which were equally devastating. Well-trained and disciplined units could do it three times

54

in a minute. The whole theory of warfare was dependent on being able to mass the fire of the infantry units on an opposing force, and kill or wound so many of the enemy that they would be unable to withstand a bayonet charge.

Today, Sweesley's squad and the rest of the regiment were going to see what that meant when the whole division assembled. When all was in order among the companies, Brown gave the order, and the companies stepped off to the beat of the drum. They marched to a cadence. It was the most efficient way to move a large body of men a long distance in a short time. Speed was predictable, and they weren't tripping over each other. Each time the bass drum was struck, one thousand left feet struck the ground, and the whole formation moved along in an orderly, manageable mass.

They marched two and one half miles to a huge open field. On the right was the division's artillery. The four batteries were drawn up, with the twenty-four guns wheel to wheel. The eight-man gun crews were standing by each gun. Behind each gun were the caissons and the horses, attended by their drivers.

Torbert formed up his First Brigade of six regiments. Soon, Colonel Cake appeared and marched in the Second Brigade with his four regiments. Then Brigadier General Russell's brigade of four regiments marched in to complete the assembly. When all were in place, nearly twelve thousand men were assembled on the field. The men in H Company gawked at the spectacle. Forests of bayonets gleamed in every direction.

It took over two hours for General Brooks to review his division. He and the staff and three companies of cavalry rode up and down the ranks, inspecting each formation. He ordered the division through several maneuvers that would be used to attack a position.

Even the lowliest private could see what was going on. Sweesley's boys were finally starting to understand what drill was all about. The parade broke up, and they were back at their tents by early afternoon. All had been suitably impressed.

After the parade was over, General Brooks summoned his brigade and regimental commanders to a meeting. He looked them over and began, "Lee has assembled eighty-five thousand men across the river at Opequan Creek. He reorganized the Army of Northern Virginia into two corps, and named Jackson and Longstreet the corps commanders. It seems he also promoted the boys to Lieutenant General. In a few days, we will move south to engage them. I want you to prepare your baggage trains to move in seventy-two hours, and be ready for a fight. I also expect every one of you to make sure your guards are alert. I don't want Jeb Stuart knocking on our door like he did at Frederick last week." The group nodded in agreement.

The meeting broke up, but the usual coterie of officers hung around to visit with each other. None would publicly criticize the commanding general, but it was openly spoken that he had let Lee escape across the river. Friends in the War Department let it be known that Lincoln was so astounded that McClellan had not pursued Lee after Sharpsburg, that he left Washington and personally went to the Commanding General's headquarters. The President ordered McClellan to cross the Potomac on October 6th. So far, the General had delayed. Secretary of War Halleck had telegraphed McClellan on the 21st demanding to know when and what route he would use to enter Virginia.

Lincoln was becoming impatient, and so was the rest of the country. Twenty days of perfect campaigning weather had been wasted. The public and the Administration wanted the war over as soon as possible. They were unhappy that an opportunity to end it quickly had slipped away. It was obvious to the commanders that something had to happen soon. They returned to their units and made ready to move.

After the parade, Howard was almost jumping up and down with excitement. "I want to go see the cannons."

Sweesley said, "You boys have some free time. Hexamer's battery is over there, and some of our neighbors are in it. Go ahead. Look for Henry Myers and Henry Buckley. Myers is a bugler, and Buckley is a private on a gun crew."

Crispin, Sharp, Goodenough and Howard all headed off for the artillery park and soon found Myers. Myers was from Masonville, and lived about two miles from Crispin's farm.

"Hello, Henry, how's life in the artillery?" grinned Sharp.

"Well, I'll be. Hello fellas, good to see ya," laughed Myers, shaking hands all around. "What brings you around?"

"We saw you in the parade and came to see the cannons," said Howard.

"We're just finishing up taking care of the horses and putting the harnesses away. Let me ask Lieutenant Parsons if I can show you around." Myers led the boys to the Lieutenant. "Sir, some of my neighbors have come to visit. Is it all right if I show them around?"

"If you are all done with the horses, go ahead, Private Myers. Where're you boys from?"

"Sir, we live down near Moorestown," replied Sharp. "How about you, sir?"

"Hoboken," said Parsons. Everyone grinned. There was no disguising the North Jersey accent. "The team's going to practice before dark, Myers."

"Yes, sir, I'll be there."

"Team?" inquired Crispin.

"Yeah, most of the men in the battery are from Hoboken, and they belong to a baseball club."

"You mean town ball?"

"Yup, only we call it baseball. Maybe you can come watch after I show you the guns." All nodded their heads in agreement.

They walked over to the batteries' line of Parrott rifles. They were 3" guns, and there were six of them. Each was hitched to its limber. Behind each gun was a second limber hitched to a caisson.

The black painted guns were cast iron, with a welded iron reinforcing ring around the breach. Unlike older cannons, there was no bell at the muzzle. These were just straight, deadly-looking barrels a little over six feet long.

"Captain Hexamer formed the battery after the war started, but the army waited until after First Bull Run to put it in service. We started out with four Parrotts and two twelve-pound smooth bore howitzers, but we lost the howitzers when we got overrun at Gaines Mill. We just got our two new Parrotts in time for Antietam."

Howard was looking down the barrel. "These are rifles, then."

"That's right. The book says they'll shoot about three miles, but we consider the effective range about two thousand yards." The boys were astonished. "When the gun is fired, you can see the shell fly down range. I never get tired of watching it. It goes so fast until it's out of sight, and then you see it hit."

"I am a bugler, but everybody in the battery cross trains on all of the duties, so if somebody gets hurt we can still service the gun. Each gun is supervised by a sergeant, and he has eight crewmen, and each guy has a special job."

"What kind of job?" asked Howard. Myers had the boys' rapt attention. The size of the guns and the details of all of the equipment around them were mind-boggling.

"Well, each man has a number, and we load the gun by the numbers. When we are ordered to fire, the gunner starts to sight the piece. Number one sponges out the bore to make sure no fire is in the gun. Number two gets the right round for the mission and puts it in the muzzle. Number three puts his thumb over the vent."

"Why does he do that?" asked Elwood.

"It keeps the powder from going off early, if there is any fire in the gun. Really pisses off the guy with the rammer staff when that happens," grinned Myers. "Then number one rams the round to the breach. Number three pokes a vent pick down the vent to open the powder bag and four primes the gun, and we are ready to fire."

Howard just couldn't keep his hands off the guns. "Where do you keep the shells?"

"They are in the ammunition chests, over here on the limber. Each chest holds twenty-four shells, and each gun has four chests. The shells are all made up in bags, so the loader doesn't have loose things to carry when he serves the gun. All the tools and things we need to do our job are in these boxes."

"We even have a traveling forge, farrier and harness maker to take care of any iron or leather work that needs to be done. The battery has about one hundred and seventy-five horses, and we need to take care of them every day. Between training, maintenance and taking care of horses, our days are full."

"How much does one of those guns weigh?" asked Sharp.

"They tell me the gun with its carriage and wheels weighs about eighteen hundred pounds. When you add the limber, the ammunition chests, the ammunition and tools, the horses are pulling about forty-five hundred pounds, plus the gun crew."

"You even have a spare wheel on the caisson."

"We sure do. We have spares of almost everything. The generals get really upset when one of these things breaks down. It's getting late, fellas; I need to get over to ball practice. Why don't you come on over and see what we are doing?"

They all walked over to a corner of the parade field. There were a lot of people standing around what looked like a square that was bounded by four white sacks. Each sack was about eighteen inches square and two inches thick. A man was standing next to one with a long stick in his hand. Another, standing in the center of the square, threw a ball toward him. The man with the stick hit the ball, and it sailed out into a field, where somebody caught it.

The boys and the 23rd Regiment were introduced to baseball.

October 26, 1862 - near Dam #4, Mercerville, Maryland

Rue, Crispin, Lloyd, Hibbs and Howard had their guns half cocked. They were at a listening post near the flour warehouse on the north side of the Potomac, a quarter of a mile upstream from Mercersville. It was dead quiet. The Rebs were less than twenty miles away across the river at Opequan Creek, and trouble was expected.

It had rained all the previous day and last night, so everyone was cold and wet. They had been sitting around the fire trying to stay warm when the word came down to be ready for picket duty in an hour. Picket duty was not just guard duty. Guard duty was used to secure property or a post on the regimental or brigade perimeter.

A picket line was an early warning system. It was actually the front line of the Army of the Potomac, and it was manned with enough force to delay an attacker until units in the encampments could get into defensive formations.

The squad drew three days' rations. They packed up their equipment, and were ready to move at the appointed time. They had marched quietly toward Mercerville and were joined by a general and a guide. Something was up. Generals didn't do picket duty. For the first time the new troops were deployed ahead of the company. Sweesley spread them out as scouts, and they were told to move as quietly as possible.

Eventually, they moved down a steep and very narrow stone lane to a village by the river. They had passed silently through it and traveled along the empty bed of the Chesapeake and Ohio Canal at the base of a steep hill until they came to their present position. All that could be heard was the water flowing over Dam Number 4 further up the river.

Dam Number 4 was built in 1856 and considered an engineering marvel. It replaced a rubble and brush dam used for flood control and for improved navigation. It was built with hand-hewn limestone blocks that were about one foot thick by three or four feet long by two feet deep. The constant noise from water falling eighteen feet lulled many a man to sleep.

The five waited motionless through their two-hour detail until they were relieved. They rolled up in their gum blankets and slept on the ground. In the morning, they were covered with ice. Nothing had happened during the night.

They pulled the same picket duty the next night, but got to sleep on straw in a nearby barn. They slept fully armed, with their guns nearby and their cartridge belts on.

They awoke for breakfast and found they would not have to go back on picket until the evening. The river was visibly higher from the last week's rains. Infantry and artillery needed slow water no deeper than forty inches to safely ford a river, and this only if the artillery had waterproof ammunition boxes. Cavalry could use a ford if the water was less than fifty-one inches, or in a pinch the horses could swim. The water was obviously deeper than that. No infantry or artillery from either side would be using the Potomac fords until spring.

"Sergeant Sweesley?"

"Yes, Josie?"

"Sarge, we don't go back on duty until 6 o'clock. Can we go look around Sharpsburg for a while this afternoon?"

"Guns cleaned? Got your kit looked after?" The boys nodded yes.

Sweesley nodded his head yes. "Be back by 5." He watched as Crispin walked off with Conover and Terhune. Sharpsburg was only a mile and half away. They could easily see the sites and be back in time. Sweesley thought the boys were turning into pretty good troops. Three weeks ago, they would have just disappeared.

The boys stopped by a little hotel on the way into town and were promptly kicked out by a miserable old woman. 'You dirty no-count Yankee bastards get the hell out of here. This is a decent place, and I don't want you thieving sons a bitches muddying up my floors."

"Quite a lady," mumbled Terhune as they walked out the front door.

They made their way to the Hagerstown Turnpike and walked south toward Dunker's Church. "My gawd, look at that," cried Terhune, pointing to a heavy oak timber that was nearly shot in half. They looked at it curiously. It was shot full of bullets, grapeshot and canister holes.

They gazed around them and were speechless at the destruction. Full grown oak trees had their branches shot off. Every tree in sight was riddled with bullet holes. One had a cannon ball hole all the way through it. One of the locals told them the cannon ball had passed through the tree and still had enough force to kill two Rebels.

They spent the afternoon viewing the battlefield. Dead horses, wrecked gun carriages and caissons, broken equipment and fresh graves littered the area. The crops were trampled into the dirt, and the fields were wrecked. The stench of death was thick.

October 31, 1862 - Bakersville, Maryland

Sweesley's picket detail returned from Mercerville early in the evening, dead tired. They had gotten lost on the way back and wandered around in the woods for several hours. One of the local farmers finally led them back to camp.

Everyone turned in early and was sound asleep when the drummer beat assembly at 2 AM. It was a typical nippy late October morning, but the sky was clear and the moon was up. They broke camp by firelight and each picked up 3 days' rations. Sounds of other units getting ready to move out were all around them.

At 3 AM, Hartman called them to fall in. They were slow and he erupted, "I told you men to fall in, and I mean it. When I tell you to do something YOU DO IT! You move like a bunch old women. Straighten up or I'll have you sent to over to Harper's Ferry with the penal battalion to clean up the mess the Rebs left."

Somebody in the back of the company mumbled, "Jesus Christ, Reuben, its 3 o'clock in the morning."

"Knock that shit off and fall in," bellowed Hartman.

McCabe, Root and Carter looked at each other and grinned at the tirade.

They took the road to Keedysville. By daylight they joined General Franklin's Corp of four divisions. Close to forty thousand men were on the march.

Each division needed six to eight hundred wagons to carry its food, ammunition, supplies and equipment. Each wagon needed four horses or mules. The artillery batteries needed six horses per gun, six horses per caisson, plus others for supply wagons and forges. Officers and cavalry also had horses. In all, it took close to five thousand head of horses and mules for each division.

All of this manpower and horsepower added up to one noisy, dusty, smelly mass of blue moving eastward at about two and a half miles an hour. The men could march in cadence and sing, which helped break the monotony, but that in itself became hard to do for very long. Most of the trip was made at a shuffling route step.

The veteran regiments moved off first, and the 23rd brought up the rear. This was the first time the vets had marched with the "cruits." They remembered the "Yahoos" who had come into camp three weeks earlier singing "We'll Hang Jeff Davis from a Sour Apple Tree." The pace they set was brisk. The day grew hot. Soon, the rear guard had its hands full of stragglers from the 23rd.

H Company was moving along well, and at mid-morning halted for a ten minute rest. Hartman found Sweesley and Miller clustered in the shade of a maple that was well into its fall color change. "I have a detail for your squads." They sat up.

"Captain wants us to spread out and help the rear guard herd these stragglers." This was a good deal. It meant they could move at their own pace and quit eating dust from the columns ahead.

Miller looked at Sweesley and asked, "Who's gonna herd us?" This brought peals of laughter from the men. The sergeants got up and looked around, "You heard the man. Let's get up and help these fellas. Where we going, 1st Sergeant? Where do we meet up if we get separated?"

"We are going back to Keedysville, then through Crampton's Gap to Burkittsville. Camp's gonna be near there. I'll see you there."

The infantry generally marched cross-country so the wagons and guns could use the roads. The rear guard was spread out on both sides of the road trying to urge, cajole, goad, sweet talk, order, and force, or whatever else would work, a growing group of short tempered, hot, exhausted men to keep moving. Sweesley's squad joined in.

The heat of the day and the fifty-pound packs were a torture to the troops, and they started dropping heavier items from their rucksacks. Goodenough, Hibbs, Kimball and Terhune were salvaging dropped equipment and putting it in a supply wagon. The steep narrow valley to Crampton's Gap restricted the traffic some. The column finally gained the top and found it easier going downhill to Burkittsville.

The rest of the squad was going from straggler to straggler to keep them moving. They were greeted with everything from gratitude to some of the most creative profanity anyone had ever heard.

Crispin found three men lying helpless along the road. They were having difficulty with the heat. He got them into some shade, loosened their clothing, and gave them water from his canteen and cooled them off.

Soon, he saw a four-horse Tripler ambulance approaching. It was a heavy, four-wheeled wagon. It could carry ten men. It had a heavy cotton duck tarp supported by iron hoops that provided shade from the sun or shelter from the weather. Hanging from the bottom was a water barrel known as a butt. It was about 14 inches in diameter and 3 ½ feet long.

Josie flagged the ambulance down and talked to the private driving it. "These men are all done in with the heat. Can you give them a ride?"

"Are they sick? The sergeant's has been downright nasty about letting people ride in the ambulance or putting their packs on it. We got orders that only sick people can ride. Are they sick?"

"They are heat sick. They are too heat sick to walk. I found them passed out and gave them all my water. They need a ride, and I need to refill my canteen."

"Well, I guess it will be all right. Help me get 'em in the wagon, and you can fill up from the water butt."

Crispin filled his canteen from the water barrel and went back to herding stragglers. The wagon moved off slowly down the road.

Late in the afternoon, a Captain rode up to Sweesley and Miller. "Sergeant, I am Captain Grubb from Colonel Torbert's staff, where are your officers?"

Miller saluted, "Sir, they are with the column. We have been detailed to help the rear guard round up stragglers."

Captain Grubb grinned. "Well, you got your work cut out for you. The regiment is spread out for 4 miles. Carry on," he said as he rode toward Burkettsville.

"Who the hell was that?" Miller asked Sweesley.

"Beats me. He didn't look a day over fifteen, though." The sergeants looked at each other and shrugged.

And so, the rear guard proceeded across the landscape of Maryland, a loud, cantankerous, argumentative mass of humanity united only by their shared misery.

———————

Torbert was waiting at Burkettsville when Lieutenant Colonel Brown rode into camp with 24 men. The remaining 950 were straggling for miles across the Maryland countryside. This was the last straw for Torbert. He rode to the hospital at Burkettsville to find Doc Oakley and requested Ogden Ryerson be released. When all was said and done, Ryerson was released from the hospital and ordered to take over the regiment. Torbert had the orders published.

The squads finished their rear guard detail and got back to H Company after the evening formation. The regiment was finally setting up camp and was abuzz about Ryerson. Orders had been read that permanently transferred him from the 2nd Regiment and appointed him Acting Commander of the 23rd. Word was he would be appointed to full Colonel in a few days. Nobody shed a tear about Cox. The men got their tents up and drifted off to a much-needed blissful sleep. The march for the day had been twelve miles. How far they had actually walked was anyone's guess.

November 1, 1862 - Burkettsville, Maryland

While Crispin and his friends were getting ready to march, Lieutenant Colonel Ryerson was meeting his officers. The company commanders, their lieutenants, Chaplain Abbott, Major Thompson, Adjutant Winans and Doctor Cook had reluctantly assembled at the headquarters.

"Gentlemen," opened Ryerson, "by orders of General Brooks I am temporarily taking command of the 23rd. Are there any questions about that?" There were none. Major Thompson and Adjutant Winans looked like they were about to burst blood vessels. They had assumed that they and Brown would succeed Cox if the old man was really losing his command, and this meant Ryerson had been moved in ahead of them.

"I was very disappointed with yesterday's march. The lack of discipline and marching skill was an embarrassment, and men in your sister regiments are making fun of you. This doesn't have to be. Not one of the men in the 2nd or the 4th were any different than your men when they entered the Army, yet all of them now have the discipline and skill to take care of themselves and each other. You have heard of how bravely they fought in the Peninsula Campaign and at Bull Run Bridge, and you have met the men who bought Crampton's Gap with their blood. Jersey men have a reputation for being tough fighters. However, it would be criminal to send this unit into battle right now." Ryerson looked around the room, and the officers' expressions ranged from heads shaking in agreement to steel-eyed fury.

"They are so ill-trained that if they were put into a fight, they would run or die before they could get off the first shot. If that happens, that leaves the men in the other units around them in danger. That could lose a whole battle. You and I have to fix that. We are going to start a regular training schedule. Reveille will beat at 6 AM. Every day we are not marching, you will have one hour after reveille to feed your troops and get them cleaned up. You will then take one half hour to police your company area. You will then take one hour to practice the manual of arms and go over your infantry commands. After that, there will be two hours of company drill. After lunch there will be two hours of battalion or regimental drill, and there will be a dress parade every night at 5 o'clock. Roll calls will be held by the book."

A hand timidly rose. "Is there a question?" asked Ryerson.

"Sir?" squeaked the anonymous voice. "Why are we doing this?"

Ryerson looked at the officer coldly for a minute, and then his gaze softened and he looked around the room. "Has no one told you why we drill?"

A room full of officers shook their heads no. Just two months ago they had been civilians who had no intention of being soldiers. They had answered a call from their President. They were volunteers with no clear idea of what they had volunteered for, other than the glorious idea they would be heroes. And now they were officers with no clear idea of the responsibility that entailed.

"We drill because there is safety in numbers. Our purpose is to shoot the maximum number of rifles at our enemy each time we fire. The massed fire will cut a path through their formations and allow us to close with them and defeat them. The only way to move a large number of men across the field in an organized manner is to drill until reaction to orders is instinctive. We don't do this for entertainment. In a fight, it is a life-or-death proposition. The commander who can get the most rifles to the critical area the fastest wins. The 4th Regiment won at Crampton's Gap six weeks ago because they marched into the battle like they were putting on a regimental parade. The Rebels shot cannons and hundreds of rifles at them, yet they held their formation for 400 yards in a double quick charge, and the Rebs couldn't stand up to them. Those men saw you come in here yesterday and they are not impressed. Their experience tells them you can't do it. You gentleman are blessed with some very fine men. They will do almost anything you ask, if you give them a good reason. They trust you to be their leaders, but you dare not abuse that trust. The best chance you can give them to live through a battle is to teach them how to fight, and that means drilling them hard. They want to be led. As officers, you need to make sure they eat, sleep, are well, check their equipment and feet. Keep an eye on their morale. You don't have to do this by yourself. Make sure you use your NCOs and corporals to help. You aren't the first officers to ever find yourselves in a job you aren't used to. Talk to your friends in the other regiments. They can give you good advice, or come see me. My door is always open to you. We will be marching towards Berlin today. There will be no more straggling, and there will be God-damned sure no abandoning equipment. It's your job to see the men stay together and don't throw things away. If they drop something and you let them leave it, you will have to pay for equipment they discard. Is that clear?"

Sheepish nods of acknowledgment showed they understood.

Another hand went up. "Yes?" questioned the new Colonel.

"Sir, why weren't we paid in October?"

Ryerson patiently explained that they would not be paid until the march was over. Some looked skeptical about the news.

"One final thing. I expect each of you to get a copy of Hardees' or The Military Handbook and Soldier's Manual. It will give you some good pointers about your duties as officers. Remember, you are responsible for everything your unit does or fails to do." That concluded the officer's call.

———————

The regiment marched twelve miles and set up camp near Berlin. As the Lieutenants were walking back to their tents after supper, the conversation was all about Ryerson. Just who was this man who had been so suddenly thrust into their lives? A short walk over to the 2nd Regiment was all that was needed to get the story.

They found a group of officers around a warm fire and introduced themselves. The 2nd Regiment officers invited them to sit down. "Pleased to meet you," drawled one. "This is Gene Guindon from H Company, Joe Jenkins from G Company, Augie Linder from E, Charlie Lockwood and Marty Monroe from K, Billy O'Connor from C, got Bill Williams here from A, and I am Albert Frank, D Company. What brings you boys around on this crisp fall night?"

"Just coming around to visit. None of us have been in the Army before, and Colonel Ryerson said we should ask you for help if we had questions about our job."

"Ohh! You fellas are with that bunch of yahoos that waltzed into Burkettsville yesterday. You're from the 23rd?"

One of the 23rd Lieutenants started to get up, and Frank looked at him. "Easy, friend, no offense, all of us were just like you when we started."

Lockwood looked over at Frank and deadpanned, "Oh, bullshit, Albert, none of us were ever as bad as you when we started," which was received with guffaws by all of the 2nd Regiment officers. Lockwood took a swig of brandy from a flask and passed it around.

"AHHHH, stop it, Charlie, my wound only hurts when I laugh," cried Lieutenant Williams.

Linder leaned forward and poked the fire. "We've all been here in the 2nd since the beginning. Old Frank over here is the only one who started out as a Lieutenant. The rest of us came up through the ranks. Monroe and Lockwood were our Sergeant Majors for a while."

The flask was passed around the fire, refilled and passed again. The 23rd Regiment officers noticed several slings and bandages on their hosts.

"What happened to you?"

"Ahhh, some of us ran into a few Rebs up at Crampton's Gap..." sighed Frank.

"And Frayser's Farm and Malvern Hill and Bull Run Bridge and Antietam Creek," sighed another. The new lieutenants exchanged looks.

"Here's to Plume, God rest his soul," toasted Frank.

"Who was Plume?"

'He was our 1st Sergeant Major. Wonderful friend! Got promoted to Lieutenant and sent to D Company. Cannon ball took his head off at Bull Run Bridge. His brother, Joe, is Adjutant over at the 3rd Division in the 2nd Corp. He's taking the death hard, and I doubt if he will stay in."

"How did you learn all of these jobs and commands if you were not in the Army before the war?" questioned one of the 23rd's officers.

"General Kearny trained all of us," recalled Frank.

"YOU KNEW GENERAL KEARNY?" asked the Lieutenants.

"Sure did. He called us his pets."

"And we called him General," chuckled Lockwood.

"In fact, the first time we met him, we looked just like you did when you came in. Our boys were all strung out on both sides of the road, no formation at all. We strolled up to this house by a peach orchard and started picking peaches when this one-armed fella dressed up like a farmer comes out and starts yelling at us. We didn't know he was General Kearny until he arrested us," grinned Frank as the other 2nd Regiment men smiled.

"Arrested you?"

"Yeah, sent us to our camp and placed all our officers under arrest. Then they had dinner with him, and everything was fine. He taught us all about soldiering, how to march, set up camp, keep clean, stand guard and fight. He learned it from the French Army. He actually fought with them in Africa. He used to charge the enemy with his horse's reigns in his teeth so he could wave his saber with his one arm."

"Finest man I ever met. Took money out of his own pocket to make sure we were taken care of, bought us food and equipment. Once, he turned down a promotion to command a division so he could stay with the First Brigade. Might be alive today if he had taken that promotion," drawled Frank as others nodded their heads.

The small talk eventually got around to the 23rd's new CO. Lieutenant Franks and his friends were happy to tell the tale of Henry Ogden Ryerson. The story was related with near reverence.

Ryerson had been a lawyer in Jersey City when the war started. He had volunteered and entered the Army as a private in the 2nd Regiment.

The men in Company B elected him captain, and the Governor signed his commission. By the time the regiment was in the Peninsula Campaign, he was a major leading six of the regiment's 10 companies. He was shot through both thighs with the colors in his arms as he tried to rally his troops at Gaines Mills. His men thought it was a mortal wound and left him on the battlefield. The Rebs didn't find him for ten days. The first three were without food or water. Eventually, he was captured and taken to Richmond. His captors tended his wounds, but they put him in POW camp, and he caught the fever. Finally, he was paroled. Somehow, he made it back to the 2nd Regiment just after the attack on Crampton's Gap. He had been shot, left for dead, imprisoned, survived the fever and gotten back to his unit in less than four months. It was whispered by the regimental surgeon that one of his wounds was still open.

The lieutenants from the 23rd thanked their hosts, excused themselves and were about to start back to their camp when Lieutenant Lockwood stopped them. "I was the Sergeant Major when Colonel Ryerson was our Major and Lieutenant Colonel. You "Yahoos" better take good care of our colonel, he is a good man. We don't want him wasted on a bunch of no-counts."

The story spread through the 23rd like wildfire. Ryerson was a real soldier, and a hero at that. Men wondered how anyone could function with a wound still open. How could someone be wounded and go without water for three days? What was it like to be a POW? When the sun came up the next morning, everybody in the New Jersey Brigade was calling the regiment the "Yahoos", and Ryerson's word was law.

Crispin was sitting on a fence not far from camp, tear tracks on his face. Yesterday had been going well until the 1st Sergeant yelled mail call. Everyone piled out of their tents to see if a letter had come from home. Josie was ecstatic; he had one from his sister, Mary. He quickly opened it and his world collapsed around him. Mary wrote that his little brother, Frank, was dead.

Josie had just held the letter and sobbed. Frankie had been his favorite. After the death of his mother, Frank had been stepmother Hannah's first child. Everyone in the family spoiled him. Even though Josie was ten years older, he and Frank had been special playmates. They made sand castles, chased frogs down by the creek and spent hours playing on a rope swing Randy built for them. The last thing

Frank had asked for was a Rebel sword. Josie lay awake all night with his broken heart.

November 2, 1862 - Lovettsville, Virginia

At dawn, the company packed up and marched to Berlin. At 8:30 in the morning they crossed the Chesapeake and Ohio Canal and the Potomac. New York's 50th Engineers had laid two pontoon bridges side by side. The men had never seen a floating bridge, and they were all eyes. The bridge rode on the deep and clear waters of the Potomac. They could see the rocky bottom and jagged bedrock outcroppings stretched up and downstream as far as they could see. Whole trees and piles of brush littered the rocks from previous floods. Engineers with ropes and grappling hooks rowed back and forth above the bridges to intercept floating debris that might damage the bridge. Guards were posted at the end of the bridge, and several more on the bridge. They were shouting "route step, route step march" to make sure the infantry remembered not to march in step. Marching in step could create waves that would break it.

All eyes took in the nine blackened stone piers that jutted thirty feet out of the river just upstream. They dominated the landscape. "What happened to the bridge?" asked Conover.

Lieutenant Root was nearby and he explained, "In the spring of '61 when the war started, Stonewall Jackson came up here and burned this bridge. Of course no one called him Stonewall, yet. He also burned the one at Harper's Ferry and the one down at Point of Rocks. The Rebs didn't want us to be able to use them to cross the river."

Conover thought about that for a few minutes as he looked down at the bridge deck laid over the pontoons. He listened to the clump-clump-clump of soldier's feet on the bridge deck. "Sure seems stupid, a terrible thing to destroy a big beautiful bridge like that." Root nodded.

"When we step off the end of this bridge, you will be in Virginia, boys," said Root. "Enemy territory." The boys all stood a little taller. They started a long, climbing march out of the valley toward Lovettsville. They left the road and went cross-country as soon as the valley widened out.

Conover noticed Josie was marching ten yards ahead. His head was down and he wasn't paying attention to what was going on around him. He was just going through the motions.

Sweesley was marching nearby, so Joe sidled over to him. "Sarge, I am worried about Josie."

"What's wrong?"

"He got a letter from his sister last night. His little brother died."

Sweesley looked at Conover, then looked ahead at Josie's back.

"You mean Hannah's little Frank, Little Frank Crispin?" asked the sergeant incredulously.

Conover nodded.

"Christ, I better tell the First Sergeant and the Lieutenant. Thanks, Joe, keep an eye on him."

Sweesley turned around and got Hartman's attention and motioned him over to Root. He told them what Conover said. Both of them sighed. With the army on the move and in enemy territory, all knew there was no way they could get him a furlough. Root walked on a few steps and said, "I'll let Captain McCabe know. How about you send Conover to find the Chaplain, he'll know what to do." The men nodded and moved off.

The column ended its march at 11 AM near Lovettsville. They pitched camp in woods nearby and spent the afternoon cleaning their guns, repairing equipment and resting. They had marched thirty-five miles in three days.

Conover was not able to find Chaplain Abbott until late in the afternoon. Abbot walked back to H Company with Joe. Sweesley showed them where Josie had gone, and together they walked up to the fence where he was sitting.

"Son, I am Chaplain Abbott. I heard about your brother and I am terribly sorry. Is their anything I can do for you?" Abbott knew Crispin was a Quaker, and some of that group did not approve of clergy.

"Sir, I thank you for coming," and he poured out his heart. Abbott comforted him and they prayed together.

After a while, other men from the company joined them. One brought Josie his supper and another gave him a piece of candy. They spent the evening making sure he was not alone.

The same mail call that brought devastating news to Crispin brought an anxiously awaited letter for George Howard. After George paid his respects to Josie, he returned to his tent and pulled out his treasure. It was a little yellow Beadle's Dime book called, *Baseball Player: A Compendium of the Game, comprising elementary instructions of this American Game of Ball.* Howard had enjoyed the game at Hexamer's Battery so much that he had gotten the address of the Beadle Company from Henry Myers and sent for the rules. He studied the book in the fading light. As a great harvest moon rose big in the east, he, Conover and Goodenough were plotting about how to get a bat and ball, and enough canvas to sew together the bases.

November 4, 1862 - near Snickers Gap, Virginia

The army continued south toward Front Royal. General Franklin rode with them for a short time to boost their morale. The land was forested and hilly, and marching involved a lot of climbing and descending that made it tough to keep a formation. Sometimes, they could see the long low barrier of the Blue Ridge Mountains from the tops of the hills they'd climbed. Hundreds of pieces of artillery and thousands of cavalry were over there to make sure the Rebs did not get through the Blue Ridge Mountain gaps and attack the flank or the rear. Hancock's troops seized Snicker's Gap on November 2nd, and a lot of firing had been heard in that direction. Sometimes the troops could hear the sounds of battle as Union and Confederate cavalry probed each other's defenses. Franklin's men had fought off a determined attack yesterday afternoon. Every army has rumors, and this one did, too. One minute the Rebs had won and the end of the world was coming, and the next they were beaten and all was well.

The 23rd marched past an old gristmill and some log cabins at a place called Wheatlberg, and halted at 2 PM. Camp was set up in a wood. They were headed southeast toward Thoroughfare Gap, and the marching was difficult. The drummers drummed assembly at 4:30 that afternoon. The regiment formed up with the rest of the division in a nearby field. The Division Aide de Camp read court martial charges for Privates Secord and Oliver of the First Regiment, Bradley of the Second, and White of the Fourth. They had been tried and found guilty of cowardice and direct disobedience of orders of an officer. Their sentence was public humiliation and dishonorable discharge from the army. In front of the twelve-thousand-man division, their heads were shaved, and they were drummed out of the camp.

Elwood Goodenough wondered if that wasn't too harsh. Rue said, "Elwood, when we get in a fight, we have to rely on each other. If the man next to you runs or won't do what he's told, that puts you and the rest of us in danger. We have to stick together."

Elwood gazed around at the twelve thousand men on parade. He knew Rue was right. He didn't see how anything could stand up to a host like that if they stuck together.

Torbert grinned at General Brooks as he handed him Colonel Cox's resignation. It was signed and dated November 1, 1863. Torbert and Brooks both noted that Cox had started the resignation with "Dear" and crossed it off. The official note began "Sirs." The man was still unrepentant. Torbert quickly approved the resignation with a note saying "Approved and strongly urged. This officer is totally incompetent and has been ordered before a Board of Examination."

General Brooks approved the resignation.

"General," began Torbert, "I have a petition from the officers of the 23rd saying they elected Ryerson as Colonel of the regiment. What do you think of that?"

Brooks looked up. "Not much," he growled.

Torbert thought he knew where this was going, but wanted to be sure. "General, I think I know what you are going to say, but I need to hear you say it."

The general gazed at Torbert and nodded. The volunteers were in a hazy realm between state militias and regular Army units. Each had its own rules. The Army had never faced a Civil War, and was breaking new ground when it came to handling state units. Some of the new ground had not been easily broken. There had been trouble. Some officers had been relieved for being incompetent, and a few units had rebelled when that happened. On occasion, entire regiments had been punished because of it.

Brooks spoke. "Volunteer units in the service of their states are entitled to elect their officers. But the 23rd has been federalized. They do not have the right to elect their officers." He paused. "Alfred, you are to reject the petition. They are in the Army now, and they are subject to U.S. Army regulations."

Torbert disapproved the petition. Ryerson was appointed Colonel by order of the Commanding General. The volunteers had been federalized.

November 6, 1862 - near Union, Virginia

The Army of the Potomac was creating a traffic jam in Virginia. It took Captain Noyes of the First Division six hours to squeeze his squad-sized security detail into the traffic crossing Berlin's pontoon bridges. The thousands of wagons and hundred of cannons were limited to traveling on the roads. Columns of infantry and cavalry trampled fields and fences as they marched cross-country, but still managed to cover nearly ten miles a day, and camped near the Hampton & Loudon

Railroad. Mixed in with this mass were several herds of cattle to feed the troops. Herds of spare horses and mules also were in the march. These animals all needed forage, so their movements had to be coordinated according to the availability of pastures. The only railroad that could help supply the army was the rickety old Orange and Alexandria. It was a poorly maintained single track that would become more and more exposed to Rebel action as the army moved further into Virginia.

The pleasant Indian summer weather the march had enjoyed for the last few days was ending. Cold winds from the North hinted it would snow soon.

The company was not able to get on the march until noon, due to a large herd of cattle being driven forward by the quartermasters. The squads were huddled around their fires in the late morning when they met their first slaves. An old black man came up and spoke with them. He had been gathering abandoned clothing along the march. Hullings asked him, "You know if any Rebels live around here?"

"Oh, yes," he replied. "All these folks round here is secessists."

"He means 'secessionists,'" frowned Terhune.

"Yes, sir, that's what they is. All the men folk and their sons is in the Rebel army. There is lots 'a us slaves around here to work these plantations."

"Looks like these folks are quite rich."

"Tha's right sir, quite rich, they is quite rich."

"Where are the Rebels?" asked Hullings.

"We heard they is over in the Shenandoah."

Root came up, and said it was time to go. Hartman called them to fall in. They route stepped off toward the east. They marched until 9 PM. A piercing wind was blowing from the north. Nobody had to be told to put their tents up.

November 7, 1862 - White Plains, Virginia

Josiah came awake to utter silence. The tent was lying on top of him. "Ed - - Ed," he rasped, "wake up. It snowed, and the tent fell on us."

Ed groaned, "OHHH, damn. What's wrong with your voice?"

"Got a sore throat. Can hardly swallow." He crawled out from under the tent, and looked around. There was three inches of snow on the ground, and it was still snowing and blowing very hard. He could hear the subdued sounds of other men coming awake. The snow muffled all noise. Occasionally, he could hear swearing from one of the others companies as men woke up. Some had been too tired to pitch their tents the night before, and now they were paying for it. Finally, reveille sounded at 6:30, and everybody got up for roll call.

The squad cooked up its coffee and crackers for breakfast. The coffee was strong and burned his already sore throat. The crackers were hardtack biscuits. Each was a square three inches on a side. One day's ration per soldier was twelve ounces, so a company of a hundred men ate seventy-five pounds a day. They came in a wooden box that weighed fifty pounds. Crackers could be fried or broken up and mixed with water to form a pancake, or just eaten as is. Weevils were knocked out by tapping the cracker on a pan, or just ignored and eaten.

They were just finishing up when Hartman came by and said they were not marching today. That didn't break anybody's heart. He also announced they were on short rations. The further they got from Maryland, the more trouble the quartermaster was having distributing supplies to so many units.

Crispin went on sick call. He waited in the hospital tent and noticed it was almost as cold inside as out. Hetzell and Elmer were complaining to Doc Cook that no one had issued them a stove, and it was difficult to treat sick men in the cold. Finally, Doc Elmer examined Josie and gave him some medicine. It was pretty much honey mixed with whiskey, and strong enough to knock a nineteen-year-old teetotaler out. Crispin took his medicine, crawled into his tent, wrapped up in his blankets and overcoat, and slept for the rest of the day and the next.

Lloyd and Howard went for a walk in the snow, and found the Washington and Manassas railroad. The camp was between Salem and White Plains, at the fifty-three mile marker. They were fifty-three miles from Alexandria. It snowed until late that night. The Blue Ridge gleamed like it was coated with pearl when morning dawned sunny on the 9th.

The regimental surgeons had been called to another meeting by the Medical Director. Major Letterman had issued another circular. It was dated October 30th, and was the document that surgeons throughout the Army had been hoping for. It took the lessons learned from the hospitals at Antietam and created a hospital structure that might actually work.

For the first time in U.S. Army history, the order required a senior Surgeon in Chief to set up a hospital for each division facing combat. This Surgeon in Chief had the authority to detail an assistant surgeon to set up the tents, and organize the hospital kitchen. Experience in previous battles had shown that the army usually could find sufficient medical supplies to treat the wounded, but often overlooked necessities such as food and shelter. This "quartermaster surgeon" was responsible to make sure the hospital had sufficient equipment, personnel and supplies of bread, beef stock, arrowroot, tea and other foods to quickly prepare palatable and nourishing meals for all of the patients.

Another assistant surgeon was detailed to keep a complete record of every case brought to the hospital. This officer was responsible for recording the name, rank, company, regiment, nature of injury and treatment given. These surgeons were separate from the doctors who actually performed the medical procedures. The circular ordered each to be provided with an assistant and a properly organized and maintained operating table. Military medicine was finally moving into the 19th Century.

During the snowstorm, late that night, Brigadier General Catharinus P. Buckingham arrived at General Ambrose Burnsides's headquarters, and woke Burnside from a sound sleep. Buckingham informed Burnside that the President was relieving McClellan, and Burnside was to be his replacement. When Burnside protested, Buckingham told him the next choice was Hooker. Burnside's hatred of Hooker was well-known. Burnside dressed and accompanied Buckingham to McClellan's headquarters. McClellan read the orders. Lincoln and Halleck had lost faith in him. He immediately turned over command of the Army of the Potomac to Burnside.

November 12, 1862 - New Baltimore, Virginia

The Company had been on the march for the last two days, and had pulled into thick oak woods near New Baltimore The country had been very hilly. Marching had been slow and miserable. They passed several small towns. There were very few people around, and none of the businesses were open. Most of the populations had fled to larger communities.

The men were cooking a very meager breakfast when Miller sidled up to Sweesley. "Things are getting a bit hungry around here, John."

"You're tellin' me," growled Sweesley. "I must have lost fifteen or twenty pounds since we left Beverly. The rest of the boys are looking a little lean, too."

"O'Neill told me they will be butchering some of that beef that passed us the other day."

Miller had Sweesley's attention. "What say we go down there and get our ration before they run out?"

John was all for it. He picked three men, and went with Miller to the butchering site.

When they got there the quartermaster had several cattle already down, and a detail was shooting others in the head. Teams of horses were dragging the dead cattle to nearby trees. The bodies were hung up with blocks and tackles to be gutted and skinned. The meat was carefully weighed out before it was distributed, so each man got his twenty ounce ration for the day. The men helped with the butchering, and got their rations for H Company.

As they were leaving, Miller glanced over his shoulder saw a crowd going through the entrails and picking out plucks. Plucks were the liver, kidneys, lungs, stomach and intestines. Others were working at the hides with jack knives. When they were done, every speck of edible material was on its way to a frying pan. Things were indeed getting hungry.

After the men had cooked their beef and crackers, Hartman called them all together. Captain McCabe explained that President Lincoln had ordered General Burnside to replace McClellan. There would be a good-bye review for the outgoing commander in the afternoon. He also explained that the Army of Northern Virginia had split. Part was still back in the Shenandoah under Stonewall Jackson. The other part was twenty miles to the south at Culpepper. The artillery they were hearing was from fighting between cavalry screening the flanks of both armies.

The meeting broke up, and the men noticed a commotion in the field to west of them. Hundreds of men were running around chasing hundreds of rabbits. With meat as short as it was, it didn't take long for H Company to get into the hunt. By the time it was over, the regiment had taken nearly a hundred rabbits to add to its larder.

———————

At noon, the drummer beat assembly, and the regiment lined up on both sides of the road. Soon, Generals McClellan, Burnside and Franklin rode by with their staffs. They were escorted by a bodyguard of 1,000 cavalry. The well-groomed horses, the flags and banners from the various regiments were a magnificent sight. A chorus of bugle salutes heralded the progress of the group.

Later in the day, the regiment assembled for the dress parade. Adjutant Winans announced the resignation of Colonel Cox. This was an anticlimax. Cox had been gone since General Paul arrested him at Fredrick. They had not seen him for some time. They hadn't missed him. General Brooks and Colonel Torbert then called Ryerson forward, and Winans read the orders promoting him to full colonel. Brooks and Torbert each removed one of Ryerson's Lieutenant Colonel shoulder boards, and replaced them with the boards of a full colonel. Then they all stood at attention while they read the orders making Ryerson the Commander of the 23rd Regiment. The "Yahoos" had a new "Old Man."

The boys had some free time after the parade. A group of men from most of the companies in the regiment gathered to watch Howard, Conover, Goodenough and four or five other men learn to play baseball. They had found a ball, and someone had carved a bat about the right size.

They didn't have canvas bases yet, but they did find a way to lay out a field with the right dimensions. They scratched squares in the dirt where the bases were supposed to be. Conover was pitching, Goodenough was catching, and since Howard knew the rules best, he was the umpire.

It didn't take long for word to get around camp. Soon officers, NCOs and men from all of the companies wanted to borrow the book, and learn to play. Sweesley was puffing away on his meerschaum next to McKee, Hartman and Miller.

O'Neil was up to bat. Howard carefully took the time to explain the rules, and show him how to swing the bat. Conover threw the ball for him several times. Soon, he was hitting it regularly. Howard grinned quietly to himself. When the game was over, O'Neil carefully took the bat back to the supply wagon, and in violation of Army regulations, put it safely away. The baseball equipment was secure. No officer ever questioned the wagoner about why it was there.

November 16, 1862 - New Baltimore, Virginia
The regiment had halted between New Baltimore and Warrenton for five days. Since idle soldiers are the devil's playground, the normal daily training schedule was being followed: company drill in the morning, battalion drill after lunch and regimental parade late in the afternoon. Manual of arms training, musket loading and bayonet drill

was fit in between. During their free time the men had sat around their fires, played cards and checkers, and visited. Some had become good friends with Chaplain Abbot, and attended prayer meetings with him. Abbott was continuing to help Crispin deal with little Frank's death. Many in the squad noticed. They had a special respect for the Chaplain's way of helping each of them through the trials they faced every day.

The chaplain was a balding, middle-aged man with a full beard, and he actually looked like a chaplain. He appeared to be at peace with the world. His faith and gentle demeanor inspired confidence in the men, but they knew he was no pushover when it came to speaking out about vices in the ranks.

Yesterday afternoon at the Regimental Parade, Lieutenant Winans announced that Major Thompson had resigned. Several of the men asked Hartman, "Top, what's with all the officers resigning?" Hartman was about to chew them out for questioning what went on in officer country, but he stopped. "Fellas, most of these officers are political appointees. You know what that is?" Some nodded no, so he continued. "That means they got made officers because they knew the Governor or somebody important. Sometimes they know what they are doing, and sometimes they don't."

"I don't know if all the things they say about Colonel Cox are true, and I don't know why Major Thompson resigned. I can tell you this. The people that are replacing them are fighting soldiers. I'd rather be following one of them in a pinch. Now, I expect you to respect every officer you see, whether you like him or not. Understand?"

"Yes, Top Sergeant."

Lincoln ordered Burnside to come up with a plan to move on Richmond and end the war. The general transmitted the plan to Washington on November 9th. He got a reluctant approval on the 14th. The plan was put in motion the next day. All over the north, men and equipment started moving toward Fredericksburg.

Brooks called his commanders together early in the morning and outlined what they were going to do. "Gentlemen, we find ourselves in an interesting dilemma. The Army could attack Lee at Culpepper and move on Gordonsville to cut the rail line to Richmond, but our supply lines would be at Tom Jackson's mercy. You might have noticed supplies are a bit thin." Everyone nodded.

"General Burnside sent plans to President Lincoln to cross the Rappahannock at Fredericksburg and march on Richmond. It allows us to get our supplies through Aquia Creek, and if we move fast enough it will shorten the war. Gentlemen, the President's approval of that plan arrived yesterday. General Sumner's men moved out yesterday, and his leading elements should be in Falmouth tomorrow. Get your men ready to march, we are going to Fredericksburg. Don't spare the horses. We have to get there before Longstreet does. We can't have the roads tied up like we did last week, so you will be moving out in order and going cross-country. You need to stay with your schedule. We have a lot of army wagons and guns to get over a narrow highway. So, it's a forced march, gents. Before you go, I have an announcement to make. I want all of you to join me in congratulating Brigadier General Al Torbert* on his promotion. It should be official by the end of the month"

Torbert was taken by surprise. He was immediately surrounded by cheering, back-slapping colleagues. They knew he was wounded, so they didn't slap him on the back too hard.

The 23rd was not scheduled to move out until the morning of the 17th. Ryerson wanted to make sure they were ready for the march and a fight, so he ordered an inspection at 10 AM. The officers and NCOs made sure the guns were cleaned and the equipment was in order. Colonel Brown from the 4th New Jersey helped the new Commander look over his troops. It took an hour and a half, and when all was said and done, the Yahoos had measured up. They got the rest of the day off. The baseball game started quickly.

November 18, 1862 - Stafford's Courthouse, Virginia
By the evening of the 18th, the regiment had covered almost forty

*The Crispin diary says Torbert's promotion to BG of Volunteers happened on 11/27. Wikipedia cites Eichler's book and says the promotion was on 11/29/62. A 12/25/62 letter in the New Jersey Mirror refers to him as General Torbert. It may have been an "acting generalship", for Slade's book on Torbert shows numerous correspondences in early 1863 encouraging the promotion. Ryerson's letter to sister Maggie dated 3/6/63 says the U.S. Senate Committee rejected the promotion, and that every officer in the Brigade had signed a petition supporting Torbert, but Slade says he was officially promoted around 2/27/63.

miles in two days. The country leveled off after they left New Baltimore and marching was a lot easier. The soil in this part of the country was poor, and it looked a lot like the New Jersey pinelands. Stunted pines and oaks with catbriers and sassafras stretched off in all directions. Most of the leaves had fallen off the trees. They stopped a quarter mile from Stafford Courthouse. The November darkness fell around 5 o'clock, so everyone wanted to get their camps set up quickly.

It had been cold during the two long nights on the march, and it had rained all of the time. The companies had forded several streams, and the constant wetness from rain and immersion was taking a toll on feet and footwear. Shoes were beginning to fall apart. Cook and his assistants were busy treating blisters, sore throats and colds.

H Company made fifteen miles the first day. They went through Greenwich and Catlett's Station and, after fording Cedar Creek, bivouacked on a hill in the rain on the south side of the creek.

The next day they did it again and camped in a pine forest. It rained all day again.

During the day, the company crested a small hill. Sharp had his head down watching his footing when he glanced ahead for an instant. He did a double take, and froze. The company followed his gaze, and stopped in its tracks.

"Holy mother of God, look at that," gasped Sharp, pointing away to the east of them. The whole army was in sight and moving. It looked like some huge, quivering blue mass covering the countryside. Units were marching to the east as far as they could see in every direction.

"There're near 150,000 men out there, boys. That's Franklins, Porters and McDowell's Corps. You will never see the likes of this again," said Lt. Root, almost with reverence.

"How can the Rebs stand against this, Lieutenant?" asked Hibbs.

"I am afraid somewhere south of us, there is a gray mass that looks just like this one, John," answered Root. The men stared at the spectacle for a few more seconds and moved on.

———————

Crispin was not doing well. He woke up with a cold the morning after he forded Cedar Creek, and was unable to keep up with the unit. He caught up with them in time to bed down for the night, but woke up sick again in the morning. He had lost the sole of one of his shoes fording Aquia creek. He was in danger of falling out with the hundreds of soldiers who were lying along the road. Finally, he came to a homestead, and bought some apples. Eating them made him feel better.

He caught up with the Company at Stafford Court House as darkness fell.

———————

Doc Elmer was also having a rough time. He was traveling with the regimental supply train, ambulances and medical wagon. The roads were miserable, and the wagon trains were having a terrible time keeping up with the regiments. The column had to stop when a wagon overturned. All hands pitched in and got it righted. A little later, another sunk to its axles. Teams were arranged, and shovels were used to dig it out of the muck. Within minutes, a second wagon sunk, and the whole exercise was repeated.

One of the wagon drivers threatened to lighten the load by throwing out the men's camp chests. Elmer and O'Neil refused to let that happen. They understood the cooking utensils and incidental equipment in each chest was absolutely vital to the men. After hours of strenuous effort, the wagons finally caught up with the 23rd at the camp near Stafford Courthouse. The docs got together and made arrangements to set up the hospital tent and hold sick call.

November 22, 1862 - Stafford's Courthouse, Virginia

It had rained steady since the minute they arrived at Stafford's Courthouse. The men turned out for reveille roll call, and then stayed under their tents until full daylight. They built crude lean-tos near smoky fires, so they could fix breakfast under as much shelter as possible from the pouring rain. They sat in silence. The only sound came from the beating rain. Activity in camp was limited to the constant effort to trench tents, and make repairs to shelters made uninhabitable by the pelting rains. A desperate gloom settled over the camp as the soldiers thought of home.

Several things conspired to break the gloom, though. First, the morning paper usually arrived at 10 AM. It was the New York Herald, and the men were famished for the news. This morning it was right on time. Mail had been slow catching up to the unit after the forced march, so the bellowed "MAIL CALL" certainly brought everyone running. Everyone felt bad for the fellas that didn't get a letter, the ones who did felt blessed.

It stopped raining in the mid-morning, and the sun showed upon the army. Drowned rats couldn't have looked more pathetic. They started about their duties when off toward the headquarters tents sounded a couple of drum beats, a few hoots on some instruments, and the brigade band struck up a tune. A veritable stampede of New Jersey soldiers descended on the scene. General Torbert and the regimental commanders greeted them with grins. For a while, all thoughts of the march and the miserable rain disappeared. After the band concert, the men had gone back to their units to start putting their equipment in order.

Torbert gathered his Commanders together after the men had gone. "Bad news, gentlemen, Lee and Longstreet arrived at Fredericksburg yesterday, and they are digging in along Marye's Heights." He didn't have to tell them that Fredericksburg was only ten miles to the south. "Cavalry scouts say Jackson is moving this way from northern Virginia. Jeb Stuart was in Warrenton before the last of our men were out of sight. It took the War Department more than a week to get the pontoons here. We missed our chance for an unopposed crossing. General Burnside thinks it's too risky to use the fords. With the weather the way it's been, we would not be able to reinforce or supply a force across the river if the water came up. So, we are waiting for pontoons. I want you to have your men take the rest of the day to get their equipment dried out and cleaned. Get it done, and have everyone take tomorrow off. Chaplains can have their services and give the men a chance to have a decent Sunday. Monday, I want to have a full brigade inspection. General Burnside wants to go into action soon, and I want everything ready." The meeting broke up, and the colonels made small talk as they walked out the door.

Ryerson hung back. "Can I have a word with you, General?"

"I am not a general until Thursday, Ogden," grinned Torbert. "How are you? How are those Yahoos doing?"

"I am finally healing up. The men made it through the march, but they are tired. Tomorrow will be good for them. I hope it doesn't rain again."

"Me, too," said Torbert as he looked at his Colonel expectantly.

"Sir, you know Major Thompson and Lieutenant Winans have resigned."

Torbert nodded. "Not surprising. He claimed it was for health reasons, but I don't know. Thompson thought Brown should have gotten the regiment instead of you, and he should have moved up to Brown's job. Winans and he are friends. I approved the resignations."

Ryerson continued. "I want to move Lieutenant Perkins out of G Company and make him Adjutant. He has the background to do the job. I don't see a captain capable of moving up to major. Do you have any suggestions?"

Torbert thought for a minute. "The biggest problem you have right now is that you are the only man in the regiment that has been in a fight. That's why I picked you instead of Brown. I think you need someone who has some battle experience and can help you with your staff work."

Ryerson thought for a minute. "How about Barz Ridgway, sir? He's a Captain over in the 4th."

Torbert hesitated, and shook his head no. "I know Barz; I don't think he would do a good job. How about Burd Grubb?"

Ryerson brightened, he knew Burd Grubb. Grubb had been in most of the fights the Jersey men had seen since the beginning of the war. He served on General Taylor's staff, and Torbert had kept him on after the general was killed. "That would be very good, Sir, I could use the help."

"I'll have the orders drawn up. Have a good day Ogden."

———————

Sergeant Major McKee was waiting for the Colonel when he got back. "Sir, Doc Cook tells me we got a lot of people on sick call."

Ryerson nodded. "That's not surprising, given the weather and the march. How many?"

McKee handed him the list. "Near fifty, sir. Cook is outside, and would like to see you."

Ryerson took the list and said, "Send him in, Top, and you come in, too."

Cook came, and stood in the doorway. Ryerson motioned him in as he read through the list. "So, Doc, looks like you have been busy." The Sergeant Major stood with him.

"Yes, sir, we have a lot of sore throats, colds, lots of blistered feet and a few infections. I am a little worried that we have serious fevers showing up. I have three troops who need to go to a hospital." The Colonel looked at him, and he went on. "Jacques from B Company has the fever, Lippincott from E Company froze his feet, and Corporal Bussom from D Company has a double hernia. I can't help them here."

"You talk to their company commanders yet?" asked the Colonel.

"No, sir."

"You need to do that. You need to use the Chain of Command." Cook nodded. "Anything we can do help you out?"

"Elmer and Hetzell could use some help getting them to the train station. There could be a lot of troops on bed rest for a few days until they get rested up. I thought you should know first. Sir, I had to send a

Private Johnson from C Company back to Philadelphia a few weeks ago. I thought he had galloping consumption."

"Yes."

"I was right. We got word today he died at the General Hospital on the 12th."

Ryerson looked at McKee. "Top, make sure Dr. Cook gets all the help he needs. Let's get the orders together to move these men to a hospital." He paused. "Let Captain Carr know about Johnson. His men will want to know."

"Yes, sir, shall I let Chaplain Abbott know, too?" Ryerson nodded yes.

"Anything else?"

"Yes, sir, there's something wrong with that molasses we got from the Quartermaster. Everybody who's had any has got the runs."

Ryerson had just had molasses on his pancakes, and he knew what the doctor was talking about. He groaned. "I noticed that. Sergeant Major, have Lieutenant Nichols send any we haven't used back, and tell the Captains to let their men know not to eat any more."

———————

McCabe, Root and Carter were busy watching Hartman and the NCOs supervise the men in the company. Blankets, knapsacks, rucksacks, clothing and everything they owned was hung up or spread out on gum blankets to dry in the sun. It was chilly. The grass was turning brown and most of the leaves were off the trees, but direct sunlight could warm a man. Tents were set straight and cleaned.

The men emptied their cartridge boxes and inspected every paper round. Anything that looked suspicious was replaced. The men learned to be very careful about this. The cost of any cartridges unaccounted for was deducted from their pay. When that was done, they turned to their weapons. The guns were disassembled, and each piece examined and cleaned. The barrels were swabbed out, and burnished along with the bayonets. No rust was tolerated. When the metal parts were clean, they were coated with a mixture of bees wax and tallow and wiped down. The corporals and sergeants looked at every piece before a man was given permission to put his rifle back together, and then checked it again to make sure it was assembled properly.

Next, the men started repairing their clothing. Missing buttons were replaced. Holes, tears and broken straps were mended and brass polished. Shoes were repaired as best as possible. Then they were oiled and blacked, along with the leather belts and slings. Finally, their canteens and cooking utensils were cleaned and inspected. By the end of the day, H Company was looking good.

November 24, 1862 - Stafford's Courthouse, Virginia

Torbert personally inspected each regiment in the brigade. It took all day. H Company was ready in the morning, but he didn't get to them until 3 o'clock. The 23rd was the biggest regiment and last in order.

General Brooks accompanied him. Both arrived and marched up to Colonel Ryerson at the front of the regiment. Ryerson called the regiment to attention and exchanged salutes. The command was given for the regiment to stand at parade rest. Over 900 men simultaneously assumed the parade rest position. Ryerson nodded to Adjutant Perkins, and he began to read, "Attention to orders! Effective this instant, Captain E. Burd Grubb is transferred from staff, First Brigade to Staff, 23rd Regiment New Jersey Volunteers. Effective immediately, Captain E Burd Grubb is promoted to Major, by order of A.T.A. Torbert, Brevet Brigadier General, U.S. Army."

Back in the ranks of H Company, Miller hissed to Sweesley, "Johnny, ain't that the captain that stopped and talked to us when we were on the rear guard?"

Sweesley whispered, "Sure is."

"Knock off the BS in ranks," growled Hartman. "You sergeants know better than that. You bunch of dammed Yahoos." Fortunately, Hartman was out in front of the company with McCabe, so he didn't see them grin.

The commanders approached A Company. The men in the company being inspected were called to attention when the officers approached the Company Commander. The officers walked through the ranks and randomly picked troops to inspect. After two hours, they finally came to H Company. They snapped to attention at McCabe's command.

Eyes were supposed to be straight ahead, but Crispin was looking down the rank from the corner of his eye. Major General Brooks was over 6 feet tall and a little stout, with a commanding continence and a slouched hat on his head. His uniform was simple, consisting of a plain blue coat with a white star on an epaulette on each shoulder. A neat white silk sash circled his waist, and he wore plain blue pants and nicely polished boots. He dwarfed Torbert.

As he stopped and turned to face Crispin, Josie executed a perfect "Inspection Arms." His right hand lifted the rifle until it was in front of him and at a forty-five degree angle to his body. His left hand grasped the fore stock, and held it in position while his right hand slid down the weapon, cocking the hammer, and ended by grasping the stock.

General Brooks took the weapon, inspecting it carefully.

Crispin's heart was in his throat. Would he find something wrong? Had some spider or insidious dirt clod found a way on to the piece he had missed? There was always an element of doubt in these inspections. Was he going to get in trouble?

The general handed it back. He looked Crispin in the eye, and said, "Nice presentation, soldier," turned, and moved on down the ranks. Crispin just barely kept his sigh of relief to himself. The General had complimented him. Crispin was on cloud nine.

November 27, 1862 - Stafford's Courthouse, Virginia

The Governor of New Jersey had issued an official proclamation calling for a Thanksgiving holiday to be observed on Thursday, November 27th.* He had written to General Brooks, and asked that the troops be given the day off. The past two days had been spent drilling intensely. Brooks was agreeable.

Chaplain Abbott held services at 11 AM. He took his scripture from the 27th and 136th Psalms. It was a very impressive sermon, and gave the troops great comfort.

After the service, the regiment went back to their tents. Lloyd, Conover, Rue, Crispin, Sharp and Terhune were lounging around as Lloyd said, "What's for dinner?"

"Well," opined Rue, "Looks like hardtack, fresh beef and maybe some ham."

"Well, that's what we had for breakfast."

"Yup. It's what you get for supper, too."

"But, it's Thanksgiving. We should be having turkey and mince pie and mashed potatoes and butter," crooned Crispin. "I'll bet they are having just that at the Cooper Refreshment Saloon. I'll bet Mary and Paul and the kids are eating right now back at the farm."

Sharp glared at him. "Why'd you have to bring that up? I get hunger pangs just thinking of it."

"Oh, it was just something on my mind, George, don't think nothing of it," said Crispin, trying to keep a straight face.

Just then, Hartman bellowed, "Chow call."

As the company ran to get in line, Rue grinned. "Looks like a great big pot of vegetable soup."

* Federal recognition of the Thanksgiving holiday was extended by President Lincoln in November of 1863.

Crispin grinned. "That's wonderful. We haven't had vegetables since we left Bakersville."

"It sure beats salt pork and hardtack crackers. Hey, what's going on over there?" smiled Conover.

"General Torbert sent us a barrel of whiskey to celebrate his promotion."

"Well, I don't want any whiskey. I don't drink. I resolved not to touch any spirits or associate with immoral persons, and to abstain from game and other vicious habits when I left home." The group of friends looked at Crispin, and each other, and burst out laughing.

"So, what are you doing here with us, Mr. Quaker Innocence?" The laughter continued.

"Now, I have it on good authority that men who refrain from liquor heal faster from their war wounds than those who imbibe."

At this, the whole group laughed even harder. "Sure," jibed Terhune, "that's why the first thing they do after you've been shot is give you a drink of whiskey."

Crispin blushed. "Well, that's to stimulate your system and help with the pain."

By now the group was laughing even harder, and Terhune added, "If it's all the same to you, I would just as soon get stimulated without having any pain or a hole in my hide."

Sharp exchanged glances with Terhune. "Well, can I have your share?"

Rue could see the wheels turning in Sharp's head. Josie was just about to say "yes" when he saw Rue grin and shake his head no. Then he caught on.

He scratched his chin for a second, and asked, "What will you trade me for it?" Out of the corner of his eye he saw Rue grin even wider and nod his head yes.

Sharp had not expected this. Crispin was usually a pushover when it came to deals. It took a few minutes to conclude the deal. In the end, a quantity of sugar was exchanged for Josie's share of whiskey.

The trading of whiskey rations became quite brisk around the regiment that afternoon. Sugar, pork, beef, hardtack and tobacco were the common units of exchange.

George Howard's crowning baseball achievement was teaching Milt O'Neil how to play. The carefully lobbed pitches over the previous weeks had made the man a fanatic. The Wagoner made sure the ball, bat and newly sewn bases were kept in the wagon with the company supplies. The game had caught on so well, the officers and NCOs were starting to play. The weather was nice enough for the men to lay out a diamond and play a few innings. Those who weren't playing or watching enjoyed playing catch off to the side. General Doubleday rode past, and was obviously pleased to see the boys having a good time.

"Who the hell is Burd Grubb? For crying out loud, he's only twenty, and he's a major already?" asked Terhune after several shots of General Torbert's whiskey.

"You wouldn't know him," said Conover. "He's from Burlington. Our people along the Delaware know him. He joined up when the Army formed the 3rd Regiment last year. He graduated from college in Burlington, so they made him a 2nd Lieutenant."

"He's been in a lot of battles, 1st Bull Run and the Peninsula Campaign. He was with General Taylor when he was killed at 2nd Bull Run, and he was with Torbert at Crampton's Gap."

Sweesley was listening, and added, "Me and Miller met him when we pulled that rear guard detail on the way to Burkitsville." He puffed on his meerschaum pipe. "He rode up to us to see how we were doing. Said the regiment was spread out for four miles. He wasn't mean or overbearing, just checking to see if we were all right. I liked him."

"Yeah, but he's only twenty years old," carped Terhune. Sharp looked like he was going to jump in and agree.

"Well, boys, you can complain about Thompson, who has resigned, and gone home to Bordentown, and never was in a fight, and got made a major because he knew somebody. Or," he paused to puff on his pipe and look into the fire, "you can have Grubb, who earned his way up, and is still here. It will be good to have a major who knows what it feels like to get shot at, even if he is only twenty." Terhune looked at Sharp, thought for a minute. He nodded yes.

Grubb was sitting at a fire with Kirkbride and Parmentier. They hadn't had much time to get to know one another. It was late in the evening when Parmentier said, "Major, do you know anything about this rumor that Torbert's a Reb?"

Burd looked over the fire at the two men, and they clearly were uncomfortable. This was strange, because Parmentier looked like old Saint Nick. He had a reputation for being a cut-up. Kirkbride had a reputation as rock-solid officer. Grubb sensed the question was sincere.

"Yes, I've heard it. I don't believe a word of it. J.P. Freeze up at the Trenton Star Gazette has made it his personal mission to ruin the man. The first time I met the Colonel was just after the Manassas Bridge. I tell you, it was the strangest thing. We were laying on the ground, firing at the Rebs from the prone. Smoke got so thick we couldn't see them. Thought they left. We kind of half got up, and I guess they could see us. All of a sudden I hear "AIM – FIRE." Just that quick, and they just raked us. It shook up the boys so bad there was no controlling them. They broke and ran. Can't blame them, Rebs caught us completely off guard. The officers finally got them settled down after they ran about a mile. The companies were all mixed up. I got orders to put them back in order, but I couldn't do it by myself. Next thing I know, there's Torbert on a stretcher. He had to be the only man in the Army carried to the battle. He had rheumatism so bad he could barely walk, but insisted on coming. He got off the stretcher and helped me get the companies straightened out. It took almost all night; sometimes he was on his hands and knees. He doesn't sound much like a Reb to me."

"I heard he's from Delaware," said Kirkbride.

"That's right, Milton, I think. He got appointed to West Point from there. He graduated in the Class of 55. Spent some time fighting Indians, and then came back and helped organize the Jersey volunteers. Word is some Confederate sympathizers from Delaware put him up for a Confederate commission without his knowledge. He stayed Union, said it would be terribly ungrateful to fight against the country that paid for his education. Some newspapers have tried to make it rough for him, but he's true blue. You should have seen him at Crampton's Gap. The Union couldn't ask for a better commander."

December 2, 1862 - Stafford's Courthouse, Virginia

The training schedule was being relentlessly exercised. The regiment had drilled every day since Thanksgiving. Everyone expected a battle soon, and drills were dress rehearsals. There was squad drill, platoon drill, company drill, battalion drill, regimental drill, and even brigade drill. There were right flank marches, oblique marches, left and right wheel marches, column right and left marches, and dozens of commands and maneuvers for the troops to learn and practice. The whole aim was to make sure the men practiced so often that they reacted instantly to the commands.

That was until today. Winter set in with vengeance. A wintry blast struck that was so severe it stopped the army in tracks. It froze hard at night and didn't warm up enough for things to thaw during the day. The roads from the ports to Falmouth worked only because they were frozen. A thaw would disrupt the wagon trains. It was so cold that a number of men at a drinking party went to sleep and froze to death.

Steamboats and tugs were moving materials in from ports all over the north. Supplies were coming into Aquia Creek at an amazing rate, but ice on the Potomac was two to four inches thick, and some were worried it would hinder the Army's supply lines.

William White had rebuilt Herman Haupt's famous "cornstalk and beanpole" railroad bridge over Potomac Creek. The army was not dependent on the roads from the ports, because trains could once again run the twelve miles from Aquia Creek wharf all the way to a depot near Falmouth.

A rail car could carry ten tons of supplies. A barge could carry eight railcars. A tug could push two barges, and an engine could pull sixteen railcars. General Haupt and Superintendent White had the railroads organized so well that a railcar could be pulled by horses across the Long Bridge in Washington, loaded on a barge in Alexandria, moved by steam tug to Aquia Creek, offloaded, and pulled by a steam engine to Falmouth in twelve hours. The railroad was moving in over 800 tons of supplies a day.

Just as important, this meant that sick or wounded soldiers could be moved from Falmouth back to hospitals in the north just as fast. The knowledge that troops could get to a hospital and first rate medical help when they needed it was a tremendous boost to Union morale.

The ease of travel from Washington to Aquia Creek had several immediate benefits for the troops. First, mail became more regular. Second, civilian sutlers could come into camp and sell their wares.

"MAIL CALL," bellowed Hartman. Men came boiling out of their tents, even though the temperature was brutal. They swarmed around him and grabbed their letters as he read off the names. Crispin had three, along with a package. He snatched up the items and headed back for the tent. George had his, and they sat there reading the news from home. Sharp was chortling about his letter from Mary. His son, Allen, had turned one on November 7th, and both were doing well. Others were reading and sharing the news from home.

"Look at Sharp," laughed Lloyd, "he acts like a big, tough man of the world, but Mary sure has him under her thumb."

Crispin smiled and grunted his agreement.

"How's the family, Josie?" asked Lloyd quietly.

"Mary says Hannah and Dad are still having a hard time about Frank. I wish I could go back and see them."

"Me too, but with a battle coming I don't think they will let you go."

"Me either. The neighbors sent me a letter, too. You know, the Witcrafts. Said they had a nice Thanksgiving, and they miss us. I might have to look in on that Mary Witcraft when I get home."

"You've been hangin around Sharp too long," grinned Edwin. Josie just smirked. Ed Lloyd actually leered.

"What's in the box?"

"Hmmm, well, let's see." It was from Mary and had an official seal on it. Josi looked at the seal and read, "Repacked by U.S. Sanitary Commission. Wonder who they are?" Most soldiers weren't aware that the shipment of packages through the mail to the troops early in the war had been a disaster. Inexperienced families all over the north had sent preserves and a variety of food items that arrived spoiled or broken. This wasted resources and hurt morale. So, the U.S. Sanitary Commission procured a warehouse in Washington, intercepted the gifts from home and repackaged them, so the fragile contents would not break.

Josi opened the box. "Peaches!" he yelled.

"Shhhh, you'll have everybody in here," hissed Ed.

"Sorry, there's sugar, and some candy and some newspapers. New Jersey Mirror, so we can see what's happening home, and some apples. Oh, grape jam. Mary did good."

"She sure did," grinned Ed.

Conover ran past the door of the tent. "Sutler's in town. He's down at the end of the street."

Josie carefully repacked his box, and joined Ed on the way down the street. There was quite a line by the wagon. They crowded in and saw the usual assortment of dry goods. It was amazing how much people forgot how cold it was when new food items showed up in their midst. "Those prices are awful."

"Yes, but he's got cheesecake," moaned Ed. "Cheeeeeeesecake."

"Yeah, at one day's pay. I am not paying that."

"I'll split it with you. We buy one slice and share it. Each pays half."

Josie thought for a minute, and a mischievous grin came over his face. "All right, but just this once."

The mail brought news on a number of fronts. Quakers in the regiment were relieved to hear that the Longwood Yearly Meeting had declined to disown members who were fighting in the war. The meeting disclaimed all disciplinary authority over individuals and local associations. It posited that each individual should be governed by his or her own conscience, and not some external authority. Josie and the other Quakers in the regiment breathed a sigh of relief. They were still members of their meetings.

The mail also brought disturbing news from some families. They were depending on the men to send their pay home. Men away soldiering were not bringing home the accustomed wages and salaries the families needed. November 30 was the second payday in a row the Army had missed. Some families were approaching the holidays in dire straits. Officers started getting inquiries from their troops about when to expect payday.

December 4, 1862 - Stafford's Courthouse, Virginia

Crispin and the squad were stepping along at two miles an hour in the dark. The sun wouldn't rise for another thirty minutes. Last night, McCabe had told them to be ready to move out at 6 AM this morning. Josie was sick again. He went to bed early to try and get a good night's sleep. He and Ed had awakened at 3, cooked breakfast, hardtack with fresh pork and coffee, and packed their gear. The drums sounded assembly at 5:30, and off they went.

"How are you feeling, Josie?" asked Ed.

"Sick," rasped Josie. "My stomach is bothering me."

"Are you going to be all right marching?"

Josi grunted an affirmative. He had some difficulty for the first mile. As he warmed up, it got easier. He had learned that each time he took a step, he could throw a foot forward a little and let gravity pull it to the ground. Once he settled into a pace, he could easily keep going as long as it wasn't interrupted. The rest of the squad had discovered the same thing.

Daylight came slowly in early December. The winter sun rose far to the southeast. Today it rose clear and bright. It revealed an army marching through a countryside coated with frost. Each man could see his breath as he exhaled in the cold air.

They marched past Stafford's Courthouse just after sunrise. Conover glanced to the side as they went by and puffed, "This place is a real dump."

The dilapidated single-story courthouse was built with long windows and a porch supported by massive columns facing the road. It did have an impressive double front door with sidelights that added some dignity to the structure. The courthouse had been pilfered. Papers and legal documents were scattered on the ground and blowing about the neighborhood. Across the street was the county jail. It was a twenty by thirty foot building built of gray sandstone. There were only two small grated windows on either side. It would be a very dark, cold place.

Hibbs and Howard followed Conover's gaze. "That jail is enough to make a man go straight. How would you like to spend time in that thing?"

"Not me. Wouldn't want to spend time in that old hotel, either," gasped Hibbs as he pointed to a tumbled-down old building further down the road. "Bet that place has bedbugs big as Barnegat Bay crabs." Laughter echoed up and down the column as word of Hibb's giant bedbugs spread.

The column halted a mile down the road for a few minutes as pioneers cleared several trees that had blown across the road in the last day's storms. As soon as that was done, they were off again.

They crossed a newly constructed rail line linking the docks at Aquia Creek with Falmouth. The march continued southeast.

At one o'clock, they came in sight of the Potomac, "Holy cow, Ed, look at that," exclaimed Josie. He was looking at an expanse of water he never expected to see. They were marching past the bustling port of Belle Plaines Landing. "It's sure bigger than the river we slept by back at Mercerville."

"Look, there's a steamer tied up at the wharf." There was no wind, and blue smoke rose straight into the clear blue sky from the steamer's stack. Men were unloading cargo. "It's the Major Reybold. It's from Philadelphia." Gunboats and steamboats were moored in the bay.

The port looked brand new. It was. The Department of the Rappahannock had been at Aquia Creek the previous spring for the attack on Richmond and the Peninsula Campaign. When they had to retreat back to Washington, Burnside had ordered those port facilities burned to keep them from falling into Confederate hands.

Navy gunboats and Army engineers returned on November 15th within hours of Burnside's decision to attack Fredericksburg. They knew from experience that Aquia Creek could not handle the volume of materials consumed by the Army, so they had built this second major port in sixteen days. In spite of the icy conditions, steamboats and barges full of supplies were unloading at the docks.

The 23rd marched past hundreds of laborers building new warehouses. Stacks of boxes, barrels, cannon balls, ammunition, and building materials were everywhere. Supply wagons trundled off towards the railroad.

Guardhouses, tents and shacks of every description covered the area. Smoke rose from hundreds of chimneys and campfires. Horse, wagon and artillery parks dotted the landscape.

"Hey, 1st Sergeant, how about a break so we can look around?" called someone from the squad.

"Captain'll tell you when you can have a break. Keep going," droned Hartman.

A few minutes later they came to a large, flat plain and another amazing sight. Huge wagons loaded with pontoons were parked in a field along the road. A large number of engineers and soldiers were guarding them and the stock that pulled them. Each wooden pontoon boat was built of stout wood. Each was 31 feet long, 5 ½ feet wide and 27 inches deep. Both ends were squared off like a pram. Each contained the tools, oars, ropes, anchors and equipment the engineers needed to assemble the floating bridge. There were also wagonloads of lumber for the spans between the boats, called balks, and the decking for the bridge. More wagons were loaded with tools, rope and chain to hold it together in the current.

The most weight a four-horse team could efficiently pull was carefully calculated by the Army to be three thousand pounds. These wagons were so heavy, they were drawn by teams of six horses or mules. Several thousand head of draft animals grazed behind massive stacks of fodder, harnesses and tack.

They marched past the pontoon train, and finally stopped 4 miles down the road at 3 o'clock, about ten miles from King Georges Courthouse. The place was known as Devil's Hole. They pitched their tents on a bleak, barren hillside with no shelter from the wind. The place was frozen solid. They were just about to turn in when word came they were to go on guard. So, they tore everything down and repacked it.

Ed looked at Josie. "You look done in. Why don't you go on sick call?"

"I'll be all right if I can get on 3rd relief and get some rest." Sweesley saw to it he did. The guard station was only ½ mile from camp, so they had time to pick pine branches, and make themselves as comfortable as possible. It was still a cold sleep.

Josie stood guard, even though his throat was so sore he could not have called for the Commander of the Relief. He wore his long underwear, his wool pants and blouse, his overcoat and fatigue cap. The overcoat was knee length. It had a collar and a cape that could be buttoned into a hood. Even dressed like this, it was hard to stay warm during the two-hour shift.

Doc Elmer was left to get the sick into ambulances, and follow as best he could. Trouble was, he had twenty-five or thirty men and could only carry half that. So, he loaded the worst cases, and the rest had to walk. The weather was so bad they only made it the single mile to the Stafford Courthouse. He waited to see if he could arrange more transportation, but it was quickly apparent that all of the other units were in the same condition. The courthouse was not locked, so he opened the doors.

General Franklin's staff had been stabling their horses in the court room. The place was a mess. County records were strewn all over the floor and grounds. He cleaned it up as best he could, made the men as comfortable as possible and pushed on to catch up with the regiment. In spite of miserable roads and heavy traffic, he was able to deliver his charges to the regimental encampment that night.

December 6, 1862 - Devil's Hole, Virginia

The last two days were the most miserable guard detail the men could imagine. They spent two hours walking their posts, and then 4 hours at the guard station where they could be mobilized as a ready reserve if needed. The squads spent most of the off-duty time huddled in their two-man tents on piles of pine boughs to get up off the frozen ground and melting ice.

Yesterday, sleet started falling at daylight and changed to snow around noon, and back to rain later in the afternoon. The rain and three inches of melting snow turned the roads to mush and muck. The roads were so bad that Sgt Dobbins had to stash most of the tents and the pioneer's knapsacks along the road to lighten the load for his mules. The mud was ankle-deep each time the Sergeant of the Guard made his rounds to post his reliefs. It was dangerously slick, and sucked at their already failing shoes.

The only saving grace was the issue of some rice, beans, fresh bread and sugar in addition to the tedious ration of beef, pork and hardtack. The men were thankful for any variation in their diet.

In their spare time, the boys visited a Negro family in a small hut, and traded some coffee and sugar for some hoecakes. The cakes were about the size of a man's hand. The fried corn bread and buttermilk biscuits were a welcome treat.

Later in the day, at the regimental parade, several court martial sentences were carried out near the camp. The court found five or six men guilty of stealing hay from a local farmer to feed their starving horses. They were made to walk around a ring six feet in diameter for hours. Another man was hanged by his thumbs in the storm. The squad was outraged by the treatment of these men, with the weather the way it was.

The rain changed back to snow after dark, and the storm grew windy. The stations were in open country. There was no shelter from the brisk north wind. Men came back from their posts, swathed in snow from head to toe. They brushed it off and crawled under their blankets wet. Finally, in the morning another company came up to relieve them. They marched back to camp through three more inches of snow. They scraped the white stuff off of the ground, placed several inches of pine boughs on the ground for insulation and settled in for another cold night. Each group crowded together to share each other's body heat.

———————

Elmer and Cook went to Ryerson on the night of the 4th to tell him about leaving the sick at Stafford Courthouse. Ryerson detailed Dobbins to take the regimental wagons to assist the ambulances in bringing the troops back to the 23rd. Dobbins had to go back for the knapsacks and tents anyway.

They had started back to Stafford yesterday morning. The roads were jammed with troops. They had to go several miles out of the way. It rained and snowed all day. Between detours, traffic, bad roads and the weather, they didn't get back to the courthouse until after dark. Elmer tended the sick as best he could, and then went back the sutler's tent at the old camp and slept there.

In the morning, they loaded the sick into his wagon train and started out for the regiment again. Along the way they picked up the materials they had stashed. Conditions were just like they were yesterday. The journey took all day. Doc Elmer finally drove into the regimental area well after dark, with four wagons full of sick soldiers. Cook had the few available hospital tents set up and waiting. Helping hands unloaded the men. The men's shelter tents were useless in these conditions. Ryerson had permitted the officers of each company to keep one wall tent, and ordered all of the rest to be used to shelter as many men as possible.

Elmer was about to doze off when Chaplain Abbott and Grubb came bursting through the tent flap. They were grinning. Doc Elmer was a father again. His wife, Mary, had given birth to a healthy baby girl named Lizzy on December fourth. Oscar and Mat had a baby sister to play with, and Mary finally had her daughter. Doc Bob Elmer went to sleep happy.

December 8, 1862 - Devil's Hole, Virginia

The bleak, freezing wind continued to blow from the north. The storm had raged for 3 days, and now the ground was deeply frozen. Men used picks to hack at the frozen earth. The ringing sounds of the work echoed back from the frozen woods. The gravediggers finally broke through the crust, and quickly finished the grave with their shovels.

Soon the medical staff arrived with Chaplain Abbott, Grubb, Brown, McKee and Ryerson. The Regimental band marched up and took position near the grave. At 10 o'clock, a drummer beating cadence could be heard approaching, and I Company marched up with a crude wooden casket they had built bearing the body of their comrade, George Gilbert. Men in the regimental bivouac who were not attending the funeral stopped what they were doing, and watched the ceremony from afar.

Chaplain Abbott spoke. "Today we place a fellow soldier beneath Virginia's cold, damp clods. However, while we thus bury one of our men, we have the assurance that an offering has been laid upon the altar of our country. A sacrifice made of a true patriot, a brave soldier, and a good man. George, may you rest in peace."

Abbott comforted the men, and the band played several funeral hymns. An eight-man firing squad broke open their paper cartridges, poured their powder into the muzzles, dropped the buck and ball on the ground next to the grave, capped their pieces and fired their salute. The three volleys echoed across the frozen ground. No one thought to pick up the one-ounce lead balls lying near the grave.

The headquarters staff met afterwards with I Company's Captain Burnett and 1st Sergeant Scattergood. "What was it, Doc?" demanded Ryerson.

"Sir, I talked with the Brigade and Division Surgeons. He's been sick for two weeks. He kept up with us until a few days ago. We moved him into the hospital tents, but he went downhill fast. He had a high fever, headache, loss of appetite with a stomachache, rash on the stomach and chest congestion. It was typhoid pneumonia."

Ryerson thought for a minute. "We lost a lot of men to disease in 2nd last winter. I sure don't want to go through that again. Anything we can do?"

"Sir, the shelter tents just don't protect the men in this weather. That march and the rain and snowstorm didn't do them any good. There're a lot of people on sick call. I had to send Pvt. Hosure from E Company back to the hospital yesterday for frozen feet."

"Can you tell who is sick and who is faking it? Brigade says we are going to attack soon. I don't want a lot of malingerers trying to get out of the fight.

"I can tell if someone has a fever or sore throat. It's easy to tell if you have a rupture or broken bone. It's not so easy to tell what's going on when someone says they don't feel good or claim they are weak."

"Sir?" said Grubb. "The best thing to do is have the NCOs and officers keep an eye on their men. They need to look after them. They need to know them well enough to see an illness developing. They are responsible for them."

Ryerson looked at McKee. "Sergeant Major, I want you to get the 1st Sergeants and NCOs and have them check their men morning and night for health problems. Nobody goes on sick call without permission. I also want to have a foot inspection every day. If they can't march, they can't fight. We need to keep an eye on their feet."

"Cook, I want you and Bowlby and the Assistants to go with him, and tell them what to look for."

"Yes, sir." They left to follow the colonel's orders. When they completed their rounds three more soldiers were on their way to the hospital. Harrison, D Company had a high fever that looked like typhoid. Speer and Grass were both from B Company and had uncontrollable diarrhea. A man who couldn't control his bowels was a man who couldn't fight.

Crispin had awakened yesterday morning to the coldest morning yet. All of their clothes, two wool blankets and their overcoats as covers had not kept him and Ed warm in the little two-man tent.

They drew firewood detail, but Sweesley took one look at Crispin and sent him back on sick call. Josie told the sergeant he had a toothache and his face was swollen. Doc Bowlby checked him out. He had a headache, sore throat, stomachache and swollen glands in his neck. Fortunately, there was no high fever. He was definitely not malingering. Bowlby didn't think he had typhoid, so he sent him back to bed in the two-man tent.

This morning he was better and got up to attend Gilbert's funeral. After it was over, he stopped at the sutler's. The man was shameless. He was selling cheese at 40 cents a pound and very small tin cups for forty cents. Even though the prices were exorbitant, he enjoyed a brisk business.

On the way back, he walked a mile south of the encampment, and found a bedraggled old house where he could buy some hoecakes. The woman of the house had three young children. She said her husband had been pressed into service in the Southern army. All she had for her and the children was some corn meal. She baked hoecakes with it and sold them for twenty five to forty cents each. Some of the men who came to buy shared their rations with her. Crispin was too naïve to question whether anything else was exchanged.

Late that afternoon, Grubb and Sergeant Major McKee were walking through H Company and found Sweesley's squad sitting around their fires. They jumped to attention when he walked up, and then went back to what they were doing when he told them, "As you were." He warmed his hands over the fire, and struck up a conversation with the boys. All were flattered that a staff officer would visit with them. As he looked around, he noticed McCabe and his lieutenants visiting other fires.

December 10, 1862 - Devil's Hole, Virginia

Ryerson was sitting on his horse as he watched the regiment complete its afternoon dress parade. The companies marched in review. When they reached the end of the parade, they were not dismissed.

They were formed in a hollow square. This was unusual. The men sensed something extraordinary was about to happen.

When the last company was in its place, he ordered the men to gather around him. They did. "Can you all hear me?" was greeted with a loud "YES SIR."

"Men, tomorrow is the day we have been preparing for. Tomorrow we are going into battle. I want you to draw three days' rations, and I want you to cook your meat and put it away properly. Lord knows you will need it." The men started looking at each other. They had known the day would come, but now it was really here. It was more than a little scary.

"Each of you will draw sixty rounds of ammunition. I want you to look at every single round carefully. If it is wet or broken or you just don't like the way it looks, I want you to turn it in for a replacement. Your life may depend on it."

"Two months ago, General Torbert asked me if I would take command of this regiment. He didn't order me to do it. God help me, I volunteered," moaned Ryerson. This was greeted with laughter. "The first time I laid eyes on you; I looked at Torbert and said, 'You expect me to command that bunch of YAHOOS?' " This was greeted with more laughter. Ryerson paused for effect.

"He said, 'Yes, there is no place to go but up.' He was right." This was greeted with even greater laughter.

"I want you to know, you have earned my admiration and respect. Your performance in drill and on picket and guard and during the march to get here has earned the notice and respect of the veterans in the other regiments and brigades. You are no shirkers. You hold up your end of the job. Three cheers for the Yahoos!"

The regiment cheered as one.

December 11, 1862 - Fredericksburg, Virginia

Pickets heard a cannon shot echo far off to the west. Seconds later, another fired in the distance to the south. Unbeknownst to the men of the 23rd, Confederate pickets had heard the noise of pontoon wagons approaching the Rappahannock. Lee had arranged to have two cannons fired to alert the Confederate Army if an attack was discovered. It was. Within minutes, Confederate drums were beating assembly. The Battle of Fredericksburg had begun.

An annoying drizzle was falling on the frozen ground as sergeants quietly awakened the regiment at 4:30 in the morning. The 23rd marched out of Devil's Hole at 6 AM, and turned toward Fredericksburg on the River Road. The rain stopped before daylight.

The day dawned clear and warmed up. Within a few hours the earth thawed, and the regiment found itself marching in slippery mud an inch deep.

Josie was still sick. He had not gotten very far before he had to fall out of the march. He found a dry place to rest for a while. At daybreak, an intense artillery barrage erupted to the west and lasted half an hour. Most every friend he had in the world had marched off in that direction. He got up, and started after them. Several thugs watched him go. They didn't need to follow him; there were easier pickings back toward Devil's Hole.

Doc Elmer looked around the hospital tent. The First Brigade had one hundred and twenty two men who were too sick to go to the battle. He was left in charge of them. Cook had taken most of the supplies to the battle. On top of that, Elmer was not feeling well. It was cold and it was easy for the chill to creep into one's bones. He watched the brigade march off toward the river. Rumor had it there were robbers in the neighborhood. There were not many guards for the hospital. He thought of the Navy Colt six-shooter near his medical box. He crowded into one of the hospital tents to try and get warm. He still didn't have a stove to heat his tents. He hoped no one would freeze.

Lieutenant Colonel Brown and Lieutenant Perkins were leading the column. Ryerson, Grubb and McKee had ridden ahead to get orders for the crossing. Ryerson and Grubb were waiting for them about a quarter mile from the end of the bridge when they showed up just before noon.

"Colonel Brown, the Sergeant Major will show them where to assemble. Have the Company Commanders turn their units over to their officers and meet me here."

Brown saluted, and rode back to the A Company Commander and gave the orders. He was back with Ryerson in few minutes as the companies began to fall out into a field near the Pollack House.

Ryerson, still on his horse, saw Brown looking puzzled, so he explained, "They don't want us to cross yet. The engineers are having trouble finishing the bridges upstream because of snipers."

Grubb was looking toward Fredericksburg. What little vegetation there was along the river had no leaves. It was easy to see the town two miles to the north. "Look, Sir, the engineers are going to try again." Ryerson turned in time to see a group of men running across the unfinished pontoon bridge. They had pushed the bridge more than three hundred feet across the river, but there was still a gap of eighty feet to be completed. They had barely reached their workstations when a thunderous volley of musket fire erupted from the buildings in the town. Great tongues of fire and clouds of white smoke burst from hundreds of windows in buildings along the river.

"Those aren't snipers. That's an infantry unit," muttered Ryerson. "There's at least a regiment in there."

Bullets hit the water and threw curtains of spray eight feet in the air. Others blasted splinters from the bridge deck and the boats. Some hit their targets. Men fell to the bridge deck, into the pontoons; into the water. Those still standing ran for their lives back to cover on the bank. A Union infantry regiment immediately returned the fire to cover the escaping engineers.

"General Torbert tells me that this has been going on since daylight." By now the company commanders were gathered around the horses and everyone was dismounted. All eyes were on the bridges. Intense rifle fire continued from the town.

"Gentlemen, we are going to be here for awhile. General Franklin does not want us to cross until the upper bridges are in place. He is afraid that if we get over there and tangle with something we can't handle, we won't be able to get back. If the other bridges are up, we can get support from other units up there, or we can fall back to those bridges if we need to."

"Get your men fed, and I want their guns loaded. Don't put the caps on until we cross. Put the tompions in and the leather patches on the nipples to keep the barrels dry, so we are ready to shoot. They are out of Confederate artillery range. Keep them together so we can move out as soon as we get our orders."

"Is there any word of what is across the river, sir?" came a question from the group.

"The engineers said a couple of companies from the 18th Mississippi were shooting at them earlier, but our artillery drove them off. They finished the bridge around noon, and there is a regiment over there guarding the bridgehead."

Josie was just walking up to his friends in H Company when the officers returned to their companies at 12:45. They explained the situation to the sergeants, and the sergeants passed the word to the men. The troops started to spread out their gum blankets on the ground and cook lunch. All had a chance to gaze around the valley.

Fredericksburg looked like it had been a prosperous town. It was laid out with straight streets leading away from the river up a gentle hill. The cross streets ran parallel to the river. Church spires, mills, warehouses, mansions and homes gave it a small town skyline. The buildings extended to the river's edge. A big mill building hung over the shore, just downstream from the charred pillars of a burned-out bridge that jutted out of the river.

On the north side of the river was a narrow plain that rose quickly to a row of hills called Stafford Heights. Union artillery was set up all along the heights to command the river crossing and the town. On the south side of the river behind the town was a low area of fields and a drainage ditch. These fields behind the town rose slowly to Marye's Heights. South of town, the heights angled away from the river between Hazel Run and Deep Run for two miles. Then they angled back toward the river for another two miles until they reached Hamilton Crossing. Fields covered the river bottom and ran up gentle slopes, where they joined thickly wooded areas that covered the heights. The men could easily see the Richmond Road and the Richmond Fredericksburg and Potomac Railroad grade running through the fields across the river.

Conover had just handed a mug of coffee to Josie when all hell broke loose. At 1 PM, 150 pieces of Union Artillery simultaneously opened fire on Fredericksburg. The roar brought everyone in the valley to their feet. Horses reared in fright, people stood to get a better view, and officers reached for their field glasses. Josie spilled the coffee.

Shortly after Union troops returned to the banks of the Rappahannock, in early November, Rebel sharpshooters started shooting at them from buildings in Fredericksburg. On November 20th, General Sumner had given the mayor an ultimatum. Surrender the town or be shelled at 9 AM on the 21st. The mayor and General Lee had refused to surrender the town, but they did agree to stop the sniping. They also ordered the civilian population to evacuate. Most of the citizens were already gone. Within minutes, a small column of those who remained made their way out of the city and up the hill toward Marye's Heights.

Over 8,000 shells were sent into the town to dislodge the riflemen who were shooting at the engineers. At least one gun fired every second for two hours. The men cheered, but soon the magnitude of the destruction sobered them. Few thought the destruction of so many homes was something to be happy about. Chimneys fell, walls collapsed, whole brick buildings collapsed into the streets. Fires started in the wood frame buildings. Soon, the smoke from the fires and bursting shells and the dust raised by the solid shot obscured the view of most of the town. The top of Stafford heights was a mass of white smoke, with the flaming discharge of cannons shooting out of it. This was followed a few seconds later by the flash of exploding shells lighting the dust cloud over the city.

At 3 o'clock, the barrage ended, and two Michigan Infantry regiments marched to the bank. The engineers crept out to renew their work on the bridge, confident no one would still contest the crossing after such a brutal bombardment. They were not even in position when another massive fusillade of rifle fire riddled their ranks. The undaunted Confederates were still there.

By now, Torbert and his Colonels had gathered in a group to watch the spectacle. "Now what are they going to do?" asked Hatch from the 4th.

Soon they had the answer. A wave of blue charged the riverbank in a rush. They grabbed every pontoon they could find. The huge thirty-one foot boats were carried to the river by crowds of now furious men. They had had enough. Every oar in sight was appropriated, and the impromptu assault river crossing was on. Men were paddling with boards, oars, paddles, their hands and anything else they could find to get across the four hundred feet of open water. Some were shooting from the front of the boats, while others further back loaded the empty weapons and handed them back to the shooters. The Rebs were not idle. Rifle fire came from every window that had a view on the boats. Bullets raised a steady curtain of spray and splashes around every one. Some found their targets, and men fell into the river or slumped over to the floor. Everyone on both sides of the valley stood and watched the whole unforgettable ordeal.

By 4:30 a mass of blue had landed on the enemy side. They were sheltered from fire by the riverbank. It took a while for the boats to bring over a battalion. When they finally had the strength, they charged the first row of houses. Firefights blazed back and forth, from house to house and street to street.

While all of this was going on, a column of Union troops marched past the 23rd and started across the lower pontoon bridge. "Who are they?" asked Brown. "Looks like Devon's Brigade going to reinforce the bridgehead," someone answered.

Heavy fighting continued as the winter sun set and darkness descended over the broken town. Muzzle flashes lit up the town for brief instants through the growing darkness. Not long after dark, the firing died off. The troops were abuzz. It had been an amazing day. Later, orders came down to cross the river under cover of darkness, but it was so dark and foggy that the effort was abandoned. They were ordered back, and spent the night in an open field behind Bill Hexamer's battery.

December 12, 1862 - Fredericksburg, Virginia

The troops were roused at 5 AM. They were masked from the enemy by a thick fog. The squad got a fire going and brewed coffee and fixed a cold breakfast. Josie could swallow the coffee, but not the hardtack. At 7 AM they quietly groped their way down the bank across the dangerously slippery pontoon bridge to join the expanding 6th Corp bridgehead.

There were no safety lines, so it paid to stay away from the edges. A five-inch by five-inch sill was the only thing that separated a man from a quick trip to the bottom, with a sixty-pound pack for an anchor. Hay was spread over the bridge to make it less slippery and reduce wear on the deck planks. Ryerson led his horse across the deck at a slow walk. Cavalry had to cross the same way. It was essential that artillery and wagons stick to the center of the roadway. Only a driver was permitted to be in the vehicle, unless it was an ambulance carrying wounded. They found out crossing a pontoon bridge was not just a walk on a deck. They had to spread out and travel slowly at "route step", so the bridge would not rock. If it started to sway, everyone on it had to halt until it stopped. Guards were posted whose sole duty was to command "route step, remember, route step" to remind the infantry not to march in step.

The engineers were justifiably sensitive about this. Some idiot colonel had ordered his regimental band to strike up the music while his regiment was crossing. They unconsciously started marching in step, and almost sank the bridge before a staff officer galloped across the deck and shut them up. The bridgehead was fully established in the fog by mid-morning. An eerie quiet before the storm descended over the battlefield.

———————

H Company stumbled blindly into the regimental line of battle in the dark. Torbert's brigade was on the right of the bridgehead near the bridges, and H Company was on the right of the Brigade.

Josie's condition had not improved. He was massaging his swollen face as he noticed the double lines of the 23rd disappearing into the fog in both directions. He knew they stretched one hundred twenty yards to his left and thirty yards to his right.

Just before daylight, the troops heard a lot of horses moving around between them and the river. Some of the officers went to see what was happening, and found most of General Bayard's Union Cavalry Brigade moving back across the river in the fog. They had come over during the night to screen the bridgehead while the infantry deployed. Bayard was keeping a small cavalry reserve in an orchard near the Bernard house.

The fog masked the lower valley for most of the day. Around 4 PM, the brigade pushed a mile forward from the river. Officers scouted the land in front of them and reported to Ryerson. The Deep Run ravine was running parallel to the line of battle, just ahead of the 23rd's line. It was about seventy-five feet wide and twenty feet deep, with very steep sides.

Ryerson and the rest of the regiment noticed the visibility improve, and within a few minutes saw a cedar tree about fifty yards in front of them. It was about thirty feet tall, and if anyone noticed the filthy red and white flag in the top, nobody questioned it.

The Rebel artillery batteries on the hill beyond the railroad grade sure saw it, and the Union troops drawn up for battle under it. They opened fire. Everybody in the 23rd saw a white puff of smoke pop out of the trees 1,200 yards away. Less than two seconds later, a screeching shell hit ten feet from the base of the tree, ricocheted over their heads and exploded behind them. Within the next few minutes, a half dozen more shells were fired. It was evident the Rebs were using the tree for a ranging post.

Torbert ordered Ryerson to move his troops into the Deep Run ravine. They didn't have to be told twice. Everyone piled over the edge, careened down the slope, and was just approaching the creek when many stopped to try and find stepping stones. They were tired of wet feet and wanted to stay dry. This caused a huge traffic jam of men still in harm's way.

Ryerson rode down on his horse, waving his sword, shouting "Forward, you Yahoos, forward," when a shell came screaming close over their heads and buried itself in the bank they had just descended. Close to 900 pairs of feet simultaneously charged through ice cold, knee-deep water, and dived for cover against the sheltering bank.

McKee had crawled up next to 1st Sergeant Hartman, and both turned to look back at Ryerson, who was looking pleased with himself. Deafening artillery fire erupted along the lines in front of them, and Union guns to the rear responded. Adding to the din were the screams of a wounded man off toward A Company. Elias Gibbs was severely wounded in the elbow.

They watched the Colonel ride through the ravine to where an orderly was bandaging the wounded man. Ryerson sat on his horse and watched the orderly work.

An instant later they heard a strange sound. A shell came screeching in out in front of the ravine and plopped into the ground, but did not stop. They could hear the nearly spent cannon ball bouncing closer and closer. Ryerson saw it coming. He calmly leaned over the neck of his horse, his hat fell off, and the 12-pound ball flew over his back and missed by six inches. It smashed into the far bank and buried itself in the dirt. Ryerson was still in the saddle, hugging the horse's neck. He reached down, calmly picked up his hat without dismounting, and sat back up. He looked at the hat, put it back on his head, and rode across the stream to safety.

McKee and Hartman looked at each other. Their eyes locked. "Did you see what I just saw, Reuben?" gasped McKee.

"I sure did, John, I sure did." The story was all over the Corps before the end of the day."

While the regiment was scrambling for cover, Bill Hexamer's battery was firing back at the Rebels. His guns had been brought across the river overnight to support Torbert's Brigade. They were set up on a little plateau just north of Deep Run. A full-fledged artillery duel flew back and forth over their heads.

Crispin and Howard could hear Henry Myers' bugle back by Hexamer's guns, mixed in with Gibbs' screams. The battery's six guns were lined up at the prescribed interval, fourteen yards from wheel hub to hub. They covered a front nearly eighty yards wide.

Myers watched as the officers received their firing instructions, and directed their gun crews to open fire. The much-practiced service of the piece drill swung into use. Each gunner started sighting his gun while the barrels were swabbed. A man took the proper round from the ammunition chest on the limber, and handed it to another. That man carried it to the gun, and handed it to the loader. He placed it in the muzzle, and the rammer rammed it to the breach. The powder bag was then pierced, and the friction primer placed in the gun's vent. When all was ready, the officer commanded fire. The gunner pulled the lanyard, and the friction primer sent a spark down the vent, which ignited the powder and fired the gun. The drill was repeated until the order to cease fire was given.

The Rebel position was dug in well. Only the muzzles of their cannons could be seen. There were at least a dozen guns. They were very small targets, so the Union guns used a combination of solid and exploding case shot to try and destroy them. A case shot was a hollow iron artillery shell filled with tar, sulfur or flammable resin and lead musket balls. After the filler cooled, a hole was bored in it big enough to hold a one-ounce black powder bursting charge. A time fuse inserted above the bursting charge allowed the gunner to select the distance the shell traveled before it exploded. The desired effect was for the shell to explode shortly before it got to the target, so the enemy would be showered with hot burning material, lead and iron fragments. Normally, all guns in a battery fired at an enemy gun until it was destroyed. Then, they moved on to the next. These Reb guns were so well dug in, there was little chance of success.

The Rebel artillery had opened fire on the infantry, but once the formations had taken cover, they shifted their fire to Hexamer's and the rest of the division's guns. Rebel time fuses were notoriously inaccurate. In fact, they were so bad, the Confederate Army refused to allow them to be fired over their own troops, but firing over Yankees was fine.

Some shells hit the far bank, and some went further to the rear. Some exploded overhead and showered the area with iron fragments and lead balls. The shells whooshed and screamed and shrieked over them. Different shells made different sounds. Solid shoot whooshed. Case shot with time fuses shrieked and hissed. Rifled cannon had a higher muzzle velocity, and they made a sound like ripping cloth. The considered opinion in the ravine was that the sound of outgoing Union shells was much more comforting than the incoming Confederate shells. After an hour of unsuccessfully trying to knock out each other's artillery, the duel petered out.

Ryerson briefed his company commanders at dusk. "Brooks says Jackson got back from Port Royal and Skinker's Neck last night, so the whole Rebel army is over there. We are going back across the stream, and bivouac on the river side of the Richmond Road. Also, there has been a lot of looting and vandalism up in town. I want you to make it very clear to everyone in your command that I will not tolerate this kind of behavior."

December 13, 1862 – Franklin's Bridgehead, Fredericksburg, Virginia

The entire 1st and 6th Corps were spread out for two miles between the bridges and a creek just north of Hamilton's Crossing. Their front was along the Old Richmond Road. A thick fog hid them from the Rebels. It could only muffle the noise they made. The ground was frozen, so every hoof, cannon and caisson gave off a tremendous racket. By 8:30 in the morning, everyone in the valley could hear the shouted commands, band music and the noise of artillery moving and feet marching as forty-six regiments and eleven artillery batteries moved into position.

By this time the Yahoos had crawled through the ravine, and had been lying concealed in the rows of a corn stubble field for an hour. They were in a slight depression between the ravine and the railroad embankment two hundred yards to their front. The 15th New Jersey was to their front skirmishing with the Rebels. It was dangerous to raise one's head for very long. They were limited to listening to the progress of the battle. The fog cleared around 10 AM. Minutes later, drums and bugles sounded. Soon after that, Rebel artillery fire came from the south, and seconds later, volleys of Union fire answered. Another artillery duel started and lasted two hours. Near 1 PM a huge explosion heralded what sounded like a Union infantry charge.

Over the course of the next hour and a half, the location of the rifle fire to the south seemed to shift into the Rebel position, and then back out toward the Old Richmond Road. By 2:30, it sounded like an attack had been initially successful, and then thrown back. Firing from both sides was coming from the direction of the Old Richmond Road.

All of this artillery fire made it difficult and dangerous to see how the battle was going. The ever-present Confederate sharpshooters added to the hazard. The 23rd could only guess what was happening around them by the sounds they could hear.

The noise from the north dwarfed what was happening in the south. At noon, drums and bugles could be heard assembling Union troops in Fredericksburg for an attack. Shortly after came a fusillade of fire so violent that the men could only look at each other and shake their heads. Again, and again, volleys of unimaginable intensity echoed through the valley. Artillery fire was a frightening nonstop roar from all types of guns.

At 3 PM, Ryerson got word from Torbert to get ready to move. He sent out a quick vidette to the front, and called the company commanders together. Firing immediately broke out where the vidette had gone. They came piling over the edge of the bank, and back into the position. Rebs were between them and the railroad.

"The 15th has a line of skirmishers between the brigade and the railroad. The Rebs are giving them a hard time, and we have orders to run the bastards off. The General is sending us to support a 4th Regiment attack on the railroad embankment. Colonel Hatch is the senior officer. He will command the action. The 4th is on the other side of the ravine we were in yesterday. The ravine makes a ninety degree angle over here on our left flank by that woods," he said, pointing toward the flank, "and goes up to a culvert under the railroad embankment. There is a ditch running along our side of the embankment. Our mission will be to take the embankment and ditch on our side of Deep Run with our three left companies. The next three companies are to take the embankment and ditch on the other side. The last four companies are to hold the woods in the center. We are going to double-time along the edge of that ravine in a column of fours. When you get to the ditch, you will form your line of battle. Major Grubb will lead our attack from the left. Colonel Brown has the right. Any questions? Good luck to all of you."*

* **This account of the battle appears in Ryerson's letter to his sister dated 12/19/62. It does not match the account in the <u>History of the Reunion Society of the 23rd New Jersey</u> or the Foster narrative. I have been unable to locate an account that lists the order of companies from left to right. A 12/25/62 New Jersey Mirror article places A Company on the right flank along with I, D and G. The article also places K Company as the left flank company. Crispin writes about participating in the attack, so H was one of the left companies. Foster notes exceptional bravery by members of companies A, C, F, G and K in his chapter about the 23rd. The regimental casualty report showing KIA/WIA/MIA and other notes show K lost 13, F 8, H 7, C 5 and G 2. Company A shows two wounded, but Gibbs was wounded by a shell fragment on December 11th when the regiment first went into the Deep Run ravine. Accounts of a Rebel battery raking the attack from the left, combined with the number and nature of the wounds, suggest that K, F, H, B, C and E were the first six companies into the fight. This makes the regimental order of battle, from left to right: K, F, H, B, C, E, G, D, I, A. NJM12/25/62 and the Ryerson letter says all were on the move, and Torbert directed the last four right companies (G, D, I & A) out of the artillery fire and into the woods before they could come on line.**

"Good luck, Burd," smiled Ryerson.

"Thanks, Ogden. Thanks for the confidence."

The commanders scrambled back to their companies. Within minutes, Colonel Hatch and the 4th made their move. They stood up, and with the help of the 15th's reserves and skirmishers, charged up the south side of the ravine for the railroad embankment. They were greeted with a severe fire of grape and canister. They fought their way through it, and pushed the Rebs in front of them over the railroad. Within minutes the Rebs were counter-attacking and pressing hard.

The 23rd already had their knapsacks on and were lined up in column of fours. Two days of Confederate shelling had removed every vestige of cockiness. They were ready to do their duty. They approached it coolly. Grubb ordered, "Fix bayonets." 800 eighteen-inch bayonets clattered into place.

"LEFT FACE." He watched with satisfaction as they faced left. He drew his saber. Tears came to his eyes as he watched the company officers and sergeants draw theirs.

The moment of truth had come. "COLUMN DOUBLE QUICK, MARCH!" He led the column around the corner of the ravine at a dead run and started for the culvert.

They hadn't gone twenty yards when eighteen hidden Confederate cannons and hundreds of rifles opened fire on them. Storms of iron solid shot, grape, case shot, canister and lead bullets zipped by them.

It took almost two minutes to double-quick two hundred yards to the culvert. Just before K Company reached the culvert, a shell burst in their ranks. Fortunately, it burst high. The shock knocked many men to the ground. Ten were wounded. Those who could, finally staggered to their goal, and Grubb started them to the right to form their line along the embankment.

A Rebel battery raked them with canister. It appeared to those watching from the rear as if a giant fly swatter had smacked the ground along part of the line. A big gap opened as at least twenty-eight men went down. The formation started to break down; the line wavered. Panic set in, and the men fell back forty or fifty steps. Ryerson galloped up, got them reformed, and pushed them back towards the ditch. Grubb was just about to direct the next three companies to the left when Ryerson rode up and told him to send them to the right along with the first three. Hatch was worried the Rebs would flank them, and wanted a stronger right.

Crispin was in a bad way. Although he was quite sick, he had made up his mind to keep up with the company as far as he could. He was almost to the culvert when the airburst hit K Company. He saw the men fall. A hot shell fragment set one of the wounded on fire, his clothing burned furiously. The poor man writhed, screaming helplessly on the ground. The men in K, F and H Companies had just gotten into the ditch when a Rebel gun on their left raked them with canister and grape shot. They fell back about fifty paces, and then rallied and charged back into what little shelter the ditch and the embankment provided.

Captain Carr was leading C Company as they double-timed toward the ditch when he saw a 12-pound case shot explode right in front of him. It blew him off his feet. Carr shook himself and tried to stand up, but his left foot wouldn't work. He looked down to see what the matter was, and almost fainted. A ball from the case shot had gone clean through his foot. He could see daylight through the hole. Worse yet was the sickening sight of bone fragments and blood dripping out of what was left of his boot. Men were running past him. He struggled to join them. Strong hands grabbed him by the armpits, while others grasped each leg and carried him to the shelter of the ditch.

"Don't worry, Cap. We gotcha," gasped one of the men. Carr gazed around to see Alcott, Batchelor and Goreman all in a pile in next to him. They had seen him go down, and weren't about to leave him out in the field of fire. The group of them cringed into the smallest entity they could possibly be, and waited for the shelling to stop. Shot and shell whistled overhead. Men all up and down the line moved into position, firing and reloading as fast as they could. The firing was so constant and loud, it was barely possible to hear voices unless men shouted in each other's ears.

Ryerson galloped up and down the line, swinging his saber to rally his men. Parmentier, Grobler and the officers also rallied the troops. After what seemed an eternity, they plowed through to the cover of the embankment. But, in the panic, the second three companies had bunched up near the culvert. Instead of covering a front of one hundred twenty yards, they only covered forty.

Grubb jumped up and down, waving his arms and yelling at Parmentier. "Parmentier, Parmentier, shift them to the right, to the right. Fill the front!"

Parmentier finally heard him, looked at the jammed mass of men in the ravine, and then back at Grubb. The K Company Commander nodded his head that he understood, and started giving orders. McCabe and Root heard him and took up the cry. Ryerson dashed up and helped them start moving their men where they belonged. As soon as they were on their way, Grubb turned and glanced back the way they came. Several blue shapes were not moving. Something was on fire in the field. A trail of bloody tracks, abandoned knapsacks, blankets and packs littered the field. He could tell a lot of men were missing.

He stopped and took stock of his men. Captain Carr was shot through the foot and couldn't move by himself. Lieutenant Budd was on his hands and knees, gasping for air and bleeding heavily from a foot wound. Grobler was gasping for breath. Some men were still limping or crawling toward the bank. The officers and NCOs were seeing that they got to safety. They also made sure steady fire was directed at the enemy. The Major turned to meet Hatch at the culvert to coordinate their next action.

Meanwhile, Torbert and Brooks were watching, and knew there was no way they could force the position. The enemy artillery and supporting infantry were too strong. The Jersey men were being cut to pieces. A Confederate gun crew was moving a 12-pound Napoleon to enfilade the entire ditch. The last four companies were ordered to set up a blocking position in the woods on the far side of the ravine. Orders were sent for the rest to pull back to the cornfield.

———————

Hatch was rushing across Deep Run when Grubb got there. Massive hand-hewn blocks of stone had been cemented together to create a rectangular railroad culvert about twenty feet wide and sixteen feet high. Rebels were firing through the culvert, and their shots kicked up splashes all around Hatch. He jumped quickly out of the line of fire. Both were out of breath and gasping for air.

"Torbert has ordered us to break off the attack," yelled Hatch. They had to shout in each other's ears to be heard above the battle. Grubb nodded that he understood.

Hatch shouted, "I want you to screen our withdrawal from the railroad with skirmishers and get your men ready to go back down the ravine on the same side you came up. I'll take mine back the way we came. We both go at the same time, on my command."

"YES SIR."

"Make sure they all load their guns. The Rebs are coming and will try to flank us when they see us leave. We need to discourage them."

"YES SIR." Grubb had obviously been dismissed, so he saluted and turned to go.

Hatch started back across the stream. Grubb hadn't taken a step when he heard a flurry of shots and the smack of a bullet hitting flesh behind him. He turned to see Hatch go down in midstream.* The frigid waters of Deep Run were instantly stained red. A group of men ran to help the colonel. Shots dropped two more before everyone was out of the line of fire. Hatch was hit in the thigh and bleeding badly. Someone wrapped a rag around his leg, and several men started carrying him to the rear.

Grubb paused to look around.

Nobody in the 4th knew what to do. He managed to get across the stream to them without getting shot. He found a Captain, and told him what he and Hatch planned to do for the withdrawal. He ordered the Captain to arrange for the skirmishers, and get the 4th ready to move at his, Grubb's, command. He ran back across the stream with bullets splashing all around him. He got his skirmishers set up and his companies ready to pull back. Companies C and E had the duty. He was just finishing up when he saw a clerk he knew from Torbert's headquarters running toward him.

The man dived into the shelter of the embankment. Grubb rolled him over, and said, "Goldsmith! What the hell are you doing here?"

Goldsmith took a quick look around. He looked at Grubb. "Sir, I got promoted to Lieutenant and now I am Torbert's Aide de Camp. Hatch is hit real bad, and the General wants you to take command of both units and get them back to the cornfield." That made it official. Burd was in command.

"You go tell Ryerson that. I'll get things started here." Goldsmith nodded and flagged down Ryerson.

The officer from the 4th sent word he was ready. Grubb saw that the 23rd companies were, too. He gave the signal, and the 4th started

*HRS23 says Hatch was wounded at the culvert. "Ryerson's Letter 12/19/62" says he was wounded by a stray shot in a field behind the 23rd's position after the 4th fell back through the ravine.

back down the ravine. Nobody had to be told twice. The Confederates continued to pour rifle and cannon fire into them.

They had not gone far when two small Rebel regiments came streaming over the railroad to the south. The enemy obviously thought they could flank the retreating troops and capture them. The Rebs formed their lines, and started moving eastward down the south side of the ravine. Grubb signaled Ryerson and pointed toward the Rebels. Ryerson saw them. He ordered the six companies to wheel to the right so they could take the Rebels in the flank, but performing a wheel is difficult and the men were not well-drilled. The maneuver broke down in confusion. They started to flee to the rear. The unit could not be reformed before it got back to the cornfield.

———————

The four companies left behind in the woods heard the battle, but could not tell what was happening until a wounded man from K Company stumbled down the ravine. He was holding his right hand and arm. He told them that K Company was on the left and the regiment was heavily engaged at the culvert, and even out to the far end of the ravine. They directed him back down the ravine to the big red flag marking Cook's dressing station. Wounded men from the 4th and 15th started to stream by. Soon, three men carrying Captain Carr appeared. Carr told them it was a tough fight at the culvert.

They watched as Jersey men from the other regiments retreated through their position. First came the wounded. Then, small groups filtered to the rear. Finally, a massive stream of men raced through the position. Some Yahoos on the right of the woods watched as their six companies started what looked like a right wheel march. They saw the maneuver fall apart, and another mass of panting men streamed past them. A smaller group followed, carrying or dragging the dead and wounded.

———————

Crispin started for the rear with the column. He was so sick, he couldn't keep up. He was sick to his stomach. He couldn't catch his breath. His throat was raw. He couldn't cry for help because he didn't have a voice. He watched helplessly as the 23rd moved further and further away. He lay down in the mud. Gradually his, breathing slowed. The loudest sounds of the fight were off across the ravine. He could hear Rebel skirmishers nearby, and cautiously looked around. He had fallen in a shallow depression that shielded him from enemy eyes, for the time being. Help wasn't coming, nobody knew he was down. He was going to have to get himself out of this mess. If he stayed here, he was going to freeze to death or get captured. There was less than an hour of daylight left. He had to get back to the company before dark or risk being shot by his own nervous men. It took fifteen minutes for him to catch his breath. He gathered his strength, and crept to the edge of the woods.

The Reb fire kept coming closer after the six companies streamed by. Captain Ridgway saw Parmentier coming and flagged him down. "What happened, Bill?" he shouted.

"Couldn't hold the rail line," panted Parmentier, "Too much artillery. Colonel ordered us back to the cornfield. Got two Rebel regiments coming down the far side of the ravine right behind us."

Just then Grubb reached them. "I want a line of battle formed at the edge of the ravine, facing that way right, now." He pointed to the south. "Do it NOW!"

"Yes sir," shouted Ridgway. He ordered G Company forward. The other three followed. Parmentier watched him swinging his saber over his head and shouting, "Follow me, Company G!" as he led the way to the south edge of the ravine. Grubb set the line just inside the woods and opened with a volley. Their attack hit the Rebs square on the left flank. The Rebs halted, and one regiment started to wheel to face them.

Ridgway watched as the men frantically reloaded. The Rebs were getting closer. The next volley was almost ready when Lieutenant Kirkbride ran up to Grubb. "Sir, Colonel Ryerson says to disengage and return to the cornfield." Grubb nodded his head, and started to turn toward the men when they heard a Rebel officer command, "Aim, FIRE."

The Rebs' return volley was deadly. Captain Ridgway flipped over backwards in a heap not four feet from Kirkbride as a bullet hit him between the eyes. At least nine other men went down. Kirkbride looked in stunned horror at the body of his friend. He quickly rolled him over to see if there was anything to be done. There wasn't, Joe was dead. Grubb looked around for a Lieutenant. He saw Riggs and remembered he had been with G Company less than two weeks. He grabbed a private, pointed at Riggs. "Mister, you get Lieutenant Riggs, and tell him to get over here, now." The man took off as fast as he could run.

By this time the men were firing at will. The Rebs were reloading and firing back. Riggs came running over, and stooped to see Ridgway. His anguished look said he knew what his eyes refused to believe. Grubb yelled to him, "Ed, you have to take over. We are to pull back to the cornfield." Riggs mumbled he understood, and gave the order.

Captain Milnor and A Company were closest to the cornfield. They covered the other three companies as they pulled back. The ravine was a natural rifle pit that allowed them to maintain an annoying fire on the Rebs. Milnor's lieutenants, Hambrick and Sibley, were everywhere. They cheered their men and pointed out targets. Sergeant McKee and Privates Browne and Taylor organized loading parties that loaded muskets, and handed them to sharpshooters as fast as they could fire. The Company became a galling sore on the Confederate flank.

The Rebel regiment started marching toward them. There was no way a single company could stand off a regiment, so Milnor gave the order to fall back. They grabbed all of the dead and wounded they could find and left. There was no way to get to Ridgway's body. Just as it looked like all was lost, a horrific volley of rifle fire erupted from just in front of the Union lines as the 4th Vermont marched forward and opened up on the enemy. The Rebs pulled back over the railroad embankment. Loud Confederate cheers greeted the returning Rebs.

———————

It took only minutes to get back to the shelter of the cornfield. Ryerson and the other companies were waiting in fighting formation, ready to make sure no enemies followed. None came. It was near 4 PM. The unending crescendo of battle from Fredericksburg continued. For a short time the noise they made from their own fight had drowned it out. Now, it was the background for everything that went on around them.

The doctors and Chaplain Abbott were having a rough time at the dressing station. Hugh Capner was already on the ground, screaming in pain, his arm shattered. Two men from I Company were being half carried, half guided toward them. Several men were bending over John Crane. He was unconscious with a chest wound. Men cried, men laughed, men cursed, men stared off into space, men screamed in pain. As loud as they were, all sound was dwarfed by the incredible noise of the battle to their north at Marye's Heights.

Hetzell was treating Charlie Broome with a bullet wound in the leg. The orderly gave Charlie a good drink of whiskey to help with the shock, and an opium pill. He sprinkled some opium powder in the hole. He stuck his finger in to see if he could pull out the bullet. He couldn't.

Charlie didn't like that much, and let everyone in the regiment know what he thought of the orderly's ancestry. The orderly quickly packed the wound with moist lint and bandaged it with a wet cotton wrap. As soon as he was done, he moved on to the next man, and did the same thing. The booze and the opium pill started to make Charlie feel better. The lint packing and tight bandage staunched the blood. Someone helped him up, and they started for the rear.

Cook quickly took stock. Chaplain Abbott was tending three dead and one dying. He had half a dozen torso or head wounds that probably would not survive. He had two men with arm amputations, one missing a leg and one man with a gun shot wound that had caused a compound fracture of the lower leg. There were over thirty walking wounded. He treated their wounds as best he could, and started them for the ambulances. The sun was going down. Soon it would be dark. Cook wanted desperately to get his wounded to the division hospital at the Bernard House as soon as possible.

The bleeding from Rue's deep arm wound had stopped, but his bandage was full of blood. He was in a daze and struggling to walk back to the ambulances when he felt faint and went down on both knees. Barz Errickson reached down and pulled Joe's good arm over his shoulder, and lifted him to his feet. Together they struggled on. Barz had been hit in the hand, and was wrapped tight with his own bandage.

Hetzell and another lightly wounded man were carrying Obie Fish on a litter. Obie had a hideous head wound. Two men he didn't know were carrying Joe Tetlow. Tetlow was missing a leg and gasping for breath. Other walking wounded were helping their more seriously wounded friends. Everyone knew the rules. If you could walk, you got to the hospital on your own. If you could help, it was your duty to do so.

Sergeant Peck was waiting with his Tripler ambulance. Within minutes, the sergeant and his two stretcher-bearers had Tetlow and Fish loaded. As they were working, two more litters with Sam Pool and a man from D Company named Crane were brought up. As soon as they were loaded, Sergeant Peck put six walking wounded on board and drove off.

More men were coming to the loading point, and more Triplers arrived. Some two-wheeled Finleys came up, but no one would ride in them. Each ambulance could carry four litters. There were more litters coming. The four-wheeled ambulances were loaded and left. The last litter was placed in its ambulance, and the most injured walking wounded climbed in for the ride. Within half an hour they were at the brigade hospital that had been set up at the Bernard House. Pool and Tetlow were taken into the hospital before anyone thought to ask about the other two in the wagon. Crane had passed out, and Fish was unconscious. They were taken from the ambulance while the driver was still inside. Nobody knew who they were or what unit they came from.

Soon, the other ambulances arrived. Capner was taken to surgery and the remains of his arm removed. Crane and Pool both had bullet wounds to the body and were placed on straw mattresses until it was their turn for the surgeons. An assistant surgeon came by and recorded their names, units and extent of their injuries.

The hospital was Bernard's private home, and it had been taken over by the Army. The less seriously injured were settled under the trees around the house, while the critically hurt were taken inside. Rue, Errickson, Buzby and the rest of the walking wounded were placed under the trees. Orderlies recorded their names and units. They quickly checked their injuries and began dressing their wounds. If they were in pain, they were given brandy or opium pills. A cold night was coming on, and they had little shelter. They were fed bread, hot tea and beef stock. Extra hospital blankets were distributed. Most had left their packs where they fell, so this improved their outlook on life.

Crispin noticed skims of ice were forming on the puddles. He quietly moved down the edge of the ravine toward the cornfield. The sounds of battle on the other side of the ravine had petered out a few minutes before. There were still a lot of Rebs moving around out there. Just before dark, he hailed a skirmisher, and was brought back into the Union lines. He was obviously sick, but there was no place to send him. Fortunately, he still had his equipment, so he curled up for the night and went to sleep.

The evening chill crept through the men's sweaty clothing. Collars were turned up and shirttails tucked in. Men with overcoats buttoned their hoods over their heads. Men without could see their breath in the frosty air and shivered. They huddled together with their company mates and prayed for safety.

The sun set over the battlefield for a third day at 4:45 PM. It was already below freezing when it did. The attacks at Marye's Heights ceased at dusk, and the silence was broken only by an occasional musket shot. Volunteers quietly searched the 23rd's sector for wounded and bodies. A bright aurora borealis, something rarely seen in Virginia, lit their way.

Within an hour, Ryerson had a preliminary report of his losses. He made sure command was intact in every company. It took a few hours. By midnight, the Yahoos were ready for whatever the morning would bring.

Ryerson found Grubb in the semi-dark of the aurora. "Burd, we are pulling back into the ravine for the night. I want you to come with me. Nothing is going to happen tonight that Colonel Brown can't handle, and we have some things to do. " With that, the Colonel led him out of the ravine. After a while they came to an orderly holding their horses. Chaplain Abbott was waiting for them. They all mounted, and Ryerson led the way back toward the Franklin's Crossing pontoon bridge. Bivouac fires showed them location of various units, and eventually these helped them navigate to Franklin's headquarters at the Bernard House.

This house had been established as Franklin's Division Headquarters. Under the orders of the Letterman Plan, Surgeon Doctor Crandall of the 16th New York had also designated it as the division hospital. It was set up and ready for patients before the battle started. It was getting plenty of business. The three rode into the firelight in front of the house and dismounted. An orderly tied their horses to a tree. Almost immediately, Charlie Buzby saw them.

"Sir, it's me, Charlie Buzby, we're from the 23rd."

"Buzby, you sure are. How are you? Who else is here?" Grubb, Abbott and Ryerson knelt down by a group of 23rd men lying around several fires under some leafless trees. Those who could, introduced themselves.

"Sir, we are fed and safe. We have blankets and we are warm, and they gave us something for the pain. We are just laying here watching those strange lights in the sky. The doctors took good care of us. They aren't the sawbones some of us were afraid of."

"That's good to hear," said the Colonel. "You men did a fine job today. I am grateful for the work you did. I brought Major Grubb and Chaplain Abbott to see you. We are all praying for you to be well."

"Thank you, sir," came mumbles and comments from under the blankets. The officers spent a few minutes with their men, and then went into the hospital. After they left, Buzby looked around the group from the 23rd. "Imagine that, they came to see us in the dark."

The officers entered the great hall of the house, and were immediately surrounded by wounded. Wounded packed shoulder to shoulder on the floor, on the furniture and in every place a man could lie. As they walked down an open path in the center, Grubb saw an amputation being performed in a room to the left. The stench was horrible. Blood, vomit and feces fouled the floor. An orderly passed them carrying a leg under each arm. Men called for water, friends, mothers, wives and God. Moans, sobs and screams came from all directions.

They found Doctor Crandall taking a break a little further on. The man was exhausted. He quietly showed them to Colonel Hatch. Hatch's leg was gone, and he was ghostly white. Ryerson took his hand as Abbott and Grubb watched. "Bill, Bill, its Ogden, Ogden Ryerson."

Hatch was delirious and rambling. "Get Torbert to let me charge one more time, one more time, Torbert, just one more time."

"Bill, I am here. Grubb and Abbott are with me. Bill?"

"Colonel, he's really doped up on morphine and opium," said an orderly. "He may know you are here, but it might take him hours to understand it."

Ryerson looked at Crandall, and silently questioned if there was any hope. Crandall shook his head no.

The three of them took their time to comfort Hatch as best they could. They spoke to him quietly and stroked his head. They prayed together for him. After a while, Ryerson asked Crandall to lead him to General Bayard. They went up a set of stairs to the second floor. They passed dying Federals and Confederates. In the first room to the left at the top of the stairs, they found Bayard. It was a miracle he was still alive. One leg was gone, and what was left of that thigh and lower abdomen were pulp. It was a mortal wound. His aide was very protective, but not so protective a full colonel couldn't get in to see him.

Ryerson knelt next to the stretcher and took his hand. He whispered in his ear, "George, its Ogden Ryerson. Al Torbert asked me to look in on you." Ryerson felt a slight squeeze.

"We are all praying for you. Is there anything we can do?"

"Father, get my father," whispered Bayer.

"He's on the way, George. Al Torbert said to tell you that you were the best rider he ever saw. George, those West Point cadets love you. You are the best cavalry instructor they ever had." Ryerson blinked tears as he brushed Bayard's face.

Bayard managed an expression that might have passed for a smile. He squeezed Ryerson's hand again and drifted back to sleep.

December 14, 1862 – Franklin's Bridgehead, Fredericksburg, Virginia

During the night, the Yahoos carefully pulled back to the ravine they had occupied on the 12th. The regiment was close to Rebel lines, but the men could light fires in the ravine without enemy snipers seeing them. The men were cooking their hardtack, salt pork rations and making coffee. Those with rations, shared with those who had none. The men were abuzz with tales of the things they had seen in the battle. They waited all day on the 14th for an attack that never came.

Sweesley's squad gathered and talked quietly. "What the hell was yesterday all about?" growled Sharpe. "Run out in a field and let the Rebs shoot at us, and then run back?"

Sweesley and Conover looked at him. "I guess the Generals wanted to know if there were any Rebs in front of us."

"Well, damn it, they sure as hell found out. Do you think Rue is going to be all right?"

Sweesley nodded. "Yes. I am worried about Fish and Ellis, though. They were hurt bad. George, have you cleaned your gun yet?" The sergeant knew he hadn't. "That would be a good thing to get done, goes for the rest of you, too. Get your stuff cleaned up and quit sitting around complaining."

They reluctantly reached for their equipment.
Later in the day, Josie crept out of the position and visited an abandoned house that contained some fine furniture. In spite of the edict about looting, he took some old documents and a sack of flour. The men cooked up a huge batch of pancakes for everybody.

The weather had warmed up, which was fortunate, because everyone had to sleep on the steep sides of the ravine. Some fell asleep at the top of the slope, and woke up in the morning at the bottom.

McKee came by in the afternoon and had three men from each company go back to meet O'Neil and Quartermaster Nichols by the pontoon bridge to bring up rations. They got seventy-five pounds of hardtack and seventy-five pounds of salt pork per company, and a little coffee.

Ryerson and Grubb looked up as Perkins and McKee walked up shortly after daybreak. The Colonel returned their salute. "What's the butcher's bill?"

Perkins handed him the list. "It looks like 5 dead, 36 wounded and 9 missing, sir. That's 50 altogether. Sergeant Allen and Corporal Vandegrift from B Company and Private Coer and Private Gaskill are dead. They were from I and K Companies. Captain Ridgway is still out there. We know he's dead, Riggs and Kirkbride saw him die."

"Yes, General Brook's authorized us to put up a white flag, and go find him if the Rebs will let us. I'll need volunteers."

Grubb said, "I'll go talk to Riggs and find some volunteers. The wounded we can't take care of here are back at the hospital in the Bernard House. We are still looking for our missing."

While they were talking a messenger rode up the ravine. He got off his horse, and handed Ryerson a dispatch from General Torbert. Ryerson read it. He shook his head and handed it to Grubb. "They are trying to move Hatch and Bayard back to Falmouth. It doesn't look good," was all he could say.

Grubb looked at the message, got up and excused himself. He dejectedly walked down the ravine. Ryerson watched him go.

Perkins said, "Sir, we have one other man missing. Private Burton from B Company fell out of the march on the way from Devil's Hole to the bridge. No one has seen him since. He was sick, didn't seem to be the kind to desert."

"Let the Provost Marshal know." He looked at McKee, "Top, when we get out of here I want you to go back over the route and see if you can find him. Maybe he's laid up somewhere." McKee nodded.

Ryerson got up and walked after Grubb. He found him near the stream with tears in his eyes. "You all right, Burd?" asked the Colonel.

"Sir, two commanders have been killed beside me since spring, and I was right there when Ridgway got shot."

"Well, come on Burd, Hatch would be proud of you. You saved a lot of his boys yesterday, saved a lot of mine too."

Grubb looked at the ground. "I've seen men fall and been in a few fights, but ..."

Ryerson interrupted. "You did well. That's why I sent you instead of Brown. You think you've got hard luck? Look at that poor Hambrick. He's only been with us 3 days from 1st Regiment, and he's already been through this mess." He paused a whole minute. "I need a new G Company Commander. I don't think Riggs is ready."

"I agree, sir." He paused. "Henry Risdon did a good job today, how about him?"

"Do you think he is ready to handle a company?"

Grubb hadn't known these men very long. He thought back about the attack. His recollection was that C Company didn't falter when Sam Carr went down. Risdon kept them going.

"Yes sir. C Company never faltered, even when Carr was wounded. I think he will be fine."

"Good. Now I want you to find Riggs, and make arrangements to go get Ridgway. I just won't leave him out there like they left me."

"Yes sir," said Grubb, and set off for G Company.

Ryerson called his company commanders together at 9 AM. Lieutenants Risdon and Sever were there, too. "I need you to make sure you appoint replacements for your lost NCOs this morning. If we get into a fight today, I don't want any gaps in the Chain of Command. Let Perkins know who you are promoting so we can make it official. Make sure your men know what you have done, so they know who to look to."

He paused. "You all know that we lost Joe Ridgway yesterday. I am sorry for that, he was a good man. He was easy to get along with, and he cared about his men. I want you to know that I am promoting Henry Risdon to take his place. Henry," he looked at him. "I have faith in you and know you will do a good job." The other captains nodded their agreement.

Risdon said sadly, "Thank you, sir."

"Also, Lieutenant Sever will be in command of C Company until Captain Carr gets back from the hospital. I put him in command last night."

"I want you to tell your men they did a good job yesterday. However, we will be working on that wheel maneuver when we get back to the parade ground." The captains each shared a sheepish grin.

"Are you going to have someone shooting at us when we do it?" piped up one of them.

Ryerson thought for a minute. He was unhappy with the performance of his officers. He felt there were only three Captains he could count on. At least a dozen lieutenants needed to be replaced. However, the battle was not over, and he was not about to create more problems than he already had. "I could," he deadpanned. His off-the-cuff remark broke some of the tension.

The Colonel looked at a small notebook and said, "I need to see the K and H Company Commanders, thank you, gentlemen, dismissed." Ryerson noticed Captain Grobler did not look well. He watched as the German immigrant walked stiffly away.

Captains Parmentier and McCabe waited as the others filed out. "You fellas had a rough day yesterday. How are you and your boys doing?"

"My men were lucky, sir," said Parmentier. "If that Reb shell had burst out in front of us a little more than it did, we would have lost a lot more men."

Higgins nodded. "Same thing happened to us, Sir. A few of my men will probably be discharged. Most will be back."

"Good, keep an eye on them. Things could get rough around here, and we will need every one of them. I'll be around to see them in a while."

"Sir, we have a big problem," sighed Parmentier.

"What's that?"

"Most of my men dropped their knapsacks during the attack. They have no tents, blankets or food."

Ryerson was dumbfounded. "How many?"

"I am not sure, but I think a lot."

"Find Colonel Brown, and tell him I want a report of how many men dropped their packs."

"Yes, sir." They saluted and left.

Ryerson, Riggs, Risdon and four privates from G Company were moving through the fog quietly. They had a white handkerchief tied to a stick, though it was doubtful anyone more than ten feet away could see it.

A branch cracked in front of them. They froze. Risdon called out softly, "Yo, Rebs, you out there?"

"We's here, Yank, what do you want?"

"I got a white flag here. We are under a flag of truce. Our Captain got killed, and we want to take him home."

There was some mumbling from not too far away, and another voice came back. "Who authorized the flag of truce?"

"General Brooks."

"Well, all right, we'll honor your flag if you honor ours. We are looking for some boys, too."

"Agreed," said Ryerson, and they went their separate ways.

It took a while to find the body in the fog. The Rebels had stripped it. The body was frozen, and scarcely resembled the friend they knew. They treated Joe tenderly. He was a friend and neighbor before the war. He would be missed by the regiment, as well as the folks back home. They laid him on a litter and covered him with a blanket. Then, they slowly carried him back to the regiment. When they came to a safe place, they set him down. Men filed by to pay their respects. They were furious that Rebels had stolen his valuables, weapons and clothes. The body was placed in a wagon and taken to Falmouth.

While this was going on, a detail went back by the Old Richmond Road and dug four graves. Chaplain Abbott held a short service for Allen, Coer, Vandergrift and Gaskill. They were quickly buried on the battlefield. The only grave markers they had were pieces of hardtack boxes on which their names were burned.

———

Ryerson was just about to say 'you have to be kidding' when he realized how ludicrous it would sound. Lieutenant Colonel Brown had just told him 182 of his men had lost their knapsacks during the attack. That meant almost a third of the people who attacked the embankment had dropped their gear. That meant 182 of his men did not have a two-man tent, blankets or extra clothes. It meant they were headed toward winter quarters, and twenty percent of his command didn't have the equipment they needed to survive. This was not funny – given the weather conditions, it was life-threatening. He immediately ordered a reallocation of all food and materials in the regiment. All food, blankets, tents and clothing were to be shared. The boys were going to get to know each other up close and personal at a level they had never considered. They had to, or they were going to die of exposure.

———

The sun was setting on the battlefield once again. Torbert called the regimental commanders to the rear just before dark. "I want you to know that your regiments did a fine job yesterday. General Smith and General Brooks and I are very proud of you. You tell your men I said so." He paused, and bit his lip. "I don't want this to get out yet, the rumors are around already…"

He stopped, and looked at each of them. "We lost near 8,000 men in front of Marye's Heights yesterday." The pronouncement was greeted with open-mouthed astonishment and mumbling. "Oh, my God" and "Sweet Jesus" were quietly expressed.

"Six divisions are shot up so bad, they cannot attack again without replacements and reorganization. We are at a stalemate here. Our artillery can't reach theirs, and they can't reach ours. The fuses on their shells are horrible, so it's not safe for them to shoot over their own troops. They can't hurt us unless we attack them. Hatch's attack yesterday showed us how good the Rebs' position is here. We can't breach them in the south, and their position is even stronger in front of the heights. You need to know that Burnside's headquarters is in an uproar. There is a lot of politics going on, and a lot of hard feelings. If you know what's good for you, you'll keep your mouths shut, and stay out of it. Make sure your men do, too." The colonels nodded.

"We are going back across the river tonight, and we will take up positions on the other side. Do it quietly. Be careful you don't leave anybody, and make sure your men don't leave any equipment the Rebs can use. Ryerson and Campbell, you will put out skirmishers and cover our withdrawal. That's all, gentlemen." With that, the colonels were dismissed and went back to their units. The word was passed down to get ready to move, and do so quietly. The air was warmer than it had been the night before. A thick fog returned.

December 14, 1862 - Falmouth, Virginia

Capner was awake, but drugged. He had been evacuated from the Bernard House just after daylight. He vaguely remembered the orderlies dismounting, and walking the four horses pulling the ambulance across the pontoon bridge. They joined a long line of ambulances that were bringing wounded over from Franklin's bridgehead further south of Deep Run. The line slowly made its way to the rail sidings at Falmouth. They arrived late in the afternoon.

A group of men removed his stretcher from the ambulance. Two carried him into a boxcar. He dreamily gazed around the car. The floor was covered with hay, and it smelled good. Other seriously wounded men were being carried into the car and placed gently on the floor. Critical cases were not removed from their mattresses. The mattress was picked up with the patient on it, and hand-carried to the train.

A medical officer with an attendant and supplies was detailed to accompany each car. They would travel with the patients to Aquia Creek, and then to Washington by steamship or barge.

Capner recognized some of the men in the car. Swaim from I company was there with a bandaged shoulder wound. It looked like Joe Malsbury with the bandaged jaw. Goff and Andrews from K Company each had one hand wrapped up. Crane, Tetlow and Pool were drugged and sleeping. The train whistle blew, and the steam engine slowly puffed off to Aquia Creek. The sound of the rain drumming on the car's roof and the morphine tablet the orderly gave Hugh before they left put him to sleep long before the train finished its twelve-mile journey.

December 15, 1862 - Fredericksburg, Virginia
Word came through the fog for the squad to be prepared to move at 1 AM. A strong south wind came up just before midnight. The noise of the wind and rain masked the sound of the retreat. The men gingerly picked their way out of the ravine. It took forty-five minutes to negotiate the fallen logs, cat briars and steep slippery slopes to get out and form up by the Old Richmond Road. The regiment crossed the pontoon bridges at 2 AM. Crispin was in a bad way. He fell out of the march shortly after crossing the river. At dawn he followed Birney's Brigade and eventually caught up with H Company at 10 AM. The roads were jammed with ambulances, retreating men and equipment. The columns halted out of Confederate artillery range and waited. The men were unhappy. They did not like to skedaddle again.

Torbert watched as dawn slowly illuminated the valley. The rain and fog covered everything, just as it had two days before. He wondered how long it would take for the enemy to realize they were gone. Their skirmishers would slowly feel their way across the battlefield, and marvel at the detritus of war, lost knapsacks, dropped guns, broken equipment and dead horses.

Meantime, he watched a defeated army slowly march by. The last to come had been the engineers with their precious pontoons, and then the rear guard. The army was withdrawing behind Stafford Heights. Almost two hundred Union artillery pieces guaranteed there would be no pursuit. It was just as well. The bitterness among the officers and men over the mishandling of the battle was growing more vocal and vicious by the hour. Morale in the retreating columns plummeted as word spread of the carnage and missed opportunities. Every man in the army had lost friends or relatives.

Torbert had lost many, too. His friend, George Bayard, had been wounded near Franklin's headquarters at the Bernard House on the 13th by an artillery shell. He lingered a few hours, but the shell had taken off a leg. Bayard was the 6th Corps' Cavalry Brigade Commander and the best horseman Torbert knew. They had met at West Point. Torbert was a First Classman and George was one year behind him. After graduation, Bayard was Jeb Stuart's 2nd Lieutenant in Company G of the 1st Cavalry at Fort Riley. They rode together protecting settlers on the Santa Fe Trail, until Bayard took an arrow in the face and was sent back to West Point to recover.

As the war progressed, Bayard and Stuart both became generals on opposite sides. The story was they had met under a flag of truce after the Battle of Cedar Mountain and had drinks while they talked about their adventures on the frontier. As they talked, Bayard noticed a wounded man nearby and asked Stuart to hold his horse's reigns while he got a drink for the man. The joke in both armies was this was the only time in history Jeb Stuart had "played orderly for a Union General." Longstreet, Jackson and Lee would never let Stuart forget it. Bayard's last post before the war was cavalry instructor at West Point. The shot that killed him was said to have been aimed by one of his pupils, Major John Pelham, Stuart's Horse Battery artillery commander, West Point, class of 61.* Torbert wondered if Stuart knew.

*Several accounts suggest Pelham's guns fired the fatal shot (http://members.aol.com/lmjarl/civwar/battle.html). **Harper's Magazine reports Bayard was wounded 50 yards from the "Burnard House" sometime in the afternoon. Reports show Pelham delayed the Union attack with two smoothbore Napoleons near Hamilton's Crossing for at least an hour between 10 and noon that morning. The direction of fire is correct, but the time is wrong and the distance to Bernard's House is well over the weapon's 1,600-yard range. The injury was caused by a solid shot to the thigh NJM12/18/62. Bayard's location at Bernard's House, the time of injury and the range involved suggests the shot may have come from one of two Confederate 20-pound Parrotts belonging to Pogue's Battery. A source quoted as E.A. Moore on page 357 of Lee's Lieutenants places Pelham at the Pogue battery that afternoon. Website http://richmondthenandnow.com/Newspaper-Articles/John-Pelham.html suggests Pelham sighted at least 8 separate batteries that day. It is possible he aimed the shot.**

Chaplain Francis B. Hall, 16th NY Vols, saw General Bayard and Colonel Hatch on the night of the 13th at the Bernard House and reported on the critical nature of their wounds in his Journal.

Earlier in the morning, word came that his trusted friend Bill Hatch had died on the way to the hospital in Falmouth. Torbert had known Bill since before they mustered in. Last year, most of the 4th was surrounded and captured at Gaines Mill. The Rebs had taken their brand new Springfield rifles and, in an increasingly rare gesture of humanity, sent them home under parole. Most had rejoined the brigade. Hatch assumed command after the parole and served with distinction.

The War Department had rearmed the 4th with old 1842 percussion-capped smoothbore muskets. This really chafed the troops. Torbert could still picture Hatch leading the charge through Crampton's Gap. The regiment was so poised; it looked like it was on parade. They charged four hundred yards across a plowed field through a cross fire and never broke ranks. They took the position and captured two stands of Confederate colors, and enough new Springfield rifles to outfit the whole regiment. How proud Bill had been to rearm his men with the captured Springfields, and send those worthless smoothbores back to the War Department. He looked at the retreating men. How many were wondering who was safe and who was gone? He guessed it was all of them. He was right.

December 15, 1862 - Alexandria, Virginia

Hugh Capner was amazed. It was late in the evening and he was at the US Army General Hospital in Alexandria, Virginia. He had arrived around noon and the remainder of the day had been spent cleaning up and getting settled. He was bathed. He was warm. He was dry. He had clean pajamas, a soft bed and a belly full of good, warm food. He was not in pain. The only thing missing was his arm. As he looked around, he noticed almost everyone in the ward was suffering from the same problem. Some were missing more than one limb.

He didn't remember much about the trip. The train pulled into a siding at Aquia Creek. There was some jostling as the freight cars were loaded onto a barge. A steam tug pushed them up the Potomac to Alexandria where the cars were unloaded. A new engine pulled them into a siding, and an ambulance carried him to this hospital.

It was hard to believe that he had been shot just two days before in a cold, damp, dirty field, and now, here he was between clean sheets. And, there were women here.

When they took him off the train, he remembered being awake enough to say goodbye to Malsbury and Swain. He didn't know where they were going. Crane, McAninie and Tetlow were here with him. He would be able to visit them and keep in touch. He heard that Sam Pool and a fella from K Company he didn't know named Andrews had been sent to a place called Harewood US Army Hospital in Washington. Capner didn't know the others. Bill Goff and Jim Adams ended up in the Army Hospital in Newark, New Jersey. Mica Ellis was sent to the one in Chester, Pennsylvania.

The trains were not just carrying off the wounded. The mortuary services were busy at Falmouth preparing the dead for shipment home. The Ridgways arranged for Joe's body to be returned to Beverly. Colonel Hatch was taken to Camden, and General Bayard to Princeton.

December 16, 1862 - White Oak Church, Virginia

The regiment waited two days for its turn to march to camp. It marched down River Road in a heavy downpour, and turned left on the road to White Oak Church. Just before it got to White Oak Church, it halted, turned right and moved into a pine woods with rest of the 1st and 2nd Brigades. Hexamer's six guns trundled by, and the battery set up camp near the creek at the back of the property.

H Company immediately went on guard. No fires were permitted, so there was no hot coffee or food. The men curled up together for warmth under their blankets. After a long, cold night, they were finally relieved.

Marion and Esau Montieth and sisters Jennie and Lucy watched from their farmhouse as the long column of soldiers and wagons came up the road through the mist and rain. Soon a Union officer informed them he was commandeering the house for General Torbert's headquarters, and the brigades were occupying the farm. A few minutes later, Doc Hetzell moved two sick officers in and made them comfortable. General Torbert arrived a little later and was pleasant enough. He apologized for the intrusion and told them he would share food and firewood with them, and that the Army would pay for any damages to the property. Soon the ambulances pulled in, and Doc Cook started putting up the regimental hospital.

Torbert and the staff were laying out the regimental camps. Each regiment was allotted an area. Within that area, each company arranged its tents in a straight line along its company street. The company officer's tents were in a line across the back of the ten company streets. The regimental commanders' and staff tents were behind them in the center. After the men got their tents set up, it was time to get a fire going. The weather was cold, and they had been without hot food for days. The only source of dry firewood around was Montieth's split rail fences. The fences started disappearing immediately. It wasn't long before the aroma of wood smoke and coffee filled the neighborhood.

December 17, 1862 - White Oak Church, Virginia

McKee found the Regimental Headquarters wagon, and got Ryerson's tent set up in the pine woods just to the east of the White Oak Church. The Sergeant Major found a table and a chair and got a lantern lit so the colonel and the adjutant could get some of the famous Army paperwork caught up.

Ryerson looked at the letter Perkins had prepared for him. It started out: "I have the honor to report the following casualties in my regiment in the battle of Fredericksburg on the 13th day of December." It was a funny way to start a letter that reeked of death and destruction. How do you feel honor when you tell someone that fifty-one people in your command are dead or hurt or missing? It seems like it should start: "I regret to inform you of the loss of my men." He stopped. This wasn't the first time he had signed one of these letters, and probably wouldn't be the last. It was pointless to think about it, and he certainly couldn't talk to his subordinates about it. The letter went on to list the killed, wounded and missing.

Ridgway, Allen, Vandergrift, Coer and Gaskill were gone. Ryerson knew Joe Ridgway well. He was one of his best commanders. They had visited and shown pictures of their families to each other. He would have to write to his family and tell them what happened. He'd met Sergeant Allen once or twice. He couldn't picture the others.

There was a list of thirty-seven wounded. Perkins said thirty-six, but he counted them and would make the correction. The list failed to mention four would probably die and eight more were so injured they would have to be discharged. So, twenty-five might return for duty. Then there were nine missing. With luck, they would be in Confederate hands or at a hospital or just straggling. He hoped they would turn up. The colonel pondered the report for a few minutes and finally signed it. He knew his counterparts on both sides of the river were doing the same. Soon the Generals would total up the frightful cost of Fredericksburg.

Early in the day, H Company was ordered back to the regimental reserve. Plenty of good fires and the first hot meals some had seen in eight days were waiting for them. They had some free time and found they could catch rabbits in a nearby field to augment their rations. The hunt was on, and soon the field was overrun with laughing soldiers. It was good to have a chase to take their minds off their troubles.

Just before dusk, the company was ordered to the regimental camp and told to set their tents up along the H Company street that had been laid out for them. It was extremely cold, and the men went to work to put their dog tents up as fast as possible. The frozen ground made it difficult. Hatchets rang through the woods as men cut tent stakes and poles. Then the woods rang with profanity as they tried to drive the stakes into the frozen ground. More stakes were cut and driven, until eventually the shelters were built. Soon cooking fires warmed them and their food. Water was becoming a problem, too. The streams and ponds were frozen thick with ice.

Some of the men had lost all of their equipment in the battle. All they had was on their backs. These fellas were in dire straights. They were in danger of freezing to death. Others in the regiment shared their equipment to keep them alive. Big fires were built to keep the men warm, but it was so cold that a side nearest the fire got too hot, while the opposite side froze.

Sweesley's squad was sitting around a big bonfire. Crispin was a mess, but it was the first time he'd been warm since the 10th. The sickness he had struggled with since before the battle had translated into a severe swelling of one side of his face. **(10 days of headache, low fever, swollen glands and face, loss of appetite, and stomachache all point to mumps – fortunately, no swollen testicles, although he might not record these. Also could have been strep throat.)**

Sweesley was puffing on his meerschaum. "So, Terhune, what do you think of our young major now?"

Terhune grimaced. "Sarge, you were right. Grubb was really something. When Hatch was shot, he took right over. Nobody in the 4th knew what to do. Thompson couldn't have done that. He would have just stood there. The Major saved a lot of lives. Got the whole 4th out and our six companies, and he's only twenty."

"Conover, when is Rue coming back?" asked Hullings.

"I expect he'll be gone at least a week," replied Conover. "It took a lot of stitches to fix him up. He's hurting. I hear him, Buzby, Wood, Shinn and Erickson are all over at Falmouth Hospital. What bothers me is they can't find Obie."

A collective set of grumbles arose as everyone leaned forward to gaze at Conover. "What?"

"Hetzell and some of our wounded carried Obie to the ambulances. He was hurt bad. His head was crushed and his face was swelling real bad. The drivers say they took him to the hospital, but nobody knew who he was. They don't know what happened to him."

They all glanced around at Sharp as he said, "I hear Micajah might not lose his arm."

The group muttered approval at the news.

"They put a splint on it and stopped the bleeding fast. I hear they put him on a hospital ship. I doubt if he'll be back."

"Well, I am glad he's going to be all right," said Elwood. "At least he's in a warm bed tonight with some good food. It'll be Christmas soon. Maybe he can go home. Too bad about Capner, though."

"Yeah, Hetzell told me they had to amputate his arm. He was a good troop. Didn't shirk."

Josie spoke quietly. It hurt too much to open his mouth, so he spoke softly through clenched teeth, "My friend Stacey Borton from E Company over in 4th Regiment was killed at the railroad. He was a nice boy. When we were back at Bakersville, he came over and loaned me three dollars. Just showed up and said, 'Josie, you might need this.' I need to get that back to his family." They all looked at Josie and shook their heads in agreement.

"Yeah, if the bastards ever pay us," griped Terhune.

Over the next hours, days and weeks around the fire, they all spoke of the friends each had lost in the battle. They mourned their dead and worried about their injured and missing friends. Thousands of other men were sitting around thousands of other campfires on both sides of the river, doing the same thing.

When it was all said and done, the Army of the Potomac had lost almost 13,000 men killed, wounded or missing. It was nearly one out of every ten Union soldiers on the field. When the word spread of the horrific casualties, the officers found they were not alone when it came to being critical of how the battle was handled.

Ryerson was in his tent looking over a series of reports. The world had continued to turn while the regiment was at Deep Run. Two men who were in the hospital when the regiment moved out had died. Private Harrison from D Company died of typhoid on the 12th and Private Speer of B Company died of dysentery on the 14th. Private Grass from B Company had been discharged from Fairfax General Hospital for a service-related disability. Private Hosure had been discharged from Cliftburne Hospital in Washington on the 9th for his frostbitten feet.

Captain Milnor reported that Private Carr had deserted from A Company sometime on the 16th. George Lippincott was gone from E Company, too. Ryerson had Perkins turn the cases over to the Provost Marshal. Milnor mentioned he and Hambrick were getting along well. Hambrick had held up well during the attack, for only having been with the company for three days.

Doc was worried about Lieutenant Newbold from D Company. Newbold had been sent directly from the Montieth House to the hospital almost as soon as the regiment got back to White Oak Church. He probably had typhoid. That would be hard on his brother, Reading, the D Company Commander. Lieutenant Kirkbride was temporarily taking his place.

The word on his officers, Carr, Budd and Grobler, was not good. Carr and Budd were not terminally wounded, but the wounds to their feet would take a long time to heal. Grobler was deathly ill. It would be weeks, if not months, before he would be back.

Private Charlie Broome was being kept at the hospital in Falmouth, along with the rest of the walking wounded from the regiment.

All of the men reported missing in the fight returned except William Henry. The men who were with the attacking force had good reasons for being missing. They had been separated during the attack and been trapped behind the lines, and escaped or fought their way out with the 4th.

Three of the missing men had turned up at Aquia Creek with only minor wounds or feigned injuries. They had gotten across the river, and hopped a hospital train to the rear. Everyone, from the Sergeant Major to their officers, first sergeant, sergeants, corporals and fellow soldiers, were making their lives miserable over it. They wouldn't do it again. Nobody liked malingerers.

While he was contemplating all of this, the orderly came in and said Lieutenant Colonel Brown would like to see him. "Send him in," said Ryerson.

"Good evening, George, how are you?"

"Colonel, ah," he stammered. "Ogden, I have been doing a lot of thinking since the battle, and I don't belong here."

Ryerson sat up and turned up the lamp. "Why don't you have a seat, George? Would you like some coffee?" Brown nodded yes. Ryerson called the orderly to bring some for both of them. "This is a big decision, George. Once you make it, it can't be unmade. Are you sure you want to do this?"

Brown sighed, and slowly shook his head yes. "I have tried to learn this soldiering job. There is a lot more to it than one would think. Just learning the commands to move the men on the field is difficult. Then there is the administration and the day-to-day command responsibilities, and the fighting. I just don't feel I am up to it."

"You have been helpful and ..."

"Thanks, Ogden. You have been patient and kind, but when I saw what Grubb did in that attack, I knew I ... I knew that if something happened to you and I ended up in command, I would not know what to do. I don't have the background. If I had been out there, we would have lost a lot more men. I want to resign my commission."

Ryerson thought for a minute. He didn't want to be impolite. Brown was right. While Brown was a genial man, he seldom took the initiative expected of a commander. He had been no help at all in the battle. At the same time, he had been a solid friend to all in the regiment. They drank their coffee and discussed the resignation for an hour before Ryerson acquiesced, and said he would recommend that General Torbert give his approval.

Brown left, and Ryerson called the Sergeant Major. Together, they walked to the General's headquarters.

———

Torbert was reading when the orderly showed them in. The Montieth house was comfortably warm. It was made of logs that were hewn square and chinked together. Kerosene lamps lit the space. The General invited them to have a seat. "So, what brings the 23rd to see me tonight?" drawled the General.

Ryerson noticed the General was wheezing. "Are you all right, sir?"

"Ah, I caught a cold when were over in that damned ravine, and it settled in my chest. Oakley is taking good care of me."

"Well, I certainly hope you start feeling better. Sir, Lieutenant Colonel Brown wants to resign his commission. I have spoken with him about it, and unless you have an objection, I will approve his request."

The General looked at Ryerson for a minute and said, "Has he learned enough to handle the regiment if you are hurt?"

Ryerson shook his head. "No, I don't think so."

At this point, Sergeant Major McKee asked to be excused. "Sir, I don't think it's appropriate for me to be here while you discuss senior officers' affairs."

Torbert started to nod his agreement, but Ryerson shook his head no. "Sergeant Major, you are the senior NCO in this regiment, and your opinion about these matters is important to me. You also figure in my plans for addressing this vacancy, and I will need your thoughts."

Torbert looked at them for a minute and said, "I agree. Go on, Colonel."

"Sir, this is an opportunity to create a battle-tested chain of command in the 23rd. I request you permit me to promote Burd Grubb to regimental executive officer as a Lieutenant Colonel, and promote and move Captain Milnor to regimental major."

"Those are good choices, Ogden. Who would you replace Milnor with?"

"Hambrick was absolutely rock solid at Deep Run. He could do the job."

Torbert nodded. Ryerson continued, "I put Henry Risdon in temporary command of G Company after Ridgway was killed. Sir, I need your approval to make that permanent. That means I have to move Severs up to 1st Lieutenant to replace Henry."

Torbert nodded, "And who do you replace Severs with?"

Ryerson looked at Torbert. Torbert looked at Ryerson, and then they both looked at Sergeant Major McKee. McKee suddenly suspected he had been set up. "Oh, no. Not me, sir. I am the Top Sergeant in this outfit, and I like it that way."

"Now, Top," soothed Torbert. "Every officer and man in the 23rd respects you. You have earned it. I think you would be a great choice for an officer. You are a gentleman; of course, everyone knows that, but Congress will make it official."

McKee was uncertain. Ryerson looked at him. "John, you are a gifted leader. We may have a lot of fighting ahead of us. I need you to pass on what you have learned to the other young officers. You've seen it from the enlisted side. You can't do it unless you are an officer. They just won't listen to an NCO, but they will listen to an officer, and as Second Lieutenant McKee, I can assure you nobody is going to cause you any trouble."

"All right, now who replaces McKee as Sergeant Major?" asked General Torbert. The general was clearly getting excited about the conversation.

"This is unusual, sir," said Ryerson. "I suggest we promote Private Sam Browne from A Company to Regimental Sergeant Major."

"That is unusual. Why?"

"First, he is older than most of the men in the regiment, and they respect him. Second, Private Browne served with distinction at Deep Run. He helped Milnor and Hambrick get our line re-established. Then, he made sure the troops reloaded so they would keep firing. When it was all over, he helped get our wounded back to the dressing station. The men do look up to him, sir."

McKee nodded in agreement. "If you take Browne, sir, the NCO chain of command in each company stays intact. For what it's worth, I think it's a good choice."

Torbert thought for a few seconds. "I am not going to interfere with your internal promotions, Colonel. You have good reason for advancing the people you have suggested. But, Burd Grubb just turned twenty-one years old. Will the men follow him if something happens to you?"

"Yes sir, I believe they would."

Torbert looked at McKee. "Your thoughts, Top?"

"Yes, sir. The men think very highly of Major Grubb. They saw what he did at Deep Run, and they talk about it every day. I think he will be fine."

"All right, then. I will approve the promotions and Colonel Brown's resignation. It will take a few days. Hopefully, we can have it done just after Christmas."

With that, the meeting ended. Ryerson held the door as McKee stepped out of the house. Ryerson looked back at Torbert. The general winked and grinned and broke into a coughing spell.

December 20, 1862 - White Oak Church, Virginia

This was a happy day for Doc Elmer. He finally was able to break up the brigade hospital at Devil's Hole. Wagons were sent from each regiment to take the soldiers to the regimental hospitals. It was a relief to take down the tents, and ride back to the regiment at White Oak Church. The Doc had taken care of one hundred twenty two men for nine days. He didn't have much help, and was very short of supplies. It was a real testament to his skill that most of them made it. He had finally cobbled together a stove out of sheet metal he had found. It looked like a dunce cap with a hole in it. Add some chimney material, and it was possible to keep the hospital tolerable.

Hartman and Sweesley were waiting for Josie when the company formed up for morning formation. "Private Crispin, what is wrong with your face?"

Several other men in the squad started laughing. Then they looked at Josie and saw his condition was no laughing matter. His right eye was swollen almost shut. Ed Lloyd had helped him wrap a handkerchief around it. The wrap's warmth and support gave Josie some relief.

"Sweesley, Crispin has been sick since before we went to Deep Run. I want him on sick call, and I don't want him back until he is well. You make sure Doc Cook knows that."

Sweesley answered, "Yes, 1st Sergeant."

They started to walk away, but Hartman stopped them, "Crispin, you did well to keep up with us. We all know how sick you've been. Go get well."

Josie mumbled a thank you and headed off to find the surgeon. The sick call line was quite long when he got there. He got bed rest in his tent.

Sergeant Major McKee was in a foul mood. He had just spent his final two days as a Sergeant Major visiting every unit and house between Devil's Hole and the abandoned pontoon bridge crossing on the Rappahannock, looking for Private John Burton from B Company. Burton was sick when the regiment marched to Fredericksburg. He fell out of the march, and no one had seen him since. After two days of searching, he couldn't find him either. Several unidentified bodies had been found and buried. Nobody knew if it was Burton. Just as he was sitting down to figure out how to tell the Colonel, the news came that two more soldiers were missing: Private Fish from H Company and Private Henry from F Company.

He stalked off to H Company and found Hartman. After talking to the First Sergeant, they both stalked off to find Doc Cook. Soon the three of them were stalking off to find Sergeant Peck and the ambulance drivers. They found one who remembered picking up a man with a head wound late on the thirteenth and delivering him to the division hospital. They stalked off to find the people who had worked in the hospital.

The Assistant Surgeon in charge of records remembered someone who might have been Fish. The man had died, his face swollen beyond recognition. He never regained consciousness. Nobody knew who he was. No equipment was with him, and there were no name tags sewed into his clothes. The body was taken away and buried with a number of other unknowns.

Tracking down Fish had taken most of the day. When McKee got back to camp, he found that his inquiry about Henry had been answered. Henry was last seen as F Company was attacking toward the railroad embankment. His friends saw him go down, but lost track of him. Confederate troops reported finding a burned Union body near the place he was last seen. They buried it with their own.

McKee was vexed. He went to Colonel Ryerson. "Sergeant Major McKee reporting, Sir."

"Yes, Top, what is it?"

"Colonel, you asked me to look for Private Burton."

Ryerson noted the Sergeant Major's voice, pushed his papers aside, and looked up at him. "Yes?"

"Sir, we have a problem. Burton is probably lost, and we have two others in the same boat."

Ryerson frowned, and so did McKee. McKee continued. "Burton was known to be sick, and fell out of the march around Devil's Hole. It froze that night. There are some pretty desperate characters around there. He could have died or been killed, and the body stripped. No one has seen him or a body that we could identify as his. During our fight on the 13th, Private Fish was wounded in the head and unrecognizable. Our orderlies got him to an ambulance and he was taken to the division hospital. No one there knew him, and he had no identification on him. I think he died and was buried with a bunch of other unknown soldiers. Henry was last seen as F Company was charging toward the railroad embankment. Several men claim they saw one of our men on fire during the attack. The Rebs claim they buried a Union body that was all burned up near there. It could have been Henry." McKee paused and pursed his lips. "Sir, we did everything we know to keep track of these men, and we still have three unknowns in less than a week."

Ryerson looked at him for a minute. "Sit down and talk to me, Top. This is happening all over the Army. From what I hear, it is even worse on the Confederate side." He paused. "Upsetting. A man who dies out here shouldn't just disappear forever."

"I agree, sir, it is shameful, but I am hearing this from every NCO I know."

140

Ryerson said, "I have heard of men buying metal disks to wear around their neck. Each disk has their name and home on it, so if they are killed or injured, their family can be notified. The sutlers are selling them. I can't order the men to spend their money for these things, especially since we haven't been paid yet. I wish I could get the government to buy them."

He smiled. "But, Sergeant Major, I can order them to put their names on their clothes and write their name and address on a piece of paper and keep it in their pockets."

McKee nodded and smiled. "Sir, I will get that done right away, and Sir?"

"Yes."

"Thank you for recommending me for promotion."

"You did well, Sergeant Major. I look forward to you being one of my officers. Thank you."

Ryerson was not surprised by the news McKee had brought. He knew that since the beginning of the war, well over 30 percent of men killed in battle were listed as unknown. It was a figure that disturbed him greatly.

December 21, 1862 - White Oak Church, Virginia

It was a chilly Sunday morning, and the men were gathered around their campfires. Conover looked over at Josie and asked, "How are you feeling, Josie?"

"A little better, Joe, my face isn't as swollen," rasped Crispin through his hoarse, sore throat.

"Are you writing in your diary again?"

"Yup, I try to write every day. I promised Mary. It will be fun to read some of this to the folks when we get back home. They will never believe all this."

George Sharp and Corn Terhune walked up with arms full of sticks and roots they had gathered for the fire. They set them down and fed a few into the blaze. Just then, a gray squirrel ran by.

Terhune yelled, "Come on, George, let's get it," and the race was on.

They chased the squirrel up a small tree. The little animal scolded and chattered at them. Heads turned at the various fires, and men grinned at the distraction. Sharp and Terhune started rocking the tree back and forth. This just made the squirrel more upset. He chattered louder.

"What are you fools doing? The thing's too little to eat," laughed Conover.

"We just want to catch him," grinned Sharp.

Men got up from their fires, and ran to see the developing circus. They cheered and yelled as tree rocked harder and harder. The squirrel finally jumped to the ground, and everyone scattered to get out of the way as it ran to another tree. Sharp and Terhune were right on his tail. By this time, the new tree was surrounded by soldiers and laughter echoed through the camp as the spectacle unfolded before them. The two men started climbing the tree, and the squirrel continued scolding them all the louder.

"That damned thing's going to bite both of you," laughed Conover, and then the tree broke. Down came the squirrel, the branches and two grown men, all in a heap. Suddenly it dawned on everybody that they were in close proximity to an angry little rodent with teeth. The two men were trying to keep the beast from getting on them, and the beast was just trying to get away. In the end, all three exited the area in different directions.

The audience loved it. People were slapping their legs, holding their sides and laughing so hard, they cried. Conover couldn't stop giggling, and Josie was gasping to catch his breath while he held his swollen face. The officers were just shaking their heads in amazement.

The hunters wandered back to the fire and sat down. "Almost had the damned thing, but George let it get away," said Terhune dejectedly. The hilarity started all over. The men relaxed for the first time since the battle and enjoyed a quiet Sunday.

December 22, 1862 - White Oak Church, Virginia

The Provost Marshal found Private Carr trying to get on a boat at Aquia Landing. They arrested him and brought him back to Colonel Ryerson's headquarters. McKee was chewing Carr out when Ryerson came in, and Carr wasn't the least bit intimidated. In fact, Carr was defiant.

Ryerson listened for a minute, and finally took over. "Carr, you have been arrested as a deserter. This is a serious charge. You could be sent to prison or even shot if you are found guilty of this in a court martial."

Carr looked Ryerson squarely in the eye. "Colonel, then just shoot me. I have tried everything I can do to be a good soldier in that squad. No matter what I do, I get picked on. I get all the dirty details. I get all the worst guard posts and all the extra duty. I ain't no God-damned contraband slave. I signed up to soldier, and I ain't being treated fair." The boy was standing at attention and had not violated military courtesy. Something was different here.

Ryerson looked at McKee. Both of them were thinking about the big changes in the chain of command that A Company would be going through in the next few days. Between the defeat at Fredericksburg and problems paying the men on time, morale in the whole regiment was pretty touchy right now. Whether Carr was right or wrong, the problems he brought to the men of A Company were not needed.

"So, you don't think you have been treated fairly?"

"No, sir, I have not."

"I don't like to pass my problems off to someone else, Carr. Regulations give me a few days before I have to prefer charges for a court martial. I will talk to the other regimental commanders, and see if anyone will give you a fresh start. You mess this up, and I will process the court martial papers as soon as I hear about it."

"A fresh start would be welcome, sir. I thank you for that. I just could not take the abuse down there anymore."

Ryerson looked at McKee. "Find a detail to keep him busy around headquarters today. I will talk to the others during battalion drill after lunch."

The news came from Washington during the afternoon drill. Lieutenant Newbold had died of typhoid the previous night. Ryerson and Chaplain Abbott walked out on the parade ground and found Captain Newbold. Lieutenant Kirkbride took over the Company for the rest of the day.

The Colonel gave the Captain a furlough, and Reading was on his way to Washington before dark to pick up his brother's body, and take it back to New Jersey.

Shortly after Newbold left, Doc Cook stopped by headquarters. The orderly showed him to Ryerson's office. "Good afternoon, Doc."

"Hello, sir. I heard about Lieutenant Newbold. That's a sad thing. He was a fine officer and a nice young man." Ryerson nodded, and Cook went on. "Sir, I had almost eighty people show up for sick call this morning, and most aren't faking it. We have some serious sickness starting to develop. We can't leave these men outside for two weeks and expect them to stay healthy."

"I noticed the ranks looked pretty thin during drill this morning and this afternoon."

"Sir, I have at least ten cases that look like typhoid. Several more look like rheumatic fever. I am sending people back to the division hospital, and they are shipping them back to Washington. We could be looking at a lot of sick men very shortly. We need to get some huts built, so we can get them out of the weather. Those dog tents just won't do in the winter."

"Doc, it looks like we are going into winter quarters here. I will have the men start building more permanent shelters. I turned in requisitions to replace the lost equipment and for new shoes and trousers, but they haven't come in yet. Please keep me informed about the men's health."

"One last thing, sir, we had two men injure themselves with axes in the last two days. One lost a finger and the other had a big cut on his leg. Can you please have the Sergeant Major make sure the NCOs show these people how use a knife and axe safely?"

Ryerson nodded yes. After Cook left, he slowly shook his head in wonder. How could these people live through a battle, and then risk killing themselves with a careless swing of an axe?

The weather was dry but damp, as construction of the regimental winter quarters began at Camp White Oak Church. Generally, four men pooled their resources to build a shelter. The shelters were not very big. Each man carried a shelter half that measured 5 feet 2 inches long by 4 feet 8 inches wide. Buttoned together, two shelter halves made a two-man tent a little over 5 feet long and at most 90 inches wide. The problem with this was it only stood 33 inches high, and it had no flaps. The accommodation could be improved by overlapping two more shelter halves to make the shelter 10 feet long. If the shelter was going to accommodate four men, this meant the roof either had to go up or the floor had to go down. Men started digging out the floors under their tents, so they could stand inside. Some elaborate foundations went down 7 or 8 feet.

Other structures had shallow foundations, and the additional needed height was constructed by building walls above ground. Any unoccupied structure was assumed to belong to a Rebel family who had fled. Abandoned houses, barns or any other structure or fence were stripped of their fence rails, lumber, bricks, field stones or anything else usable for construction. Men carried anything they could find back to camp and pressed it into service. Timber was cut and logs were split into boards, or notched into cabin walls and chinked with mud. There seemed to be an endless supply of chinking material. Once these walls were built, the shelter halves were erected over them to shed water. On occasion canvas tarps and bigger tents appeared, normally followed by someone from another unit trying to recover them.

A hut without heat was a problem, and building chimneys was a big challenge. They had to be tall enough to keep sparks from setting the canvas roofs on fire, and strong enough to face the elements. Bricks were prized, and used whenever they could be found. When those ran out, more enterprising builders gathered sticks and wove them into chimneys, which they covered with mud. The mud kept the branches from catching fire. Some officers liked to use pork or beef barrels covered with mud. These had a tendency to catch fire. A fire like that always livened up an evening in the camp. All of this allowed the shelter to be heated, and the men to cook their meals out of the rain.

Marion Montieth watched his fence rails and eighty acres of timber vanish before his eyes. Woodlands all over Stafford County faced the same fate. What wasn't used for logs or lumber was used for fuel. The 250,000-man army was quickly denuding the entire countryside.* First they collected all of the fence rails and firewood they could find. Then, they gathered sticks and branches off the ground and even piles of leaves. Then they cut the trees off at the butt and burned all of that. Then, they cut the stumps off at ground level. Eventually, they became so starved for fuel; they dug up the roots and burned them, too. If nothing else, Stafford County would be ready for plowing in the spring.

December 24, 1862 – Camp White Oak Church, Virginia

Sweesley felt horrid. He had fever and a terrible headache. He stumbled into sick call at the surgeon's tent. Elmer took one look at him and led him to a cot. Bowlby made him as comfortable as he could, and then went to find Doc Cook.

Doc came in and examined the sergeant. Hartman was called and came to the hospital tent soon after. Cook looked at him and said, "He's got a fever, diarrhea and a rash on his upper body. The fever appears constant because he's not getting chills. I would say he has typhoid.

"Think he'll be all right?"

"Hard to say, we will dose him up with calomel and quinine. That will help his system purge the miasma. He can have opium pills and

*Stafford County Historical Society says there are fewer than 20 trees in the county that predate the Civil War.

whiskey to keep him calm and help him sleep, and some oral turpentine to help him breathe if he gets congested. He's got a good chance, we only lose about one out of five."

December 25, 1862 – Camp White Oak Church, Virginia

Christmas was a holiday for the Army of the Potomac, but there wasn't much of a celebration in the 23rd. The normal daily drill and parades were cancelled, and guard duty was made as easy as possible.

Some of the troops gathered pine boughs and made Christmas trees decorated with hardtack and salt pork and pieces of tin cans. Occasionally, a sprig of holly would adorn the doorway of a tent.

The weather was warmer than usual, so the boys got out their baseball equipment and played ball, cards or football or pitched pennies. Many wrote letters home or read, and others spent the day visiting relatives and friends in other units.

The regimental bands held concerts. Impromptu choirs gathered to sing Christmas carols.

Chaplain Abbott was away, so there were no regimental church services. Other chaplains did hold services in the White Oak Church. It was a small white clapboard building that needed a lot of work, about a quarter mile from the camp.

Fortunately for Josie, his Christmas box from home came early. Many other men were disappointed theirs did not arrive on time.

Christmas dinner for the enlisted men was hard tack and salt pork, unless you were lucky enough to get a ration of fresh beef from the hundred head of fine fat cattle seized from a Rebel sympathizer in Westmoreland County the previous week. Some officers were lucky enough to have a turkey or roast of beef.

Army regulations prohibited sutlers from selling liquor to enlisted men. This regulation was relaxed during the holidays. An enlisted man who had the money or credit could go to his sergeant and ask for a note. The note would say, "The sutler will sell so-and-so one canteen of whiskey." The sergeant would sign the note, and the man would then take it to his lieutenant for his signature. Then it was off to the sutler's. Drunkenness was frowned on, but it could be entertaining. And, so it was, that a crowd gathered on Christmas night to watch a major of the engineers try to spur an oak log to a fast gallop. The mirth continued as the hapless officer threatened to report a pontoon wagon for failing to give the countersign to a hedge he mistook for the Major General. Eventually the men gathered the engineer, took him back to his unit, and put him to bed.

It wasn't the best Christmas they ever had, but it was one they would never forget.

December 26, 1862 – Camp White Oak Church, Virginia

The weather was cooperating with the regiment's efforts to put up winter quarters. Little rain had fallen since the men returned from Deep Run. Daytime temperatures were tolerable, but fell well below freezing at night. The quarters would never be called luxurious. They would provide marginal comfort during all but the most horrendous weather.

General Torbert was insisting on an aggressive training schedule to bring the brigade up to a better standard of marching and maneuver. The usual company drill in the morning was followed by regimental or brigade parades late in the afternoon. The short period of daylight in December made it vital to use every hour of daylight wisely.

Morale was a problem everywhere. The loss of friends and family members at Fredericksburg weighed heavily. The men had hoped to win the war in one decisive engagement and go home to continue their lives, only to see defeat after defeat dog their efforts through 1862. They were not happy being on the losing side of so many battles. Antietam was the only thing close to a victory, and that had been so costly, and the resulting opportunities lost, that it hardly passed for a win. On top of that, the 23rd had still not been paid and was short on tents, blankets and shoes. Army payday was the last day of the month. October, November and December passed, and tempers were getting short. Most of the men had families at home who needed the money.

The walking wounded started coming back from the hospital. This did boost morale. They were greeted with joy as they rejoined their friends. Although most were on light duty for a few more weeks, everyone was glad to have them back.

The troops from Bordentown talked about seeing their old school teacher, Miss Clara Barton, at Chatham. She was becoming well known for volunteering as a nurse, and the boys were proud of her. Others talked of meeting an author named John Greenleaf Whittier who was helping the wounded at the Falmouth hospital.

Training had resumed this morning and battalion drill was completed. Now, the troops were marching to a regimental parade. Ryerson was up front with Perkins and Sergeant Major McKee. Perkins was posting the orders of the day. "Attention to orders. Effective immediately, Lieutenant Colonel George C. Brown's request to resign his commission is approved." The announcement was greeted with stunned silence. The men were becoming alarmed by the number of officers leaving the army. "General Brooks, General Torbert and

Colonel Ryerson wish to publicly thank the colonel for his service to the nation, the state of New Jersey and the men of the 23rd New Jersey Volunteer Infantry Regiment."

"Effective immediately, Major Burd Grubb is hereby promoted to Lieutenant Colonel, and assigned Regimental Executive Officer." Murmurs of approval spread through the ranks.

"Effective immediately, Captain Francis V. Milnor is hereby promoted to Major, and assigned Regimental Operations Officer." Again, murmurs of approval were heard in the ranks.

"Effective immediately First Lieutenant Paul Hambrick is hereby promoted to Captain, and assigned to command A Company. The A Company change of command ceremony will take place at 9 o'clock tomorrow morning." Murmurs of surprise were heard from A Company.

"Effective immediately, Sergeant Major John F McKee is promoted to 2nd Lieutenant, and assigned to C Company." Now the troops were really listening.

"Effective immediately, Sergeant Forrester L Taylor, A Company, is promoted to 2nd Lieutenant, and assigned to G Company." There were nods in both companies.

"Effective immediately, Private Samuel Browne Junior, A Company, is promoted to Sergeant Major, and assigned to regimental headquarters." A Company cheered.

"There will be a memorial service for Lieutenant Newbold and Private Ridgway at Regimental headquarters at 5 o'clock."

"Somebody stole Mr. Montieth's horse last night. Anybody with any information about it, contact your company commander."

"By order of Ryerson, Henry O., Colonel, New Jersey Volunteers, Commanding."

The parade passed in review, and the NCOs marched the troops back to their quarters. The officers assembled at regimental headquarters to congratulate the new officers and toast the promotions. Brandy and cigars were provided. General Brooks and General Torbert dropped in to add their good wishes. Torbert was obviously not well.

"How come I can't resign?" moped Terhune at the campfire.

"Because you are a private, and you agreed to serve for 9 months when you signed up," answered Rue as he stared into the fire.

"Don't seem fair." The others were listening as Cornelius complained.

148

"You knew what you were getting into," said Rue.

"I did not know I was going to have to live in a hovel and eat hardtack and salt pork every day."

Rue stared at the fire and said patiently, "None of us knew, but we all signed a contract and swore to do our duty. Our contract is different than an officer's contract." He wasn't telling any of them anything they didn't already know, but he told them anyway to avoid an argument.

"The volunteer regiments belong to the state militia and the governor. He issues the commissions to the officers. Part of the deal is that they can leave when they no longer wish to serve. That's not how it works in the Federal Army. Those officers accept a term of service just like we do, and have to stay until it is over."

Miller was listening and added, "They don't like to talk about it much. Some of these people are leaving because they don't want to face the Board of Examination."

All eyes turned to Sergeant Miller. "What's a Board of Examination, Sarge?" asked Massey.

"The Army knows that some of these governor-appointed officers are no good. They have a group of colonels who go around and test them. Those that don't pass the test can resign their commission honorably without anyone knowing why. Word is there will be Boards of Examination this winter here in White Oak. We might see a few more officers leave."

Rue spoke up. "I must say I am more confident in Ryerson, Grubb and Milnor then I was with Cox, Thompson and Brown." The whole audience mumbled their agreement. No one wanted to think of Colonel Cox trying to lead them though the attack at Deep Run.

"I wonder when they are going to pay us?" fretted Conover.

"Me too, I don't understand why they don't," frowned Sharp. "Mary could sure use some of that pay." Everyone knew there were families all over New Jersey who were having a rough winter because their breadwinners were not bringing in an income. Neighbors had created soldier's aid societies in Burlington County to help the families as much as they could.

"They are not paying us because the government doesn't have the money yet," said Ed Lloyd quietly.

"How do you know?" asked Sharp.

"I have some relatives that work at a bank. They told me. It takes a lot of money to pay for this war. They have to clothe us, arm us, feed us, shelter us, take care of us if we get hurt or sick, and pay for all of the supplies, transport and construction that go with it. They had enough to get started, but the treasury was empty by spring."

"That's why Congress passed the Internal Revenue Act in July to raise taxes to pay for the war. It says everybody who makes between $800 and $10,000 has to pay the government 3% of their income. If they make over $10,000, they have to pay 5 percent."

"You saying I have to pay this tax, too?" growled Terhune.

"Not unless you make over $800, Corn, and at $15 a month I don't think that's likely. Everybody who does, including the President and the officers, has to pay. The paper said President Lincoln paid $1,220."

"So, the government got us to volunteer, and knew they couldn't pay us?" bristled Terhune.

"Corn, would you rather have Robert E. Lee in Philadelphia?"

"Guess not," said Corn.

"The new law didn't take effect until September 1st, so it's going to take some time for them to raise the money. We will get paid, but it might be a while yet."

"I just hope they hurry up," growled Sharp.

Ryerson, Grubb and Milnor were going over the day's events. Doc Cook notified them that two more men had died of typhoid. Private Ridgway from E and Dubell from G Company would be buried in the morning. It had been a rough month for the Ridgways. The Colonel had written to the family about Joe's death. Now, he would have to write again.

The Army had sent word that Privates Craft and Scatterwaite had been medically discharged just before Christmas. Craft had been discharged in Philadelphia. Hopefully, he had made it home for the holiday.

Lieutenant Colonel Collet of the 1st New Jersey had agreed to give Private Carr a second start. Perkins completed the transfer papers before Christmas. Carr was now with A Company, 1st New Jersey.

Ryerson was feeling good. He was confident his new staff officers would work well with him. They were good men he could count on.

The orderly came in. "Sir, Captain McCabe is here to see you."

"Thank you, send him in. Hello, Henry, how are you?"

"Not so good, sir. I would like to talk to you about resigning my commission." So much for that good evening, thought Ryerson.

December 26, 1862 - Alexandria, Virginia

Hugh Capner had a comfortable Christmas at the Alexandria hospital. It had been thirteen days since he lost his arm. He was still dealing with the pain and emotion of the amputation. He constantly forgot his arm was gone, and kept trying to reach for things with it. Sometimes there was intense pain in the place where his arm and hand used to be. That didn't make sense to him. How could your hand or arm hurt when it wasn't there? But it did.

His emotions were a mess. One minute he was thankful he had survived, and the next minute he was raging about his lost arm. Some of the amputees who had been there longer than him watched knowingly as he grieved. They had all faced the same thing.

Several befriended him. It helped to talk about what happened. A loose-knit group started to look out for each other.

Capner's arm was healing nicely. There had not been a lot of pus or infection. The pain was starting to go away. The morphine tablets worked whenever it really hurt. Others in the ward were not so lucky.

The ward was part of an impressive pavilion hospital complex. There were fifty long, narrow clapboard buildings fifteen to eighteen feet wide arranged in an O-shaped pattern. The roofs were covered with cloth that was covered with tar and sand. Ridge ventilation made sure any inflammation-carrying noxious vapors were vented outside.

There were sixty to one hundred patients in each ward. The wards were whitewashed, provided the best care available, were easy to clean, and had big windows that provided plenty of light. Each hospital had its own kitchens, a butcher shop, not to be confused with the operating rooms, laundry, guard house, chapel, morgue or ice house, pharmacy, and barracks for the staff and offices. Coal stoves kept the wards warm for the patients. There were special small wards for those who were critically sick and needed special care.

The staff and the Sanitary Commission and numerous volunteer groups visited the hospitals daily. Women throughout the North and South sent preserves, canned goods and baked goods to help the wounded recover.

Capner's ward was decorated with flags and garlands of Christmas greens. Carolers made their way through the hospital to cheer the men. The kitchen provided a fine Christmas dinner for all who were up to it.

He visited Crane, Tetlow and McAninie. McAninie was improving. He would probably keep his leg, but the war was over for him. Crane and Tetlow were very sick. He prayed they would start to get better.

December 28, 1862 – Camp White Oak Church, Virginia

There was free time for the troops on Sunday morning. Some used it to improve their shelters, so the continuous sound of axe and shovel work echoed through the countryside. Others took a break to attend Private Dubell's funeral.

There was a dress parade in the afternoon. The regiment was formed in a square, and Chaplain Abbott preached a wonderful sermon about Matthew 24, verse 55. The men's spirits were down. He reminded them that heaven and earth shall pass away, but the Lord's Word goes on forever. The men found comfort in his words.

In the evening, the squads gathered around their fires to sing and tell stories. Sometimes they put on skits, played checkers or cards, or went off to visit other units. All of the regiments in the brigade were from New Jersey. A good part of General Brook's cavalry and artillery also came from New Jersey, so there was a decided camaraderie among the Jersey men.

Sharp, Terhune, Crispin and the rest of the squad were talking by the fire when a voice came out of the night. "So, how's life in the lowly infantry these days?"

Sharp recognized the voice, jumped to his feet grinning and tossed back, "Without hemorrhoids, you no-good horse-abusing son of gun. Bill Leath! By God, how are you?" Bill and George were neighbors in Moorestown, not far from Crispin's farm.

Leath stepped into the firelight with Parker North from Mount Holly. Both men were from C Company, 1st New Jersey Cavalry. "Pull up a stump and sit a spell, boys," smiled Sharp. "Glad to see you. What's the news?" Josi and Terhune grinned at the guests with pleasure, introduced themselves and shook hands all around.

He yelled over his shoulder, "Hey Elwood, Bill Leath's here." Someone called back that Elwood was asleep.

"Well, we're back here on light duty. Colonel Wyndham took off toward Dumfries this afternoon with everybody that could ride and had a horse. They say there's a Rebel cavalry force up there."

"Where's Dumfries?" asked Terhune.

"It's up north of Stafford Courthouse," replied Leath. "The Rebs were raiding up there during the battle, and they've been doing it ever since, even during Christmas."

"Sounds like they had a better Christmas than we did. All we had was hardtack and salt pork and no boxes from home," groaned Terhune.

"Yeah, one of our scouts said the Rebs were really whooping it up on the south side of the river. Had horse races, played games and fired off cannons."

"So, how did you boys get through the battle?" said Sharp.

Parker North took out a pipe and lit it. "We didn't see much action. We led our horses across the bridge in the dark and fog. That was tricky. The horses don't like those damned pontoon bridges."

"We got over and rode picket while the Grand Division assembled for the attack, but got pulled back before it started."

Crispin nodded. "Yes, you were behind us for a while just before daylight. I remember hearing the horses."

Leath was poking the fire with a stick. The night was clear and cold, so everyone was huddled close to it, and everyone took a turn tending it. "Most of the regiment crossed the river before the fog lifted. General Bayard kept a few of us in reserve back by the Bernard house. The house was General Franklin's headquarters."

"The fellas had the horses back in the orchard. There weren't no leaves on the trees, so they weren't hidden. They watched the battle for a couple of hours and felt safe. Then all of a sudden, here comes this damned 20-pounder cannon ball bouncing toward us.

"Only three men got hurt. General Bayard was one of them. It hit him in the thigh. It tore him open and pretty well took his leg off. They did what they could, but he died the next day. Too bad, he was a good man. He looked out for us."

"I heard he met Jeb Stuart," said Terhune.

"Yup, he and Stuart met after Cedar Mountain. The story's true. Some of our men saw the whole thing. Imagine Stuart holding the reigns for Bayard," answered Leath with a chuckle. "Sure is a screwed-up war."

"Bayard was supposed to go home and get married over Christmas. What a shame. I hear they buried his body back in Princeton."

Leath looked over at Crispin. "How'd it go for you boys, Josie?"

"We spent most of the battle under cover up near Deep Run ravine. We took some shelling for a couple days, and then we attacked late in the afternoon. The Reb artillery shot a bunch of us up pretty bad. Most of them are back from the hospital already. Mica Ellis almost lost his arm, and probably won't be back."

Sharp chimed in, "The brass ordered a probe late in the afternoon to see what was in front of us. You knew about Captain Ridgway?"

Leath and North nodded.

"That's where he got killed. Colonel Hatch got shot there and died in Falmouth the next day. We had 5 killed and 45 wounded or missing. All of the missing are back except Bill Henry, and they think he got burned up. Probably never find him."

Leath winced.

The conversation trailed off for a few minutes. "I hear we may be moving out soon. I guess Burnside wants to attack again."

"Not back to Fredericksburg?' groaned Sharp in disbelief.

"No, word is back up towards Warrenton." Everybody groaned at that. The memory of the march from Warrenton was still fresh in their minds. The conversation moved away from the war, and turned to good-natured kidding between the horsemen and the ground-pounders. They all turned in fairly early. It was very cold.

December 29, 1862 – Camp White Oak Church, Virginia

The beating of reveille by the drummers was greeted with the usual moaning and groaning heard on any morning. The camp slowly started to come alive as men climbed out of their beds and stoked up their fires for breakfast.

Crispin and Lloyd were up and kicking their fire together. The others were starting to come out when they heard Conover fussing around about three tents down the row.

"Time to get up, Elwood. Come on, Elwood, roll out. Elwood? Elwood? ELWOOD?"

Joe came tearing out of the tent. "Holy shit, something's wrong with Elwood. Somebody get Doc."

The whole squad was converging on the tent. Miller ducked in and yelled for Rue to get McCabe and Hartman. Somebody else ran off to find Doc Cook. Within minutes, they were back.

Cook went in and felt for a pulse on Elwood's neck. There was none. He sat back and frowned. He stood up in front of the tent, and looked at the men. He shook his head. "He's gone, fellas. I am sorry."

Conover was devastated. He had known Elwood since childhood. He burst into tears. Crispin and Lloyd led him away to the fire, and made him sit down. He cried and cried. Most of the rest of the squad had tears running down their faces, too. Elwood Goodenough had been a solid friend to all. He carried his weight, and was just a peaceable, good-natured boy.

Soon, Grubb came by and paid his respects. Later Ryerson and Milnor stopped by, too. Chaplain Abbott came over, and helped the squad make the funeral arrangements. It was a painful day for everyone. Lots of men were sick, and several in the regiment had already died, but Elwood was the first from H Company. Work could not stop in camp for a death. The details of the day and drill had to continue. Neither the officers nor the men really had their hearts in it.

At 5 o'clock that evening, the regimental band, Colonel Ryerson and his staff conducted a graveside ceremony. Ryerson made a point of attending each of his boys' funerals. He felt it was the least he could do for someone who was being laid to rest far from home. Chaplain Abbott read a Psalm that seemed like it was written just for Elwood, and eight men fired over the grave.

Abbott spent the evening with the squad. Conover was in bad shape. The Chaplain made a special effort to spend time with him.

Ryerson, Grubb and Milnor spoke with Doc Cook after the funeral. "God Almighty, Doc, was there no warning that something was wrong with him?"

"Sir, Conover says he was out of sorts yesterday, and went to bed early. He had some of the symptoms of typhoid. I don't know. When somebody gets typhoid, they usually don't die overnight. Conover grew up with him. He says Elwood was sickly when he was young. He could have had rheumatic fever, and that might have hurt his heart."

"How are the rest of the men?" asked Grubb.

"Sir, I have a dozen men down with typhoid right now. Out of 850 men in the regiment, I have near one hundred on sick call every morning and my hospital is full. If we stay here, and they can get some rest and good food and stay dry, we might see some improvement."

Ryerson said nothing. He already knew they weren't going to stay long. He was afraid the regimental cemetery on the little hill by the stream was going to get bigger. It was.

December 30, 1862 – Camp White Oak Church, Virginia

The previous two days had been tough on everybody. The weather had grown noticeably colder.

Crispin visited the regimental hospital to check on Sweesley the morning after Goodenough's funeral. He had spent a lot of time there before Christmas, and decided to check on some sick friends. Elwood's sudden death reminded him not to take friendship for granted.

The regimental hospital consisted of three hospital wall tents. Each was about sixteen feet long and fourteen feet wide. A pole at each end gave an eleven-foot peak and four and a half foot walls down the sides. They could be joined end to end to form a hospital ward, if necessary. Each could hold twenty men. A rain fly covered the roof of each to help shed water and improve ventilation.

Before Josie could step into the tent, he detected a disgusting odor. It seemed to be a mixture of wood-smoke, putrefied flesh, human waste, vomit, blood, and decaying swamp material. He stepped into the tent, and it was even worse. The tents were closed up for warmth, and the lack of ventilation made the atmosphere inside absolutely sickening. The hospital was full. Many men had fevers. Some were lying quietly, while others were obviously delirious. The odor was so bad that Josie cut his visit short, and returned to camp.

———————

Miller was saying, "Well, boys, we've got guard duty tomorrow night."

"Ahh, not New Years Eve," growled Sharp.

"Oh, were you going somewhere, George?" drew chuckles from all.

"Well, ah," he paused. "No," frowned Sharp.

"Good, you need to look sharp out there tomorrow night. The Rebs are trying to capture pickets up north, and we are worried they will try here. Our scouts spotted six Rebel cavalry down near King George Courthouse two nights ago."

"Where's King George Courthouse?" asked Terhune.

"Cornelius, you dunce, it's back down by Devil's Hole, don't you know no geography?" ribbed Sharp.

"Just asking," pouted Terhune.

"Well, if we can't celebrate the New Year tomorrow night, we better do it tonight," grinned Miller. A jug appeared as if by magic. The singing and jokes and laughter drew a crowd as the boys threw an early, impromptu New Years party.

December 31, 1863 – Camp White Oak Church, Virginia

They all marched off to guard duty in the afternoon. Now, Josie was walking his post on the 11 to 1 shift. He was in a pensive mood. 1862 had been a rough year in his young life. He hadn't experienced anything like it since his mother had died. He never expected to be in the Army. He never dreamed he would see some of the horrible things he had seen, friends blown apart or burned. Little Frank was gone, and so was Elwood.

Josie's post was in a particularly exposed place. It was difficult to stay warm, but he was getting by. He could see over most of the New Jersey Brigade's camp, and he could hear a massive party in progress. At the stroke of midnight, the camp erupted in fireworks, firecrackers and gun fire. Ripples of muzzle flashes lit up the sky as black powder smoke spread over the encampment, and detonations echoed across the countryside. Similar sounds could be heard from other encampments in all directions.

This racket was followed by the incessant shouting of officers and then NCOs trying to stop the gun fire. Eventually, order was restored.

Josie chuckled every time he remembered the sight. At least the boys weren't totally devoid of levity.

January 1, 1863 – Camp White Oak Church, Virginia

Josie and the squad were relieved from guard duty at 9 AM and marched back to their tents. Every one of them was laughing about the New Years fireworks display and all the shouting that went on to stop it. It was even funnier when Hartman called them into formation and tried to chew them out about it. "You men are accountable for your ammunition. Any ammunition unaccounted for will be deducted from your pay."

Normally, there is no talking in ranks when standing at attention, and especially when the 1st Sergeant was speaking. However, this was so outrageous, the men laughed out loud. "Oh, come on Rueben, we were on guard duty and none of us was involved."

"Besides, they never pay us anyway," jibed someone else, to more laughter.

Hartman just looked at them and shook his head. "Damned bunch of Yahoos." Then he chuckled.

The day was a holiday, and the troops were served a ration of whiskey to celebrate the New Year. Somehow, Doc Cook got a gallon and the hospital staff really celebrated. By evening the Doctor was quite drunk. Several of the men wondered if allowing him to have the liquor was the right thing to do.

January 2, 1863 – Camp White Oak Church, Virginia

The day dawned clear and crisp, throwing a red luster over the encampment. The usual morning activities, formations and details were assigned. Just before lunch, Hartman bellowed, "Mail call." The troops came running. Letters and several overdue Christmas boxes were handed out. Those lucky enough to get boxes were surrounded by their squads as they opened them.

Letter writing was one of the troops' most important pastimes. Military post offices were set up in camps, so troops could buy stamps and send out their mail. The U.S. Postal system continued to function in the north. It generally took three to five days for a letter to reach a camp from the cities. The South was trying to salvage what was left of the Union postal system in their territory and set up their own. It took letters much longer to reach Confederate troops, if they got there at all. Neither side recognized the other's stamps, so correspondence between families in the North and South could be difficult. Mail could be smuggled, sent through a ship to another country, or exchanged under a flag of truce. All required the proper Union and/or Confederate postage for the particular route it was destined to follow.

———————

Lieutenant Root stepped forward and took the report from Hartman.

Hartman saluted, and the company was dismissed. Terhune and Sharp looked at each other. "So what is that all about?" asked Sharp.

Terhune replied, "I doubt if we will ever know. Rumor has it Captain McCabe resigned his commission, and just walked out of camp without saying a word to anyone."

"Lieutenant Root will be promoted to Captain and take command of the company. Lieutenant Carter will be promoted to 1st Lieutenant, and 1st Sergeant Wright from C Company will be promoted to 2nd Lieutenant and assigned to the company."

"You think Root can handle the job?"

"Don't know, but I doubt if Carter can. I don't know Wright. How about we go ask the C Company boys about him?" The men strolled over to C Company.

———————

The orderly stepped into Colonel Ryerson's Headquarters tent. "Excuse me, sir, there are some gentlemen here to see you."

"I am a little busy, son, who is it?" said Ryerson without looking up from the papers he was reading.

"Sir, he says his name is Andrew from the U.S. Sanitary Commission." *

Ryerson's head snapped up. "Show them in, Private." He stood up to greet the gentlemen.

"Sir, thank you for stopping by, what can I do for you?"

"Colonel, my name is George Andrew and this is my assistant,

*Dr. George Andrew and his assistant Mr. Clampitt were at Sharpsburg after Antietam with Dr. Steiner. Page 146, <u>The Sanitary Commission of the United States Army, A Succinct Narrative of Its Works and Purpose</u> places them at Fredericksburg at the time of the battle, and indicates they were assigned to the Army of the Potomac, and had accompanied the army on its march from Antietam.

Mr. Clampitt. I have been asked to visit the brigade's facilities, and make recommendations to improve the health of the men."

Ryerson could have kissed him. "Sir, please have a seat. I am so happy to see you. I understand Dr. Steiner was wounded in Fredericksburg. How is he?"

"Dr. Steiner was shot in the arm and is recovering nicely. Do you know him?"

"Only by reputation. That was a nice of piece of work he and the commission put together to get those medical supplies to Antietam."

He waited until the gentlemen were seated and continued. "Last winter I was an officer in the 2nd New Jersey, and we had a terrible number of deaths from various diseases. I am afraid the same thing is happening again right now. My surgeon appears to be a good man, but he tells me we have almost one hundred men a day showing up for sick call, and our hospital is full. I have already lost more men in the last month to disease than I have in combat. I have heard of the Sanitary Commission's work, and I could use your help."

"Well, thank you, Colonel. I don't always find a welcome like this. I am a doctor and I have been with the Sanitary Commission for quite some time. I would like your permission to inspect your camp and hospital and, if I find causes for concern, make recommendations to help you improve conditions. Camps that have implemented the Sanitary Commission's recommendations have seen a decrease in disease."

"I would welcome the assistance. May I accompany you?"

"Certainly, but I want you to understand, I am not here to denigrate you, or your officers or men. I want only to suggest improvements that might improve the welfare of the troops."

"Please give me a minute." Ryerson excused himself, and sent the orderly to find Grubb, Browne and Cook. It took a few minutes to round them up. When they were all together, they started their inspection of the camp.

Doctor Andrew observed a number of items that could be improved. First, and foremost, use of latrines had to be enforced; the men could not be permitted to defecate anywhere they pleased. The pits were to be dug eight feet deep, and human waste was to be covered with six inches of dirt daily to prevent flies. Not that there were many flies at this time of year. Next, drinking water was to be drawn from wells uphill from the latrines. Doctor Andrew assured everyone it would taste better.

Tents and shelters that were in swampy areas or places that might flood in a storm needed to be moved to higher ground; the further from a swamp the better, to keep the men away from the miasmatic vapors that caused diseases. Finally, the hospital tents needed to be moved to a place with better ventilation. They certainly were not to be in the direct path of storm winds, but they had to be in a place where a breeze could remove any inflammation-carrying noxious vapors.

The inspecting party returned to Colonel Ryerson's headquarters for coffee and some bread with jam. Doctor Andrew discussed his findings with Colonel Ryerson, Grubb and the Sergeant Major. Ryerson ordered Grubb and Browne to take the recommended actions as soon as possible.

Andrew left and Ryerson breathed a sigh of relief. The U.S. Sanitary Commission had the ear of President Lincoln and support in Congress. It had been formed in 1861, and was ridiculed as a women's "do-gooder" organization. Lincoln, when it was originally presented to him, called it the 5th wheel on a carriage. Halleck thought it was useless, but finally allowed it to help volunteer regiments, as long as it didn't interfere with regular Army units.

It proved its worth during the Peninsula Campaign, at 2nd Bull Run, Antietam and Fredericksburg, when it brought medical supplies and personnel to the battlefield days before the Army medical service could fully mobilize. In fact, the Confederates captured nearly all of the Union medical supplies at 2nd Bull Run. The surgeons had little for the wounded except the civilian medical supplies provided by the Sanitary Commission. Fortunately, when handing out the supplies, they didn't make a distinction between regular Army and volunteer units.

As a combat veteran who had lain wounded and unattended on a battlefield for over a week, Ryerson was ready to help the Sanitary Commission any way he could. When he was sure the 23rd was on the way to implementing Doctor Andrew's recommendations, he sent the orderly with messages to Torbert and Brooks saying he was doing so. The orderly came back to say Torbert had been sent to Philadelphia with severe bronchitis. Brown was temporarily in charge of the brigade.

Josie and Ed visited Sergeant Sweesley as the hospital was being rearranged. Sweesley appeared to be better. He wanted his meerschaum.

January 4, 1863 - Alexandria, Virginia
Hugh Capner seated himself in the hospital chapel. The last few days had been as upsetting as the battle.

Johnny Crane had been the first to die. His gunshot wound to the chest had let the air out his left lung, and it never refilled. The bullet had been removed, but no one dared open his chest to do any more. The doctors kept him quiet, and hoped his blood's normal clotting activity would stop the internal bleeding. Meantime, bits of clothing, bullet fragments, and dirt still in the wound became infected. Johnny had slowly deteriorated, and mercifully passed away on the 29th. Hugh tried to comfort him and give him hope. He knew there was little. Johnny's constant struggle for breath in his single lung was painful to watch. He had drifted into a coma, turned very pale, and finally stopped breathing.

Joe Tetlow had been nearby. He was in sad shape, too. The doctors had trimmed the ragged amputation from the shell fragment, but they couldn't control the sepsis. The infection steadily dragged him toward the same inevitable conclusion. Tetlow passed away four days later.

So, he had come to see the chaplain. Although he was getting better, the events happening around him presented him with an overwhelming set of very upsetting contradictions. He was thankful to be alive, but angry about losing his arm. He was thankful to not be in pain, but angry at watching people around him die in agony. He was glad he would not have to go back to war, but ashamed his friends were still out there. He was relieved when the chaplain took the time to talk and pray with him.

Capner's condition was improving. Soon he would be expected to help around the ward and the rest of the hospital. The work would be light at first. Simply going for supplies or carrying messages. As his strength increased, he would be expected to help with bedpans or other duties within his capabilities. He was not looking forward to this duty, although he did feel he owed the hospital something for the care he was getting.

January 4, 1863 – U.S. Army General Hospital, Baltimore, Maryland

Noah Dennis walked away from the laundry room of the general hospital and was soon out on the streets of Baltimore. He was deserting from the army. Bill Logan, a friend of his from C Company, had given him the idea. He and Bill had both come down with typhoid before the Battle of Fredericksburg. They were too sick to fight, and the regimental hospital was packing up to go to the battle. They were too sick to be taken care of at Devil's Hole, so the Army had evacuated them to Baltimore. They both survived the terrible fever, and the

161

hospital had assigned them to light duty in the wards while they convalesced.

The duty was drudgery. They were detailed to empty bedpans, clean up after sick patients, give people baths, change bedding, wash floors, stand fire watch, stoke stoves, and anything else the nurses could think of. The supervisors were unpleasant, and most of the patients were ungrateful.

Noah and Bill had been friends since the day they met at Camp Cadwalader. Each was shocked when they fell sick at the same time and ended up in the same ward. Bill decided he was not going to keep emptying bedpans, and had no interest in going back to Virginia. He quietly informed Noah he was leaving, and four nights earlier he had simply walked off. There was little security or chain of command to stop him. It was hours before anyone noticed Noah was missing.

January 5, 1863 – Camp White Oak Church, Virginia

Quartermaster Nichols reported to Ryerson. "Sir, the material we requisitioned for the men has still not come in, and no one seems to know where it is."

"Have they lost the requisition, Lieutenant?" asked the Colonel.

"I don't know, sir. Sergeant Dobbins filled it out and personally delivered to Aquia Creek three weeks ago. If the stuff hasn't come by now, for all practical purposes it is lost."

Ryerson had promoted Dobbins to Second Lieutenant and sent him to I Company the day before to replace Frazier. "Who's filling in for Dobbins?"

"Private Alcott from I Company has been filling in. If he works out, I would like to have him promoted to Quartermaster Sergeant."

"All right, get Alcott to make out another complete requisition just like the first one. The rumor is we are going to march soon, and half my men's shoes are falling apart, not to mention we still don't have the replacement gear we lost in the battle." Ryerson was getting angry. "I keep reading in the papers about how well supplied this army is. It's been three damned weeks since I sent that requisition. I just wish those hidebound bureaucrats in Washington would get off their dead asses and come see what is really going on down here."

"I'll have to take this up with Colonel Brown and General Brooks," huffed the Colonel.

January 7, 1863 – Camp White Oak Church, Virginia

Colonel Ryerson was sitting with Grubb, Abbott and Milnor when Sergeant Major Brown brought in the morning report. "Sir, we started out in September with 955 enlisted men and 39 officers. As of this morning, we have 900 enlisted men and 39 officers."

Ryerson watched him carefully; the new Sergeant Major was meeting all expectations. Brown continued, "During the last week, two of our men deserted from the General Hospital in Baltimore. That would be Logan and Dennis from C Company. Both were sent up there with typhoid before we went to Fredericksburg."

Ryerson thought for a minute. "I understand duty in those hospitals can be very unpleasant when one is convalescing. Still no excuse for desertion, go ahead and make sure the Provost Marshal knows about them. I would guess the hospital turned them in."

"Yes, sir, they did."

"All right, what else?"

"I am sorry to let you know that three of our men who were wounded at Fredericksburg died in hospitals. Privates Tetlow and Crane died in Alexandria, and Private Pool died at Harewood in Washington."

Ryerson looked at Abbott. "Bill, would you please tell their company commanders, and make arrangements for services for them? Those boys were hurt bad and we hoped they would recover. I am sorry they didn't. Their friends will want to know, and I would like to be there for the services."

"Yes, sir, I will let you know as soon as I have spoken with them."

"What else, Top?"

"E Company reports private Morrain went AWOL on the 4th and is now reported as a deserter. Reed from K Company died of typhoid up at Armory Square on the 2nd and Pope from D Company died of typhoid here in our hospital on the 5th. Wilson from H Company is being discharged this morning for a disability. Sir, that brings us to 900 enlisted and 39 officers on the rolls. We have nearly a hundred men sick or on light duty."

The Colonel looked at Grubb and Milnor. "If we had to fight today, we would be short one hundred fifty rifles. That is fifteen percent of our firepower. The 2nd regiment went through this infernal sickness season last year. It won't get better until spring. We need to make sure every man that is healthy practices his place in ranks over and over again, until he knows what to do by instinct. This is going to get worse before it gets better."

All nodded agreement.

"Gentlemen, Lieutenant Perkins has resigned his commission, and that will be effective on the 14th. I am promoting Lieutenant Downs to 1st Lieutenant, and appointing him as Adjutant to take his place."

"That leaves McKee as acting 1st Lieutenant," said Grubb.

"I know, Burd. It's just too soon to promote him to 1st. He's only been an officer for two weeks."

"Sir, the men are getting very restless about all these officers resigning. What should we say to them?" asked Milnor.

Ryerson thought for a minute. "The best thing you can tell them is the men replacing them have been their leaders in a fight and lived with them on the march. They have advanced because of merit. They will make good leaders they can trust."

January 10, 1863 – Camp White Oak Church, Virginia

"We commend the spirit of our dear friend and your faithful servant, John Sweesley, into your hands in the name of the Father, the Son and Holy Ghost," concluded Chaplain Abbott. The officers of the regimental staff stood with H Company and Sweesley's friends.

The four sergeants, Miller, West, Wood and Hartman, carefully lowered the body into the grave in the slippery mud. It was already getting dark at 4 PM, and gloomy enough without the steady cold rain that was falling on them.

Crispin blinked back tears as he and the other five riflemen bit the ends off their paper cartridges and poured the powder down the barrel of their rifles. They dropped the buck and ball on the ground, primed their pieces and fired on command over the grave. They dropped the spent caps next to the grave. They went through the drill two more times. The funeral ended, and the company slipped and slid back to their quarters.

Sweesley was deeply mourned. His good nature and kindness made him a leader people enjoyed serving with. The weather was dreadful, but the squad managed to find enough shelter to hold a suitable wake. Whiskey appeared and toasts were offered. The sergeant's meerschaum pipe was ceremoniously lit, and passed around to be smoked by all.

Several men spent the evening reading from their New Testaments. The little books had been distributed as gifts from the US Christian Commission the day before. Books were scarce. They were quite popular among the troops from a very Quaker part of New Jersey. Captain Root and the lieutenants stopped by to pay their respects. Root let the company know that Rue was the acting sergeant in Sweesley's place. The wake broke up around midnight, and the men retired to their canvas-topped huts. The steady drumming of the rain and the whiskey ensured they slept soundly.

January 11, 1863 – Camp White Oak Church, Virginia
Church services were cancelled due to the downpour and the mud. It cleared off just before noon, and the daily afternoon dress parade was held as scheduled. Colonel Ryerson announced the regiment would go on picket duty at 11 AM on Monday.

Rations for the day were twenty ounces of fresh beef per man, some potatoes and some flour. Flour was highly sought after. It presented budding young chefs with a myriad of ways to vary their diets. Since there was no yeast and few ovens, it seldom went into bread. It did provide opportunities to make gravy after one fried up his beef or salt pork and lobscouse. Lobscouse was a thickened stew with meat and vegetables. Hardtack was used to make a dumpling, and for once, was edible.

It was possible to make an oven by digging a hole in the ground and lining it with rocks. A fire was built on the rocks and allowed to burn down to coals. Then a pot with navy beans, water, molasses, some onion and salt pork was placed on the coals and covered. Some boughs were placed over the oven to hold up an old piece of canvas, and the whole thing was covered with dirt. Twelve hours later, the pork and beans was served.

Pancakes were always a hit, and a cook's prowess was often judged by his ability to flip pancakes. A considered opinion was that one could make the flapjacks lighter by aeration, since there was no yeast. Men gradually acquired the skill of juggling the wheat cake in the air by using a deft flip of the wrist to send the cake skyward, and have it land back in the pan on the opposite side. Tongue-and-cheek stories were related around the regiment about some chefs who were so good that they could flip a pancake up the chimney, and have time to step out of the shelter and catch it before it hit the ground. There were numerous recipes for what do with pancakes once they were cooked. There was the always-popular steak sandwich, the stack with fruit preserves or jam and, of course, flapjacks and pork or beef gravy.

Men on a fixed diet of rations often sought to vary their menus with whatever they could buy or hunt out of the local farm and wild game supply. Life for a critter with four legs, two wings or gills in Stafford County during the winter of 62-63 was always a near-death experience.

January 12, 1863 – Camp White Oak Church, Virginia

After much hustle and bustle, the regiment marched off for picket duty on time. It had taken some time to convince everyone that it was prudent to leave the shelter halves in place, so that the huts would be there when they got back.

The picket line of the Union's left flank stretched from near Pollock's Mill on the Rappahannock across Stafford County to just east of Belle Plain. The 6th Corps was responsible for the western end, and the 1st Corps handled the eastern part. Picket duty was shared by all the regiments in the corps, and usually lasted three days.

The 1st and 6th Corps were lucky; they were on the south side of the Army. The depth of the Rappahannock River south of Pollack's Mill made it much more difficult for Rebel cavalry units to cross. Union pickets on the northern flank of the army were under constant threat from Rebel guerillas or cavalry. Still, vigilance was part of the job.

The march to the picket post was difficult. The roads of Stafford County already had a poor reputation for being dusty in the summer and wagon-rut deep in mud in the winter. They were starting to live up to their reputation. After struggling through the mud for two miles, they came to a group of "shebangs" and found the 27th New Jersey. The 23rd relieved the 27th, and soon the 27th marched back to its camp.

The "shebang" was a little hut made of pine boughs. Woven and constructed properly, they could provide a warm, comfortable shelter in all except the worst weather. The troops gathered small sticks from the nearby pine woods and built small fires in front of them. They were comfortable even though the night was very cold with heavy, soaking dew.

H Company was in reserve during the first interval. They were not to go on duty until the next day at noon. During the morning, Josie walked over to a neighboring house to see if he could trade for some food. The owner had no food to trade, but he did have a desirable commodity: inulah meal. Josi returned to the regiment and told Bowlby what he had found. Almost immediately, Bowlby talked Doc Cook out of two pounds of coffee and returned with Josie to the farm.

The bargaining was difficult. The farmer's southern accent made him almost unintelligible. Eventually, they traded the coffee for a like quantity of inulah meal. They went straight to Doc and turned it over. Inulah is elecampane, an aromatic medicinal plant more commonly known as fleabane. Doc put the fleabane in a safe container. Josie watched as he put three pints of water in a pot and added a coffee cup of inulah meal and a half coffee cup of white hoarhound. The mixture was steeped like brewing tea until there was only a quart of liquid. Doc strained the liquid through a cloth and put it back in the pot. Then he added a lump of tartaric acid about the size of a small hickory nut, and half a cup of honey. When all was finished, it produced a very effective cough syrup. The accepted dose was two tablespoons every half hour until the cough broke up. As soon as the syrup was done, it was bottled and on its way back to the regimental hospital with the container of unused meal. Josie had found enough to help a lot of sick men.

January 14, 1863 - Stoneman's Station Rail Siding, Falmouth, Virginia

Lieutenant Nichols, the regimental quartermaster, brought three wagons from the regiment over to Stoneman's railroad station twice a week to pick up supplies. Each time Nichols made the trip, he brought a squad with him to help unload the railcars and load the wagons. Today, Sergeant West's squad had the rail station work detail. O'Neil gave them a ride to the station in the H Company wagon.

It had not rained for several days, so the roads were in fair shape. The mud had dried and wagons were moving well. The men rolled up the canvas sides and watched the scenery go by. The country was flat. You could see a long way in every direction. There were nearly 200,000 men camped around Stafford County. Tent cities occupied part of almost every open field. The rest were used for parade grounds, wagon and artillery parks, and pastures for horses and cattle.

The whole area was covered by a pall of wood smoke from all of the cooking and warming fires. In fact, the whole county smelled like the forest does after it has burned and been rained on; a constant, damp odor of charred wood. This blended with the odor of stock and an occasional latrine that needed its daily covering of dirt.

There were some nice farms and plantations in the area. They generally were in the 400-acre range, and had grown corn, produce, cattle and pigs before the war. The majority of the men were off serving in the Confederate Army. Generally, families that could not manage the farms with their men gone had moved away earlier in the war. Those left were mainly women, children, older folks and freed slaves working some of the farms or doing jobs for the Army.

The area was not completely abandoned, but there were many empty houses and structures. These were in danger of being torn down to meet the Army's insatiable need for building materials for winter quarters. Some of the nicer homes were commandeered for headquarters or hospitals.

The men saw all kinds of activities. Infantry units were drilling. Artillery units were cleaning their weapons and practicing battery drill. Wagons, artillery, marching troops, dispatch riders and civilians going about their business clogged the roads. Blacksmith shops, harness makers and wheel rights were making or repairing equipment.

It took a little more than an hour to get to the station. There was a station house, water tower and wood supply for the engines. A telegraph office made sure the trains ran on schedule without accident. There were a number of barns to keep the supplies out of the weather.

The steam engine *Washington* had just pulled into the station on the main line, with 16 cars. There were switches that allowed the engine to park the cars on sidings on both sides of the main line. A line of telegraph poles along the tracks stretched out of sight, back toward Aquia Landing.

Heavy timber loading docks had been built on the outside of each of the sidings. These platforms were the same height as the floors of the rail cars. This allowed workers to move freight quickly off the cars. The army was using nearly 800 tons of supplies a day, which meant the engines were pulling eighty cars a day from Aquia to the Falmouth and back.

Lieutenant Nichols was waiting when the regimental wagon train pulled into the station. Wagons from other regiments were lined up in front of and behind them. Lieutenant Nichols had ridden down on his horse and presented his reports and requisitions to the Divisional Quartermaster. The regimental morning report showed rations would be requisitioned for the 892 enlisted men and 37 officers present for duty. Rations would not be drawn for the two officers on leave and the five enlisted men in the hospital.

Enough food for that many men for 3 days came out to just over one ton of hardtack and one ton of salt pork. Each man could expect 20 ounces of fresh beef per day, if the butcher was butchering. If available, they might get 270 pounds of rice or 400 pounds of peas or beans. If the Commissary had potatoes, they could get 14 bushels. Roasted coffee for three days would be about 216 pounds, or 8 pounds per 100 men per day. Sugar, salt, pepper and molasses might also be available, with quantities for each 100 men carefully calculated.

Nichols found O'Neil and directed him to a loading dock. West got his men busy loading the supplies into the wagons. As soon as they were done, O'Neil and the other wagoners started back to the regiment with Nichols.

West and his squad stayed to help the stationmaster unload railcars. They were not alone. Details from many other regiments were helping, too. The work was done by a combination of two-wheeled carts, wheelbarrows and good old-fashioned muscle. By mid afternoon, the men were bushed. They had unloaded a number of cars, and each time they were done, an engine would move the empties out and push more full cars up the siding to the loading dock. They headed back to the regiment at 4 PM. The roads were tolerable.

Nichols watched the wagons being unloaded at each company street. It was heavy work in the slick mud. One of the details was having trouble with a barrel of salt pork. They had to be careful to not drop it off the wagon and break the barrel. They were struggling when one of the men slipped. The barrel teetered on the edge of the wagon, and toppled over on one of the men. Shouts echoed around the scene, and the barrel was quickly lifted off Private Chambers. Men tried to help him up. Nichols strode over. Chambers needed a doctor. The 23rd was down another rifle.

January 18, 1863 – Camp White Oak Church, Virginia

Ryerson lived in a hospital tent with Grubb and Milnor. The tent was erected on top of a three-foot tall footwall. A pole at each end gave a fourteen-foot peak and raised the walls to seven and a half feet, so there was standing room under the whole structure. Grubb and Milnor built a bunk bed on one side, and Ryerson had his own bed on the other. A small tarp made a partition which separated the living area from the headquarters office. One end of the tent had been cut to accommodate a mud and stick fireplace.

It was just before daylight. Grubb and Milnor were brewing coffee when the orderly brought a telegram for Ryerson. He read it and burst out, "Oh, for God's sake."

The major and the lieutenant colonel looked up at him.

"Peter Garridan is dead. For crying out loud, he got run over by a train."

"How'd that happen, Sir?"

"The hospital in Philadelphia gave him a few days off before sending him back to us. He was trying to go home and hopped a freight train in Camden. He fell under the wheels and lost his legs. They couldn't save him."

Milnor handed Ryerson a cup of coffee. "He was H Company, wasn't he?"

"Yes, that's what Doc said. I think he had typhoid and we had to send him north. This just seems so ludicrous. Survive a battle, survive the weather and the march and survive the fever, and get killed by a stupid train."

"I guess Abbott's right; it's just not given to us to know when our time is up."

Ryerson silently struggled with his thoughts. He'd lost many men in battles. He'd seen many die of disease. Why did this death bother him so much? Was he growing jaded to the normalcy of death, or was it because this one was so unexpected and so grotesque?

He would tell the men of the death at morning formation. He would also make a point of addressing safety issues at officer's call. All were living in dangerous circumstances and dangerous times. There was no point getting through a battle if you were going to be maimed or die from some stupid accident afterward.

Sergeant Major Browne came in with the morning report. "Sir, Doc discharged Corporal Ridge from H Company yesterday. A musket went off next to his ear during our fight at Deep Run. We were all hoping his hearing would come back, but he can't hear a thing in that ear, sir. Doc says Keene from D Company died at our hospital yesterday, chronic diarrhea, and the Army discharged Lovett from I Company back at Columbian Hospital yesterday."

"So what is our strength this morning, Top?" Ryerson asked. He knew Brown was still not used to being called "Top Soldier." In spite of the bad news, the colonel enjoyed seeing the confused expression on Brown's face when it happened.

"Well, Captain Newbold is back, but Captain Grobler is still recuperating, so we have 38 officers present. We have 892 enlisted on the rolls, but 14 men have been evacuated to hospitals in the north and probably won't be back. That puts us at 878, and we have at least 90 men on sick call. Sir, we can march less than 800 men."

Ryerson thought for a few minutes. Grubb and Milnor knew what was going through his mind. The regiment had been alerted to issue and cook three days of rations. They would move out for an attack in forty-eight hours. What would happen to those who could not march?

Ryerson called Doc Cook and explained what was going on. Cook started evacuating anyone he thought would be in peril if they went on the march.

While Doc went to work, Ryerson told Browne about McKee's project to provide identification for the men by marking their clothing and equipment. Browne promised to remind the 1st Sergeants to get it done before they marched.

A little later in the morning, Milnor found Lieutenant Nichols. Together, they rounded up the company supply sergeants and started issuing the rations and what replacement equipment they could find. Grubb took over the afternoon drill, while Ryerson rode up to brigade headquarters to get the orders. Grubb was waiting when Ryerson returned. Drill this afternoon had been difficult. The men were in a foul mood. While they were not insubordinate, they were clearly unhappy. The recent defeats and officer resignations, combined with the payroll being late, were causing very hard feelings in the ranks. Families were struggling back home, and the men were worried. Ryerson listened carefully, and then went to discuss the issue with Colonel Brown. They had not been paid since they mustered in, and something had to be done.

January 20, 1863 – Camp White Oak Church, Virginia

Orders came to strike camp at noon. The men packed their things and dismantled the shelter halves from their huts. The companies formed and were marched into a square formation.

Colonel Ryerson addressed the troops and read General Order Number 7 from General Burnside. "The commanding general announces to the Army of the Potomac that they are about to meet the enemy once more. The late brilliant actions in North Carolina, Tennessee and Arkansas have divided and weakened the enemy on the Rappahannock, and the auspicious moment seems to have arrived to strike a great and mortal blow to the Rebellion, and to gain that decisive victory which is due to the country. Let the gallant soldiers of so many brilliant battlefields accomplish this achievement, and a fame the most glorious awaits them. The commanding general calls for the firm and united action of officers and men, and, under the providence of God, the Army of the Potomac will have taken a great step toward restoring peace to the country and the Government to its rightful authority. By command of Major-General Burnside."

Ryerson called for three cheers for the Union. The troops responded well. They marched back to the river, and then turned upstream and joined a column marching parallel to it.

Rue and Miller had the group stepping along. "Some of the boys are disappointed. They thought we would be going up to Washington to guard the capitol," breathed Josie.

Rue was watching his footing and glanced at Josie for an instant. "I heard that rumor too, but never put much stock in it."

"How is your arm?" asked Josie.

Rue replied, "The wound finally closed up last week, but boy am I going to have a scar."

"Hartman sure has a bug about writing our names on our stuff," puffed Josie.

"I know. I heard him talking to Sergeant Major McKee before McKee was promoted. McKee thinks we'd never have lost Obie or Henry if their names had been with their stuff. The doctors or whoever found them could have identified them, and let us know where they were. McKee was really upset that they were listed as unknowns."

"That makes a lot of sense. I labeled all my stuff and put my name and address in my diary, and in my waterproof case.

"Still keeping up that diary, are you?"

"Every day. How far you think we will go tonight?"

"I doubt we will go very late. With all the horses, cavalry, artillery and wagons on the move, we will have to pull off early enough to get the roads opened, so the pontoons can come up."

He was right. They marched past some fine farms and a small village with two or three hospitals. Finally, at 4 PM, 4 miles past Fredericksburg, they stopped and set their tents up in a thick oak forest. Bartlett's second brigade camped right next to them. Fires were lit and coffee brewed. The men brought out their rations and ate their precooked meat between two pieces of hardtack. It started raining about two hours later. It was night one of the Mud March.

Doc Elmer was setting up the division hospital for those who could not march. The sickest men had been sent back to Aquia Creek to be moved north. He had just gotten his tents up when it started to rain. He was attending to one of his patients when several men pushed through the tent flap.

"Who are you?" asked Elmer.

"Private Williams and Peters from the 4th Regiment, Sir," rasped Peters. "We were sent back to the hospital at Aquia Creek, but there's no place for us there. The rest of the men are on their way back here."

Elmer looked them over. Both had sore throats, fevers and rashes. They should never have been out, let alone forced to walk all the way from Aquia Creek in the rain. Elmer wanted to give these men some medicinal liquor. He noticed his whiskey supplies were low. They had been full earlier in the day. Doc Cook had been sorting through the supplies. Elmer sighed. He wondered if Doc had taken the whiskey. He was just getting the two men from 4th regiment comfortable when a steady stream of very sick people started coming into the tents. By morning he had two hundred and twenty.

January 21, 1863 - Rappahannock River, 4 miles above Fredericksburg, Virginia

The drummer tried to beat reveille at 6:30 AM. The drumhead was so wet, it barely made a sound. The gale out of the northeast drowned out all of the sound anyway. Word was passed from tent to tent to get up and get packed. The rain came in torrents. Periodically, the rain changed to sleet and snow, and then back again. The Jersey men knew the signs. This wasn't going to be just a march on a rainy day. An entire army was trying to move in a full-fledged "Nor'easter."

The rain blew across the fields in sheets and almost horizontal to the ground. The wind howled wildly, trees were breaking and crashing to the ground. Limbs and branches were snapping off and hurdling through the air. The rain beating on the wet ground and puddles was audible. Understandably, nobody wanted to move.

Men cooked what breakfast they could, and the march started early. Bartlett's brigade went first. They didn't get very far. The roads were jammed with bridging wagons buried to their axles.

The storm hit the army at the worst possible time. Stafford County was notorious for having terrible road conditions in the winter, and the lesson was about to be hammered home in Biblical proportions.

Pontoon trains were heavy and cumbersome. They took up a lot of room on a road. That is why they normally traveled at the rear of an army, and only moved to the front when they were needed. The plan was to move the army into position by late afternoon, so the roads could be clear for the bridging equipment to come up during the night.

Five separate pontoon trains were on the move to the bridging sites when the storm hit. Within an hour, trouble started. Each train consisted of 34 pontoon wagons, 22 chess wagons, two forge wagons and four tool wagons. Each pontoon wagon was drawn by eight mules. The rest were drawn by four or six animals, depending on their cargoes. Each bridge's supply wagons, nearly 100 men, officers on horseback and spare horses also traveled with the group.

As the stock heaved their shoulders into their harnesses to pull the heavy loads, their hooves churned ever deeper into the muck. Each iron-rimmed pontoon wagon wheel cut a furrow in the wet earth like a plow. The next set of 32 churning hooves mixed the loose dirt into the deepening mire and started the vicious cycle all over again. Within hours, the pontoons were stuck to their hubs. Supply wagons, ambulances, artillery pieces and caissons, and any other vehicles which fell into line were in the same fix.

To get around the wagons, Bartlett's 2nd brigade started to march along the roadside. Almost 3,000 sets of human feet churned through the wet Virginia clay. By the time the 1st Brigade and the 23rd started marching, the mud was already ankle deep. It was slippery, and tried to suck the shoes off men's feet. As horse teams, dispatch riders and officers tried to move up and down the road to deal with the situation, the roadsides got wider and the mud got deeper. In some places, only the muzzles of cannon could be seen sticking out. Triple teams of mules and horses with 150-man details hauling on ropes could not move them.

Soon, the situation was recognized as an emergency. It became apparent the horses and mules were in danger. The drivers had beaten them to exhaustion. Some collapsed and couldn't find their footing. They submerged and drowned. If the driver couldn't cut the harness fast enough, one animal could drag a whole team under. Luckier animals were hauled out by ropes and placed on high ground, where they could rest and recover their strength.

More and more stragglers from every regiment in the division could be seen resting along the road. Harsh words were common as men threatened to desert. Many did.

Shortly after 2 PM, the regiment halted and pitched their tents. The storm had subsided a little by then, but the boys hoped it would continue. The lowliest private knew it would be suicide to continue the attack in the current conditions. By nightfall, the most skilled fire builders in the regiment had succeeded in getting small, smoky fires going. Men were able to warm their rations and boil a little coffee. Rain drummed steadily on the shelter halves, gum blankets and tents. Nearly 200,000 Union troops gazed at the world forlornly from under anything that would keep the rain off them.

Rue and the squad were huddled by a campfire trying to get warm. It didn't provide much heat, but it threw off enough light for the squad to gather around. They had buttoned their capes over their heads to keep the sleet off their necks. "I sure wish we were back at the Cooper Shop Refreshment Saloon, having boiled ham and cabbage and potatoes," mused Crispin.

"Yeah, with fresh bread and butter and cakes," chimed in Lloyd.

174

"You two are doing this on purpose just to make us miserable," barked Sharp.

"Oh, no, we were just ... daydreaming. Sorry."

"Daydreaming my ass, you two are trying to ruin our evening."

"No, actually, I was trying to think of something pleasant to get my mind off the ice cold water flowing down my spine from the rain and sleet which is blowing in my face," deadpanned Crispin. The others grinned. Crispin and Lloyd's constant interplay with Sharp and Terhune was everyday entertainment for the troops.

Lloyd added, "Yes, me too, nothing like thinking about all that good food and nice ladies and warm weather to make you forget your troubles."

Sharp just brooded.

"Did you hear about the shooting over by White Oak Church?" asked Lloyd.

"Shooting, what shooting?" asked Hibbs.

"It happened while we were on picket duty. The provost marshal had a guard posted at Bullock's house. I heard some teenage boy got the guard's pistol, and it went off and shot the Bullock girl." Lloyd had everyone's attention.

"The bullet hit her in the stomach, so there was no hope. She died a few hours later."

"Well, what did they do with the boy? Was it murder?"

"Nobody knows, but it sounds like they are treating it like an accident."

"I hear Colonel Brown got drunk and fell off his horse and landed on his face," said Hibbs.

"So that's what happened to him," chuckled Lloyd. "I saw him. His nose was all skinned up and both eyes were black. Looked like a raccoon." They all grinned.

Hullings got up to urinate while Terhune was filling his canteen in the storm water flowing by them. "Hey George, do that downhill. We don't want the smell around where we sleep, and it will make the water taste better. Goes for the rest of you, too."

The squad chuckled. Hullings started to walk away from them. Over his shoulder, he tossed back, "OK, Rue, but there's just about 10,000 men uphill from us."

In unison, every head in the squad swiveled to look upstream. Terhune quietly poured the water out of his canteen and asked Sharp for a drink.

Sergeant Major Browne managed to get a small headquarters tent up for Ryerson in spite of the high winds and rain. Late in the afternoon, he was able to brief the colonel on the status of the men. Their condition was terrible. They had one full day of rations left, even though most of the food was soaked. Even hardtack was chewable. Morale was poor. A Company reported that Privates Clarke and Falkenburgh had deserted on the 20th along with Private Borden from G Company. I Company reported three desertions on the 21st. Ryerson and Grubb looked at each other. They could understand an occasional man going over the hill, but multiples leaving at the same time from the same units smacked of a conspiracy. "Send for Captains Hambrick and Burnett."

When the captains arrived, Ryerson let them know quite clearly that they needed to impress upon their officers, NCOs and men that desertion was a serious crime and would not be tolerated. Ryerson also let them know that this was now a Military Law matter, and the men would be sent to prison when they were captured. He instructed Sergeant Major Browne and Grubb to make sure every man in the regiment was told that desertion would not be tolerated at all. The word was passed. So, started night two of the Mud March.

January 22, 1863 - Rappahannock River, 5 miles above Fredericksburg, Virginia

The storm finally subsided about 2 AM. In Washington, the weather station at the Smithsonian recorded a total rain fall of 3.2 inches in 30 hours, winds at gale force and a barometric pressure of 29.75 inches.* It was truly a great storm.

Dawn came. It was almost deathly silent. The rain-soaked muddy ooze projected an overpowering gloom in the camps. Tens of thousands of men peered out from under their rubber blankets or shelter halves to see what the day would bring as darkness turned to light. There was little recognizable order. Anything that could hold up a gum blanket, shelter half or chunk of canvas had men under it. Rain mixed with sleet

*Washington Weather; Ambrose, Henry & Rice; Historical Enterprises, 2002.

had fallen so fast that it flowed over the ground in sheets, sometimes inches deep. Tents kept some of the downpour from falling directly on the men; however, there was no place to go to get up out of the water and mud. Men slept in flowing streams, sometimes inches deep. Some nearly drowned. The soaked ground exuded a cold that penetrated their wet wool clothing. People were grumpy, and since there was nowhere to go, tempers grew short. They had no confidence in a commander who attacked an impregnable position, lost 12,000 men, couldn't get them paid on time and marched them in weather like this. Grumbling became vocal and dangerous. Burnside was the target.

The regiment was ordered to be ready to move back to White Oak Church at 1 PM. Major Allison would be waiting with their pay. All was made ready, but the order never came. Instead, the regiment was marched to the road. The emergency was growing worse. Orders from General Woodbury required that bridge pontoons and other equipment be moved out of the roads. The infantry regiments were ordered to help. The command was worried the mud would freeze and trap the equipment until spring.

Unfortunately, most people don't know much about roads. The material under them is not uniform. Some places are harder than others or drain better than others. Wet areas tend to break down before dryer areas and the dryer areas tend to be hilltops or places that are raised above the wet areas. Drainage is the key to building an all-weather road. There wasn't any here. So, a wagon might be able to move easily over a hill for a few hundred yards, only to become mired in a mud bog when it came to the next low portion of the road. Animals churned some of the mud bogs 8 feet deep and hundreds of yards long. These places were a danger to man and beast alike. Creatures of either sort unable to find their footing might as well be in quicksand.

This was not a problem happening on just a single road. Virtually every road north of the river, from the United States Ford to Aquia Landing to Belle Plaines and back to Pollack's Mill on the Rappahannock, was in the same condition. Supply wagons could not deliver rations, and regiments were sending company-sized details to backpack rations to the troops and fodder to animals.

What had been considered an emergency the day before was quickly deteriorating into a disaster. Franklin's Grand Division consisted of Gregg's cavalry and the 1st and 6th Corps. It numbered over 50,000 men and 15,000 animals. Every item the Division needed, from food and fodder to medicine, was delivered from the rail line to the camps by more than 1,400 wagons. If the wagons could not bring the needed rations and fodder, the Grand Division might have to evacuate. Two other Grand Divisions were in the same shape.*

Engineers were waiting for the regiment when it got to the road. They had the ropes and chains and timbers from the pontoon trains. The work was unbelievably difficult. The pontoon had to be untied from its wagon. It weighed about 2,000 pounds. Crews then took the 27-foot long, 5"x5", 110-pound timber bridge balks from another wagon in the bridge train and placed them on the mud like a railroad tie. When enough balks had been placed, the regiment got the word to heave-hoe on the ropes, and the one-ton boat moved forward a few yards.

When the pontoon was pulled as far as it could go, the crew went back to the starting place, pried the balks out of the mud, carried them to the front of the boat and reset them for the next pull. Entire regiments were able to move one pontoon an astounding 100 yards per hour. When the pontoon was safely placed on a set of logs, so it would not freeze to the ground, the whole group went back, and started the process all over to bring up the wagon. All of this had to be coordinated so the precious boats were out of Rebel artillery range. When all was safe, another detail camouflaged the equipment with pine branches.

General Burnside decided to distribute whiskey to boost the troop's spirits, but morale was so low it did the opposite. Troops not involved in hauling equipment grew bored. The commander of the 118th Pennsylvania bet the commander of the 25th New York that his pioneers could fall a tree in a given direction faster than the New Yorkers. The Pennsylvanians won the bet. Later, poor sports among the New Yorkers claimed the ax was stolen and tried to seize it. A drunken brawl erupted between the two regiments. The 22nd Massachusetts tried to break up the fight and suddenly found itself in a 3 regiment donnybrook. It took a battery of artillery loaded with canister aimed at the rioters to get them to calm down.

Rebel pickets watching from across the river near Ellis' Ford were delighted. Word of the debacle and the fight spread through the Rebel

*WOR, Series 1, Volume XXI, page 984.

camps, and hundreds came running to see the spectacle. They started taunting the Army of the Potomac and painted a giant sign. It said, **"Burnside stuck in the mud."** The final insult came when a Rebel voice echoed across the river, "HEY, YANKEES, WE BE'S THE REBELS. YOU'S SPOSED TO BE FIGHTIN US." The peals of laughter from the Confederate side only served to deepen the malaise. At nightfall, the exhausted, mud-covered men went back to their cold rations and wet tents. They spent a third night in the mud by the Rappahannock.

January 23, 1863 - Rappahannock River, 5 miles above Fredericksburg, Virginia

The fourth day of the Mud March dawned foggy and damp. The rain stopped and the air warmed. There was no thought of drill, as most everyone was assigned to details hauling equipment out of the mud. Josie was still on light duty, so he took the time to walk toward the river and see the disaster firsthand.

He walked through a soaking wet, leafless forest. Some places were very thick and impenetrable, while others were quite open. The low areas were full of standing water, and the higher areas were covered with makeshift tents as far as one could see in all directions. The sound of trees falling from the storm was replaced by trees falling from axes and hatchets. Shouts and yells to stand clear as the trees fell could be heard from all directions.

Plenty of wagons and pontoons were still sunk in the mud. Dead horses, sometimes entire teams, littered the landscape. Broken boxes of cartridges, hardtack and abandoned equipment littered the ground. After a mile or so, he came to an amazing sight. Thousands of men were trying to free the vehicles. Entire regiments were working to pull single pontoons or guns or wagons out of the mud with long ropes. Timbers and chess planks from the pontoon train and any logs that could be found were being used to bridge the all-consuming muck.

Crispin noticed most men wore low shoes. They were laboring in mud up to their knees, so the shoes were useless. They were sweating, covered with mud and wet to the bone. When they stopped working, they quickly became chilled. Steam rose from their clothes. Many lost their shoes as the cold mud pulled them off. Those who did were in trouble. January in Virginia with wet feet could be fatal.

By the time Josie got back to camp, he was overjoyed not to have been chosen for the hauling details. Many from the 23rd had been sent to help. After dark, they struggled back to camp, exhausted, hungry, sore and wet. Some were hurt. Whiskey was issued to help them deal with sore muscles and strains. Doc Cook drank some, too. As they settled in for the 4th night of the Mud March, word came to be ready to move out at daylight. Nobody had to be told twice.

January 24, 1863 - Rappahannock River, 5 miles above Fredericksburg, Virginia

The regiment was packed up and ready to march back to White Oak Church long before dawn. Those who had most bitterly hated the old campground seemed to be the ones who longed the most to get back. Fortunately, the weather seemed to cooperate - - - at first.

The march started well after daylight, but it took off in the wrong direction. The men struggled through deep mud for half a mile until they came to a corduroy road. Once this objective was reached, morale improved as they started back to White Oak Church. Within a quarter mile, things went wrong. The road was plugged with abandoned pontoons and wagons. Dead animals were mired in the mud. It was so deep it was almost impossible to navigate. The regiment took a rest break.

General Brooks and some of his staff rode slowly toward them while they were resting. Their horses were obviously struggling as they labored across the field in mud at least a foot deep. All were covered with muck and sweat.

"How are you men doing?" asked the General.

"Sir, we are hungry, wet, dirty, unpaid, tired and HERE," yelled a voice from the middle of the group.

Whoever had made the comment was very close to insubordination. Brooks looked at them for a second, looked at his muddy uniform and his lathered horse, and answered, "We sure as hell are," and grinned.

It took a second for the troops to realize the General was not going to be angry, and suddenly they laughed, too. Tension was broken, if only for a minute. Brooks asked Captain Root how things were going.

"Sir, we are marching in a circle. The men aren't happy, and I have never heard of a mess like this in my whole life."

Brooks paused for a second. "Me either, son, never heard of the like in all of history. We will get you and your boys back to White Oak Church as soon as we can." He started to spur his horse toward the road. "I am counting on you to take care of them. You hear?"

"Yes, sir, sir you might not want to go that..." The horse fell into what seemed a bottomless hole. Brooks was thrown head-first into the mud. Root and his troops looked on for a few seconds before it dawned on them he wasn't coming up. Ropes and guns and human chains were formed, and the General was grabbed and unceremoniously saved from certain death. In the luckiest move of the day, several men managed to free his horse. General Brooks was so covered with mud he couldn't open his eyes. He was barely able to breathe, before men poured their canteens over his face to clear his nose and mouth. Eventually, he could open his eyes, and saw that men had covered him with blankets. One said, "Begging your pardon, Sir, this the first time I ever saw a general look like a God-damned contraband." Brooks slowly turned toward the voice, then he looked down at himself and over at his horse. As cold and shivering and miserable as he was, he burst into laughter and the men around him did, too.

It took a lot of water to get the general and his horse cleaned up, but the men pitched in and helped. Brooks had been good to them, and they bore him no ill will. Eventually, they got most of the mud cleaned off and his clothing rinsed and wrung out. They got the saddle and tack off the horse and got that cleaned up, and the animal rinsed off. The general was just saying thank you and getting ready to leave when Major Milnor rode up.

Brooks yelled, "Milnor! No…" but it was too late. Milnor and the horse fell into the bog, and the second rescue of the day was made.

Finally, after saving a General, a major and both of their horses, the regiment marched back to the place it started that morning. They set up camp for the night. Grumbling that might have been subdued earlier in the march turned noticeably vocal. The men were pleased they had rescued the officers, but they were incensed about being made to march in a circle in the mud. General Burnside was the officer they blamed. To add insult to injury, it started raining again at dusk, and the squad had to stand guard.

January 25, 1863 - Rappahannock River, 5 miles above Fredericksburg, Virginia

The squad was relieved from guard at 8 AM. When all were in camp, Grubb assembled the regiment. The rain and sleet stopped just before dawn. The temperature and humidity made it raw.

"Colonel Ryerson and I want to personally thank each of you for the extraordinary effort you have made to move our equipment and pontoons to safety. Colonel Ryerson is meeting with General Brooks to find out when we will return to camp. We have been told we will return to our site at White Oak Church. I expect Major Allison to be waiting for us with your pay. I want you to know you deserve every penny of it. Colonel Ryerson and I are sorry it has been so long coming."

JAMES G. BUCK

All soldiers like to be told they are doing a good job. Morale was as bad as the weather, but a personal pat on the back from the colonel and an apology about the late payday soothed some of the hurt feelings.

"Now, attention to orders, General Orders Number 20, War Department, Adjutant General's Office, Washington, D.C., January 25, 1863. The President of the United States has directed: That Major General A.E. Burnside, at his own request, be relieved of command of the Army of the Potomac. That Major General E. V. Sumner, at his own request, be relieved of duty in the Army of the Potomac. That Major General W. B. Franklin, at his own request, be relieved of duty in the Army of the Potomac. That Major General J. Hooker, be assigned to command of the Army of the Potomac ... By Order of the Secretary of War: E.D. Townsend, Assistant Adjutant General."

A muttering in the ranks showed the troops approved of the change. No one had faith in Burnside. They knew something serious had been going on for the last 6 weeks. Few knew the details of the vicious power struggle that had occurred in the General Staff and reached all the way to the President. They could sense the tension in the officers, but officers didn't discuss such things with enlisted men. Their only sources of information were rumors and newspaper reports. General Order 20 brought hope that things would settle down.

Grubb told them they were going to stay where they were for another day, but the order was countermanded around noon.

Captain Root called the officers, sergeants and corporals together as soon as he knew they were marching. "Fellas, this is going to be a very difficult march. The colonel wants us to stay together as much as possible, but he understands many will not be able to keep up. It is up to each of you to look after your men, and make sure they get through this. Do not leave anyone alone. Anyone who has to stop must have someone stay and make sure they are taken care of, any questions?"

There were none, "Make sure your stronger men help the weaker ones. We need to get everyone back under shelter at our camp at White Oak Church."

As the men moved off, Doc Elmer sidled up to Root. "Sir, you're limping. What's the matter?"

"Ah, Bob, it's those goddamned veins in my legs."

Elmer looked at him. "Pull your pant leg up and let me see."

Root did, and Elmer gasped. Thick blue veins protruded from the skin the size of ropes. "Sir, you've got to get off your feet as soon as you can. Keep them clean and keep them elevated."

"I will, Bob, but first I have to get these men back to camp."

Elmer nodded in agreement. Root had the worst case of varicose veins he had ever heard off. Root needed a wagon, and there was none to be had. Elmer went off to find Bowlby.

By 1:30 they were on the move. The roads were so bad they moved across country over fields and valleys, fording streams and jumping ditches.

Marching was an exhausting affair. The mud was often knee-deep, so it took an effort to pull one's foot from the mire and an additional effort to lift the water-logged shoe and the mud that clung to it like a leg iron. On top of that, almost everything they owned was heavier because it, too, was water-logged. After a short time, anything not already soaked with water was soaked with sweat.

The regiment started as a group. Soon, the weak and the injured began to straggle. The men knew they should not fall out of the march, but some grew so tired they stopped when they were only halfway to the next rest. Sometimes they would climb a steep hill and fall to the ground, without caring if it was dry or muddy. Eventually, nearly 500 of the 800-man regiment fell out of the march. The first troops arrived at the regimental area at Camp White Oak Church around 6 PM. They had covered ten miles in the worst conditions in a little over five hours. They cheered in the dark when they got there.

January 26, 1863 - Camp White Oak Church, Virginia

The 23rd's Regimental Camp at White Oak Church had been primitive. It was not a place most people would choose to live. Under the circumstances, it was as comfortable and serviceable as the men could make it. At least it had been when they left five days before.

Now, the holes and low walls they had worked so hard to build and chink were full of snow, sleet and water. The troops who arrived during the night simply covered themselves with everything they had and curled up together for warmth. They slept the sleep of the exhausted.

As daylight broke, they arose and made fires. They warmed themselves and cooked what coffee, hardtack, and salt pork they had. Once this was done, they started draining the water from their huts. Boards substituted for shovels. In places where there was standing water, drainage ditches were dug. Sometimes dryer dirt was thrown in.

After it soaked up the water, it was thrown out and replaced with more, until all of the water was gone.

Only then were the shelter halves and canvas tarps put back over the frames of the huts. Fires were lit, and the long process of warming the structures and drying the equipment began. Quick inventories showed anything left in camp by the troops was pilfered. All of their boxes from home, personal effects and little bottles they had hidden away were gone.

The reconstruction of the camp became a continuing saga as the day went on. It took most of the daylight hours for the 500-odd stragglers to make their way in. Sometimes, officers or NCOs had to detail men to go back and help their compatriots come in. Everyone was covered with a thick layer of Virginia. Sometimes, those with their huts already reconstructed helped the latecomers fix theirs. By evening, the camp was as it had been before the Mud March started.

Colonel Ryerson had his tent set up on its old footwall. It took a while to get it right. Once it was done and the fire lit, the Colonel was able to start making a reasonable effort get back in control of his regiment. Milnor's near drowning and the effort to recover all of his stragglers and reset camp had kept everyone in the regiment busy for the day. The lamps were lit all of the time because of the short winter days. He was reading reports at his desk when Browne and Cook came in. "Good evening, Sir."

"Sergeant Major, Doc, nice to see you."

"Sir, I have the morning report updated, and Doc has some news for you."

"Go ahead."

Cook started. "Sir, we might as well have been in a battle. I was over at the hospital, and we have at least eight injured that we have to evacuate or keep in the tent."

"A horse fell and crushed two; two sprained their backs jumping over ditches and at least four got hernias trying to pull those pontoons. There are more coming on sick call all the time. Got a couple of broken legs, a crushed hand and a lot of sprains and torn muscles."

"A man can be discharged for a hernia?"

"Yes, Sir. If he can't pick up a sixty-pound pack and a ten-pound gun without his insides poking out, he's not much good to us. Most probably will have to be evacuated."

"The man has a point," said Ryerson as he looked at Browne. "Anything else?"

"No sir," said Cook. His words sounded a little slurred. Ryerson said good night, and motioned he was dismissed. He watched the doctor go and frowned.

He paused, looked at Browne and asked, "Do you have any good news?"

"Yes sir, Major Allison will be here on the 30th to pay the men."

"Well, thank God for that. We will need two days to get cleaned up for muster and inspection. Top, when the men get paid, see what you can do about keeping the gambling down. Some of my younger charges used to get fleeced every payday. Make sure anybody who needs help sending money home gets it."

"Yes sir," replied Browne and continued, "I've been keeping track of the news on the Mud March, ah, that's what the men are calling it. Not everyone caught up to us until this afternoon, and we still might be missing some. While we were gone, we had three men die in hospital and three discharged for injuries or illness. We have six more in various general hospitals. Counting the desertions that puts," pause, "that puts our strength at 872 enlisted and 39 officers, with Grobler still convalescing. That's not counting those in our hospital or on bed rest. We can field about 800 men. We are lucky the Rebs can't get to us, and we sure can't get to them. I think we will be here a while."

"Top, who were the three men who died?"

"Broom from K Company, Holman from H and Shreve from B, Sir."

"Please let their Commanders know, and Chaplain Abbott, too."

The Top sergeant nodded and started to leave, but Ryerson stopped him. "Do you have something you want to tell me, Sergeant Major?"

Browne straightened and took a deep breath. "Sir, something happened at the hospital at Aquia Creek, and all the men we sent over there before the march had to walk back. Apparently, no one made arrangements for them to go there. Bob Elmer's got over 200 men up at the division hospital and he's out of food and medicine. He says somebody stole some of his hospital liquor."

"Any thoughts on who that could be?"

"Not my place to guess about things like that, Sir."

"Is Cook hitting the bottle again?"

Sergeant Major Browne slowly nodded his head yes. "That's what the men are telling me, sir."

"Top, get a detail together and get up there and get Elmer some help." The Sergeant Major nodded.

January 27, 1863 - Camp White Oak Church, Virginia

Crispin found Hartman shortly after the morning formation. "Top, can I talk to you for minute?"

"Yeah, Crispin, what do you want?"

"Top, Mr. Brock's our undertaker back in Moorestown. He came down to take Elwood's body home for burial. He will need help opening the grave. Can you please cut me and a few men loose to get Elwood, and can you find a detail to send Joe Conover on so he won't be here when we do it?"

The 1st Sergeant had a reputation for being tough. He stared at Josie for a minute and shook his head yes. "Thanks, Crispin, that's a good idea. Tell Rue I said you can have four men. I'll take care of Joe," and off he went to find something for Conover to do for the rest of the day.

Crispin found Rue. While Rue rounded up the men, Josie went and found Chaplain Abbott. Together they joined a few friends at the grave. They removed the body and put it in the coffin Brock brought with him.

It took Crispin, Brock and the four men a while to get the coffin to a usable road. Brock and Elwood were on their way to Aquia Creek by 3 o'clock. There was sadness, but comfort knowing that Elwood was going home.

When Conover returned from his detail and found out what happened, he was quiet for a while. "Did you see him, Josie?" he asked quietly.

"No, Joe, the shroud we sewed around him was intact. He is at peace."

Joe nodded and walked to his tent.

The regiment was formed for the daily dress parade. Adjutant Downes called, "Attention to General Orders Number 9."

"By direction of the President of the United States, the commanding general this day transfers command of this army to Major General Joseph Hooker. The short time that he has directed your movements has not been fruitful of victory, or any considerable advancement of our lines, but it has demonstrated an amount of courage, patience, and endurance that under more favorable circumstances would have accomplished great results. Continue to exercise these virtues; be true to your devotion to your country and the principles you have sworn to maintain; give to the brave and skillful general who has so long been identified with your organization, and who is now to command you, your full and cordial support and cooperation, and you will deserve success. In taking an affectionate leave of the entire Army, from which he separates with so much regret, he may be pardoned if he bids an especial farewell to his long-tried associates of the 9th Corps. His prayers are that God may be with you, and grant you continual success until the rebellion is crushed. By command of Major General Burnside."

Downes turned and saluted the Colonel, and the Colonel ordered the regiment to march back to camp. The men in the 23rd didn't know Burnside very well. They remembered the send-off the Army of the Potomac gave McClellan in November when Burnside assumed command. They sure didn't feel the same affection toward Burnside that the Army felt for McClellan. The forced march to Stafford Court House, the fight at Fredericksburg and the Mud March debacle had destroyed their confidence, and with it any regard they had for him. They walked quietly back to their huts and hoped Hooker would be better.

January 30, 1863 - Camp White Oak Church, Virginia

Major Allison, the brigade pay officer, sat on a sawed-off maple round. Before him was a board set up like a table on several pieces of firewood. There was an armed guard on either shoulder.

The troops, starting with A Company and progressing through the unit, lined up for their pay. The privates came first, approaching the table one at a time. As the Captain vouched for the man, Allison counted out his pay and placed it on the table before him. The man recounted the money, signed a receipt and moved off, so the process could start again. NCOs came next. Officers were paid in private.

The muster for receiving pay was onerous, but necessary. History was filled with stories of unscrupulous military paymasters padding payrolls or cheating troops. There had been some of that in the Union Army early in the war. One of the reasons for the delay in pay was implementation of procedures to make sure the abuse did not occur. Muster rolls took on the status of sacred documents, and any commander who didn't do his correctly was looking for big trouble, court martial trouble.

The effect of pay on morale is always good, especially when one gets three months' worth. The Yahoos were mired in mud and facing horrendous problems, but being paid removed one of the biggest issues they were facing. They sent most of their money home. They used the rest to buy comforts they had only dreamed of a few days before. There was a brisk business at the sutler's. With whiskey at two dollars a pint, and gambling an accepted pastime in the ranks, quite a few soldiers were as poor that night as they had been in the morning.

There were a number of ways to send money home to the families. Marcus Ward of Newark left his own business, and set up a "bureau of correspondence and collections" for the Public Aid Committee. He hired a number of clerks and established the bureau with all of the New Jersey regiments to act as conduit for safely getting the money from the field to the families. By the end of the first year of the war, he had collected and dispersed over $500,000 to families in New Jersey and every state of the Union without losing a single dime.

John Cook of Boontown and Colonel Jonathan Cook of Trenton worked with the State of New Jersey to collect and disperse military pay to the families. Troops could also count on a trusted friend going home on furlough to do the job. Doc Elmer sent $450 home to May with Major Acton.

Most of the squad was sitting around a big fire after dinner trying to keep warm. Conover, Rue, Howard and Crispin were trying to sing a few songs and keep away from the gambling and drinking that surrounded them. George Howard was just telling them the news about a huge baseball game that was played at Hilton Head, South Carolina, on Christmas Day. The 165th New York played a team of all-stars from the other regiments in front of 40,000 troops.

Joel Blakesley from H Company's 2nd platoon walked by, and Rue called for him to join them. Blakesley was much older than most of the men. He found a comfortable spot and joined them. "Joel, I heard you were in the army in the Mexican War."

"That's right. I volunteered in 1847. New Jersey raised four companies for that war. Why do you ask?"

"We were wondering if you knew General McClellan or any of the other officers."

Blakesley chuckled. "I wouldn't say I knew them. I served with a few. The army was so small, we got to see almost all the officers. Most of our senior officers now were just lieutenants and captains then, same with the Confederate officers. They were all West Pointers."

"General Brooks was down there with us. He was just a captain then, got a brevet to major for bravery at Churubusco. That's where General Kearny lost his arm. Burnside was there working on supplies. Meade was up North, and we never saw him."

"I got to see Robert E. Lee a couple times, and McClellan. They were both engineers. Stonewall Jackson and Longstreet were both down there, too."

Howard put in, "It must be tough for these men to fight each other."

"Yes, I imagine so. That story about General Bayard serving all those years with Jeb Stuart and then getting killed by Stuart's artillery is pretty sad. Say, where's George Sharp?"

"Oh, him and Terhune went off to play poker somewhere," said Conover.

Blakesley grinned. "He better win, or Mary is going to kick his ass. I got relations in Moorestown that know her, took a lot of guts for him to leave a woman as pretty as her with a ten-month-old baby and come with us."

Rue brought the conversation back. "So, what was it like down there, Joel?"

"God, it was hot, much worse than here in the summer. There were palm trees, and desert and poisonous snakes if you weren't careful." This comment brought moans from the listeners. "The dust was awful, and the people were poorer than the blacks you see around here. There was a lot of disease. I got sick a couple of times with malaria, took a long time to get well."

"How about the Mexicans, were they any good at fighting?"

"Some of their units were pretty good, but they kept trying to fight different than we did. They would form up in big lines and expect us to come fight it out with them front to front. Our officers usually flanked them or cut them down with artillery. Our guns could shoot further than theirs, and our muskets were better than theirs. When we finally got to Mexico City, there were only about 10,000 of us. General Hunt, he's our Union artillery general now, was just a lieutenant then. The man ran a 24-pounder right up to one of the gates and blew it wide open while the Mexicans were shooting at him. It was a miracle any of the crew survived. By the time it was over, there were dead horses and men from the gun crew lying all over the place. Once the gate was blown open, our infantry broke through and joined up with another column and took the city."

"Hexamer's boys say Hunt's a stuffy old fart, real old Army and goes by the book all the time."

Blakesley chuckled. "That he may be, though one thing's sure. These West Pointers know how to fight a war, and there's as many of them down South as there is up here. I think we got our work cut out for us."

"Yes, but the North has all of the factories and most of the railroads and manpower. We got more men and horses and food and ships and just about everything," said Howard.

Blakesley looked at him for a minute, and then at the fire. "Tell Obie Fish or Elwood Goodenough that. It's going to be a long war."

January 31, 1863 - Camp White Oak Church, Virginia

A pleasant evening around the campfires was brought to a close by a fall of very fine snowflakes. Within an hour it was snowing heavily. By the time the storm was over, there were more than six inches on the ground. Then it turned frigid cold.

The squad's turn for guard duty came, and each man put on every piece of clothing he had. Men who did not have shoes borrowed them from those who did. Men on guard loaned blankets to those who were not. Crispin lucked out and was chosen orderly. All he had to do was run errands for the colonel. He spent the whole guard detail in front of the fire in Colonel Ryerson's tent.

When the shift was over, Josie went back to his shelter to talk to his tent mates. Lloyd, Howard, Hibbs and he had combined their shelter halves and anything else they could find to create their four-man shelter. It wasn't very big, only about seven feet wide by ten feet long by seven feet high. The only heat in their structure was body heat from snuggling up to each other, unless they built a fire inside. That turned the shelter into a smoke house. They needed a chimney.

Josie explained what he needed to Lloyd, Howard and Hibbs. Each man set out to find as many sticks as he could. The sticks needed to be about four feet long and an inch in diameter. As they brought each load to the tent, Crispin would tie them into a rectangular frame and stack them on top of each other at the far end of the hut. Occasionally, an upright would be added to each corner and woven into place to keep it straight. Crispin borrowed a bucket from O'Neil. A clay deposit was located near the camp, and used by many who were building chimneys. He brought back bucket after bucket of clay. He used it to coat the inside and outside of the chimney to keep the sticks from catching fire. Then he built a small, flat surface out of sticks and clay, and knocked out a piece of the wall to make a fireplace in the chimney. Then, he started a little fire. The other men in the regiment who had built chimneys like this said it would take a few days to dry and harden the mud. Once completed, it would be possible to carve out a serviceable hearth. The "Crispin, Howard, Hibbs and Lloyd hearth" was well under way. They kept the little fire going.

———————

The weather was too miserable to even contemplate drilling the men, and there wasn't a shelter big enough to move people into for any kind of training. The Union Army essentially went through the daily routine of formations, roll calls, and assembled the details it needed to keep the camp going. Other than that, no one stirred out of their shelters unless they had to. Nature had imposed winter quarters, and there was nothing mere generals could do about it. The pontoons were covered with snow. The roads were so bad that units were beginning to cut every tree in sight to corduroy them just so they could get to their rations.

The artillery outfits were still trying to get their guns out of the mud. Once they did, they had to be cleaned and put back in shape for battle. Virtually everything attached to the outside of a gun carriage or caisson that was dragged through the mud had been lost. Rammer staffs, buckets, lunettes, gun carriages and ropes all had to be replaced from spares. Then, the spares had to be replaced. The precious artillery horses were given the best shelter that could be found. They were groomed daily, and when the roads were too bad for the horses to haul feed, the men hauled it for them.

Fortunately, the men were veteran enough to clean their gear without a lot of supervision. They learned in battle that a dirty weapon or poorly maintained piece of equipment was a liability. It was easier to care for equipment properly, then trust your life on something that didn't work because of your neglect. Your life might, and frequently did, count on it.

The Union Army had survived the Mud March, but they were horrifically vulnerable at the end of January in 1863. They couldn't advance. They couldn't retreat. They had plenty of supplies to feed their men and stock. Distributing them across the muddy road networks was another matter. Thousands of dead horses and mules littered the roads. The effort to keep the units supplied became the focus of the Army.

In one of history's most fortunate ironies, the Army of Northern Virginia could not take advantage of the debacle. The mud that locked the Union forces in place was just as sure to lock the Rebel forces in place if they tried to move to the west or even attack the "stuck in the mud" Union Army. The Confederates didn't have a problem distributing supplies. They had very few supplies to distribute. Confederate railroad problems and inefficiencies locked the Army of Northern Virginia into winter quarters just as firmly as mud locked in the Army of the Potomac. Shortages of food, clothing, shoes and shelter hindered the Southern forces badly, and became an increasingly strident issue throughout the south. Stalemate was the word until spring dried out the roads.

February 1, 1863 - Camp White Oak Church, Virginia

Doctors Oakley and Osborne were meeting with Ryerson in his headquarters tent to discuss Doctor Cook. Oakley was the senior surgeon in the brigade and Osborne was the 4th regiment's surgeon. Ryerson was saying, "He seemed to snap out of it for a while after the court martial, but now I am worried he's right back to drinking like he was."

Oakley nodded. "Have you noticed him drunk?"

Ryerson thought for a minute. "I wondered if he was drinking right after the Mud March, but I wasn't sure. Elmer told the Sergeant Major he was sure there was medicinal liquor unaccounted for."

"Are you satisfied with his service to the regiment?"

Ryerson sighed and slowly shook his head no. "The men really like him and they stuck up for him at the court martial, but I'm not satisfied. The Sanitary Commission inspected our hospital just before New Year's, and the stench was unbearable. We had to move it to a place with better ventilation. He should have done that on his own. Then, my sickest men had to walk back here from Aquia Creek during the Mud March because no one made arrangements for them at the hospital. If he's drinking and these incidents were caused by it, he has to go."

The doctors nodded their agreement. They inspected the hospital and found Cook with liquor on his breath during duty hours. This was enough to start an investigation, and when it was all over Oakley preferred charges for Cook's second court martial. The charges specified conduct unbecoming an officer and a gentleman, in that Surgeon William Cook "did, at various times during the month of January 1863, drink for his own pleasure, the spirituous liquors furnished by the U.S. Hospital department for the benefit of the sick of his regiment." He was also charged with "conduct to the prejudice of good order and military discipline, in that he has been, and is, addicted to the intemperate use of intoxicating drink as to produce disease, and render him incompetent to attend the duties of his position.

Hetzell, Elmer and Polhemus had stood by Cook in October, but they were not about to lie to protect him this time. Oakley named them as witnesses, along with Burd Grubb. Cook was relieved of duty and placed under house arrest. Bowlby took over as surgeon temporarily.

February 2, 1863 - Camp White Oak Church, Virginia

Josie was well and pleased with the recent weather. Most of the snow had melted and, while the roads were still impassable because of the mud, at least a few fields were dry enough to permit the resumption of the all-important company drill.

It was too cold to play baseball. It was difficult to pitch or bat or run with the heavy clothing on. On the other hand, the heavy clothing provided protection while playing another game, like rugby--more commonly known as football. On the morning after the first football game, a meeting was held between the surgeon and the regimental and brigade commanders.

Orders were published at the morning formation. "Attention to orders. Due to the large number of injuries that have occurred to men playing the game of football, the following is ordered. No game of football will be played without an officer in charge. The officer will permit no profanity from the players or spectators. The officer will eject any players observed gouging eyes, biting noses or ears, breaking arms, legs, or jaws or engaging in general mayhem. The command desires the troops engage in healthful sports activities, and reserve any hostility they may harbor for the enemy."

"Know ye," droned Sharp in an official voice, "That reposing special trust and confidence in the patriotism, valor, fidelity and abilities of Joseph Rue," Sharp dropped his voice and added, "and Edmund Scatterwaite," as an aside, "I do hereby appoint him sergeant in Company H of the 23rd Regiment of New Jersey Volunteers in the service of the United States, to rank as such from the first day of February, one thousand eight hundred and sixty three. He is therefore carefully and diligently to discharge the duty of sergeant by doing and performing all manner of things thereunto belonging. And I do strictly charge and require all non-commissioned officers and soldiers under his command to be obedient to his orders as sergeant. And he is to observe and follow such orders and directions from time to time, as he shall receive from me, or the future commanding officer of the Regiment or other superior officers and non-commissioned officers set over him, according to the rules and discipline of war."

"Well, there you have it. It's official. Rue and Scatterwaite are NCOs. What is the world coming to?" chuckled Crispin. The rest of the squad gathered around to look at the commissions. The commissions were parchment and were signed by Adjutant Downs and Colonel Ryerson. They looked very official with the Seal of the United States Government on the top.

"Don't forget, George Howard and Fenimore are both corporals now, too," added Hibbs.

"You fellas are going to earn the extra two dollars a month now, and you sergeants are going to make a whopping 17 dollars a month."

"Well, we have been doing the job since Sweesley passed away. I sure would rather have John back," answered Rue.

"We all would." said Hibbs, and then added, "John would be pleased with you. We all think the officers picked the right men to fill the vacancies. Is it going to be hard to learn all of the commands and such?"

"I don't think so. We have all been doing it so long. Guess we'll find out in a few minutes. With the snow gone, we have company drill this morning, and battalion drill this afternoon. You better start getting ready."

"Already it starts," exclaimed Sharp. Everybody around laughed and got ready for the formation.

The Provost Marshal called at the Colonel's tent. Falkenburgh and Clarke from A Company had deserted on January 20th, and been caught trying to stow away on a steamer at Aquia Landing. It seemed like every deserter wanted a boat ride. They were standing in irons out in front of the tent. Ryerson had the Sergeant Major send for Captain Hambrick. When Hambrick arrived, Ryerson stood the men at attention. The men did not appear sorry for deserting and still looked rebellious.

Ryerson hesitated for a minute, and then looked them straight in the eye. "General Hooker and the army are cracking down on desertion. You men are going to be court-martialed. Deserting in the face of battle is a serious offense. I doubt if you will be shot. If you are found guilty, you could get several years in Fort Jefferson." Both men paled. Fort Jefferson was a 25-acre island of sand in the Dry Tortugas off the Florida Keys. Inmate labor was slowly turning it into a fort. The place was so bad, they had to bring fresh water to it in barrels. It was where the worst prisoners in the Union Army were sent. The mere mention of a sentence there was enough to bring tears to some men's eyes. "I don't think you can be trusted in the unit, so I am sending you to the guard house in Falmouth until the court martial is convened. Dismissed."

"But... " started Falkenburgh.

"I SAID DISMISSED," roared Ryerson.

Hambrick led the thoroughly cowed pair back to the Provost Marshal. As Ryerson was going back in the tent, the Sergeant Major asked for a minute. "Sir, Private Borden, our deserter from G Company, came back and turned himself in this morning. The Provost Marshal says he arrested Lippincott yesterday, too."

"Must be my day for deserters," sighed the Colonel.

"He wants a fresh start, like you gave that Private Carr back before Christmas."

"Why would I do that? The man leaves on the eve of a battle, and he wants a fresh start?" asked Ryerson incredulously.

"Sir, he knows he was wrong. He had enough guts to admit it, and come back here on his own. He claims there's a group of men in G Company that bully him all the time. Downs knows him, and thinks he might turn out all right if you transfer him."

"I can't just look the other way when someone deserts like he did." He thought for minute. "General Hooker is death on deserters, and he is going to crack down hard on them."

"Sir, you could fine him a month's pay and then transfer him."

Ryerson thought about that for a minute, and finally nodded his head yes. "All right, have Lieutenant Downs arrange a transfer. I heard the 5th was short-handed. Maybe they will take him. Go ahead and prepare court martial charges for Lippincott. The charge is desertion."

"Yes, sir, before you go, we lost two more men to typhoid. Corporal Everham died in Portsmouth Grove Hospital on the 26th and Private Haines died over at Windmill Point. Privates Joyce, Thorn and Emery were discharged for disability in the last day or so."

"Where is Portsmouth Grove?"

"Ahh, that's in Rhode Island, sir."

"How in the world did one of my men get all the way back to Rhode Island?"

"I'll find out for you, sir. I imagine there was a steamer headed that way, and they had space for a sick man and took him."

Ryerson just shook his head. He could picture his regimental front growing shorter by the day.

———

Bowlby and Hetzell were looking at a bulletin the Brigade Surgeon had passed around. The Medical Director, Major Letterman, had identified a sudden increase in cases of scurvy in the Army of the Potomac. He had written to General Hooker, and Hooker had ordered the commissary to immediately begin issuing more bread and fresh and dried vegetables, especially onions and potatoes.

The bulletin also expressed concern about the physical condition and overall morale of the Army in general. The defeat at Fredericksburg, the experience of the Mud March, and the terrible living conditions were all taking a toll on the strength and vigor of each soldier. Letterman was concerned because weakened men were more susceptible to disease. The more men who got sick, the fewer were available if the army had to fight. Men who fought in weakened condition had more difficulty recovering from wounds.

There was also an increase in fevers and chronic diarrhea. The surgeons spoke with the Colonel, and then rounded up Downs and the 1st Sergeants. They passed the word that any man who experienced loose bowels was to be immediately put on bed rest. His intake of water and salt was to be restricted, and he was to be fed weak soups with rice, wheat or barley. A flannel scarf or cloth was to be wrapped around the belly to keep the patient warm. He was to avoid all physical activity until the condition improved.

Generally, these remedies would prevent the condition from worsening to chronic diarrhea or dysentery. If they failed, the man was to be brought to the regimental hospital immediately.

Fevers were more difficult to deal with. It was known that fewer men got sick if they washed regularly and drank water that had been boiled. Orders were reinforced to make sure personal hygiene was strictly monitored. This, and aggressive enforcement of latrine and camp sanitation policies, could go a long way toward preventing the deadly infections.

February 2, 1863 - 1st Division Army Hospital, Alexandria, Virginia
Private Hugh Capner awkwardly signed his name to his discharge papers with his left hand and walked out of Alexandria General

Hospital a civilian. Hospital helpers arranged for him to be taken to a U.S. Sanitary Commission lodge in Washington. The home was run by the Commission's Department of Special Relief.

Earlier in the war, newly discharged soldiers had been easy prey for con artists and criminals. The Sanitary Commission, The Young Men's Christian Association and the U.S. Christian Commission had all joined together to protect the newly discharged men from this heinous behavior. Lodges were set up in every major city to provide shelter and assistance for any veteran or soldier who needed it. Hafner had heard about the network from some of the other amputees in the hospital, and joined an ever-increasing number of veterans who were gratefully taking advantage of the assistance.

Hugh didn't know anyone in Washington. It was late Monday afternoon and the stores were closed. Although his wound was closed, he was still not very strong. The people at the lodge made him comfortable and got him a meal. Arrangements were made to take him to the pension office the next day. Hafner wanted to be sure his papers were in order before he left Washington. The Commission also made arrangements for his train trip back to New Jersey, and recommended accommodations if there were stops along the way. The lodge was a pleasant change from the hospital. The round-the-clock hustle and bustle of care that was constantly required for the sick and wounded had made it difficult to sleep there. He didn't miss the smell of infected wounds or chronic diarrhea, or the cries of critically sick men. For the first time in almost two months, Hugh slept peacefully.

February 3, 1863 - Camp White Oak Church, Virginia

Morning roll call always occurred right after reveille. This morning, the men were just lining up when the first fine flakes of snow began to fall. "Damn it, I was hoping spring would come early this year," grumbled Sharp. The men were flapping their arms to get warm.

"You must be kidding!" ribbed Rue. "You honestly think God is going to bring an early spring while we are living in these miserable huts? Sharp, you're daft."

Sharp grumbled a little more while the new corporals took roll. The 1st Sergeant called the company to attention and called, "Report." Each new sergeant droned, "All present or accounted for."

The 1st Sergeant took the reports, did an about-face and saluted Captain Root. "All present or accounted for, sir."

"Dismissed," ordered Root. The men fell out and went back to their shelters to cook breakfast. Those who were sick or injured walked over to the regimental hospital for sick call.

An hour later, the men formed up to get their work assignments for the day. Crispin was not on a detail, so he started looking for firewood. Today was the day to finish the hearth and fireplace. The snow fell steadily, and the wind began to rise. Soon it was starting to make drifts. Josie walked through the swirling whiteness for almost a mile before he came to a woodlot. He looked for old dead seasoned wood, and found some small pieces. Splitting off the wet, snow-covered outside would give some dry wood for fire starting. He put it in his knapsack. Then he picked up as many wood chips as he could find from where the axe men had been working. Finally, he topped off the load with some of the green wood, which was much more common. When all was said and done, he had nearly 100 pounds of fuel.

It took half an hour to walk back through the deepening snow. When he got to the shelter, he used a hatchet to split the dry wood into thumb-sized pieces about a foot long. Then he used his pocket knife to make a fist-sized pile of wood shavings. He placed these in the fireplace and struck a match. The tinder lit, and for the first time, something more than a tiny hearth-seasoning fire was introduced to the hut. Josie carefully added some of the dry thumb-sized wood to the blaze, and soon had a fire going about the size of a couple of loafs of bread. The tent started to fill up with smoke, so he opened a flap a little, and soon the warm air in the chimney started to rise. It pulled the smoke out of the tent. He stood some of the green wood on end in the chimney in the hope it would dry out a little. He smiled as the hut got warmer. Finally, he looked around the shelter for the first time in the firelight. He had light, he had warmth, he could cook without going outside and getting wet, and within seconds he had neighbors crowding in to take advantage of his innovation.

———————

"What do you mean, we are having evening dress parade?" groused Terhune. "It's snowing harder all the time, and it's colder than hell out there."

"Form up, boys. You think nobody ever marched in snow before? Put your tompions in your muzzles to keep the wet out and get ready," said Rue. "Why, the French marched all the way from Moscow to Paris in the snow."

"Yeah, because the Russians kicked their asses the whole way," sneered Terhune.

"They did?" asked Crispin.

"Corn and George, can I see you for a minute?"

"Sure, what's up, Joe?"

"Fellas, you are causing me some problems. When you complain, it makes it look like you are questioning my orders."

Terhune and Sharp exchanged glances. "Joe, we don't mean no harm," said Terhune. "We are glad you got promoted, and we don't want to cause you no trouble. It don't mean nothing."

"All right, I know that. But, I don't want to look like I am throwing my weight around, and I need some help from you. The men look up to you both."

Terhune grimaced. "Oh, come on, Joe."

"No, they do. You are both strong men in our group, and they know it. You and I will always be friends, but right now I have to be your sergeant. I am asking for you to help me do that."

Sharp pursed his lips, and he and Terhune shook their heads yes. Rue thanked them and called for the squad to form up. The dress parade in the snow was a partial success. Only half of the first section slipped and fell when the order for "column right, march" was given. The rest of the regiment stacked up behind them at "Mark time" while they sorted themselves out and got back on their feet. Ryerson and Grubb didn't know whether to laugh or cry.

February 4, 1863 - Camp White Oak Church, Virginia

The normally staid Howard was in a tizzy. After morning roll call was dismissed, he had gone to the stream to get water to brew coffee and it was frozen solid. Starting a day without coffee was not going to be good.

He tried to break the ice with a stick. It was too thick. He kicked at it with his feet; it didn't budge. Stafford County was frozen solid. It was the coldest day he could remember. He walked dejectedly back to the tent and looked in. "No coffee, boys, the water is all froze solid."

Josi looked up at him from feeding the fire in his new fireplace. During morning roll call, he had noticed smoke coming out of cracks and crevasses of neighboring structures without chimneys. Some of the troops were still trying to build fires in their huts without the proper ventilation. Sometimes they caught fire. Sometimes the men staggered out sick from smoke inhalation.

Once in a while, a whole group would go on sick call after some idiot tried to burn poison sumac for fuel. This usually resulted in evacuation to a general hospital, maddening itching and days of calamine bathes. If they got it on their hands, the first places to break out were their eyes, their face and their genitals. Then it spread to anyplace else they touched. The itching was uncontrollable.

"George, we can melt snow for coffee on the hearth. Don't get the yellow kind."

George left, only to be replaced by a frantic Sharp. "Word's out somebody killed Colonel Cook and took our pay. He had my money for Mary. They said he was carrying $100,000."

Miller heard this and came over fast. "Where'd you hear that, George?"

"It's all over camp." Miller took Sharp to Root, Root went to Ryerson. Ryerson went to brigade headquarters, and within an hour a telegram was sent to Trenton and returned. Colonel Cook was unaware of his demise, and busily seeing that the families got their money.

The news did two things for the 23rd. Of course, it soothed the rattled nerves of the troops, but it also established a firm relationship between the men and their new officers. The fact the officers cared about them enough to wire for information about their pay was gratefully acknowledged. The full story from Trenton was even better. In addition to Cook's $100,000, Marcus Ward delivered almost $50,000 from the 6th, 7th and 8th regiments and over $14,000 from the 23rd to people in Burlington County. Families all over New Jersey were buying food, fuel and necessities. Men in the field breathed a sigh of relief.

"Sir, I need to talk with you about a problem we are having in the regiment."

Ryerson looked up at the Sergeant Major. "What's that, Top?"

"Sir, the sutler is charging such high prices that I don't know if the men will tolerate it, Sir. He's been watering down the whiskey, too."

The Colonel looked at him. "Did you proof it?"

"Yes, sir, I put some whiskey in a spoon and dissolved a little gunpowder in it, and tried to light it with a match. It wouldn't burn, sir, so he is definitely watering it down."

Ryerson thought for a minute. "Are you telling me my men could become disorderly, Sergeant Major?"

"Sir, I am merely passing on information given to me by a number of 1st Sergeants. The sutler is charging such outrageous prices for his products that I am not sure his safety in camp can be assured."

Ryerson considered the information. Sutlers were merchants the army authorized to set up variety stores in tents in each regiment. For all practical purposes, they had a monopoly on products they offered to sell the troops. An abusive sutler could be a source of significant discontent in a unit.

Ryerson looked across the tent at where Grubb was working. "Burd, you hear this?"

"Yes, sir."

"I want you to go see if the sutler is gouging our men, and if he is, you put a stop to it. Torbert will be back in a few days, and I will have him revoke his franchise if I have to. I won't have disorderly conduct in my camp, and I won't have my men being taken advantage of, either."

"Yes, sir."

Grubb got his overcoat and fatigue cap and headed out the door with the Sergeant Major. They quietly walked to the sutler's tent and started looking at the prices. They were sky-high. Several men from the regiment were grousing to each other about the situation. The Sergeant Major caught their eyes, and motioned with a slight head-nod for them to leave. They fled. Grubb picked up a piece of cheesecake and listened to the sutler gush about how good it tasted and what great quality it was. Grubb put it back where he got it. "So, you are charging a day's pay for a slice of cheesecake that can be bought for pennies at any store in Washington?"

The sutler was a little defensive. "Well, sir, we are hardly in Washington, are we, sir?"

Grubb stared at him. "No, we are not. It's a rough camp out here. The guards have more things to look after than they can possibly watch. How much do think all of this stock is worth?"

The sutler looked around, grinning. "Oh, it's worth a fortune, I am sure."

"I am sure it is. We have word that there is talk in the camp of running you out of business because of your exorbitant prices. It would be a shame if your establishment was broken into and this was all taken."

The sutler looked alarmed. "Sir, you have a duty to protect my stores."

"Yes," drawled Grubb quietly, "I do. It is easily done when the men believe they are being treated fairly. I only have to protect you from the occasional thief who wants to steal some of your wares. That is much different from asking a guard to confront a mob who are rioting because they think you cheated them."

The sutler was getting defensive and agitated. "You, sir, are insulting, and I demand you leave my store."

The Sergeant Major watched Grubb quietly, and was clearly enjoying the performance. Grubb smoothly answered, "You wouldn't want me to do that. If I leave this store, two things might happen. First, my men might refuse my orders to fire on rioters to protect your stock. Second, Colonel Ryerson might have General Torbert revoke your franchise in the morning. That is, unless you quit gouging my troops. You can get rid of your watered-down whiskey, too. There are hundreds of sutlers out there that are looking for a chance to serve a regiment like this. It's your choice: start treating my men fair, or get out of camp."

The sutler was red-faced with anger. "I will be talking to my congressman about this. This is outrageous."

"You do that! Meantime, you'd better start packing. Torbert will have you closed down and gone by noon tomorrow. So, let me review a few things with you. Article 60 of the Articles of War, which we are required by law to read to our troops when they muster in, and every 6 months after, says 'all sutlers are subject to orders of commissioned officers under the rules of war.' Article 30 says 'the commander is required to see that the persons permitted to sutle, shall supply the soldiers with good, wholesome provisions at a reasonable price.' As I see it, my colonel has received complaints about your outrageous prices. I have investigated the allegations and found them to be true. Sergeant Major Downs is witness to this. So, under the Articles of War, my colonel is in trouble for not controlling your prices if you continue to operate the way you have in the past. He would also be in trouble if the troops riot and take your goods. I am not going to see my colonel in trouble over you."

The sutler gulped. He knew he could lower his prices considerably and still make a good living. "No need to be hasty, I'm sorry I lost my temper. I will examine my prices, and see if I can make some adjustments."

Grubb stared at him for a minute with a gaze that would cut glass. "You do that. Don't make me come back," he growled.

With that, he and the Sergeant Major left. They were barely out of hearing distance of the sutler's tent when Downs started laughing. "Sir, I've never seen anybody do what you just did. You absolutely had that man for lunch. How about a drink?"

"That, Sergeant Major, would be welcome. The rotten bastard deserved all of it." They walked back to the Sergeant Major's tent, and each had a shot.

It didn't take long for word to get around that there was a sale at the sutler's tent. Tensions in camp eased, and prices became a lot more reasonable. Grubb's reputation among the men was cemented in stone, but the sutler's greed couldn't take the pressure. After a few days, he packed his wares in the middle of the night and left. Three men named Keeler, Powell and Pitcher replaced him. They were honest people, and the arrangement sanctioned by Torbert benefited both the regiment and the sutlers.

February 10, 1863 - Camp White Oak Church, Virginia

Crispin was standing guard when morning light pushed back the night to bring on the new day. The last week had been a challenge. Snow, cold and disease had taken their toll on the regiment. Unknown to him, in the last week, four men had been discharged for disabilities from various hospitals on the eastern seaboard and three more had died of disease. Josie was on a post that overlooked a good part of the first and second brigade camps. He watched as dawn revealed the various patterns of each regiment's streets. The order shown by the streets in each camp revealed a story of each regiment.

The straight-line geometric accuracy of the streets in Seavor's 16th New York differed from the occasionally straight streets of the 23rd New Jersey in Torbert's Brigade. The contrast vanished as the rays of the morning sun illuminated the tents and shelters. Men were stirring. Soon, thin wisps of smoke rose from hundreds of tiny shelters. For a brief instant, the shelters looked like thousands of delicate cocoons festooned across the landscape. The scene possessed a beauty few could ever imagine in a time of war. As Crispin gazed over this surreal landscape, a small bird flew up and perched on a bush near him. It sang a merry tune. It was the first bird of spring. In a few minutes it was gone. Crispin wondered if he had seen it in his imagination, but he hadn't. The sorrowful groans of a patient in a nearby hospital tent showed him reality was very near.

He gazed over the camp and saw more sinister birds up in the sky. It seemed every raven and crow in Virginia had come to feed on the remains of the horses and mules from the Mud March. Vast gyres of turkey buzzards and vultures marked the scene of the disaster. Within minutes, the peaceful scene turned into a braying, neighing, mooing cacophony as the animals and soldiers started their daily routines.

———————

Ryerson, Grubb and Milnor were in a quandary. B and H Company's COs, Francis Higgins and David Root, had resigned along with Doctor Cook. Word had also come that Gus Grobler was going to have to resign for disability. He was not expected to recover from his illness before summer. All had good reasons, and they were certainly within their rights, but the constant flow of officers out of the regiment was a burden on everybody.

Cook didn't have much choice. He could resign with an honorable discharge or face a court martial that would certainly find him guilty, punish him and kick him out of the Army with a dishonorable discharge. His resignation was dated February 9th. Milnor recommended approval. It was certain the recommendation would be accepted.

Root was plagued with varicose veins. The strain of the mud march had aggravated an already bad condition. Thick ropes of braided blood vessels covered his legs from ankles to knees. There was no way he could continue his duties, and every day he spent in camp increased the danger of infection.

Lieutenant Shinn had done a good job in Grobler's absence. He would certainly have been promoted to Captain of E Company, but he'd resigned on February 7th. Brigade was talking about sending a Lieutenant Coursen from the 7th regiment to take the company. The problem was H Company. Lieutenant Carter was the logical man to replace Root. He had been with the company since it mustered in. He had taken Root's place as 1st Lieutenant when Root replaced McCabe in December. The problem was, he had not proven himself capable of taking command, and it was obvious to the men.

Milnor was explaining, "I spoke with Captain Root, and he, let me put this politely, was not confident in Carter's ability to command. Root says he is weak in drill, and doesn't show much interest in running the company. He does what he has to do. No initiative."

"We pass him over, and I think we are going to have trouble," said Grubb.

"We promote him to Captain and we'll have even more. Burd, I just can't promote somebody because they are next unless they are actually performing the job," added Ryerson.

"Who do you have in mind, sir?"

"I hesitate to move one of the other company commanders over, because that just disrupts another unit."

"What about bringing in an officer from one of the other regiments?" questioned Milnor.

"We could, if we absolutely had to, but these regiments are 9-month units. They muster out in June. A man would have to go back to his regiment with no guarantee a similar command would be available."

"That leaves us with promoting one of our Lieutenants. Wright's not ready, how about Taylor?" asked Grubb.

"Hetzell says he has a hernia that is bad enough to get a discharge for disability, but he's never let it interfere with his duties. He's moved around a lot, mustered in as a sergeant in A Company. We moved him to G Company and made him a 2nd Lieutenant in December. I am promoting Kirkbride to Captain to take over B Company, and was going to promote Taylor to 1st Lieutenant to fill his slot. I suppose we could promote him and have him take over H Company. He's a natural leader and gets on well with the troops."

"You have the final say, sir, and I am not second-guessing, you, but I think Carter will take this badly. Putting a junior 1st Lieutenant in command of a company over a lieutenant who is senior in date of rank is trouble. It makes him look bad in front of the men."

———

Lieutenant Carter saluted the Colonel, performed an about face, and stalked out of the Colonel's tent with tears in his eyes. He was furious. It didn't matter to him that he was sloppy in drill. He didn't care about learning the various commands, and he knew he hadn't gone out of his way to help Captain Root. He still had more time in grade than that damned newcomer Taylor, and he should have gotten command of the company.

He marched straight to his tent and sulked.

Ryerson and Grubb watched him go. "Maybe we should transfer him," said Grubb.

"No, with his attitude he would just cause problems someplace else. He's going to have to shape up or leave. He knows it. His feelings are hurt. He has not done a good job. Maybe this will wake him up," sighed the Colonel.

Lieutenant Wright came in from checking the condition of the huts. Carter told him what had happened. Wright kept his opinion to himself. He knew Ryerson was right. If something happened to H Company's Commander, Carter was not capable of taking over the job.

———

Forrester Taylor was standing at attention in the Colonel's tent. "Lieutenant Taylor, I have been hearing good things about you," began Ryerson. Grubb and Milnor were watching.

"Thank you, sir, and thank you for promoting me to 1st Lieutenant. I look forward to working with Captain Kirkbride."

The officers exchanged glances. "Taylor, do you think you can handle a company?"

Taylor's mouth dropped open. He stared at the Colonel. The expression was so genuine, the other two officers chuckled. "You mean as company commander, sir?"

"Yes, that's what I mean. I was thinking of having you take over H Company."

Taylor sputtered, "This is completely unexpected, sir. I always hoped to have a company someday, but never expected it this soon. Kirkbride and I have worked well together, and he's taught me a lot. I know the drill and regulations. Yes, sir, I think I could do it."

"All right then, I am giving you command of H Company. You will have Lieutenant Carter as 1st Lieutenant and Wright as 2nd Lieutenant. I want you to be careful with Carter. He needs supervision, and if you can help him improve his knowledge and performance, I would be very grateful. He is pretty unhappy about not getting the command, but he simply is not ready."

"Yes, sir, when is all of this to happen?"

"Captain Root's resignation is effective on the 16th. I would like to give you a couple of days to work with him before he leaves. I want you to move into the company by the 14th.

"Yes, sir, I will be ready. Thank you for the opportunity."

"Good luck, Forrest. H Company has a lot of potential. I look forward to seeing you bring them along, dismissed."

Grubb watched him walk out of the tent, "Well, Ogden, at least you made one man happy today."

"Actually, we have two happy men in camp today. Lippincott's court martial found him guilty of being absent without leave instead of desertion. They fined him two months' pay and thirty days' hard labor."

"That made him happy?"

"Yup, it's a sight better than getting shot or going to the Rip Raps. The court says if he had left while we were over the river, it would have been desertion, but since the battle was over he was only AWOL."

Civilian George Brown, formerly Lieutenant Colonel Brown, was back. Although he had resigned his commission, he still had firm friendships with the men in the regiment. He had spent most of January gathering boxes for them. When he accumulated a hefty number, he boarded a train and took them along as his baggage. Inspections were something Brown had not considered when he started his plan to bring the boxes to the troops. The U.S. Mail forwarded all boxes to the U.S. Sanitary Commission for repackaging, so they did not need to be re-inspected. The private freight companies did not enjoy the same privilege.

This was Brown's second visit. He had spent a week in camp during the Mud March, trying to deliver boxes to the men. All understood there was no way of delivering them while the Army was on the move. Now, he was stuck at Aquia Creek at the Provost Marshal's office. It seemed Army regulations required each box to be inspected for forbidden items, like whiskey. The PM had a backlog of thousands of boxes, and no amount of cajoling, pleading or arguing could move the 23rd's boxes to the beginning of the inspection line. Brown spent two days traveling back and forth to Aquia Creek and 10 days visiting the regiment, trying to break the bureaucratic log jam. Finally, he gave up and went back to Mount Holly.

February 11, 1863 - Camp White Oak Church, Virginia

Crispin was wondering if the little bird that sang to him on guard duty the day before had been an illusion. A cold rain suggested snow was not too far away. The squad was on firewood detail, and was on a two mile, one-way march to a woodlot. Firewood was so scarce that the entire Army of the Potomac's left flank and picket line had been extended to the south two miles to include more woodlots. Since Sharp had commented about wanting an early spring, the weather had been mostly awful. They were all convinced Sharp's comments had jinxed them. Sharp was reaping a continual stream of wisecracks and teasing about it.

The woodlot had a good stand of white and black oak. It was all of it would be burned green. It would have provided much better fires if it could have been seasoned. The demand required it be used immediately. They pitched in with the wood-cutting and splitting, and soon noticed an old black woman splitting wood for a "secessist" sitting on a cart nearby. This woman knew how to split wood. "So, is she a slave or is she free?" asked Howard.

"I think she's free," said Hibbs. "When President Lincoln announced the Emancipation Proclamation on January 1st, I think he freed all of the slaves."

"So why is she cutting wood for him?" Howard replied.

"Well, go ask her, you dunce."

"Excuse me, ma'am, are you a slave?"

She swung the ax and split an oak round. "Sonny, I don't know what I am. Yo Pres'dent Lincoln say I free, but Ol' Smart over there feeds me and my young'uns. He don't beat us and we get along fine. I delivered his wife's babies and she delivered mine. He can't pay me 'cause he got no money, and I can't live 'less I work for him. I guess you say I is his employee."

Howard looked around at the boys. They shrugged and went back to work. The old black woman kept swinging the ax and splitting wood. Pretty soon Lloyd elbowed Josie in the ribs. "I'll bet Sharp can't keep up with her," he whispered.

Josie looked around and caught Howard's eye. He winked and cocked his head toward Sharp. Howard smiled and nodded yes.

"Hey, Sharp. I'll bet you a dollar she can split wood better than you." Several other men added to the bet.

Sharp's back was to Josie. He slowly stood up straight, took a deep breath and turned around, "You have to be kidding. You actually think an old black woman can split wood better than I can?"

"Yup, I bet she splits more wood than you in fifteen minutes. In fact, I bet she splits more wood than anybody else here can."

Sharp was caught. "You're on."

The boys got Sharp an ax. They set up a green oak round about eighteen inches thick, and Sharp took a swing. The round didn't split. The old woman swung her ax and cut clear through her chestnut round. While the boys were setting up the next piece of wood, Sharp was still trying to get his ax out of the first. She swung again, and her second log split. Sharp finally split his first round after three swings.

By this time the black woman was on her 4th round. She won going away, and Sharp had to pay up. The squad never told Sharp what they had done. They made sure the black woman was given clear chestnut or pine rounds with no knots, and the logs were always placed upside down. Sharp's logs were selected because they had knots and were always placed right-side up. They were much harder to split that way. He never had a prayer of winning.

By 2 PM the weather had turned so miserable that the detail was sent back to quarters. They carried what firewood they could with them. They had to trek cross-country because the roads were impassable. They returned to camp in time for Isaac Wells' funeral. He had only been sick a week, but he died of typhoid fever. His G Company friends had painstakingly dug a grave at the little regimental cemetery, in ground that flowed like muck. He was laid to rest with all of the military honors they could render in a teeming, icy downpour.

February 13, 1863 - Camp White Oak Church, Virginia

Crispin was back on guard again. He was on the same post he had been several days before, when the sun made such a beautiful morning. Today it was just a cold gray dawn that made him shiver. The smell of green pine smoke was everywhere. It hugged the ground like a fog.

Sharp's jinxed weather continued unabated. An occasional good day was invariably followed by several days of rain or snow. The parade ground was so soft that it was impossible to drill. Troops not on detail were mostly idle in their tents. They worked on hobbies and crafts to pass the time. Some made buttons or rings out of brass or pieces of wood, others read or wrote letters home.

O'Neil had found some old canvas for George Howard. George rounded up a bag needle and some heavy twine, and was busy making bases for the spring baseball season.

Officers and NCOs were not idle. Even though the men could not march, staff officers like Ryerson, Grubb and Milnor were training the company officers in company and battalion drill. The Sergeant Major and some of the Lieutenants were training the NCOs in company and section drill. Some of the senior NCOs were training the corporals in the School of the Soldier and basic commands.

This was a complicated situation. All were expected to know 48 different bugle calls, which were supposed to transmit instructions for actions on the battlefield. The School of the Soldier contained the basic knowledge every troop should know to do his job. School of the Company, Battalion and Regiment each required much more in-depth knowledge of how to handle large masses of troops. Trying to teach this vital information in deplorable living conditions was difficult for everyone, officer, NCO and enlisted alike. There were few tents or structures that could seat more than twenty or thirty people at a time, and these were in constant demand for training by the other regiments.

Living conditions for everyone were bleak. Snow or rain often blew through the walls of the shelters and tents. Clothes and guns that had been painstakingly cleaned and dried overnight in the heated huts could become soaked and muddy in seconds. Fortunately, most clothing was made of wool and would keep a person warm even if it was wet. Warm did not mean comfortable.

There was a great deal of sickness. One man from C Company died of small pox, and all of the clothing that he and his tent mates had was burned, along with the tent. The quartermaster gave the tent mates a complete new issue of clothing and equipment.

The men were locked in a winter encampment almost as bad as their forefathers endured during the Revolution. Officers could resign. Enlisted could not. Life in the Army of the Potomac was tenuous.

February 14, 1863 - Camp White Oak Church, Virginia

Lieutenant Taylor's actions during the fight at Deep Run were well known in the regiment. His calm courage under fire was the stuff of numerous campfire conversations. The men of H Company were surprised that he had been promoted over Carter, but not dismayed. They were happy to have a leader who had performed well in combat, and the fact that Taylor had started out as a sergeant gave them added confidence.

Root called the officers and NCOs to his tent to say good-bye. He had spent the last two days familiarizing Taylor with the company, and introducing him to everyone. Only Lieutenant Carter was indifferent to the change. The weather was cold. The Company assembled for a short change of command ceremony. Drilling was hopeless. After it was over, Root said his good-byes, and climbed on a wagon to Falmouth to catch the train for home.

A runaway mule team nearly collided with the wagon. The runaway veered into a ditch, and one of the crazy mules rolled over on the driver. Root helped sort out the mess. The driver was a man from E Company named Pancoast. A stretcher team carried him to the regimental hospital.

Root resumed his ride toward the station. He noticed a thick column of smoke as he neared town. The Phillips House was ablaze. The fire in the beautiful old mansion was uncontrollable. Crowds of soldiers gathered round to watch it burn. It was being used as General Stoneman's Headquarters. They said some idiot tried to install a Sibley stove in the attic and set the house on fire. The building Burnside used for his headquarters during the Battle of Fredericksburg was nothing but smoking walls and stone chimneys.

Root thought it was a good day to leave Virginia.

February 15, 1863 - Camp White Oak Church, Virginia

Chaplain Abbott conducted his Sunday services in the morning, and Rue's squad was back on firewood detail in the afternoon. The woodlot they were working in was close to the Rappahannock, and was in another good stand of trees. A steady stream of wagons from various regiments loaded with firewood made their way back to the camps through the mud as best they could.

A box from Mary was waiting for Josie when the squad got back from detail. He was ecstatic. He had been waiting for it for four weeks. She had sent preserves, pickles, stewed tomatoes, candy, socks, underwear and newspapers. The Sanitary Commission Seal showed they had repacked the box and nothing was broken. Mary Crispin was very popular with Hibbs, Howard and Lloyd.

Boxes from home were a great morale booster for everyone in the unit, whether they got to share in the largesse or not. The mere knowledge that there were caring people in a safe place, far away from the mud, sickness and cold, brought comfort to everyone.

February 19, 1863 - Camp White Oak Church, Virginia

The Regimental Duty Officer shook Colonel Ryerson gently. "Colonel, the Brigade Officer of the Day is here. He needs to see you."

Grubb and Milnor were snoring in their bunks. The Duty officer had a small lamp, and Ogden sat up and rubbed his eyes. The wind was blowing sleet against the rain fly that covered the tent. The canvas made a mournful flapping sound. The fire in his fireplace was smoldering low, and the smell of burning green wood was heavy.

"What time is it?"

"It's 3:30 in the morning, sir."

"Where is he?"

"He's just on the other side of the tarp here."

Ryerson got up and put on his britches and blouse. He pulled on a pair of loafers, and asked the orderly to put some wood on the fire. Then he ducked under the tarp to the office side of the tent. A major he didn't know was waiting.

The Major identified himself and started, "Sorry to bother you, Colonel," in a low voice. "I have just inspected your guards, and they are not posted properly and have not been given proper instructions."

Ryerson frowned. He knew Lieutenant Carter was in charge of the guard. It only took a minute to get his boots, overcoat and hat. He woke Grubb up and told him what was going on, and then trudged off in the snow with the major.

It only took Ryerson and the Major about thirty minutes to find Carter. He was sound asleep. Carter was relieved of his position as 1st Lieutenant on the spot. The Colonel ordered the Sergeant of the Guard to place him under arrest and escort him to his quarters.

By now, Milnor and Grubb were up. Leaving a sleeping camp vulnerable to the enemy, regardless of the weather conditions, was intolerable in any army. The Union Army's rules of war were very clear on this type of thing. Carter was probably not going to be shot, but he was in serious trouble. There was no question. This was a Court Martial offense.

The officers spent the rest of the night in the snow and sleet, making sure the camp was secure. The guards had never seen so many officers out on a stormy night. They weren't sure what was happening, but they knew enough to be especially alert as they walked their posts.

"Burd, you told me so. Damn it, I should have listened to you," railed Ryerson.

"Ogden, you told him he wasn't measuring up. He had a choice. He could buckle down and learn the material, or he could continue the slipshod performance that got him in trouble in the first place. It's not your fault he did what he did."

"Why in the hell didn't he just resign? This is going to cause all kinds of problems for him for the rest of his life. He gets a dishonorable discharge and the press will publish the court martial in the newspapers at home, so he will be publicly humiliated."

"Well, maybe he'll get acquitted."

"Not a prayer. I caught him asleep on guard, and I have to testify under oath that I did. It's cut-and-dried dereliction of duty and violation of standing orders. Torbert knows Carter got passed over for company command, and he knows why. So, that shoots the asking for leniency because of extenuating circumstances."

"Sir, right now he is confined to his quarters over at H Company. I recommend you ask Torbert to keep him under arrest up at brigade or division. Lieutenant Taylor has enough problems on his hands as a new company commander without having a distraction like this right in front of his men."

"Good idea, Burd. Get Milnor on that right away. It will be at least a week before they can convene the general court martial." Carter was gone from H Company before noon.

February 19th was a day to remember for several reasons. First, heavy snow continued all day, and only necessary duties were carried out. This snow sifted through the cracks and crannies of every shelter, and the men were constantly plugging holes with anything they could find in the dim light of the blizzard.

The second reason was much more pleasant. The yeasty odor of fresh bread wafted through the camp on the winds of the storm. Captain Fitts, Brigade Commissary of Subsistence, had spent days building a baking oven. There were a few bakers in the New Jersey Brigade, and it didn't take much to talk them into making something to replace hardtack. The wonderful brown loaves were divvied up among the regiments, and sent off to be sliced up and distributed. Fitts was definitely the most popular man in camp.

Army fare had improved dramatically during the last few weeks under Major Letterman's supervision. Rations now included tea, dried apples, potatoes and onions, which all gave discerning chefs the tools to increase the variety and flavor of the daily meals. The men's health improved, and so did their morale.

General Hooker added another morale booster. He authorized the regiments to allow men to go home on furlough. Before this, there was little hope of a man seeing his family before his enlistment was up, unless he was on convalescent leave. This was especially true in nine-month regiments. The loosening of the travel restrictions gave everyone the hopes they would get a few days off.

February 20, 1863 - Camp White Oak Church, Virginia

The previous night had been the most miserable since the regiment mustered in. It started snowing on the 16th, and snowed for two days. Yesterday morning, the snow had changed to rain, and it rained all day and all night. Crispin and almost everyone else in the camps of the Army of the Potomac awoke to flooded huts, and ankle-deep slush and mud outside.

Hibbs was the first one up and had just swung his feet off the bed when he yelped, "Oh, shit, there's water in here!" Sure enough, the hearth was flooded, the fire was out and there was almost two feet of ice-cold water under the bed.

The boys got up and got out as best they could. After roll call they were excused from duty, as was most of the rest of the regiment, to go salvage their shelters. They cleaned out the trenches to keep new water from flowing in and dug a drain to lower the level inside. They started bailing water with coffee cups and cooking pots. Even so, they still had to borrow a bucket from O'Neil to bail the last of it out of the bottom. Eventually they got a fire going again. The day was a total loss.

Howard's precious baseball bases were waterlogged. He had to cut the carefully sewn stitches to dry out the already questionable canvas.

This was the last straw for Hooker. What had started out as Burnside's disastrous Mud March thirty days ago was now a life-and-death struggle to save the Army of the Potomac. Trains could bring supplies from Aquia Creek to Falmouth, but mud in the wagon roads to the regiments was eight feet deep. Men and animals were drowning regularly. Every time a new road was opened, it turned into quagmire within hours. The Stafford County soil simply would not support traffic. Food, fodder, firewood and supplies were not getting to man or animal. Hooker ordered brigade-sized details to start building corduroy roads. This doomed what remained of the already endangered woodlots of Stafford County.

February 21, 1863 - Camp White Oak Church, Virginia

Apparently, nature was not impressed with General Hooker. Almost 100,000 men struggled to cut trees, and carry them to be laid side-by-side for the corduroy roads. Woodlots and forests literally vanished before men's eyes. They were looking for trees four to eight inches in diameter, and they took them all. Trees that were bigger were left for firewood or lumber. Trees that were smaller were firewood.

After they were cut down and the limbs removed, they were cut into poles twelve to fifteen feet in length. A corduroy road was a road surfaced with poles placed side by side. One foot of road twelve feet wide required two logs six inches in diameter, or three that were four inches in diameter. The poles distributed the weight of a wagon, person or animal across a wide area like a floating dock. It made for a very bumpy ride, but the finished roads would permit supplies to reach the regiments.

Men struggled in mud up to their knees to move the poles into place. They toiled with shovels and pick axes to place the logs side by side. Still, it was not enough. By early afternoon the rain was falling so hard the effort was cancelled for the day. The men went back to their camps and spent the rest of the day trying warm and dry themselves and their clothes.

February 22, 1863 - Camp White Oak Church, Virginia

Washington's Birthday was observed as a holiday by a proclamation of the governor in each state, although there was growing sentiment to turn it into a national holiday,

Congress had more important things on their minds. The war consumed their attention. This holiday for the New Jersey Brigade got off to a bad start. The men awakened to blinding a snowstorm, with more than a foot on the ground. Men quickly scurried back to their shelters after morning roll call. Few stirred for the rest of the day.

Salutes were fired and officers gathered for a few toasts at the Colonel's tent. Conditions were too severe to assemble the troops. It was traditional to read the Declaration of Independence and cheer the country's first president and founding father. Nature's wrath required the tradition to be put off until the next suitable day.

February 24, 1863 - Camp White Oak Church, Virginia

Lieutenant Carter's court martial convened and found him guilty of dereliction of duty for behavior on guard duty during last week's blizzard. He was dismissed from the service and sent back to Beverly to be mustered out.

"General, I feel I am the reason that so many officers have resigned from the regiment," said Ryerson to Torbert.

"Oh, nonsense, Ogden. I sent you over there to crack the whip. You had a few leave who thought I treated them unfairly by promoting you, but that's not your fault. If they can't cut it here and want to leave, it's their prerogative." Torbert was quiet for minute. "Actually, with what we've been through in the last month I am surprised anyone who could leave is still here, and there is no end to this damnable weather and mud in sight. How are your men holding up?"

"The men seem to be doing as well as can be expected. The living conditions are horrible. Life will be a little more bearable when the corduroy road is finished, and I don't have to detail a whole company to backpack our supplies in. I do have to say, the fresh potatoes and onions have improved our diet. They are sure God-awful heavy to pack. We have to pack our firewood almost two miles, and it's all green, too."

"General Hooker has ordered every able-bodied man to work on the roads. He wants it done as fast as possible, so we can get back to delivering supplies by wagon," said Torbert. "Major Letterman told Hooker yesterday that over eight percent of the army is sick right now. That is 16,000 men a day. "

"Yes, sir, I have lost fourteen men in the last two weeks. Two died up north, three died here, and nine were discharged for medical reasons. The regiment is down almost a hundred men since I took over. We would have been better off in a battle than this damned mud." Ryerson paused. "Sir, I need some help."

"What can I do for you?"

"Sir, I need some lieutenants. I have promoted every qualified man I have in the regiment. I have a man I just promoted to 1st Lieutenant commanding H Company. We can't promote him to captain until mid April. These resignations are making it difficult to keep officers that can maneuver the troops in the field. Milnor and Grubb are training them every day we can't march."

"How many do you need?"

"Right now, I need two."

Torbert thought for a minute. "We can transfer a couple from our three-year regiments, but you can't count them on your muster."

"Yes, sir, I understand they have to return to their regiments when our nine months are up."

"That's right. I have to be careful about that, because I don't want their regiments to penalize them for being with you when it comes time for promotions. I'll talk to Sam Buck and see if he has someone over in the 2nd that can help you out."

Ryerson walked back to his tent to find another problem. Sergeant Major Brown, Abbott, a number of officers and most of C Company were waiting for him, and they were unhappy. "Sir, we have word from home that someone is saying Colonel Brown sold our boxes and pocketed the money," said Captain Newbold.

This news was so surprising and so unexpected that Ryerson just stared at them in dumbfounded amazement. He finally shook his head and said, "What?"

"I got a letter from home saying the rumor is around," replied Newbold.

"That's dumbest thing I've ever heard. The poor man spent almost two weeks down here trying to get those boxes to us."

"Sir, do you have any objection to us sending a letter to the Mirror clearing this up? Colonel Brown's integrity is being questioned, and we don't like it."

Ryerson thought for a minute. He couldn't think of any reason not to send a letter, and nodded his head to the men to go ahead. Several men spent the better part of the day putting a package of letters together. By evening, they were in the mail on the way to the New Jersey Mirror. The letters read:

To the Citizens of Mount Holly and Vicinity.

Numerous reports having been circulated prejudicial to Dr. George C. Brown, in reference to the boxes placed in his care for members of the 23rd Regiment, the following will show that Dr. B. did everything in his power to forward them to the men, and that no blame whatever attaches to him. He used every effort to ensure their prompt delivery, and their detention at Aquia Creek, was entirely beyond his control. Camp near White Oak Church, VA.

February 26, 1863.
We, the undersigned, do sincerely believe that Lieut. Col. Brown did all that man could do towards getting the boxes to us, sent by our friends from home, and moreover did more than many men would do, under the circumstances. This certificate was not solicited by Col. Brown, but by the wishes of the majority of Co. C. and the Regiment.

Sergt. Thomas Taylor	*Wm E Doron*
Sergt. H C Woodward	*Gen S Bott*
Benj. G Clark	*I R Folwell*
Corp. Seth Batchelder	*W Durand*
T Oakley Gouid	*Danel W Newcomb*
William R Haines	*Silas P Evan*
Patrick F Gorman	*Thomas H Phares*
Daniel Waterstreet	*John Gorman*
Sergt. J K Mulliner	*Jacob Flenard*
Samuel S Taylor	*Charles F Lindsay*
David Taylor	*Gavin Hamilton*
Daniel S KemptonElwood Shinn	*James Lippincott*
Ellis B Coles	*Thomas Ellis*
Geo P Havens	*William Brown*
Liet John F McKee	*William Reeves*
C Harry Alcott	*Josiah R Kirkbride*
Thomas Vankird	*Read Seaman*
William H Bowker	*Aaron Wood*
Corp Judson C Bowers	*Joseph K Filer*
Corp Chas W Alleway	*George Warren*
Adam Karg	*Samuel G Clevenger*
T B Haines	*William Stricker*
John L Warner	*William Newcomb*
JP Burnett Capt Co I	*Harry Polhemus, H S*
Liet RM Ekings	*John W Taylor*

Lieut Edw L Dobbins	**William W Curtis**
Thos J Alcott	**Josua P Adams**
Charles J Peters	**Robert Thomas**
Jos. G King	**Chas C Powell**
Isaac A King	**Thos E Akins**
John B Gaskill	**Benj Aaronson**
Job Ewan	**Charles Bell**
John K Scattergood	**John C Allinson**
Absalm B Scattergood	**Jason Cox**
	John Fields

Camp near White Oak Church
Q. M Dept 23rd Reg NJ Vol

February 26th, 1863
This is to certify that from personal knowledge I know that Dr. Geo C
Brown, (late Lieutenant Colonel of this Regiment) of Mount Holly,
has made every exertion in his power to procure the delivery of the
boxes sent in his care to the soldiers of this Regiment – that on the
first occasion when he came down with them, and spent a week, the
army was on the move; there was no prospect at all of his being able
to facilitate an early delivery of them; and this time he has spent ten
days, beside the time going and coming, and has made every possible
effort, doing all that could be done by him for their delivery to the
Regiment; and that all boxes and parcels have to be delivered to the
Provost Marshal of the Corps, for examination, and I believe that he
is fully justified in leaving the matter in the hands of the Provost
Marshal and Brigade Quartermaster for the completion.

This they pledge him, they will do as early as possible. The mass of
business on their hands is very great, but I have no doubt they will
keep their pledges to Col. Brown.

A.H. Nichols,
Quartermaster 23rd Reg NJV
We fully concur in the above statement
Wm T Abbott, Chaplain 23rd Reg NJV
Jos F Mount, Com Sergt 23d Reg NJV
Being personally concerned, we fully endorse the above
David G Hetzell
Acting Surgeon 23d Reg NJV
Robt. W Elmer
Ass't Surgeon 23d Reg NJV

Samuel Brown, Jr
Sergt. Major 23d Reg NJV
Having a personal interest in the boxes, we are prepared to endorse
the statement of Lieut. Nichols, Reg Quartermaster
J P Burnett, Capt Co I
Reading Newbold, Capt, Co. D
Henry C Risdon, Capt Co. G

Feb 25, 1863
This is to certify that the Express material for the 23rd New Jersey, in
care of G C Brown, will be forwarded as soon as it is possible to
examine it.
Thos. W Hyde
Major and Provost Marshall 6th Corps

That night a number of officers joined Ryerson, Grubb and Milnor in their tent. "I've been reading the papers, and I notice things are getting a little testy back home," opined Captain Burnett.

"How so, John?" asked Ryerson.

"That stunt about Colonel Brown today was just a symptom. We always had Copperheads back there, but a bunch of them got elected to the assembly, and they want to end the war and let the South secede. The men see it, and they don't understand what's going on."

"I heard some of my men complaining about it the other day," said Risdon. "Sometimes I think they don't pay much attention to the news or politics. Every time I do, they surprise me," added Burnett. "They sure were angry about that Attorney General's opinion about their right to vote."

Ryerson and the others were all ears. The New Jersey Attorney General had issued an opinion saying soldiers away from home could only vote if they planned on returning to New Jersey after the war. That didn't sit well with the men.

"Really? That's good to hear they are paying attention," said Ryerson.

"Oh, they are. They hang on every word in every paper and every letter. What I am hearing is that the Copperheads are spreading rumors that the Army is unfit. They say they will interfere with the draft and efforts to recruit volunteers, and they are actively trying to undermine morale at home and in the field. The rhetoric is growing more heated every week. Our morale has improved a lot since we got paid and that fresh food and bread started getting through. We have a lot of fine men here. I have to think that as our sick and wounded get home and talk about all this effort, folks will see through the lies," added Abbott.

February 28, 1863 - Camp White Oak Church, Virginia

Army regulations required a full inspection and muster of every unit on the last day of the month, rain or shine. The Articles of War were very specific about having this done correctly. More than one commander had seen his career end because of lax attention to mustering details. Those who intentionally manipulated muster rolls could expect jail time or worse. February 28th was a Saturday. The regiment formed at 9 AM. They paraded in review before opening ranks for inspection. Colonel Ryerson and Major Milnor inspected every man. The officers examined the arms, clothing, equipment and physical condition of each.

It was apparent that the H Company NCOs and 1st Sergeant Hartman were working well with Taylor and Wright. The Company looked good in spite of the last month's turmoil among the officers.

When the inspection was completed, each company was fully mustered in. Each person's name was read out loud, and the person answered present. This served two purposes. First, it provided the Commander with the information he needed to make the monthly report to the War Department required by Article 19 of the Rules of War. Second, the roll call was the basis for paying the troops. No name on the muster roll, no pay on payday. The entire process, from formation, to review, to inspection, to completion of the muster, took four hours. The regiment marched back to its quarters at 1 PM.

February 28, 1863 - Burlington, New Jersey

Franklin Ferguson had written a letter to the Dollar Newspaper. "Arrangements are now being made, by which the Sunday school children of Burlington County will present to the 23rd Regiment New Jersey volunteers a splendid stand of regimental colors, showing the desire that is in their hearts that this United Republic should be handed down to them, as it was their fathers, untrammeled by the traitor's hands. It is desired that every school in the county will participate in the offering, and make such arrangements as that each child may contribute, although it may be but the 'widow's mite.' Any person desiring to aid in this movement will have an opportunity of so doing, and any contributions they may desire to make, if left with Franklin Ferguson, will be placed to the credit of any designated school. All schools are requested to participate. The colors are ordered, and will be of rich blue silk, 6 by 6 ½ feet. On the front an oil painting of the coat-of-arms of New Jersey, with the inscription 'Presented by the Sunday School Army of Burlington County to the 23rd Regiment New Jersey Volunteers.' On the reverse side the United State's coat-of-arms encircled by 'Fredericksburg' and the '23rd New Jersey Volunteers' on the ribbon in the eagle's grasp; to be executed in Messrs. Horstman & Son's artistic style. A Union concert is proposed to be given in Burlington about the 11th of March in aid of this patriotic memorial to our brave boys. This regiment has had no colors. Any desired information will be given by Franklin Ferguson, Burlington, N.J." Dollar Newspaper, February 28th.

March 4, 1863 - Camp White Oak Church, Virginia

The changeable weather meant the regiment had to drill every opportunity it got. The new officers and NCOs could use skeleton formations to practice the marching commands, drum signals and bugle calls without the troops, but there was really no substitute for seeing how much time and space it took to actually perform the maneuvers. On the other hand, the troops needed constant refresher courses on the 48 different commands they needed to understand to do their job.

At 2 PM, the regiment started regimental drill. After practicing a few maneuvers, they were formed into a hollow square. General Torbert and his staff rode up, and the brigade adjutant read the results of a Court Martial for three deserters from the 3rd Regiment. They were sentenced to wear a ball and chain attached to their ankles for 10 days and forfeit $20 each. That was almost two months' pay. The word was out that Hooker was cracking down on AWOL and desertion.

The saga of the 23rd's officer troubles continued. Coursen needed Lieutenant Wright back in E Company. Sergeant Major Brown was promoted to 2nd Lieutenant and sent to C Company.

Torbert had spoken with Sam Buck, and the 2nd Regiment had provided two men to help with the officer shortage. Sergeant Richard Wilson from B Company and Sergeant William Hamilton from I Company were promoted to 2nd Lieutenant. Both went to H Company. Hamilton was placed in the unusual position of acting 1st Lieutenant. The whole company was being run by NCOs or men who had recently been NCOs. Their experience was invaluable.

221

JAMES G. BUCK

March 5, 1863 - Camp White Oak Church, Virginia

The regiment was formed into a hollow square after the regimental parade. Colonel Ryerson addressed the men. "Last September, Major Thompson purchased a set of national colors for the regiment. I have taken the liberty of altering it slightly. When we go into battle this spring, I want you to know I will be proud to lead you with this fine flag. I know you will be there with me. We will show the world how Jersey men fight. Color Sergeant, would you hand me the colors, please?"

Color Sergeant Mount handed Ryerson a cased flag on a staff. The colonel removed the case and unrolled the flag. "You can look to this standard to see we are victorious."

It took a few seconds for the men to see the banner. It was their American flag, the one they drilled with every day and had fought under at Fredericksburg. It had the correct number of red and white stripes. The blue field was in the right place, and there were the right number of stars, but the thing that stopped them in their tracks was the bold white lettering on the blue field. It read "23rd Regt NJ Vols," and under it in bold letters: "YAHOOS."

They looked at each other. Then they grinned. Then they looked at Ryerson, who grinned back, and then it started, a steady chant, rising in volume and crescendo. "YAHOOS. YAHOOS. YAHOOS. YAHOOS."

Men in the other regiments of the Jersey Brigade who were going about their business stopped, and heads turned toward the 23rd to see what all the commotion was about. New Yorkers, Pennsylvanians and men from Maine in the 2nd and 3rd brigades joined the spectators from the 1st. The Hoboken boys in Hexamer's battery climbed atop their caissons and looked too. It appeared the YAHOOS were here to stay, and not the least bit ashamed about it.

When the cheers died down, Ryerson spoke again. "I want you to know that Private William Ferguson from B Company was discharged for disability yesterday from the hospital at Frederick. The Ferguson family has organized the Sunday school children of Burlington County to purchase a stand of regimental colors. They are taking up a collection, and hope to have the flag to us soon. The flag will be of blue silk with the New Jersey coat-of-arms on one side and the national coat of arms on the other. We hope to have it soon." This was greeted by more cheering, and someone yelled three cheers for Bill Ferguson and then three cheers for the Sunday School Army.

Even though the afternoon had turned cold and the last few days had been stormy, the men seemed to have a lighter step as they marched back to camp. Knowing people at home were thinking of them brightened their spirits.

As they were getting supper ready, word spread throughout the camp that a balloon was up. They had seen a balloon over Stafford Heights in December, but never one close up. Many spent hours watching the strange contraption floating on the breeze.

Professor Thaddeus Lowe, Chief of Aeronautics for the Army of the Potomac, was doing what he loved best. He was 1,000 feet over White Oak Church in his balloon, the Washington, observing the Rebel camps south of the Rappahannock.

He had received orders on February 27th from Captain Candler saying Major General Butterfield directed him to put a balloon at the disposal of a Lieutenant Comstock, the Chief Engineer of the Army of the Potomac. Other orders followed directing Major-General Sedgwick to detail an officer, a sergeant and thirty-five men to assist him in preparing a balloon for observations near White Oak Church.

It took a week to get the balloon and its hydrogen generators from Washington to Falmouth. The equipment traveled over the newly completed corduroy roads to a position near the 23rd's camp. At the first break in the weather, the iron filings were thrown into the sulfuric acid to generate the hydrogen to fill the balloon. The specially coated silk cloth inflated beneath the cotton netting. The ropes held the basket in place, and Lowe had made his ascent. The balloon was ready for observation duty.

March 7, 1863 - Burlington, New Jersey

The Dollar Newspaper continued to help with The Sunday School Army's fundraising effort for the 23rd's new state colors. It reported:

Regimental Colors for the Twenty-Third

"At a meeting of the superintendents and those representing several Sunday-schools of this city it was thought advisable (for want of time to arrange a creditable concert) to change the programme, and take a voluntary offering from each school, of which the superintendent will give due notice. The response to the proposition from other parts of the county has been, thus far, very satisfactory. As almost every school in the county is represented, either by a pastor, superintendent, teacher or scholar in the 23rd Regiment, we hope that

every school will be represented in this patriotic testimonial.
Individual contributions are invited. "

The March 5th edition of the New Jersey Mirror also arrived with
the letter about Colonel Brown and the boxes. There was a smug
satisfaction among the men that it had been printed. There was no
sympathy for the lying Copperhead who started the rumor. George
Brown was ecstatic that his men had defended him so firmly.

March 9, 1863 - Camp White Oak Church, Virginia

March 9th was a very pleasant day, in fact, the nicest day of the
year so far. The spring warmth was a big morale booster for everyone.
At 11 AM, Professor Lowe made an ascent in his balloon. The 23rd was
in the middle of company drill, and the sight enthralled everyone. The
clear, unclouded sky allowed the troops the best view of the craft they
could have seen to date. The shiny globe floated in the sunlight like a
giant bubble. It was nearly impossible to continue drill as long as the
device was in the air.

Letterman's success with the reorganization of Army of the
Potomac's medical wing was beginning to pay big dividends. General
Hooker listened to his advice, and usually supported his directives to
the brigade and regimental surgeons. The men seemed stronger, and
there was some evidence that the introduction of fresh vegetables and
insistence on stringent personal and camp hygiene had cut the
incidence of disease in the army.

Lord knew they couldn't attribute it to improving weather or road
conditions. It should have been spring, but the weather continued to be
more cold and rainy or snowy than nice. A nice warm day or two was
invariably followed by several days of weather so bad, all unnecessary
activity had to be cancelled.

It was no surprise when Bowlby got another letter from the
Medical Director's office. Letterman had toured the camps and
observed the four-man huts the men had to build to survive the winter.
He recognized immediately that the huts were a health hazard.

"I have the honor to invite the attention of the Commanding
General to a practice prevalent in this Army: that of excavating the
earth, building a hut over the hole, and covering it over with brush and
dirt or canvas. This system is exceedingly pernicious and must have a

deleterious effect on the health of our troops occupying these abominable habitations."

"My hut is not an abominable habitation," said Hetzell with mock gravity. "I built that hut with my own hands, and it's all I've got. It keeps me and my pet lice alive."

"Damned right," said Elmer. "Ancient civilizations spent thousands of years trying to attain this level of sophistication."

Bowlby stared at the two men. Then all three of them burst out laughing. Peals of laughter echoed through the camp. He tried to read on while still laughing. "They are hot beds for low forms of fever, and when not productive of such diseases, the health of the men is undermined, even if they are not compelled to report sick."

Bowlby regained his composure and continued to read. "I strongly recommend that all troops that are using such huts be directed to discontinue their use, and that they be moved to new ground and either build new huts or live in tents."

"Well, that ain't likely for us," drawled Elmer. "The generals never moved us into winter quarters, so they never brought the tents and stoves we should have had. I doubt they even have them."

"Here's something we might be able to use," said Bowlby as he read on. "I also recommend that in huts covered by canvas, the covering be removed at least twice a week, if the weather permits, and that the men throughout the Army be compelled to hang their bedding in the open air every clear day: in huts not built over an excavation, but covered with brush and dirt or other material that cannot be removed, that such apertures, as Medical Directors deem necessary, be made in them, to allow light and ventilation."

"Leonard, my pet louse, won't like it," deadpanned Elmer.

Hetzell stopped in his tracks. "You actually named a louse?"

"Well, come on Bob, the damned thing is so big I painted his name on his back," drawled Elmer.

"Did that to a box turtle I caught once. I'll bet it tastes like crab," deadpanned Hetzell.

Elmer glared at Hetzell. "I can't believe you said that. No one ever names a pet they are going to eat. It's uncouth."

"Oh, so now it's a pet. The son-of-a-bitch was grazing on me this morning! I damned near…"

"Gentleman!" injected Bowlby with mock dignity. "Could you please pay attention to what the Major writes?"

Elmer and Hetzell put their hands over their mouths and took several tens of seconds to control themselves. The three looked at each other.

"Actually, airing out the huts is not a bad idea," said Elmer. "Our place could use a good airing, especially after that salt pork and beans you two cooked up last night." He collapsed in laughter, and Hetzell joined him.

Bowlby grimaced. The pork and beans had been good, but the after effects had - - - lingered. This was one discussion that just was not going to get any better. He nodded, took several breaths to gain his composure, and headed off to find the Colonel. There was wisdom in Letterman's missive, even if his tent-mates were incapable of appreciating it. Within hours the 23rd was airing their bedding and their huts.

Bob Elmer's pet louse was never seen again.

Colonel Ryerson and Major Milnor inspected the troops with a special eye toward arms, ammunition, shoes and clothing. After the inspection, the regiment joined the brigade for a dress parade on the parade ground on the north side of White Oak Church road. The brigade formed a hollow square.

Two wagons drove into the center of the square. Suddenly the canvas was thrown off, and there stood five deserters from the Mud March. They were dressed in black and white striped prison clothes and wearing handcuffs and leg irons. This mass desertion was an especially serious crime, because it was deliberately planned and involved many men from units in the brigade. The deserters had been tried and found guilty by court martial, and were here to have their sentences read and carried out. General Hooker was sending a message that this crime would not be tolerated.

The brigade adjutant read the charges and specifications contained in Headquarters, 1st Division, 6th Corps General Order 39. He announced the court had found the men guilty on all counts. Privates Plant, Haines and Cordery from I Company were sentenced to forfeit all pay and allowances for the time they were absent, plus the loss of $10 per month from their remaining pay. They were also to have half their heads closely shaved and parade before the regiment.

This didn't seem too out of line to the troops in the brigade, so there was a collective gasp when the adjutant concluded with, "and sentenced to two years' hard labor at the Rip Raps." The troops were stunned. The Rip Raps was a small, 15-acre artificial island in Hampton Roads known as Fort Calhoun. The adjutant continued reading the charges and specifications for Hays Falkenburgh and Charles Clarke.

These two were included in the leaders of the desertion, and they were found guilty on all charges and forfeited all pay and allowances. They were also to have half their heads closely shaved and closely parade before the regiment.

The troops were unprepared for the next announcement. "The men will be branded with the letter D on their left buttock in view of the brigade, and are sentenced to two years' hard labor at the Rip Raps." The men gasped louder the second time.

Similar sentences were read for men from other regiments. When the sentences had been read, several men with straight razors moved forward and dry-shaved half the hair from each man's head. They weren't real gentle about it. Blood flowed from numerous nicks and cuts. Falkenburgh and Clarke and several others had their pants dropped and were bent over a barrel as guards held their arms and legs. The hiss of the branding iron was heard above their screams as it burned the D into their flesh. The group was half dragged, half prodded by bayonet around the inside of the square to complete the humiliation. It would be an understatement to say the General made his point.

March 11, 1863 - Camp White Oak Church, Virginia

Former Sergeants Major Brown and McKee, now 2nd Lieutenants, were grinning at Scattergood. They were teasing him about his new promotion. He was the 3rd Sergeant Major since September. "By God, Abe, you'll be a 2nd Lieutenant before you know it, just like us," laughed McKee.

"Then you will be an officer and a gentleman by order of Congress. They'll need to work on that gentleman part, though."

The two officers ribbed Scattergood for a while, and he accepted the good-natured ribbing. The position of Sergeant Major was an honored institution in the Army. As senior non-commissioned officer in the regiment, no enlisted man would cross him and most officers stayed out of his way. Colonels picked their Sergeants Major very carefully. They knew that having a good one was like having an extra set of hands when it came to managing the unit.

Scattergood watched his friends walk away. "Damned shave-tail lieutenants," he grinned.

The detail sent to corduroy the roads had been dismissed early again. The weather was just too bad to proceed.

March 12, 1863 - Left Wing of the Army of the Potomac, Picket Duty on the Rappahannock River, Virginia

Something was up in the Army of the Potomac. The regiment had been turned out for picket earlier in the morning. They drew their three days' rations and headed for the extreme left flank of the Army. Major Milnor was in charge. Ryerson was back with General Brooks, acting as the Divisional Duty Officer.

Rumor had it that General Hooker was on the rampage. A Reb cavalry unit had sneaked across the river on February 25th and raided Hartwood Church. Word from headquarters was that Rebel cavalry units were trying to capture every picket they could. They were especially trying to capture men from new and inexperienced regiments. Hooker was furious. It was no secret that every officer in the Union army was conducting guard and picket duty straight by the book.

The 23rd's companies divided into six-man squads. Each squad took over a picket post, and manned it around the clock. The normal picket guard was tripled at night. Each three-man post consisted of a picket with one man standing about sixteen feet in front of the other two, and they were relieved every two hours. The idea was that one picket might be overwhelmed, but it was unlikely the other two would be captured before they could sound the alarm.

The guard posts were in the open and well in view of the Rebel encampments. Crispin's post commanded a liberal view of Rebeldom. It looked across a vast plain of level, cultivated land extending along the river for two to three miles. The intermittent spring sunshine and snow flurries made the sight hauntingly beautiful. About midway between the Rebel lines and the post stood a magnificent aristocratic plantation. It included a very large and high brick mansion, surrounded by other buildings and well-kept grounds. It was nicer than any of the other farms they had seen in Stafford County.

Late in the afternoon, a man walked out of the plantation and started toward the Union pickets. He was not well-dressed and the pickets thought he acted strangely. When he finally walked up to the post, Sharp challenged him. "Halt, who goes there?"

"I have come to pass through the lines, my friend."

"Do you have a pass, sir?"

"Yes, I have it here somewhere. Let me look." The man rifled through his pocket book, pockets and wallet for some time. "Well, I guess I must have left it home. Can't you let me pass just this once? I am going to visit my sick mother."

Sharp had had enough, he called out the guard. The other pickets passed the call down the line. "We been at war with you people almost two years, and you forgot your pass. You think we been standing out here looking at the weather? You just stand nice and still, and I won't have to shoot you." He cocked the hammer on his gun. The man stood stock-still.

When the Sergeant of the Guard and the relief came up Sharp explained the circumstances. "I think we got us a Rebel spy here, Sergeant."

The Sergeant put the man under guard and marched him to Ryerson, who sent him directly to General Brooks. The rest of the night passed slowly. Occasionally, the stars could be seen between snow flurries. A keen wind compelled the men to keep stirring, to keep from freezing their feet and hands.

March 12, 1863 - Camp White Oak Church, Virginia

During the night, Professor Lowe received new orders from Hooker's headquarters directing him to "make frequent ascensions during the day, moving the balloon from right to left along the river. The General desires that you make very close observations of the enemy, noticing any movements or work going on or changes made. Watch and note carefully all of the fords and along the riverbank. Report promptly any changes you may see."

Lowe took the balloon up early in the morning near Falmouth, but was unable to see enemy movements near the visible fords or along the roads. The camps around Fredericksburg were quiet until around 8 o'clock, when work parties started working on breast works on the low ground to the right of the city and in the woods on the first ridge. He descended soon after.

The balloon detail hooked the inflated balloon to a wagon, and carefully towed it three miles up the river. By the time they got to the new launching position, the wind was blowing too hard to safely make an ascent. They lashed it down and secured for the day. Lowe had positioned another balloon with the Allen brothers 6 miles south of Fredericksburg. They sent him a report that they had been able to make an ascent between 6 AM and 8 AM in the morning, and there was no Rebel activity as far as could be seen. Lowe forwarded both reports to headquarters.

March 13, 1863 - Left Wing of the Army of the Potomac, Picket Duty on the Rappahannock River, Virginia

The boys stood guard from 8 to 10 PM. Their relief came a few minutes after 10, and they marched back to the large pine bough shebang that served as their guardroom. A small fire in the middle made it quite comfortable. "What do you think is going on out there?" asked Lloyd

"I heard that Reb General, Fitzhugh Lee, sure pissed off Hooker," muttered Howard. "Blakesley told me General Averill knew Lee back at West Point. The cavalry weren't paying attention, and the Rebs took a hundred and fifty men prisoner in a raid. Then Fitzhugh Lee left a message asking Averill to bring him a sack of coffee. It got Hooker all upset. The General threatened to relieve all the officers in the Cavalry Corps if they didn't stop the raids."

"Yeah, that's why we are on triple picket tonight," added Hibbs. Clouds were gathering overhead again, and it was starting to spit snow.

They were back on post at 4 AM. Dawn revealed the Rebel camp south of the river. The hills were dotted with tents. "I wonder if they got better shelters than us?"

"I doubt it. The Lieutenants say they have seen the Reb pickets, and some of them don't even have uniforms. Some look like they are wearing civilian clothes."

The boys watched as a steam engine pulled a train of cars into Fredericksburg. Soon it chugged away south toward Richmond. The trains had been moving back and forth all night.

March 13, 1863 - Camp White Oak Church, Virginia

Professor Lowe took his balloons up at 5 AM, and they stayed up until 6:30. One was near White Oak Church and the other about three miles up river. All appeared quiet. No enemy movement was apparent. Smoke was visible from all of the camps, indicating the troops were still there. Camps were visible at Bowling Green, Scott's Dam, Golin Run and Taylor's Dam. There was also a new earthwork to the right of Fredericksburg with embrasures for guns. By 6:30, the weather grounded the balloons.

The big news in camp was all about Captain Hambrick. He had been given a brevet promotion to Major for his bravery during the fight at Deep Run. Everyone knew it was an appointment to higher rank for command purposes without the corresponding pay increase, but the men were pleased Hambrick had received the honor.

230

The brevet conferred special seniority on the recipient for sitting on Courts Martial or special details outside of the regiment. This meant that if group of Captains or Majors were being considered for a job in another corps, Hambrick would be considered a Major with a date of rank of March 13. The honor did not change Hambrick's seniority for duties he performed within the 23rd Regiment.

March 14, 1863 - Left Wing of the Army of the Potomac, Picket Duty on the Rappahannock River, Virginia

The monotonous two-hour picket detail, followed by 4 hours off, continued all day and night. The weather threatened storm. Things were quiet in the Rebel camps until sundown. Shortly after dark, drums sounded and signal fires were lit. Activity progressed all night long.

At noon on the 14th, the regiment was relieved by the 121st Pennsylvania from the 2nd Brigade. On the way back to camp, the companies were marched past the base of a large hill. Each halted, faced toward the hill. There was a series of burlap targets. The order "Ready, Aim, Fire," was given and the men fired their muskets for the first time since back at Beverly. The bank was perforated, the targets were largely untouched. Lieutenant Taylor was not impressed.

Neither were several officers in the camp. Standing orders were that no man was to discharge his weapon without permission. Any gunfire was assumed to be a Rebel attack. There was some discussion about regiments deciding to discharge their weapons without letting other units know what was happening in advance.

It took a while to assuage some ruffled feelings. It also took a while for Taylor to sort out how bad the shooting had been. Before the night was out, he had permission to use the large tents for percussion cap training. This training allowed each soldier to familiarize himself with squeezing the trigger on his rifle. The soldier's rifle was placed on a bench rest or something solid so he could hold the stock to his shoulder. He then looked through the sights to get the proper sight picture. A candle was lit and set 3 feet in front of the muzzle of the weapon. A percussion cap was placed on the nipple, and the soldier ordered to squeeze the trigger. If he squeezed the trigger properly, the blast of air from the cap would blow out the candle. If he jerked the trigger, the barrel would point off target and the candle would keep burning.

Each man in H Company was given ten caps to complete the exercise. Afterwards, leather cups were given to place over the percussion cap nipples so the men could practice without caps. The first volley of an engagement was crucial to bettering the odds of winning the fight. It did no good if the men were poorly trained and missed.

In the evening, the men washed out their guns and put their equipment back in order. The little bit of extra time was spent working on their baseball game.

March 17, 1863 - Camp White Oak Church, Virginia

The weather remained changeable. Monday had been disagreeable. Today was clear and warmer than the three previous days. The parade ground was still wet and unfit for extensive drill. A dry portion of a field near camp did permit limited drill by companies and small battalions.

The big news was that a cavalry battle had been fought near Kelly's Ford. General Averill had returned Fitzhugh Lee's visit to Hartwood Church. The Rebel pickets had held off the Union cavalry at the ford for several hours. Finally, the Rebs were driven back about a half-mile. They counter-attacked, only to be pushed back another mile.

Averill pulled back across the river before nightfall, leaving Lee his sack of coffee. The Union cavalry had taken seventy-eight casualties.

Josie wondered if his friends Bill Leath and Parker North in the 1st New Jersey Cavalry had been involved.

March 19, 1863 - Camp White Oak Church, Virginia

The 23rd held company drill in the morning, but they were sent on an unusual detail in the afternoon. The entire regiment was sent on a police call to clean the abandoned camps of the 12th and 15th Regiments.

These regiments had occupied a camp of huts built by the Confederate Army during the winter of '61. Letterman had noticed an increase of a deadly fever that resembled typhus in the two regiments. As many as six men a day had been dying, and these were the only regiments having the problem. He ordered the camps abandoned. They were moved into tents on higher ground.

The place was a pigpen, and the 23rd troops were offended. The filth among the tents was disgusting. Human waste, spoiled rations and spilt contents of boxes from home littered the landscape. They shoveled the debris and waste into the hovels, and set them on fire. The place was such a mess, they could not complete the task before nightfall. They returned to their camp with a new respect for personal hygiene.

When they got back, they found Hank Myers and Henry Buckley looking for George Howard. They were visiting from Hexamer's Battery to set up a baseball game. All gathered around the fire to catch up on the news from each unit.

George brought out his bases and beamed as the artillerymen admired his work. "The Hoboken boys don't have bases this nice," said Myers. "You did a good job, George."

"You should have seen him when the tents flooded and they got all wet. I thought he was going to cry," laughed Josie.

"I did cry. I had to tear them all apart, dry 'em out and start over."

"We came over to invite you to a ball game. As soon as the weather turns nice, the Hoboken Clubs are going to play. We have plenty of people interested. It will be a lot of fun," grinned Myers. "Did you hear about the Christmas Day game down at Hilton Head?"

"Yup," said Howard. "Over 40,000 men watched it. Can you imagine?"

"Did you hear about the battle up at Kelly's Ford?" asked Buckley.

"We heard our cavalry crossed for a while, but came back," said Hibbs.

"Yes, it was quite a fight. The river was running fifty-three inches, and they almost had to swim the horses over."

"Are you telling me they forded fifty-three inches?" asked Hibbs incredulously. "Hell, that's up to my armpits."

"Sure did, the 6th Battery of the New York Light got six guns across. They couldn't get wagons or the caissons over without getting everything in them wet, so they carried everything over. They put the ammunition and artillery rounds in their horse's nosebags and carried them over their shoulders. That's why they pulled back that night. Just couldn't get any infantry or enough supplies across to hold the ford."

"They each had a cannon ball tied around their necks? Sounds like a good incentive not to fall off your horse."

"It sure was. Did you hear about that Reb Major who fired the shot that killed General Bayard?"

They shook their heads no.

"He got killed up there. His name was Pehlam."

"Is that right?" asked Hibbs.

"Sure is. Word came from over the river he was visiting a girl, and went up to see the battle when it started. He got killed by a shell fragment in the back of the head. The Rebs said it was so small, they almost missed it," said Myers. "We always wondered if Hexamer was as good a shot as Pehlam. The story is Pehlam killed a Union standard bearer with the first shot from a 12-pound Napoleon at 800 yards. The man was an artillery artist. He caused us all kinds of problems at Antietam, and personally held up Meade at Franklin's Crossing for an hour with two old smoothbores. Our twenty-four guns shot everything we had at him, and he held the place until he ran out of ammunition. We are all sorry to hear he's dead, but we sure are glad we don't have face him anymore."

"So, who was better, Hexamer or Pehlam?" asked Howard.

"Bill's good, but an eighteen-inch wide target at 800 yards with a smoothbore? That's almost all luck, and we are never that lucky. Besides, Bill's still around," grinned Myers.

"I'd rather play baseball with him," said Buckley. "As soon as the weather gets better, let's all get together and play a game."

"We have to do that," smiled Howard.

Myers added, "Lieutenant Sims is the 1st New Jersey Battery B commander over in Birney's Division." Everyone knew they were camped just to the west toward Falmouth. "They have quite a team, and we have been trying to arrange a game with them for ages. Maybe you boys can come watch if we can get up a game."

March 20, 1863 - Camp White Oak Church, Virginia

The drummer beat reveille. Howard thought the noise sounded muffled. He had a sinking feeling as he looked out the flap of the hut and saw it was snowing again. "I don't think we are playing baseball for a while," he moaned.

Morning roll call was held in a blizzard. Only the most indispensable duties were assigned for the day. No one was unhappy about postponing the cleanup of the other regimental area they had worked in yesterday. The men were vocally angry about the conditions they had seen. The men gathered around the fires in their huts, and told tales about the Battle of Kelly's Ford. They also speculated about the impending battle, and what would happen to the Army of the Potomac when the spring weather arrived.

March 21, 1863 - Camp White Oak Church, Virginia

The boys got up for morning roll call in the snow again. All were present or accounted for. They cooked their breakfast and got ready for the day's brigade inspection, but the weather was awful. The inspection was postponed. The boys were sitting around their huts making small talk and working on their hobbies. Josie looked up from his diary.

"Say, did you hear the news about those fellas who got court-martialed last month?" The others shook their heads no. "I hear they took them from the Rip Raps and sent them to Fort Jefferson."

Lloyd gasped. "Ugh, I hear the place is so bad they don't hardly have to guard it. It's got a moat with sharks in it. I heard some prisoners tried to escape, and the sharks ate them. They say the guards just watched."

"That's awful," chimed in Lloyd. "News like that is enough to make a man go straight. What's all the racket from Sharp and Terhune?"

Sharp and Terhune were arguing in the next hut. "I say he didn't get treated fairly," groused Sharp.

"Lieutenant Carter was asleep on guard and he didn't make the right postings. That's what the court martial found, and they kicked him out of the Army for it," opined Terhune.

"Well, it was a shitty night and nobody was out and about. For Christ's sake, we had a foot of snow. They could have looked the other way and given him the benefit of the doubt."

"Oh, come on, George. Snow hasn't stopped those damned Rebs and their cavalry raids. What if it had been us? You think I want to spend time at Libby or Andersonville over some stupid guard mistake? And not only that, you think any of us would have gotten the benefit of the doubt if we had fallen asleep?"

"He's got you there, George," said Howard. "I liked Carter, but he was not someone I would be comfortable following in a fight. The Colonel saw that, and I am sure that's why Taylor is our CO now instead of Jim. It's too bad he got in trouble, but he's the one who got in trouble."

The controversy raged on for most of the day. A lot of people didn't think Jim Carter got a fair shake.

It snowed all day and didn't stop until the last roll call.

March 23, 1863 - Camp White Oak Church, Virginia

Sunday dawned cold and damp. The temperature was just above freezing, so there was fog and dripping water everywhere. Josie and most of the squad stood guard, while the rest of the regiment went to Sunday services with Chaplain Abbott. The sun finally broke through about noon and it became quite pleasant for a while. The men did the best they could to get the snow off their roofs and air out their huts. It was still too wet for the evening parade. Howard and the boys did manage to play catch with their baseball.

JAMES G. BUCK

March 25, 1863 - Camp White Oak Church, Virginia

After five days of waiting, and endless preparations, the weather finally cleared and the long-awaited division inspection was held. Most soldiers dread inspections, but everyone in the Army of the Potomac, from the lowliest private to General Hooker, knew this inspection had to happen. They prepared for it as if their lives depended on it. In this case, their lives did depend on it.

The Mud March disaster and the tribulations encountered since January 20th had compromised the Army's ability to fight. The infantry units questioned if the artillery would work, and the artillery wanted to know if the infantry could protect them. Everyone wanted to know if the cavalry, ambulances, wagon trains and engineers could support them.

Boots, leather, uniforms, guns, ammunition, bayonets, sabers, rucksacks, artillery pieces, caissons, ambulances, wagons, pontoons, horses, harnesses and a thousand other pieces of equipment needed to win a battle were checked. If cleaning could not restore an item to serviceability, it was destroyed. When everything was polished, blacked, oiled, mended, repaired or replaced, it was brought out for all to see.

The inspection didn't just check the equipment; each man was checked to make sure he was in condition to fight. In preparation for the inspection, the 23rd had discharged nine men on March 22nd who were unable to serve for health reasons. It would continue doing so as the need arose. The coming battle would not be kind to the weak. No detail was too small. When the inspection was over, the men were proud that they had been found to have the cleanest underwear and best cared for feet in the brigade. When all was said and done at the end of the day, the troops knew they were as good as they had been before the Mud March. That confidence raised morale.

The big news in the 23rd was that they were two-thirds of the way through their term of service. They were due to muster out in mid June. This presented a problem for the Department of War. The fact that Lincoln had called for 330,000 volunteers six months before meant the Army was going to lose those regiments right in the middle of the 1863 military campaign season.

Something had to be done. Congress had passed the Military Conscription Act on March 3rd, but it would not take effect until mid summer. Public support for the draft and the war was weakening.

Trouble was brewing on the recruiting front. The state of New York failed to recruit almost twenty-eight regiments it was committed to raise. Worse, a Lincoln opponent had been elected Governor, and he refused to help find the 28,000 men the Army needed.

The Army decided to make a deal with the volunteers it already had. Any unit that could find 400 men who would re-enlist was told they would march home to be mustered out. Those who re-enlisted would already be trained and schooled in the ways of the military, and the Army would not have to train them from scratch. They could go back on duty immediately. The rumor was 300 of the 400 had agreed to re-enlist. The men saw visions of home.

General Torbert had called all of the 23rd's officers to a meeting at his headquarters in the Montieth house. General Sedgwick and General Brooks were in attendance. The brigade Sergeant Major had also called a meeting of all of the NCOs in the regiment for later in the evening. Something big was up.

The men were standing at attention when the generals, along with Ryerson and Grubb, entered the room. They sat as the Adjutant ordered, "Take seats."

General Torbert walked to a rostrum, and glanced slowly around the room. "In September, I asked a wounded man if he would volunteer to take command of a bunch of Yahoos who were wilder than jack rabbits." Chuckles greeted his statement.

"That man took that rabble, and made them into a fighting unit I am proud to have in my brigade. The man volunteered to leave a three-year unit and command a nine-month unit. I swore to myself that if the officer was a good commander, and an opportunity came for him to have a similar command in a three-year unit, I would see that he got it."

Torbert had every man in the room's undivided attention. "That man exceeded my every expectation, and the opportunity has presented itself. Gentlemen, may I present the next Colonel of the 10th New Jersey, Colonel Henry Ogden Ryerson." Cautious applause greeted the announcement, and as the officers realized the tremendous honor and opportunity being give to their colonel, they rose to their feet and cheered.

Torbert waited for the cheering to die down. "You men have come a long way in 6 months. You fought a hopeless battle with both the enemy and the elements. You trained your men in conditions when others said it couldn't be done. You have brought the regiment through

237

the worst winter our Army has faced since Valley Forge." The generals noted the straightening postures and chests swelling with pride.

"You deserve a leader who has proven himself. May I present the next colonel of the 23rd New Jersey, Colonel, and I do mean Colonel, Burd Grubb." There was no cautious applause. The men were out of their chairs and cheering before the last word was out of his mouth. Sedgwick, Brooks, Torbert and everyone in the room beamed. In a short time, more cheers greeted the news that Milnor was moving up to Lieutenant Colonel and K Company's Parmentier was promoted to Major. Later in the evening, the Brigade Sergeant Major broke the news to the NCOs. They were as excited as the officers. The 23rd was in good hands, and so was the 10th. Word spread through the companies like wildfire. The men were happy, too.

March 26, 1863 - Camp White Oak Church, Virginia

The weather was back to its old tricks. Sometimes it snowed and sometimes it hailed, and mostly, it was just cold. Josie was on a fatigue detail to do odd jobs at the regimental hospital. Once those were completed, they were sent to the General Hospital to help with chores there.

The general hospital at White Oak Church was a few hundred yards from headquarters. It was arranged in very good order on an elevated piece of ground, and it was surrounded by a fence made of pine branches. The detail was directed to clean up a small ravine inside the enclosure and dig a ditch to drain an accumulation of surface water. Disease prevention through sanitation and drainage of standing puddles was a standard practice in camps, and particularly important around hospitals. The efforts were cutting down on the sick lists.

As the men were working on their detail, Letterman was writing of the improvements his efforts had made for the Army of the Potomac. Although his efforts were showing promise for the whole Army, March had not been good to the 23rd New Jersey. The regiment had lost 10 dead at the regimental hospital and one dead up north. Another twenty-nine had been discharged as unfit to serve in the Army. Disabilities ranged from wounds suffered at Deep Run to deafness to heart trouble to chronic diarrhea, to a continuing problem with hernias incurred during the Mud March. Almost five percent of the unit's strength had vanished in thirty days without a shot fired in anger.

The regiment held its change of command ceremony at the dress parade late in the afternoon. The companies formed a square, and the officers walked to the center.

Ryerson looked over his command for the last time. "I want to tell you how proud I am of you. The 23rd is a fine regiment of fine soldiers. We have suffered through a terrible winter, but we have stayed together and can look forward to a glorious life ahead. Thank you for the work you have done for me, and for your country. Farewell, Yahoos."

His comments were met with a call for three cheers for Colonel Ryerson. He got three cheers and more. Colonel Ryerson turned to the color guard. The color sergeant handed him the "Yahoo National Colors." Ryerson handed them to General Torbert. The General had given him the command, and now Ogden was giving it back. Torbert accepted the colors, said a few words to Ryerson and turned to Burd Grubb. He presented the colors to Colonel Grubb to show he was now giving Grubb the command. Grubb took the colors and returned them to the color guard.

The men cheered their new colonel. Miller looked over at Sharp and said, "Not bad for a twenty-one year old, eh, Sharp?"

Sharp grinned. "So, I was wrong. You fellas are never going to let me forget it."

March 27, 1863 - Camp White Oak Church, Virginia

Signs continued to show the Army of the Potomac was preparing for battle. General Torbert and a number of senior officers had been called back to Washington. Balloon flights were common every day the weather permitted. The brigade areas were being aggressively patrolled by the guards, and most telling of all, General Hooker had declared most of Stafford County off limits to civilians.

The brigade formed up for a brigade dress parade at 9 AM. The Commander of the 3rd Regiment, Colonel Brown, acted as brigade commander. The regiments practiced their maneuvers for the coming battle. Many men were hopeful they could avoid the fight. Pressure was on to find 400 men who would sign on for a three-year hitch.

March 28, 1863 - Camp White Oak Church, Virginia

Saturday dawned clear and pleasant. The regiment continued to try and make up for the training they had missed during the winter. There was company drill, rifle loading drill, practice at deploying and recalling skirmishers, and a dozen other useful maneuvers.

In the afternoon, Parmentier commanded battalion drill for the first time as the new major. They went through a few maneuvers and practiced their left wheel and right wheel marches very carefully. No one had forgotten the frightening few minutes in December when most of the six companies were a defenseless mob at the ravine.

The men noticed there were more men at drill these days. The better food and intense efforts at personal hygiene made deaths less common in camp, and fewer people were going on sick call.

Battalion drill finished, and the unit formed for the dress parade. They took their retreat roll call at the dress parade and were dismissed. Some went to watch the balloons over Falmouth, and some returned to camp for supper. After supper Howard got out his bases and O'Neil showed up with the bat, and the boys played ball.

Professor Lowe's balloon was quite close to camp. Some gathered to watch the activities. The balloon made three ascents. First, a colonel went up for a few minutes, then a major, and finally a captain. They said it looked like the Rebs were evacuating their fortifications and moving away. This caused a lot of excitement.

Toward nightfall, a cold wind blew in from the northwest. It brought a halt to the game and the balloon rides.

March 31, 1863 - Camp White Oak Church, Virginia

The day dawned bright and sunny. Most of the snow that had fallen in the last two days was melted by noon. The weather continued its monotonous changeability. It was hard to plan training, drill or even when to air out the huts and bedding, because one moment it was nice and the next it was awful.

The regiment went through its end-of-the-month inspection in much better shape than it had thirty-one days before. The men were healthier, and the prospect of being sent home to muster out early was the top thing on every man's mind. Morale was very good, getting paid on time made it even better.

Furloughs were another factor that helped improve morale. General Hooker had instituted a program back in February where commanders were authorized to send several soldiers home each week for a break. The men brought back important news, mail and packages, while getting a chance to visit friends and family and tell them about how things were in Virginia. The program had been a stunning success.

Grubb, Milnor and most of the regimental staff were standing in a patch of brush near the Rappahannock River. Grubb was looking at Rebel positions south of Fredericksburg through his new Army-issue binoculars. When it was time to leave, Milnor couldn't get on his horse. He tried several times and passed out. Grubb was by his side in an instant. "Frank, are you all right?"

"Ah, Burd, I think I've got rheumatism. Every joint in my body hurts. Let me catch my breath a minute. I am sorry."

Regimental staff crowded around them, and Grubb called for help. One of the aides went for Bowlby right away. The men got Milnor into an elevated position to help him catch his breath. Grubb felt his forehead; he was soaking wet with sweat and burning up with fever. A few minutes later he was shivering so hard, his teeth chattered.

"What is this?" asked Grubb.

"Remember when I fell in during the Mud March?" stuttered Milnor through chattering teeth.

Burd nodded yes.

"I caught a cold, and then this damned rheumatism came on. It's just gotten worse in the last day or two."

Burd thought back to the last few nights in their tent. Parmentier had moved in after Ryerson left. Parmentier was a sound sleeper, but Milnor had become more and more restless. Grubb was unhappy, he should have noticed. In hindsight he could see it.

"Get some blankets," ordered Grubb. "Bundle him up. We aren't waiting for Bowlby. Get him on his horse. Ride double if you have to and go to camp right now."

When a colonel gives an order like that, things happen fast. Men lifted Milnor into the saddle. When it was apparent he couldn't ride, one climbed on and rode bareback behind him. The man held Milnor so he wouldn't fall, and guided the horse to White Oak Church. One man galloped ahead to warn Bowlby. He and Abbott were waiting for them at the commander's tent. Bowlby put Milnor in the lower bunk. He covered him with blankets and put several hot water bottles in with him. Milnor was incoherent. In a few minutes, Bowlby came out to talk with Grubb, Parmentier and Abbott.

"Sir, he's definitely got rheumatic fever and a chest cold."

"Are you sure?"

"Yes, sir, it seems to come and go, especially if the patient gets run down. I can put him in the regimental hospital, but he might catch something else if I do. If you want to have an orderly tend your fire and keep him warm, he might be better off here."

Abbott added, "Burd, you know I will stay with him for as long as it takes."

"I know. I want him here instead of the hospital. Put him in my bed, it will be easier to take care of him than in the bunk."

Bowlby nodded. "I'll come by to check on him every few hours, and I'll send for some drugs to keep him quiet, and beef broth and some soft food. Make sure he only drinks boiled water, and keep him quiet." Grubb and Abbott nodded.

Thaddeus Lowe was back in camp after testifying before Congress about his balloon operations. He watched as the balloon detail assigned to him and the Allen brothers launched three balloons at the same time. It was glorious evening, and quite a crowd of troops gathered to watch the ascensions. The wonderful spring twilight and the calm air made for perfect conditions.

But Lowe had other things on his mind. A competitor named England had proposed to take over the Aeronautics Corps, and England didn't know what he was talking about. His statements about Lowe's management of the corps and its expenses were simply not supported by evidence any fool could observe every day in the field.

England stated it took fifteen hours to inflate a balloon with hydrogen, when, in fact, Lowe's crew routinely filled a balloon in two and a half hours. England further misstated that it took 12,000 pounds of acid and iron filings to generate enough gas to fill a balloon, when the lowliest private in the crew knew that amount of material could keep a bag up for two to three weeks.

England's attacks had to be refuted. The professor would have to spend the rest of the night setting the record straight. His experience at ballooning had been under almost constant attack since the beginning of the war, when he launched a balloon on the White House lawn for President Lincoln. While the President watched, Lowe had telegraphed a message through wire on the tether telling the President about the wonderful fifty-mile view from a basket 1,000 feet above. Lowe had more experience with hydrogen balloons than anyone in America. His observations saved Heinzelmann's Corps from Rebel envelopment at Gaines Mill, and were recognized by the Count de Joinville for "saving the day." He was not about to let England horn in on the Aeronautic

Corps when there was empirical evidence to support Lowe's demonstrated performance.

Colonel Grubb announced at the retreat roll call that 400 men of the 23rd had agreed to re-enlist for a two-year term. The men maintained their ranks and discipline, but they were barely able to contain themselves. Some were convinced they would march for Beverly in the morning for two months of recruiting duty. When the NCOs finally dismissed them, they cheered and cheered and cheered. Only a few skeptics doubted the Army would send them home early. They were right. Military necessity required the regiment to stay the whole nine months.

April 1, 1863 - Camp White Oak Church, Virginia
An obscure fact, unknown to those outside military circles, is that men away from home and family supervision will, on occasion, do things they might not otherwise do. And, so it was that April 1, 1863, dawned on the Army of the Potomac. Near anarchy reigned. It was April Fools Day. Almost all of the jokes played on tent mates and friends were harmless fun. Nevertheless, the proceedings were a trial for NCO and officer alike.

Buglers attempting to sound reveille found their instruments plugged, drummers found drumsticks missing, and many a man was unable to find one of his shoes or socks. In some cases, entire shelters had quietly disappeared overnight. Mysteriously, the guards had seen nothing. A favorite trick was to sew several stitches through a pant leg, so a man could not get his pants on. Later in the evening, the infamous short blanket was applied to many a bed.

Sharp was having a great time with a piece of thread and a twenty-five cent shinplaster. He would drop the note near an unsuspecting friend, wait for him to bend over to pick it up, and jerk the string to pull the note just out of reach at the last moment. This worked several times, until the thread gradually tore through the paper. The laugh was on Sharp when he jerked the line and the twenty-five cent paper note stayed where it was just long enough for Crispin to pick it up. Only Josiah's good nature and the fact that twenty-five cents was almost a half day's pay got the note back to Sharp.

Parmentier was supervising battalion drill in the afternoon when the mail came. A letter from Frank Ferguson addressed to Ryerson had been forwarded to Grubb. Adjutant Downes quietly entered the Colonel's tent and found Milnor propped up in Grubb's bed. Milnor was awake but groggy from his opium pill. Bowlby put a mustard plaster on his chest, and cup of water with a little camphor was boiling over a small candle flame.

"Sir, are you up to some good news?"

Milnor nodded his head weakly.

"Mister Frank Ferguson was supposed to be here last Friday to present the New Jersey Colors to us."

"Yes, I remember, he and his daughter were coming. We sent a horse and a cart over to Falmouth to pick them up, but the General closed the camps to civilians. I think they went home."

"Yes, sir, they did. They left the colors over there, and sent us a letter. Can I read it to you?"

Milnor managed to shake his head yes. Downes watched with concern. He read the letter.

Milnor thought for a minute. "I have to answer him. I just don't have the strength to do it right now." Downes nodded his agreement. Milnor said, "I want you to go find the flag. Let's get it back here, so it will be safe. We need to arrange a ceremony."

"Yes, sir, you get some rest and let me start to work on that." Milnor was too weak to protest. Downes made sure he was comfortable and left.

April 5, 1863 - Falmouth, Virginia

A warm sun rose on Easter Sunday to reveal the camp covered by several inches of snow. This was a distinct relief from the previous day, when the wind, rain and snow had actually blown some of the roofs off of the 23rd's huts. The standing joke was that this was part of Letterman's efforts to air out the bedding. Sharp, of course, was to blame for wishing for an early spring.

Sunday duties and services were held, and when all of the work was done, Companies C and E challenged G and H to a massive snowball fight. This degenerated into gigantic game of capture the flag. Eventually, the C & E boys stole the flag, and no matter how hard they tried, the G & H boys couldn't get it back.

By evening, the snow was all gone and the baseball equipment was brought out.

Rue and Miller were watching Howard and the boys play when 1st Sergeant Hartman came by. "Evening, Top, you come to play baseball?" asked Rue.

"No, I just came by to see how the boys were doing. I heard President Lincoln is over at General Hooker's headquarters in Falmouth."

Miller and Rue looked at each other. "Top, April Fool's Day was last week," smiled Rue.

"I ain't fooling. The President came down and brought his whole family to see us. We are going to have a Grand Parade for them as soon as the ground dries out."

The news spread through camp like wildfire. Abe Lincoln had come to see his army. The Commander in Chief was in camp. People started getting their equipment ready for the parade.

———————

Milnor's rheumatism was better, but he was still very weak. An aide helped him to the table in the Colonel's tent, so he could write a letter. Burlington County's Sunday School Army Colors were safely cased in the corner.

Dear Sir:

Your favor of March 27th reached me on the first instant, but suffering from a severe indisposition I was unable to answer it. I can truly assure you it was a great disappointment to us all, on learning that we were to be deprived of the pleasure of a visit from you and your daughter, which we had so much counted upon. I sent to Falmouth our horse and cart for your baggage and a horse for your use.

I received the flag (complete) yesterday afternoon. And have shown it to a few of our officers. It has been very much admired, and I can say the Twenty-Third has the handsomest stand of colors in this brigade. I regret exceedingly that you could not get here to present the flag to the regiment yourself. I have been unable to send for it before. Lieutenant Colonel Grubb has kindly consented to present it to the regiment. I am still quite weak, and unable to present it myself, as I had intended, but as I was desirous that the regiment should have it at once, requested him to do it. With many thanks to you and the Sunday School Army, on behalf of the regiment, for such a beautiful

245

JAMES G. BUCK

present, with the assurance to you and them that the Twenty-third will render a good account of themselves, and take good care of so valuable a charge.

I am very truly yours,
F.W. Milnor, Major Twenty-third Regiment N.J. Volunteers

Grubb came in, and Milnor showed him the letter. Grubb looked it over and then looked at his Lieutenant Colonel. "How are you feeling, Frank?"

"Better, Burd, thanks," he smiled weakly. "My joints don't ache as much, but Lord; I can hardly get across the tent without breaking into a sweat."

"Bowlby says you are going to be just fine if you don't overdo it."

"Yes, sir, I think you saved my life."

"Aw, you just needed some rest." Burd knew Milnor was right. He had nearly died.

"Well, at least I can get out to the latrine and sit in a chair for a while. How about I move back into my bunk?"

"Sure. Parmentier will probably complain about you, but I can handle that."

"Why, Colonel, I have treated our new major with the utmost respect at all times."

"Yeah, like that time you put the snowball in his boot. He's going to get you back for that, and I am going to just stay out of the way."

Milnor laughed. Burd was glad to see his friend on the mend. "Bowlby recommended that Lieutenant Seeds resign, and I agree with him. The poor man has had a fever and pneumonia almost constantly since the Mud March."

"E Company will be sorry to see him go," answered Milnor.

Grubb started to leave, but turned in the door, "Frank, we will wait until you can be with us to present the flag. That's an order."

That put a big grin on Milnor's face. "Thank you, sir. Colonel Ryerson put me in charge of the project when Mr. Ferguson first contacted us, and I would like to see it through."

"Good, when Doc says you are healthy enough to be out there with us, we will do it."

April 6, 1863 - Falmouth, Virginia

A 21-gun salute echoed across the valley of the Rappahannock. General Hooker and his Commander-in-Chief, President Abraham Lincoln, rode past twenty-five regiments of cheering cavalrymen on

246

Sthreshley Farm. It was the biggest parade of horse soldiers in North American history. All the men and equipment were clean, and the troops were well-dressed in their blue Union uniforms. The horses were rested and well taken care of, and the parade of artillery was intimidating. The Army's morale was excellent, a marked change from their condition after the Mud March. It took more than four hours for them to pass in review.

This parade and those on following days went down in history as the Grand Review of the Union Army. There was no question about President Lincoln's affection for his troops. The soldiers saw him and responded with cheer after cheer. Then, they got an added bonus. Lincoln's ten-year-old son, Tad, rode a pony alongside his father as they reviewed the troops. The thought of the Lincoln family, wife Mary and son Tad, living in tents, like the most common private, cemented a bond between soldier and President. Everyone knew he had a tent with a floor and a stove, but the fact that he cared enough to come see them with his family touched even the most cynical heart.

Soldiers were trading stories about having conversations with the great man, his wife, and even tall tales of son Tad being guided through the camps by Gustav Shuman, a young bugler from the New Jersey brigade.

The Army was so big that it could not be reviewed in one day. Torbert's brigade had to wait until Wednesday.

April 8, 1863 - Camp White Oak Church, Virginia

Crispin was annoyed. He could not go to the parade because he was on guard duty. He seldom liked parades and never liked guard, so this was a real emotional dilemma. He wanted to see the President, but nobody would trade duty with him.

He watched glumly as long lines of troops marched smartly toward Fredericksburg. The parade ground was on a plateau near the Lacey House. The reviewing stand and some of the parade ground could be seen by the Confederates across the river. The regiments formed up by brigades in a division front. A solid wall of Union infantry stretched off 3 miles. President Lincoln and General Hooker rode down the line, and then returned to the reviewing stand.

Then the Army of the Potomac passed in review. Regiment after regiment stepped off, until the 3rd, 4th, 5th and 6th Corps, totaling 70,000 men, were on the march.

The brigade band marched up to the reviewing stand and played as the Jersey men marched by. The brigade colors dipped to salute the President. In response, Lincoln removed his hat and held it over his heart to return the salute. He kept it there until every regiment in the brigade marched past. This was an honor no other brigade in the Army was given. General Torbert was eleated.*

The men were enthralled. There was the President, his wife and son, along with General Hooker and hundreds of cavalry as bodyguards. It was all true. The great man had come to see them.

The regiment paraded proudly with the Yahoos' national colors leading the way. Few knew of the state colors still safely hidden in the Colonel's tent. Grubb thought about how fine it would have been to have the full stand paraded before the President, but he wanted to keep his promise to Milnor. Bowlby said he would be on bed rest for at least another week. Grubb was almost past the reviewing stand when he did a double take. Doc Hetzell and Doc Elmer were standing near the President and waving to him. "How the hell did they pull that off?" he growled to the Sergeant Major.

The Sergeant Major replied, "Seems like nothing's sacred, sir."

Lincoln was impressed. This army was better than he had ever seen before. As he was leaving for Washington, he told Hooker "not to keep back any troops in the next battle. Put every man in."

The President and his entourage were not the only spectators. A good part of the Confederate Army lined Marye's Heights to watch the parade. Stafford Heights masked the Union camps, but it did not hide most of the parade ground. The procession of military might gave pause to even the most ardent secessionist. The army being amassed by

* April 8th is the last time Crispin refers to Torbert in his diary. There is some question about how long the general commanded the 1st brigade. Scherlman says he contracted bronchitis during the attack at Franklin's Crossing. By the end of December, he was too sick to stay at the division hospital and was granted medical leave to return to his doctor in Philadelphia. He returned to Camp White Oak Church on February 8 and was in command until a relapse forced him to go on medical leave from April 10 to June 27, 1863. The brigade had several acting commanders while Torbert was gone, which show up in orders of battle and correspondence, but officially he was in command of the brigade until his transfer to the cavalry late in 1863.April 10, 1863 - Camp White Oak Church, Virginia

the North was growing into a very frightening instrument of destruction.

———————

When everyone finally got back to Camp White Oak Church, Josie was still in a bad mood about being left on guard. He'd listened to the marching music and drums and salutes all day. When Sharp told him the Rebs got to see the parade and he didn't, there was a distinctly un-Quaker, out-of-character expression of profanity. Sharp and Terhune laughed for hours. They were finally one up on Crispin.

April 10, 1863 - Camp White Oak Church, Virginia

Spring was finally coming to Virginia. Pickets could see a green tinge in the woods beyond the picket lines. Blossoms and leaves were starting to appear in the tree in the dooryard of the Montieth house. It was the only tree left on the property. Crispin was on firewood detail, and the nearest wood was more than two miles away. Pleasant weather made the work a little easier.

Crispin was walking into camp when Rue called to him. "Josie, Sam Schooley and Ed Hendrickson are over at the hospital. Doc doesn't think they're going to make it."

"I know they have been sick a while, but I didn't know they were that bad."

"Doc says they've got Chicahominy fever."

"Can I go see them?" asked Crispin.

"Yes, a few of the boys are already over there. I'll be along in a few minutes."

Josie dropped his kit at his hut and quickly walked over to the hospital. Sam and Ed were very near death. The boys surrounded the beds and prayed for their friends. They tried talking to them, but got no response. A similar group from D Company gathered around George Goodwin. Josie went back to the hut to prepare supper. Sam passed away an hour later. Hendrickson and Goodwin lingered a little longer. That evening Josie and nearly a hundred men from the regiment attended services conducted by students from the Philadelphia Theological Seminary in the newly renovated White Oak Church. The seminary, the chaplains and the Christian Commission worked together to make sure the soldiers had a spiritual home to turn to when needed. The newly renovated church was a gift to the soldiers, too. Several chaplains in the brigade made a practice of renovating churches near their camps. Sometimes the men only got to use the new church for a few days, but the chaplains never gave up trying to see that their men had decent houses of worship.

April 11, 1863 - Camp White Oak Church, Virginia

Early in the day, Lloyd and Terhune walked up to the Regimental Supply Officer, Lieutenant Nichols. Terhune started, "Sir, do you have any empty cracker boxes?"

"I have a couple, but they are pretty precious. What do you want them for?"

"Well, Sir, two of our friends died last night, and we can't find any wood to make coffins for them. We thought maybe we could knock a few cracker boxes apart and make something for them."

Nichols was speechless. He had heard every line possible from people trying to get wood for beds, chimneys, tables, huts and God knows what else, and was used to routinely denying the requests. This one stopped him cold.

"Are you serious?" he asked.

"'Fraid so, Sir, we've tried everyplace else."

He looked around. "I don't have enough empties to make two coffins, and I don't have any extra lumber, either."

"Actually, Sir, we need to make three. A man from D Company died, too."

Nichols thought out loud. "I have to issue hardtack in the morning, and that will use up a couple boxes. That won't be enough. I do have an empty barrel I could keep the hardtack in for a few days. All right, you two help me dump the hardtack in that barrel. It sure won't hurt it. Then you can take the boxes."

The boys returned to camp with the cracker boxes. Sharp, Terhune and the rest of the company pitched in and built the coffins.

Interminable drill and parades continued. The weather had gone from cold winter conditions to almost summer conditions in a week. Today it was so warm that the troops were quite tired after morning drill and dress parade.

D and H companies formed up at 3 PM, and marched out of camp carrying the cracker box coffins. Grubb, Abbott and Bowlby met them at the regimental cemetery. Abbott read a Psalm and conducted the funeral ceremony. Fourteen men fired over the graves.

After the funeral, Bowlby pulled Grubb off to the side. "Sir, word is out that Major Lettermen is about to order us to set up our corps hospitals. Doc Oakley sent Torbert back to his doctor in Philadelphia yesterday. His bronchitis is back. I need to start evacuating people who can't fight back to Washington or discharge them."

Grubb nodded. "How many are you talking about?"

"I have six I am going to discharge. They are unfit for service. I have at least three men in the hospital that we need to get out of here. I understand that Britton fella we sent home last month died in Pemberton."

Grubb winced and shook his head in understanding. Just because someone got discharged, didn't mean they got well.

"And, sir, I think you should send Colonel Milnor back, too. He's at least as sick as Seeds was."

Grubb winced. He'd suspected this was coming, but hoped it wasn't. "He's going to be all right, isn't he?"

"I think he will live, sir, but, if we get into a fight right now, he won't be able to keep up. He needs to go home, and I'm not comfortable giving him an order."

"All right, I will tell him," sighed Grubb. "He won't like it, though. I do want him here until we present the new regimental colors."

"That should be no problem, Sir. He just can't be out moving around much until he gets his strength back."

Grubb nodded and walked back to the tent to see Milnor.

April 14, 1863 - Camp White Oak Church, Virginia

All signs said the Army of the Potomac was getting ready to go on the offensive. Stoneman's Cavalry Corps had attempted to cross the river the day before, and been turned back by high water. Lowe's balloons were up every day and reported the Rebs were moving away from Fredericksburg. Special effort was being made to be sure the 6th Corps had an identity in the coming battle. Patches bearing a Red Greek cross had been issued to each man, so other members of the army could tell which corps they were from. It was hoped this would avoid the confusions of previous battles, where commanders could not tell which men were from which units.

Word was out the Corps hospitals were going up, and that anybody who couldn't fight was being discharged or evacuated to the rear. Bowlby, Hetzell and Elmer were dealing with the usual spate of sick call complaints before a battle. Few were serious enough to send out.

H Company said goodbye to John English. He never recovered from the twisted knee he got on the Mud March. He could stand guard and help around the camp. There was no way he could keep up in a fight.

The regiment went through its morning drills and parades for the day and went back to camp. Captain Taylor called the men together and told them what was going on. "We are going to be moving out soon, within a week or so, depending on the weather and the height of the river. Hooker doesn't want a repeat of the Mud March, so if the roads keep drying out and stay dry, we will be on the move. I want you to get ready to go. Check your ammunition and keep it dry. Pack one change of clothes and turn everything else in to O'Neil. I don't want you carrying anything that will slow you down. O'Neil will issue eight days' rations." That was greeted with wonder. They had never been given more than three. "Cook it up and keep it safe."

One of the men raised his hand. "Sir, what happened to the deal we had that if we got 400 men to re-enlist, we could go home and muster out?" Others around him growled and shook their heads in agreement.

Taylor looked them over. "I have heard a lot of people talk about that deal, but the Army can't spare us right now. I expect we will be here until our nine months is up, unless we beat Lee so bad it ends the war. Let's break this up and get ready. We could leave at any time."

They were ready to go by nightfall. Taylor let Grubb know about the questions concerning re-enlistment.

April 18, 1863 - Camp White Oak Church, Virginia

The Special Orders for guards gave another indication that a battle was coming soon. As Crispin and the squad went on duty, they were informed that the camp was sealed. No one was allowed in, and no one was allowed out without permission of the Officer in Charge. Josi was walking his post as the regiment formed up and marched to the parade ground. The brigade band was waiting for them. He could see them form into a hollow square. He went back to walking his post.

Colonel Grubb walked to the center of the square with the rest of the staff and ordered the men at ease. He glanced at his men and smiled. "Today is a great day for the Yahoos. The children in the Sunday schools that many of us attended back home have sent you a gift."

He uncased the colors, and slowly unrolled a beautiful blue flag with the coat of arms of the state of New Jersey. The men craned their necks for a better view. Grubb made a speech about preserving the Union and each man's duty to his country. He spoke of his confidence in the 23rd, and the support and expectations shown by the people back home. He spoke of wives and sweethearts and folks and Sunday school children who had come together to send this wonderful standard to the men.

"Corporal Price, front and center," commanded Grubb.

Price came to attention and marched to the Colonel.

"Corporal Price, I appoint you lance sergeant. You are not to say you protect this color with your life, for that is nothing more than any of these would do," said Grubb pointing around the square. "But I do say, protect it as your honor, for to any here I trust honor is better than life." Grubb looked around the square and could see the pride in each man's face. These men would give their lives to protect that flag.

The band played the Star Spangled Banner. Then there were three cheers for the Sunday School Army. Then, three cheers for Grubb and more band music. Then, three cheers for the New Jersey Brigade and Torbert and old Jersey. When it was all over, the troops marched back to camp, and the officers had refreshments at Grubb's tent. All the through the evening, men from the 23rd and other units in the brigade stopped by to admire the flag. Songs, toasts and conversation stretched deep into the night. Grubb and Milnor had a great time.

April 20, 1863 - Camp White Oak Church, Virginia

H and G companies came back in from picket around 1 PM. The Army was lucky it was not on the march. It had rained as hard as it did during the Mud March, and the roads were still delicate. They knew they had the next day off, so they were enjoying a baseball game and a quiet evening until the mail came. The men were reading their mail when Sharp exploded, "Why, that turncoat Copperhead son of a bitch!"

All eyes turned to George. Strong language was not unusual in camp, but the vehemence of his outburst could not to be ignored.

"Geez, George, what's got you riled?" asked Terhune.

Sharp was fuming. "I got a letter from my neighbor in Moorestown, and the son of a bitch has gone completely Copperhead. Wants to end the war, let the South secede, and asked me to help oppose the draft when I get home."

Terhune looked at Crispin and Lloyd. They all knew the writer and gathered around George to see the letter. Pretty soon they were just as upset as George. Word spread through H Company, and more men gathered. The rest of the evening was spent crafting a reply. It went out in the next day's mail, along with a copy to the New Jersey Mirror. The

JAMES G. BUCK

boys of H Company were not about to let a shirker question their service and sacrifice to save the Union, and they wanted their feelings expressed in public.

Letter from a Private in the 23rd Regiment

"Camp at White Oak Church: VA. April 20, 1863
Mr. Editor -The following letter is in answer to a letter from a Copperhead of Burlington County, to a soldier of the 23rd Regiment of NJ Volunteers. I hope you will find room for it in your columns: White Oak Church: VA. April 20, 1863

Friend H – Your cowardly letter is just received. You can better imagine, than I can define, my disgust at receiving such a contemptible and treasonable letter from one claiming to be a citizen of the American Republic; a man raised and educated under the best Government ever enjoyed by an people, who has so degenerated in the state of morality and love of Country, as to become an object of contempt, rather than of sympathy.

I blush to think that one of my old acquaintances, who, but a few months ago, boasted of love for his country and her free institutions, is today, from motives of dastardly cowardice, cringing in the attitude of supplication at the shrine of the Southern Confederacy. What has so recently come over the spirit of your dreams, that you can thus meanly repudiate both your God and your Country – The sentiments you express, savor very much of humans depravity. Have you lost all the pride of your manhood? Have you become so demoralized as thus to acknowledge yourself at once a traitor and a disgrace to the country that gave you birth?

May God, in his infinite justice, prosper and glorious cause for which our arms are contending – while to the wretched torments of fire and brimstone, in the deepest gorges of H – I, consign not only the Rebels that are in arms against our Government, but the tenfold more deserving, the cowardly wretches who openly avow themselves traitors, but who have but the moral courage to take up arms and meet us face to face on the battlefield, where we can have some means of redress; but stay at home, and while we are fighting an enemy in front, cower and spout treason in our rear.

254

If such men as Cox, Wall, Vourhees, Vallandigham and their followers, expect to receive mild treatment at the hands of this Army, they are laboring under a false delusion. The scorching flames of H – I would be to them a welcome relief, if they should be so unfortunate as to fall into the hands of our justly indignant army. You greatly mistake the loyalty of those that freely gave their blood at the battle of Fredericksburg, if for a single moment, you entertain the opinion that we will justify you in resisting the draft.

We will with one accord, lay down our lives in support of the cause for, which we enlisted; but never, till the last armed foe expires, will we ingloriously lay down our arms, as you intimated in your letter. After our term expires, we will return home, and if need be, bayonet and exterminate all such treason-mongers as you describe; and since you have taken the liberty to write such an insulting letter to me, I propose to deal plainly with you; and, in so doing, allow me to say that all of your talk about resisting the draft, and dying on your doorsills, &c, is merely cowardly bombast. You and all of your stripe, lack the courage to lift an arm to oppose the draft. Besides, you say you are for peace; to oppose the draft: I suppose you think is peace. I think not. I despise a coward, as I despise a traitor; and forever hence, in my estimation, you are a cowardly traitor of the lowest order.

Only think for a moment, of a man so contemptible as to express the wish that us soldiers would join you in resisting the draft, when we came home. Go on in your mad career against the prosecution of the war, but remember the day is fast approaching when you will gladly give your right arm, to be able to recall the treasonable acts, or sentiments contained in your disgraceful letter. I have shown it to several of our Company, and they all denounce the author of such a treasonable letter, as a mean, contemptible coward, who dare not fight for, or against, his country.

With every sentiment of profound disgust, I subscribe myself forever the enemy of traitors at home, and Rebels in arms, while I am unalterably for the Union:

Moorestown,
Company H, 23d Reg., N.J. Volunteers

Near nightfall, the boys watched K Company parade toward the cemetery with another cracker-box coffin. Jim Couch died early that morning. This was K Company's second funeral this week. Jim Thomas had died while the squad was on picket.

April 22, 1863 - Falmouth, Virginia

Grubb and Parmentier saw Milnor off early in the morning. He didn't want to go, but knew it was the right thing to do. They put him in one of Lieutenant Nichol's wagons and detailed a man to drive him to the train station at Falmouth. He had orders signed by General Brooks to report to Surgeon R. B. Abbott at the hospital for officers in Georgetown.

Herman Haupt quietly surveyed the ruined railroad bridge across the Rappahannock. This would be the supply link that had to be fixed in order to supply Hooker when the Rebs were pushed out of Fredericksburg. He had stockpiles of timbers, ties, prefabricated shad belly trusses and the myriad of supplies he needed to bridge the river and push the railroad toward Richmond. This was much different than the supply situation in December. Back then, he was fighting and scraping for every piece of wood he could get his hands on. He could have bridged the river if Burnside had carried Marye's Heights. It would have been another cornstalk and beanpole bridge, but it would have worked. Probably would have torn down a lot of houses in Fredericksburg to get the lumber he needed, though. Hundreds of railroad men from all over the north were mobilizing at a camp near Falmouth. Haupt watched the river flow by and laid his plans for the bridge.

Professor Lowe was observing the Confederate positions late in the afternoon. Unobstructed views he had taken for granted several weeks before were now masked by the spring's new crop of leaves. He reported, "I should estimate that they are about three to our four. I should estimate their supports to their batteries immediately back of the city of Fredericksburg to be 10,000. Immediately opposite where General Franklin crossed, say from two to three miles from the river, and from the railroad station to the heights about one and a half mile, I should say there are 25,000 troops camped. Still farther to the left and south of the railroad, there are also several large camps. During the time I was up, I noticed many regiments on parade, near the various camps, and at one place there were three, while still farther back, I judge four miles from the river and one mile from the railroad, I saw a column of infantry moving to the right which required about twenty minutes to pass a given point, after I discovered them, and I counted what looked like seven regiments. They had no colors flying, as those that were on parade."

Crispin watched the professor from Camp White Oak Church as he made the observations. He could see two balloons up at the same time.

April 27, 1863 - Camp White Oak Church, Virginia

H Company was back on the picket line, and things were tense. The officers were warning of a Reb cavalry attack. Everyone was nervous.

Crispin walked down to the riverbank with Rue and Lloyd when they were off-duty. The Rebel pickets were visible on the other side. A kind of unspoken agreement had been reached that they wouldn't shoot at the Yankees, if the Yankees didn't shoot at them. The boys were reasonably safe.

The Rebs looked like they were in good spirits. "Look, they are playing baseball, too," pointed Lloyd. Some were playing, while others watched or just relaxed in the open.

"They don't look much like soldiers," said Lloyd. "Look, they don't even have uniforms. Looks like some of them don't even have shoes."

Rue rubbed his arm and said, "They may not look like much, but every time I see one, my arm hurts. They don't have the equipment we do, but they believe in their cause. They drill and fight in bare feet and they have less food than we do. Don't underestimate them. You saw what happened in December."

Lloyd and Crispin just nodded.

A lot was going on in the Army of the Potomac. The 5th, 11th and 12th Corps started moving toward Kelly's Ford, thirty miles above

Fredericksburg. The cavalry corps was also on the move. The boys back at Camp White Oak Church watched as two pontoon trains moved down the road toward Franklin's Crossing. Time was getting short.

April 28, 1863 - Camp White Oak Church, Virginia

5 PM - H Company was relieved from picket duty by the 5th Maine around 11 AM. They had just gotten back to camp when word came to saddle up. They checked their rations, turned their last personal items over to O'Neil and were on the march at 2:30. They set up camp at 5 PM about a quarter mile from Franklin's Crossing. The entire 6th Corps was assembled around them.

Reynolds's 1st Corps was to the south near Pollock's Mills, and Sickles 3rd Corps was between them and the 6th and slightly to the rear. The entire movement was masked by Stafford Heights. Fires were forbidden. The Rebs were in for a surprise.

11 PM - General Henry Benham was fit to be tied. Hooker had order him to have two pontoon bridges across the Rappahannock by 3:30 AM tomorrow morning, and things weren't going well. Benham had watched helplessly as sharpshooters cut his men down in December when they bridged the river. He didn't want to see it happen again. He had spoken with General Sedgwick, and suggested that a forced river crossing using the pontoon boats could provide a safe bridgehead. Sedgwick was a soldier's general, and he looked after his men as best he could.

When Benham suggested that the pontoon boats could be quietly carried to the river without alerting the Rebel pickets, Sedgwick asked him to prove it. Benham found that 72 soldiers could carry a pontoon boat in two relays. That meant 36 men would carry the pontoon part-way to the river, and be relieved by the other 36. The boats could carry 72 men each, so it was possible, if all was organized properly, to boat 6,000 men across the river very quickly. These could secure the bridgehead while the bridges were built.

Sedgwick approved the plan. There were to be two bridges at Franklin's Crossing, and two more a little further down stream near Pollack's Mill Creek. Sedgwick ordered General Pratt to be the carrying force, and General Brooks was assigned to be the crossing force. Pratt was to have his men ready to carry the boats, and they weren't there on time. Brooks was supposed to have his crossing force ready to follow each boat to the river to minimize everyone's exposure to enemy fire. The boats were ready, but the carrying force and crossing force were not. Benham could find no one in charge, and the unit commanders would not accept his orders.

The 1st New Jersey trudged into the brigade position. They were returning from Gray's Farm, where they had been the covering force for some guns from the artillery reserve. The Jersey men dozed off and on all night while Benham fussed and fumed.

April 29, 1863 - Franklin's Crossing, Fredericksburg, Virginia

0420 HRS – The first wave of twenty-three pontoon boats crossed the river with the 119th, 95th and 49th Pennsylvania regiments and part of the 32nd New York from Russell's Brigade. There was thick fog that muffled all sound. The men were within feet of the Rebel pickets before they were discovered. They captured 2 Rebels, but lost 2 killed and 8 wounded in the short, sharp skirmish. Just as the skirmish was over, heavy firing could be heard from the south as the Rebs repulsed the 1st Corp's crossing at Pollock's Mill Creek.

The remaining Rebel pickets near Franklin's Crossing retired to an earthwork. Within minutes, the Pennsylvanians mounted a fierce charge and seized the fort. While this was going on, the boats returned and picked up hundreds of Union reinforcements. By full daylight, all of Brook's Division was across. The New Jersey Brigade brought up the rear, and Doc Elmer was in the last boat. As soon as the last load was across, the engineers went to work on the bridge. In an amazing feat of pioneering prowess, the men built two floating bridges over 300 feet long in less than 1 1/2 hours. The 6th Corps started crossing right away. Later, a 3rd bridge was added.

0900 HRS – Firing was heard toward Pollack's Mill Creek. General Benham noticed very few Rebels were opposing the crossing there, and convinced General Reynolds to try again. This time the troops crossed in overwhelming strength. The bridgehead was secure by 10 AM, but by now, the engineers were tired. It took them a whole hour and forty-five minutes to build two more 300-foot bridges.

The 6th Corps consolidated its position as it listened to an intense cannonade from the direction of Fredericksburg. The picket line ran in a semi-circle from where Deep Run entered the Rappahannock to behind the ruins of the Bernard House. The Third Brigade was positioned in line of battle behind them. Later in the day, it extended its left to link up with the Pollock Mill's Creek bridgehead.

1700 HRS – The 23rd moved up to the front to relieve skirmishers from the 119th PA. H Company was stationed near a wrecked mansion.

"Feels like I've been here before," whispered Sharp. A hard rain muffled all sound.

"We have, George," answered Josie. "Deep Run's just over there a little ways, and I think that wrecked mansion is the Bernard house. Looks like the Rebs are right in front of us." He could just make out what was happening through the pouring rain and mist. It looked like men frantically digging rifle pits behind a screen of skirmishers.

"Yeah, I see 'em. Can't be more an a hundred yards away. Should we shoot?"

"Nah, not without orders. No need to kick over the apple cart just yet."

Rue and Conover came in quietly behind them. Crispin and Sharp looked around. "What's wrong?"

"Brooks put Brown in charge of the brigade and told Grubb we are too exposed out here. He wants us to pull back to a ravine by the river."

"Suits me, you want us to go now?" asked George.

Rue nodded yes, and together they quietly crept through the rain back to the ravine.

May 2, 1863 - Franklin's Crossing, Fredericksburg, Virginia

Noon - "It just don't make sense," mumbled Sharp.

"What don't make sense?" asked Terhune.

"We're supposed to be in this great battle, and we've been laying out here on the ground for two days."

"Well, George, I am sure we can find some Reb to shoot at you, if that's what you really want," piped up Lloyd.

"That's not what I am saying. I just don't understand why it's so quiet. You'd think we could hear something."

"It's alright, George. It just means the battle is out west somewhere. Somebody said they are fighting near a place called Chancellorsville. Don't worry; you'll get your chance."

"Wouldn't hurt my feelings any if we didn't get into a fight at all," replied Terhune. "We only got forty-three days left in this army. Home and free in '63 is what I say."

Lloyd grinned. "I think you got something there, Corn, 'Home and free in '63.' That could catch on."

1500 HRS – Brooks' Division was formed up for an attack, and the boys were in reserve way back in the 4th line of battle. They watched as firing broke out in front of them. The 5th Wisconsin opened up on the Rebel pickets and drove them back into their lines. A few minutes later, the 31st New York burst out of the Deep Run ravine.

They turned the Rebs' right flank in a flurry of musket fire. Drums and bugles calls echoed across the fields, and the rest of the 2nd and 3rd brigades moved forward. They stopped, loosed their volleys and pushed the Rebs back to their old positions along the railroad grade.

"There sure aren't as many Rebs there now as there were last winter," said Rue.

"Sure looks that way," answered Crispin. "Those boys charged right through the same place we got the livin' daylights beat out of us."

The conversation was interrupted as a Reb shell came screaming in and buried itself in the ground a few yards in front of them. A large fountain of dirt flew up in the air. "Hey, Sharp! You feel better now?" laughed Lloyd.

Another shell burst over the 5th Maine in a shallow valley below them and blew a man's cap high into the air. There was a strained silence as all in view looked to see if anyone was hurt. The man retrieved his hat, and a burst of laughter showed that he and his friends had gotten by unscathed. Men couldn't break ranks, but they did struggle for a better view from their lines as Hexamer's guns and the rest of the artillery opened up on the Rebel guns. The artillery duel lasted quite a while.

Within a few minutes, stretcher-bearers came by carrying several men. They saw one man carried by with a hideous face wound. Another man on a stretcher was set down near them as a doctor opened the man's blouse to look at the wound.

They heard Captain Taylor tell Lieutenant Wilson, "It's Michel." Wilson just shook his head.

The squad could see the entry wound in the man's chest just below his left nipple. The doctor tried to stop the bleeding, but the lieutenant didn't last long.

By nightfall, the ground up to the Richmond Road was secure. The boys fell out and cooked their supper and coffee.

2200 HRS – The Yahoos weren't getting much sleep. Newton's Division and the rest of the 6th Corps were crossing the pontoon bridges and marching north out of the bridgehead along the ridge crest just above the river toward Fredericksburg. A sharp smattering of rifle fire echoed through the darkness as Union and Rebel skirmishers traded fire. Marching feet, muffled commands, hoof beats on the bridges and roads and the sound of moving wagons and artillery were constant. The men were "sleeping on their arms," that is, just rolled up in their wool and gum blankets with their guns ready at an instant. Rue came by and told them they would be moving soon.

May 3, 1863 - Franklin's Bridgehead, Fredericksburg

0400 HRS – Rebel artillery was firing on Newton's columns as they were marching toward Fredericksburg in the dark. The boys had occasionally heard cannon fire at night as signals, but had never seen an outright artillery battle in the dark. The muzzle flashes and exploding shells lit up the night.

0500 HRS – The drums beat assembly and the regiment formed up just before sunrise. It marched cross-country to the Old Richmond Road south of Deep Run and joined the rest of the First Brigade.

McCartney's and Rigby's batteries were in front of them shooting it out with Confederate artillery about 1,200 yards away. The brigade stood in the line of battle behind the gun line, just in case the Rebs tried to rush them. It would take only a few steps forward with an "aim" and a "fire" to unleash 3,000 ounces of lead on any attacking force.

The fight intensified as the sun slipped over the horizon at 5:13. "Looks like four brass 12-pounders in that little earthwork," said Rue. Shells were zipping back and forth. Some were shells with percussion fuses, and others were case shot timed to explode over the enemy gunners.

"Look, our boys knocked one of the Reb guns off its carriage," pointed Hullings. A cheer went up.

Minutes later, a Rebel shell burst in McCartney's position. As the smoke cleared, the crew of one of the guns picked themselves up and surveyed the damage. There were two men and four horses down. Doctors quickly took the men to the rear, while others examined the horses. As the gun crew was reorganizing itself, a sergeant shot each of the horses in the head. Within minutes the gun was back in action.

Other members of the battery started taking the harnesses off the dead horses. Spare animals were unhitched from the caissons or brought up from the rear and put in their place.

Soon, two guns from Hexamer's battery joined in. Each gun from both sides was firing about one shell per minute. There were so many guns that a cannon was firing, or a shell was bursting, somewhere along the line of about every three seconds.

Someone shouted and pointed to their left. A Rebel infantry regiment was marching out of a draw not a hundred yards to the left of McCartney's battery. The lay of the ground hid them from sight until the last minute. Drums and bugle calls alerted the 15th New Jersey to move forward. As they were doing so, McCartney turned his guns on the Rebels. In the next few minutes, each cannon fired eight rounds of canister into the Rebel ranks as fast as they could.

Canister rounds are made of a cloth or a thin metal sleeve containing hundreds of 58 caliber lead balls. They turn the 3-inch ordnance rifles into giant shotguns. The first volley hit the Rebels when they were less than seventy-five yards from the muzzles. Union troops all up and down the line gasped as they saw the effect, some vomited and others said prayers. No one ever imagined anything so violent. Men shot with canister do not fall, as they do if they are shot with rifle fire. Canister blasts holes through an entire line. The effect over a limited area is instantaneous. Blood and body parts flew in all directions. McCartney's gunners fired at their attackers as if their lives depended on it. They did. If the infantry got into the gun position, the gunners had few weapons to defend themselves. The rate of fire exceeded two rounds a minute per gun.

As this was going on, the 15th moved up and fired a volley into the Rebs, and the Rebs returned their fire. The boys watched as a number of Jersey men were knocked to the ground. Medical orderlies came running to the wounded as the regiment stood its ground. Within four minutes, the Rebel unit broke and retreated. The field was littered with their dead and wounded. Screams and groans mingled with the piteous naying of wounded horses.

Meantime, the rest of the guns concentrated their fire on the Rebel earthwork. The Rebs finally pulled their three remaining brass guns out, and brought up two 20-pounders and a 10-pound Parrott under cover from rear. Within minutes, they joined the battle. The Rebs tried to reinforce the earthwork by moving four more rifled guns into the front. The fire from the fourteen Union guns was so severe that three enemy pieces were knocked out before they could enter the position.

"My God," cried Crispin, "What a fight."

Another Reb 20-pound shell went by one of Rigby's guns, beheaded a man and killed a horse.

"Jesus, did you see that?" said Terhune. "Sharp, I hope you didn't jinx us again when you were complaining about not being in a fight yesterday."

"Yeah, me too, Corn," answered Sharp anxiously.

Seconds later, a shell burst over C Company. They watched anxiously as three men were carried to rear. Soon, word passed up and down the line that Captain Severs and two men were seriously wounded.

It was near 7 AM when the drums rolled and the Second Brigade attacked the railroad embankment. Within minutes, the Rebs were driven out. This flanked the Confederate artillery position and things quieted down. The boys watched as McCartney, Rigby and Parsons fired over 1,200 rounds at the Confederate units in a little over three hours.

1100 HRS – General Sedgwick was pleased. Marye's Heights was carried, even though it had been costly. Nearly a thousand casualties were being taken from the field. General Brooks was standing with him as he said, "Well, Bully, are your men up to taking the point?"

"Yes, sir, the Jersey Brigade has been in reserve for days, and they are spoiling for a fight."

"Good, Newton's and Howe's men got shot up pretty bad this morning. You have fresh men, and it's your turn to prove what they're made of. Get them up front and take the lead. I know you're short-handed, so I am sending you the 95th and 199th Pennsylvanians."

"Uncle John" Sedgwick and "Bully" Brooks forgot the men were still carrying five days' rations, were an unknown number of miles from an undetermined objective, and the temperatures were inching toward the 90s.

1130 HRS – Events were moving quickly. The Yahoos had listened to the sounds of an intense fight at Marye's Heights for several hours. Late in the morning news came in that Newton's Division and Burnham's Light Division had done what six heavy divisions failed to do in December. They had forced the Stone Wall. Finally, the Rebs were beaten and the position had fallen. The men were ecstatic. Howe's Division had been waiting along the ridge by the river, and had attacked the south end of the Marye's Heights Ridge. They carried it, too. Disorganized Rebel forces were fleeing along the Plank Road toward Salem Church to the west, and Early's Confederates were retreating south on the Telegraph Road. Now, there was nothing between 6th Corps and the rear of the Army of Northern Virginia.

The boys watched four companies of the 2nd New Jersey deploy as pickets in front of the 15th New Jersey. These units would be the rear guard for the Sixth Corps. The other six companies of the 2nd formed up and started toward Fredericksburg. A few minutes later, infantry units on their right started marching up the Old Richmond Road toward Fredericksburg. Hexamer's guns limbered up and trundled off. Shortly before noon, Rigby's guns march ordered. Soon McCartney's followed. Grubb had the 23rd on the move by noon. They marched by the four graves they had left by the ravine in December. Jim Coer's cracker box grave marker was the only one still standing.

264

Herman Haupt and William White watched as Union troops and guns marched up the Plank Road out of Fredericksburg. The railroad men had come across the river as soon as the heights was carried to survey what work would be required to put the railroad back in operation. They took a side trip to Marye's Heights to look at the Confederate fortifications at the stone wall. They noticed a Rebel caisson that had taken a direct hit from a Union shell. It looked like a giant hand had smashed the horses and equipment into the ground. A photographer took their picture by the wreckage.

1515 HRS – General Brooks was sitting on his horse in the middle of the Plank road about a mile west of Marye's Heights when the first Rebs appeared. He watched as forty gray cavalrymen and three artillery pieces rushed to the Plank Road and started taking up positions in a pine woods near Downman's farm house. Their pickets covered both sides of the road.

He quickly looked around and saw the Jersey Brigade coming into a wheat field from the woods behind him. They were huffing and puffing along the side of the road. An artillery unit was coming up the road, too.

It had taken longer than expected to get Brooks' Division moved to the front. They had marched towards Fredericksburg on the Old Richmond Road, but the streets in town were jammed with ambulances and units taking roll, getting resupplied and resting from the morning's attack. It took them almost three hours to march three miles through the traffic and the heat.

Colonel Grubb rode up to him and saluted. Brooks returned it and said, "Looks like these people want a fight."

"Yes, sir."

"They shouldn't be too much trouble, there isn't supposed to be anything between us and the rear of the Army of Northern Virginia. Buck's companies are going to deploy as skirmishers. I want you to make a column left and deploy your regiment with your right flank on the edge of this road. Stay about 200 paces behind the skirmishers. The 1st New Jersey will be across the road on your right, and the 3rd will be on their right. I'll get your left covered as soon as I can." The General turned to his aide. "Wheeler, go find Bartlett and tell him to hurry up and get up here."

Grubb saluted, reined his horse around. In a few seconds the 23rd heard seven loud beats on a bass drum. Commands were given and the regiment started moving into position, just as they did in drill. Grubb had just over 600 rifles, so his regimental front would be around 200 yards wide.

Company commanders and staff met Grubb and looked over their maps. The ground ahead was mostly open farmland with low ridges and a few scattered wood lots. Unlike the Wilderness, further to the west, it was pretty good maneuvering country. The Plank Road went almost due west through the center of it. The Plank Road was a toll road. The toll gate was about a mile to their west. About a half mile beyond that, on a long low ridge, were a school and a church and a wood with a very irregular wood line. The map showed the buildings were in a clearing, with the church near the road and the school sixty yards southeast of it. The road from Hamilton's Crossing passed behind the church and intersected the Plank Road. There was a small wood at the base of the ridge east of the clearing. The church was called Salem Church.

Grubb looked at his captains. "General Brooks says we have broken through the Rebel lines and are moving to attack Lee's rear near Chancellorsville. There are small Rebel forces trying to delay us, and we need to push through them. They aren't very strong. Once we beat them, we can join Hooker's attack and catch the Rebs between us. Get ready to move on my command."

1525 HRS – Burd was checking his map to the west along the Plank Road. In the back of his mind, he heard Brooks order two Pennsylvania units to start marching off to his right, and he saw Emory Upton's 121st NY start forming on his left. The next thing he knew, he was flat on his back with his horse dead at his feet. The Rebs' first cannon shot killed his horse and hit the color guard. He shook his head and started to get to up as several men ran to help. He saw the 23rd's Yahoo flag was shredded. Lieutenant Budd was writhing in agony, and three more of the color guard were down. People were struggling to put the flag back up.

At the same time, Rigby's first gun section came galloping up the road. The Reb's second shot hit his first section's sergeant and horse. A corporal leaped off a trailing horse with a knife in his hand and cut the wounded animal free of its harness. Then he half pulled, half dragged the five remaining horses of the team and their gun into a firing position just to the left of the road. The other five guns in the battery raced by and set up on the right of the road.

Burd looked around to see he wasn't going be trampled, and went to check on his wounded. Poor old Lieutenant Budd was dying. The boy wasn't the sharpest officer in the regiment, but he was the most faithful. He worked hard, and most important, the man never used the painful foot wound he suffered at Deep Run as an excuse to get out of duty. All Grubb could do was hold him while he died. Absently, he wondered why the Sunday School children's New Jersey flag was not there. He'd left it in his wagon. Bowlby and Elmer were looking after the rest. He gazed around at the remains of his horse. Too bad, he was just starting to like that animal. He looked up and down the line of his regiment. He waved to them, and they waved back.

Rigby was almost ready to fire when Lieutenant Parsons raced into the field with Hexamer's guns. He peeled off to the right at a full gallop, right in front of the muzzles of Rigby's guns. Too late, Parsons realized he was almost cannon fodder. He owed Rigby an apology. As soon as Parsons was clear, Rigby fired. Parsons had room to set up three cannons at the end of the field. The rest of his unit chafed to get into the action, but the field just wasn't big enough.

While all of this was going on, the 5th Maine formed up to the left of the 121st. This gave Brooks a line of infantry seven regiments wide, with nine guns facing forty cavalry and three guns. More Union infantry and guns were hurrying up the road to get in line.

The Rebels held their position for about twenty minutes, then they limbered up their guns and moved back down the road about a mile to the toll gate.

1600 HRS - As this was going on, General Sedgwick commandeered the home of Mr. Guest for his headquarters. General Brooks, his aide Lieutenant Wheeler, and Colonel Brown were looking at a map. "This shows the Plank Road goes through those trees over there and into a clearing. Salem Church and a school house and the road from Hamilton Crossing come into the Plank road from the left. Doesn't look like any place for a strong position for a ways," said Brooks.

Sedgwick was looking west down the Plank Road when two prisoners were brought to him.

"Where're you boys from?"

"Why, we's from Alabama, sir, and proud of it."

"And what unit would you be from?"

"Sir, we's from the 9th Alabama."

"Cadmus Wilcox's Brigade?"

"Yes, sir. Cadmus is our General."

Sedgwick sent the prisoners away. "There can't be many of them."

"Wilcox again," frowned Brooks. "He was with me in Mexico. He was classmates with McClellan and Couch at West Point. He taught infantry tactics there. The man knows his business."

"He's been a thorn in our side since the beginning of the war. That Alabama brigade's fought everywhere. It'll be a pleasure to catch him, and get shut of him and them for good. So, today's the day we get old Cadmus Wilcox." Sedgwick smiled at Guest.

1630 HRS – The retreating Rebs set their guns up in the middle of the Plank Road by the toll gate, and defied the Yanks to come after them. Union skirmishers went first, and then came the main Union line 200 paces to the rear. The Rebs looked like easy pickings. The Union formation was approaching the Confederate guns and skirmishers at the toll gate, when two gray lines of enemy infantry suddenly advanced out of the wood line near the church. The Union line halted. Brooks and Sedgwick were conferring with Brown, the senior colonel in the New Jersey Brigade, when it happened. Brooks suddenly looked up and exclaimed, "Who the hell are they?"

"I thought there was nothing between us and Lee," said Brooks as Parsons and Rigby march ordered and galloped out in front of the Union line. Just before they were ready to fire, the Confederate infantry and artillery silently disappeared back into the trees.

"Well, that wasn't much," answered Sedgwick. "The front couldn't have been more than a brigade, and not a very big one at that."

Just as he said that, the Rebel cannons that had just disappeared from the toll gate opened fire from a position near Salem Church. By this time, Rigby and Parsons were ready, and traded fire with the Rebs for ten minutes. Eventually, the Rebel artillery limbered up and rode off. As soon as they were gone, Parsons and Rigby shifted fire and started shelling the woods to see if the Rebs would show their positions. They didn't. Parsons and Rigby shelled the woods for twenty minutes and concluded nobody was going to shoot back. The infantry was ordered forward. It was hot, and they were moving fast. Sedgwick watched as the regiments moved toward the irregular wood line. He was impressed with their spirit.

It took the Union skirmishers twenty minutes to drive off the Rebs. The Rebs were from H Company, 8th Alabama, and they knew their business. They didn't go easily. The Union main line waited until they were gone, and started toward the woods.

Brooks and Lieutenant Wheeler were riding forward to be close to the troops on the left, while Brown was riding forward on the right. Sedgwick watched with satisfaction as the 5th Maine performed an echelon left and opened a space for the Gosline Zouves of the 96th Pennsylvania to squeeze between the Maine boys and the 121st New York. Now he had eight regiments on line, with the 16th New York moving up behind the 23rd New Jersey. This should be more than enough to overlap Wilcox's meager flanks and surround him. He noticed some units were reaching the irregular wood line ahead of others. When a regiment got to the woods, they stopped a minute for a breather, then they cheered and surged forward. In the back of his mind, he knew something was wrong. This attack was not coordinated.

1730 HRS - The wood was only thirty yards wide. The bushes, vines, trees and brush had been there for years. The competition for sunlight had turned the vegetation into a tangled barrier. Catbriers, poison ivy, holly trees and all manner of thorny things were interlaced in an impenetrable obstacle course.

The Yahoos' line stopped for a few seconds to close ranks. The troops gave three cheers. The command "Advance at ready" was given, and they started to push through the tangle. Some men broke their way through, while others crawled under it. Few could see all the way through. Some climbed over.

Grubb was leading on foot. He was just starting to get his line back in order when he looked through the tangled woods. The clearing was ahead. The schoolhouse and Salem Church was right where it belonged. He looked a little further beyond it, and his blood froze. At the rear of the churchyard, not sixty yards away, was a solid wall of Confederate infantry and every one of their guns were aimed at him and the 23rd's line. He yelled "AIM, FIRE." Both lines fired at the same time.

————————

The volume of fire was much more than it should have been. Sedgwick whirled around to look down the Plank Road. He started sending aides to find Howe and Newton.

Rue's squad had already pushed its way through the wood and was ready when Grubb yelled "AIM, FIRE." The deafening roar of the muskets was followed instantly by the zip and crack of the return fire. This was followed instantly by the smack of lead against flesh, earth and trees. Ricochets whined off into the distance. The 23rd pushed its way into the clearing. The Yahoos' line was still disorganized because of the problems moving through the tangled woods. They traded fire with the Rebs for a minute and fell back into the woods. Splinters and leaves and branches fell on them as a steady stream of Reb musket balls flew through the trees.

Grubb ordered assembly, reformed his line and organized a counterattack. He could hear Upton doing the same thing with the 121st. The Yank counterattack started with a volley of rifle fire, and then a charge. The 3rd New Jersey was coming up on the right across the Plank Road. As the Yahoos burst out of the wood, they were met by steady fire from the church. It was a two-story brick building with one window facing them directly on the east side. Each floor on the north and south sides had three windows. Sharpshooters were firing from all of them, and from holes punched through the red brick walls. Marksmen were in the schoolhouse, too. It was an old log structure on the 23rd's left flank, sixty yards southeast of the church. Rebel troops inside had knocked the chinking out of some of the walls and were using the building as a fort.

The only door to the church was on the west side. The Rebel infantry on that side of the churchyard was protected by a fence and a cut made for the road from Hamilton's Crossing. Every Reb in the line had a clear shot at anyone trying for the western door. There was no way for the 23rd to rush the entrance. Josie was loading his musket when he saw a huge Lieutenant from the 121st try to break the schoolhouse door down. Someone poked a rifle through a hole and shot the officer point blank in the chest. He spun over backwards, blood spurting high in the air.

Captain Kirkbride with B Company and Captain Newbold with D Company were on their left. Josie was reloading again when Sharp nudged him. Josie followed his gaze and saw a bloody Captain Newbold struggling to the rear. Lieutenant McCarter took over and started rallying the company.

Beyond them, the boys could see the 121st sweeping forward on the flank just a few feet to the left of Kirkbride. The New Yorkers surrounded the school and poked twenty or thirty muskets through the holes in the walls. The door opened, and the Rebs surrendered. In the middle of all this, a terrified horse came stampeding through the battle lines. A frantic Union officer finally gave up trying to control it and jumped off before the horse crossed into Rebel territory. While all of this confusion was going on, the Rebs behind the church fell back about thirty paces. It looked like they were on the run.

Every Union officer in sight yelled charge, and the men started forward. They were just entering the Rebel position when a new sound was heard above the battle. It was a visceral roar of rage from behind the Rebel lines. Almost instantly, a solid wall of gray came rushing at them at unbelievable speed. The 9th Alabama crashed into the 23rd and the 121st New Yorkers and drove them back to the woods. These unexpected Confederate reinforcements came so fast, they wrested the schoolhouse prisoners from their Union captors. Within seconds, the "almost prisoners" were back in Rebel lines getting rearmed. The 9th was not about to sit by and watch their H Company boys get caught.

Rue, Terhune, Sharp, Conover, Josie, Hullings and Lloyd were running with Captain Taylor toward the church for the second time. Josie saw Hullings stagger out of the corner of his eye. He turned his head to see what had happened when something knocked the wind out of him.

He blacked out.

Rue, Terhune, Sharp and Conover made it to the shelter of the church, but they were alone. They frantically looked around for Josie, Lloyd and Hullings. There was only a sea of blue-clad bodies on the ground behind them. Some were struggling to get to the rear, and others were not moving at all.

Rue looked at Sharp. "What happened?"

"Josie and Hullings were right next to me. That volley took him and Hullings, and maybe Lloyd. I think Josie got hit in the head. Let me go for him."

"Are you crazy? You stay right here or you'll get your head blown off, too."

"Rue, it's our friends," pleaded Sharp. "Please. You have to let me go."

Rue grabbed Sharp by the collar. "God damn it, George, I'd go myself, but I can't. If we are going to get out of this mess alive, we got to stick together."

George Sharp nodded. There were tears in his eyes. Terhune just looked at the ground.

They looked around and tried to decide what to do. Everyone was trying to keep their line intact. They were loading and firing as fast as they could. As soon as someone fell, someone else moved to close the gap.

Most of the 23rd was out in the open on their right toward the Plank Road. There was no cover and no place to hide. They watched Captain Hambrick go down. He rolled to his side and laid still for what seemed an eternity. Then he struggled to his feet, and holding his stomach with bloody hands, lurched out of the clearing to the rear. Others were falling all around him.

Colonel Grubb was in the open with what was left of the color guard. He was frantically trying to move the regiment forward. It wasn't that the men didn't want to do what Grubb ordered; there simply were not enough of them left to do it. The two companies on the regiment's left were equally exposed. People were falling there, too. Rue yelled, and Sharp and Terhune looked where he was pointing. Something very bad was happening to the left flank.

They watched as a private from the 121st raced to Kirkbride and pointed toward the Rebel lines. A Confederate color bearer was running toward a tree stump, and planted his Stars and Bars in the rotten wood. Other Rebels were rallying around it. They looked back to see what Kirkbride would do just as the New Yorker got shot through the head. Kirkbride looked at the boy for a long time, and then to the flank. He ordered reload.

A stampede of New Yorkers started running into Kirkbride's company. Within seconds, Zouves from the 96th Pennsylvania were following them. They passed Kirkbride and then McCarter. McCarter grabbed one, listened to what he had to say. Then he grabbed the man by the throat and pointed to the line. The soldier nodded, joined the line and started reloading his rifle. Others followed suit.

Kirkbride looked left. He was sure glad there were no Rebs between him and the Confederate Army. If this was what it was like when there weren't any, he would sure hate to see what it would be like if there were. He ordered "FIRE," and another volley went toward the enemy.

McCarter sprinted to Grubb. He yelled, "The left flank is..." and fell dead, shot through the heart. The impact threw McCarter against Grubb, and they both tumbled into a heap. Grubb looked at McCarter. The lieutenant was Ryerson's closest friend. Ogden would be devastated at his loss.

Bullets were snapping and cracking around everyone from the front and the left. They involuntarily ducked as a terrific volley from the left smacked into the side of the church. Brick fragments sprayed all over them. Grubb got up and looked left. New Yorkers and Zouves were streaming into B and D Company. It was obvious the flank had collapsed somewhere over there. Someone grabbed his arm and pointed to the right. An officer was frantically pointing at a line of gray soldiers charging down the plank road. Solid lines of enemy infantry were pushing around both sides of the church to his front.

Grubb had no choice. He had to fall back, or be overrun. The remains of other units joined the Yahoos as they quickly pulled back through the woods. When they got to the open field, they started running for the gun line. They had been fighting just a little over ten minutes.

———

General Brooks was listening to the gunfire. He could tell things were not good on the right, so he intercepted the 16th New York and had them move by the right flank to reinforce the 1st New Jersey. Within minutes, Major Close and the rear guard from the bridgehead showed up. Brooks put them in on the right to support the 3rd New Jersey. The two regiments slowed the Rebel charge, but within minutes they too were falling back.

———

Williston's battery galloped up to the toll gate and two guns set up in the middle of the Plank Road. Lieutenant Warner set the other four guns up on the left side of the road and started firing at the oncoming enemy. Two regiments from Newton's 3rd Division hurried into position along the gun line.

1745 HRS – Wilcox's Alabamans saw the Yankees fall back. They hesitated a few seconds to be sure they weren't being tricked, and then surged across the churchyard and through the woods to the edge of the field. General Semmes and two of his regiments from Georgia joined the chase. They saw the Jersey men streaming toward the toll house. The Rebs dressed their lines and started after them.

Lieutenant Rufus Jones of H Company, 9th Alabama Volunteers, Army of Northern Virginia, stepped out the door of Salem Church. His pistol was in his hand. He quickly looked around the corner toward the schoolhouse. Wounded men from both sides were scattered across the clearing. All the fight was out of them.

"Amos? Yo, Amos? Y'all alright in there?"

Someone in the schoolhouse yelled back, "Amos is shot, and so are two more. Git Doc Minor. Git Doc Minor, quick."

Jones looked toward the rear. He saw Doc Minor and his orderlies heading for the church. He holstered his pistol and walked over to the schoolhouse.

His company was H Company. They were to use the schoolhouse and Salem Church as forts during the battle. They would not join the pursuit. Jones passed several bodies as he checked his men to make sure they could hold out if the Yankees came back. Some of the fellas were already carrying Amos and the other two to the church. He followed them.

Heavy rifle fire could be heard just a few hundred yards away. Occasionally, a bullet would zip through the trees. It didn't sound like the fighting would die down soon. Union artillery was starting to join in. Fortunately, they were shelling someplace else.

Crispin was lying facedown. Consciousness swirled close by, but was not quite within his reach. He groaned.

Jones heard him, and stopped to listen. He took a few seconds to see which body the noise came from. Finally, he saw Crispin. He knelt down and rolled him over. He saw a boy obviously a few years his junior. The boy was bleeding from the mouth and nose, not a good sign. Jones took a flask from his coat, lifted the young man's head and poured some watered-down whiskey in his mouth.

Josie revived a little. He looked at the Lieutenant and gasped, "Are you going to kill me?"

"No, friend, no I am not, you just rest easy."

Josie was having trouble breathing. Blood was trickling out of the side of his mouth. Jones unbuttoned the wounded man's blouse to look for the wound. He frowned when he saw it.

Josi glanced down, saw it and closed his eyes. He involuntarily said "Oh." The hole was just an inch below his left nipple. The same place Lieutenant Michel had been hit the day before. Jones gently rebuttoned the shirt. Both men knew it was mortal.

"Is there anything I can do for you?"

Even though it was late in the afternoon, the unrelenting sun was hot enough to make it uncomfortable. Josie gasped, "Could you help me into the shade, please?"

Jones nodded yes. He removed Crispin's knapsack and got out the blanket. There were two huge trees at the east end of the church that provided a cool place to rest. He spread the blanket in their shade and moved the wounded man out of the sun. Then he used the knapsack to prop him up so he could breathe a little easier.

Jones reached for Josie's canteen and gave him a drink. There wasn't much water in it, so the Lieutenant filled it from his. "You rest easy here, Yank, I'm going to get an ambulance for you."

"No, please don't go." Josi slowly looked across the battlefield. He saw George Hullings nearby. George stared up at the sky through lifeless eyes. Tears came to Josie's eyes. He looked up at Jones. "This war's a cruel, cruel thing."

Jones yelled to one of his men to bring a stretcher and knelt beside him. He placed the Union soldier's head on his knee, and gave him a stiff drink of brandy. He glanced around. Rebs and Yanks were helping each other around the clearing.

"Thank you, sir. Thank you so much. You are very kind." He was coughing up blood and crying openly. "My dear sister, I am never going to see her again. She's going to wait for me to come home in vain. Oh, why did I ever leave home?"

Jones didn't know what to say, so he just spoke quietly and tried to comfort him. Crispin calmed and gazed at Jones. "I know I don't have long."

Jones nodded his agreement.

"I am not afraid to go." Josie slowly reached into his breast pocket and drew out his diary. He handed it to Jones. "Take this, my friend. It's just the idle thoughts of a poor soldier far away from those he loves. You can read it if you choose, and then please send it to my sister, Mary. Her address is inside."

Jones took the diary. "I will. What is your name?"

"I am Josiah Crispin, and yours?"

"Rufus Jones."

"Give me your hand, Rufus." Jones held Josie's hand. "May God bless you for the kindness you have shown your enemy." He gasped, "Mary, my sweet sister Mary…" and then he was gone.

Jones was stunned at what had just happened. He had been at both Bull Runs, Antietam, Frazier's Farm and Malvern Hill during the Seven Days, and Fredericksburg. He was no stranger to ugly death, but the intimacy of this one staggered him. No death had ever struck him so badly. He stayed there holding Crispin's hand for what seemed hours.

Two privates ran to him. "You need a stretcher, sir?"

Jones looked at them, and then at Josie, "No. No, thanks, it's too late. He's gone."

"Do you know him, sir?"

"No, never met him till now." Jones put the diary in his pocket. He got up and walked back to the church. The sounds of the ongoing battle continued in the east.

1800 HRS – "I don't think today's the day you catch Cadmus Wilcox," drawled Mr. Guest as he watched the battle with General Sedgwick from the front porch of his house.

Sedgwick grimaced. He knew Guest was right. His estimate of the opposing force had gone from nothing, to a weak brigade, to the realization he was facing a reinforced division. His first division was being badly mauled before his eyes. Newton's Division was preparing a line near the toll gate, and Howe was coming up fast on the road. Bully Brooks had his hands full. His whole brigade was hotly engaged in everything from a route to a barely controlled fighting retreat.

Sedgwick hated seeing his men in this situation. He had been wounded five times since Antietam, and he loathed seeing his men hurt. He mounted his horse and rode to a battery on the Plank Road. He sat down in next to them and stayed there the rest of the night.

Bully Brooks was almost sick to his stomach as he watched the 96th Pennsylvania and 121st come bolting out of the woods. He watched General Bartlett, Colonel Lessig and Colonel Upton frantically try to stem the retreat and rally the brigade around their colors.

Brooks turned to Lieutenant Wheeler. "Twenty-five years in the army, Mr. Wheeler, and ruined at last. Come on, let's go help Upton." They galloped toward the 121st.

Seconds later, they watched as the 23rd backed out of the woods to the right. Most of them were running. Grubb and a few of his captains were rallying small groups to cover the retreat. There was no hope he could re-establish his line and conduct a fighting withdrawal. Upton finally succeeded in setting his line near a house about 500 yards from the woods. Brooks and Wheeler galloped up just as a brigade of Confederate infantry burst out of the woods.

Three hundred yards to the left, the 5th Maine held on by itself in the woods on the extreme left flank. Bartlett realized they couldn't hold out, and ordered them to join Upton's men at the house. Things weren't going much better on the right side of the Plank Road. More Rebs were driving the 1st New Jersey and 16th New York out of the woods towards the artillery. Only the 3rd and 15th New Jersey were holding onto a patch of thick woods on the right flank.

Williston, Rigby and Parsons were firing case shot and percussion-fused shells at the charging Rebs over the heads of the retreating Union forces.

———————

Grubb rallied a small group of men for a stand around the colors near the road. A private was waving the flag near him. They formed a small line about halfway back to the artillery. They were trying to buy time for the rest of the regiment. Williston's, Rigby's and Parsons' eighteen guns were lobbing shells over their heads at a rapid rate. Confederate troops were marching out of the woods to their right, left and center. Another line of Rebs were pushing the Yanks back on the north side of the road. A pitched battle was going in a woods north of the Rebel line. Sharpshooter fire from the woods they had just left was taking a grisly toll. Grubb watched the mass of men streaming toward the guns. They were running for their lives, scattered all over the field. The units were all mixed up.

Grubb saw Wilson, the new lieutenant in H Company, get hit. He went down on one knee then struggled to his feet, and continued back. Almost instantly, he was struck again, and staggered. He regained his balance. He was still moving when a third ball broke his right ankle.

Grubb saw a surreal scene. Lieutenant Sibley and Forrester Taylor came strolling down the Plank Road arm-in-arm, with bullets kicking up dust all around them. Grubb watched as Sibley and Taylor stopped by Wilson. Sibley said something to Taylor and pointed to where Grubb was standing. Taylor nodded and went over to Wilson. Sibley started walking toward Grubb.

Sibley was almost to Grubb when he saw the color-bearer get hit. The Yahoo flag tumbled to the ground. The lieutenant picked it up and was turning toward the Colonel when a bullet killed him on the spot. Charlie Fenton picked up the flag.

———————

Wilson was in a lot of pain, and worried about being captured.* He had already been a POW and didn't want go through it again. He pleaded, "For God's sake, Taylor, carry me off the field. I have been in

*This information is from Taylor's account found in "The Badge of Gallantry" and "Deeds of Valor, How America's Civil War Heroes Won the Congressional Medal of Honor."

a Rebel prison once as a well man. If I go back as I am, it will kill me."

"There's no way I can carry you myself." Taylor looked around and flagged down three of his men. He watched as McBreen, Ayers and Earling quickly spread a blanket and got Wilson on it. Each man grabbed a corner and started half carrying, half dragging the lieutenant toward the guns. Bullets were whining all around them.

Taylor looked up and saw a volley tear through the group of men Colonel Grubb had rallied. Several fell, and the rest broke and started running for the guns. He looked over his shoulder. A Rebel line was coming up the road thirty yards behind them. He yelled to his stretcher detail to put Wilson down and run for their lives.

"I am sorry, Dick. I won't order them to get captured trying to save you. I'll try to come back for you."

Wilson quickly nodded, "Here, take my watch and wallet. The Rebs will steal it for sure if they take me."

Taylor took the valuables and hurried off toward the guns. He grimaced when he saw Corporal Wainwright was one of the men who had gone down in the last volley. As he rushed by, he yelled, "I can do nothing for you now, Corporal, but may later."

McBreen, Ayers and Earling were waiting for him behind the guns. Fresh infantry had set up a line behind the artillery. The 23rd and the rest of the fleeing soldiers rallied behind them.

They stood together without worrying about what regiment the man beside them was from. Together, they and the artillery fought off the Rebels.

As soon as the Rebs had withdrawn, the four men raced 250 yards back out to Wilson. They were just picking up the blanket when another Rebel attack charged down the Plank Road. Bullets and shells from both sides were flying all around them, and the Rebs were closing in.

They were running, struggling to keep the blanket off the ground. They weren't going fast enough. The Rebs were catching up to them again. They were out of breath and not looking where they were going when they heard Williston screaming for them to get down. They all piled into a ditch seconds before the two guns in the road each fired a double charge of canister over them. The blast was followed by the sound of a thousand angry bees heading toward the enemy.

Taylor quickly looked around. He was fifty yards from the guns. Just fifty yards behind was a pile of Confederate bodies. The Rebs had been that close. The four were back on their feet in an instant. They rushed through the lines. As soon as they were safe, the gunners blasted double canister as fast as they could load it.

They handed Wilson off to the medical orderlies and rested for a few minutes. Taylor returned the lieutenant's valuables and gathered his stretcher crew.

"Fellas, Joel Wainwright is still out there. He fought like a trooper back there, and I can't leave him. Will you go with me?"

All agreed. They crossed the gun line a second time and rescued Wainright.

Colonel Brown was frantically trying to withdraw his brigade to the Union gun line north of the road. They were halfway back when Brown saw the 1st New Jersey's Colonel, Mark Collet, go down. Three of Collet's troops picked him up and carried him to the rear. It was clear when they put him down that Mark was dead.

Brown watched a man from Seaver's 16th New York repeatedly race into the open under fire to rescue wounded men. It was a miracle the man wasn't shot.

Union artillery was firing case shot over the heads of the retreating infantry. These shells burst among the Rebs and slowed them down. The hot fragments ignited fires in the woods in several places. Soon flames and smoke from numerous forest fires could be seen in the Confederate lines.

As soon as the Union troops pulled back to the artillery, Union guns started firing canister and grape shot as fast as they could. Broken federal formations halted their retreat at a line established by the 3rd Division just behind the guns. The Jersey men reorganized just to the rear of this line.

Brown was seeing the last of his men to safety when a ball struck him in the thigh. He fell from his horse and was carried to the rear. Command of the New Jersey Brigade passed to the 2nd Regiment's Sam Buck.

At least a brigade of Confederate infantry was coming at the Union right. Intense cannon fire drove off the flankers and pushed the frontal attack across the Plank Road behind the fleeing 23rd. Williston ordered his battery to fire solid shot down the Plank Road. The 12-pound iron balls ricocheted great distances and caused horrific injuries.

The Rebs pulled back to the woods. They regrouped, and ten minutes later charged back down the road. Brooks saw the attack was trying to overrun Williston's battery. He told Wheeler to tell Williston to hold at all costs. Wheeler galloped to the rear of the battery, yelling at Williston. Enemy bullets struck all around him. Within seconds, Wheeler's horse shuddered and crashed to the ground. Wheeler got to his feet. He gave Williston his orders. Then, he turned, waved his sword and urged the infantry to support the artillery. A stunning impact knocked him to the ground.

Brooks and Williston saw him go down. There was nothing they could do.

The Rebs were within a hundred yards of the guns. Brooks saw four men carrying a man in a blanket, staggering toward the guns. He saw Williston yelling at them. Suddenly, they dived into a ditch, just as double shots of canister blasted huge holes in the enemy line. The carnage was indescribable. The Reb attack backed off fast.

The sun set at 1847 hours. Fighting finally petered out as darkness fell. Black powder smoke wafted through the air, mixed with the smoke of burning flesh and forest fires. The screams of the wounded who could not get away from the flames haunted the night. Visibility was terrible.

1930 HRS – The First Sergeants were taking roll as fast as they could in the twilight.

They had no paper, so they used the backs of envelopes and any other scraps they could find to make their notes. When they finished, they did an about face, and faced their Captains.

Taylor looked at Hartman. "Report," said Taylor softly.

"Sir, we have 59 men present, 8 wounded or sick at the hospital and 9 men unaccounted for."

Taylor frowned. He saluted the 1st Sergeant and started to turn, but hesitated. He looked over his exhausted, sweaty, dirty men. They had fought bravely in an impossible situation. He took a minute to walk among them, and tell them he was proud of the job they had done. Then he turned and prepared to give his report.

Grubb was at the head of the regiment. The Adjutant commanded "REPORT," and voices from each company came out of the growing darkness with the grim news of the day. When it was over, the 23rd had lost more than a hundred men in a little over an hour. Some, like Sibley and McCarter, were known to be dead, and some of the severely wounded who had been rescued were accounted for. It would take weeks to sort out what happened to the rest of them. Grubb passed his

280

report up to Colonel Buck. Buck assembled the report from the ranking officers in the Jersey Brigade and passed his report to General Brooks. Brooks sent his report to General Sedgwick.

Sedgwick was sitting on the side of the Plank Road by an artillery battery. A dispatch rider with a message from Hooker had just arrived. Hooker had been nearly killed by an artillery shell the night before. Stonewall Jackson had turned the armies' flank late yesterday afternoon. Once again, the Army of the Potomac was defeated. Sedgwick's orders were to save the 6th Corps.

The Rebs he had forced out of Fredericksburg and the south end of Marye's Ridge earlier in the day had only moved a couple of miles south on the Telegraph Road. Chances were they would come back, and try to cut him off from Fredericksburg. Already, the hospitals there were being evacuated, and the engineers were getting ready to move the pontoon bridges. Haupt's plans to rebuild the railroad were on hold again.

Sedgwick knew he couldn't fight his way through the enemy division at Salem Church. That left the area between Bank's and Scott's Fords as his only way across the river.

The general knew the enemy had abandoned Bank's Ford earlier that day, and the Rebs were frantically trying to get it back.

General Benham, Sedgwick's West Point classmate, had a bridge across by 4:30 that afternoon, even though the Rebels were shelling it with long-range artillery fire. Another was ready to be laid if needed. Benham had already requested an infantry brigade and artillery to safeguard the escape route. He had bought Sedgwick a little time. Sedgwick turned to getting his divisions into a horseshoe shaped defensive perimeter around the ford. He sat by the road all night making his dispositions.

Doc Elmer and the rest of the medical staff were helping Doctor Taylor, the division's medical director, treat the wounded. They were working at a small farmhouse near the toll house. It was a mess. In addition to usual battlefield wounds, they were treating everything from heat stroke to epileptic seizures, to stark raving madness. Elmer worked to exhaustion, and finally curled up and slept in a wheat field. He was so tired he didn't even look for a blanket.

Taylor tried to retrieve Sibley's body late in the day. Grubb didn't want him to go, and took him to the Brigade Commander. Buck tried to talk him out of it, and when he couldn't, made him promise to stop the attempt if it became too dangerous. Taylor rounded up McBreen, Ayers and Earling. The men started for the body, but they were driven back by intense enemy sharpshooter fire. The regiment left Sibley and twenty Yahoos on the field. Sedgwick's Corps had suffered almost 3,000 casualties in less than 3 hours at Salem Church.*

Just a mile to the west, the Rebs were digging in. They used bayonets, frying pans, plates, boards and anything they could dig with to build a rifle pit across the Salem Church yard. The church itself was the strong point, so the trench joined it on both sides.

Word was the Yanks had taken a beating at Chancellorsville, and Lee was on the way with reinforcements to see if he could trap and destroy Sedgwick's Corp. It sounded like tomorrow would be busy.

Lieutenant Jones had Crispin buried with several other Union dead near the church. He set up a crude little rail fence around the grave. He and the regiment's chaplain conducted a short service for Josie. It was the best the Confederates could give him.

Jones watched as more graves were dug. Nearly 150 Union dead had fallen within the Rebel lines. This day was clearly a Confederate victory, but the price was steep. Cadmus Wilcox's Brigade had 75 dead, 372 wounded and 48 missing. The loss of so many friends. plus the death of a new one he only got to know for a few minutes, weighed heavily on Rufus.

May 5th, 1863 – Pontoon Bridge, Bank's Ford, Virginia

At 2 AM, orders came for General Sedgwick to fall back across the Rappahannock at Bank's Ford. He started immediately. Benham had thrown the second bridge across the river earlier in the day in anticipation of the order. Rebel artillery fired on them all day and through the night, but couldn't interdict the effort.

The 23rd was part of the rear guard. An imposing line of Union artillery guaranteed a hot welcome for any Confederates trying to

*Stockpole, pg 345.

interfere with the retreat. When most of the Corps was across, the batteries limbered up and rumbled off toward the bridges. As the last one pulled out, orders came to double-quick to the rear.

Partway to the bridge, they were halted and redeployed to face a pursuit. The Rebs fell back. Reb artillery tried to find them as they neared the ford. They caught a short sleep under the stars on the enemy side of the river before crossing at dawn. The enemy saw them and opened fire. Fortunately, no one was hurt.

Brooks was watching his exhausted troops retreat across the bridges when the 16th New York and Colonel Seavers came up. Seavers stopped and reported on his unit. When he was done, Brooks said, "Say, Joel? I saw one of your men rescuing wounded with a horse yesterday. He made two or three trips in the thick of the fight. Do you know who he was?"

Seavers chuckled. "Oh, yes sir. That's Frank Hall. He's my chaplain. The man's always in trouble." Seavers was still chuckling as he rode off.

Brooks saw Sam Buck riding toward him a few minutes later. Just as Buck reached Brooks, his horse slipped and fell. A regimental surgeon had him taken across the bridge in an ambulance. Brooks just groaned. He was running out of Colonels. Command of the Jersey Brigade passed on to Colonel Penrose.

———

The Yahoos returned to the river late in the afternoon to guard the pontoons. They spent a miserable night in a teeming downpour.

The heavy storm collapsed one of Professor Lowe's balloons and partially collapsed a second. It also destroyed a good part of the sulfuric acid and iron fillings he needed to make the hydrogen to refill them. The boys saw the damaged equipment near Bank's Ford when they were relieved the next morning. "How Josie loved to watch those balloons," thought Sharp as they marched back to White Oak Church.

May 9, 1863 – Camp White Oak Church, Virginia

The Army of the Potomac returned to its camps along the Rappahannock a dispirited, wounded and defeated force on May 7, 1863. Grubb marched the 23rd back to their old regimental area. The men who lost tent mates teamed up with other survivors and erected their shelter halves over the empty huts. More than twenty-five huts remained vacant when the work was done.

Grubb wrote his first after-action report. He dispensed with the "I have the honor of reporting" language that bothered Ryerson after the battle in December. His report started, "Report of killed, wounded and missing from the 23rd New Jersey Volunteers." It listed 3 officers and 17 enlisted men dead, 6 officers and 51 enlisted men wounded and 31 enlisted men missing, totaling 108 casualties.

Grubb also hand-wrote an order to his men. He had it posted on the tree that served as the unit bulletin board. It was the lone surviving tree on the Montieth Farm.

Regimental Order No.69
The commanding officer desires to compliment the regiment upon the gallantry displayed on Sunday last, and to return his thanks to the officers who so nobly seconded him on that occasion. It is true that, overwhelmed by a vastly superior force – outflanked, outnumbered, and in imminent danger of being of capture, you were forced to retire from the unequal contest – but, that you fought bravely, the loss of nearly a third of your numbers, among them some of our best and bravest, sadly testify. With a tear to the memory of our noble dead, and with the most heartfelt sympathies for those who have been wounded, I cannot but feel well assured that if it shall be again our fortune to be tried in battle you will not forget that you are men and Jersey men.

E Burd Grubb
Col. Commanding

"Fellas, what happened to Miller?" asked Sharp.

Rue looked pained and answered, "Captain Taylor promoted McBreen to sergeant and Earling and Ayres to corporal for helping him rescue Wilson and Wainwright during the battle. The company had too many sergeants, so he took Miller's stripes. McBreen's taking his place. Tom was a good corporal. He should be fine."

"We all thought Bill did a good job."

"He did, but it was hard on him after Sweesley died. His heart wasn't in it."

Professor Lowe's men were in a quandary. They needed to repair the balloons, but Professor Lowe was no longer around to tell them what to do. It seemed that Captain Comstock did not believe a civilian should be paid more than his Captain's pay. Without Army approval, Comstock negated Lowe's salary agreement. The Professor tried to reach Hooker, Butterfield and Sedgwick for help; however, the old Army bureaucratic Chain of Command stymied his efforts. On May 7th, Lowe terminated his government employment. The Corp of Aeronauts collapsed shortly thereafter.

May 13th, 1863 - Camp White Oak Church, Virginia

Captain Taylor was sitting in front of his tent reading the letter from an H Company private in the New Jersey Mirror when the ambulance drove up. He watched as the sergeant locked the brake and climbed down from the wagon box. The sergeant saluted, and Taylor returned it.

"What can I do for you, Sergeant?" asked Taylor.

"Sir, are you H Company's Captain?

Taylor nodded.

"Then, sir, I have a story to tell you."

"Go ahead. Have a seat."

"Sir, Major Letterman finally arranged for us to go across the river under a flag of truce to look after our wounded and dead. The engineers got some pontoons together over at Fredericksburg and built a ferry."

"I took my ambulance across and drove up towards the church, and when I got there, this Rebel lieutenant flagged me down. He gave me this diary, said it was given to him by a dying soldier who asked that it be returned to his sister."

Taylor took the little red leather-bound book. An envelope addressed to Mary Crispin had been carefully tied to the book with string. Taylor untied the string, slipped the leather flap and opened it. He read, "Diary of JBC, Sept 1, 1862," and then in pencil, "White Oak Church."

Taylor took a deep breath and shook his head. The company was desperately hoping Crispin was alive. George Hullings and Ed Lloyd were still missing. This would be a blow to them.

He called 1[St] Sergeant Hartman. Hartman came over and Taylor held up the book. "Crispin," was all he said.

Hartman's shoulders slumped. "I'll go let Rue and McBreen know."

Taylor watched as Hartman told McBreen. The new sergeant called Miller and Rue. They gathered their men. Sharp, Terhune, Conover and the others started walking toward the ambulance. Chaplain Abbott saw them and came over, too. Conover recognized the diary and started to cry. They all listened as the ambulance sergeant recounted his tale. Taylor opened the book to the last page and read, "May 3rd, Had to skedaddle from Dixie and recross the river with considerable loss. Your brother met a soldier's grave and the best the Confederates could give him."

Then he turned to the front of the book. "This book was handed to me by a dying soldier at the Battle of Salem Church fought May 3, 1863 with a request that I send it to his sister. R. C. Jones, 1st Lieut. Co. H. 9th Ala Regt. Confederate Army, Longstreet's Corps. 1863."

"Sir, the Reb told me he was worried somebody would steal the book. That's why he's put the envelope with it and tied it with the string. It's official U.S. Mail. Look at the envelope."

It was addressed to Mary Crispin and marked, "Via flag of truce." That meant it had passed through the lines legally.

Taylor thought for a minute. "We'll be going home soon. I'll deliver it personally."

News quickly spread through the regiment about what happened. The Rebs sent Lieutenant Sibley's cap and shoulder boards back for his family, too. Many came to see the mementoes. They remembered how poorly the Rebs had treated Captain Ridgway. It seemed the boys from Alabama were a different breed from the enemy they had faced in December.

May 15th, 1863 - Camp White Oak Church, Virginia

Just twenty-eight days remained before the 23rd was to muster out. Every man was counting. The daily routine of hardtack, salt beef, guard duty and drill was reestablished. The warmer weather made life easier, but with it came flies and mosquitoes. At least they weren't faced with the risk of freezing to death every night.

The survivors of the Salem Church fight repaired and cleaned their weapons and equipment. There were numerous inspections, and the unending drill.

Some of the less seriously wounded started returning from the hospitals. The more seriously hurt would go directly from their hospitals to Beverly for mustering out. Doc Hetzell finally determined that only seven of the fifty-seven officers and enlisted men wounded had life-threatening injuries. A number of others were maimed.

Hartman gave his usual "MAIL CALL" bellow. The troops came running. At least that didn't change.

"Sharp." George reached for his letter and saw who it was from. George let out a deep sigh. It was from Mary Crispin. He went back to his tent and read it. Terhune was with him.

Howard was getting up a baseball game. George quietly suggested that Terhune go join it. After he was gone, he found a pen and paper and wrote:

Camp White Oak Church, Virginia
Friday Evening May 15th, 1863

Dear Friend,

I received your letter of May 11th this morning and as you wrote to me for information concerning your brother I will give you all in my power. Josiah and I went into the engagement at Salem Church on Sunday afternoon May 3rd about 5 o'clock, and as we were going in he was wounded by my side. He said nothing that I could hear amid the battle and confusion of the day and I had no opportunity to stop and speak with him for the officers were rushing us on as fast as they could, we ought never to have went in to that woods as we did, for the Rebels were three or four to our one, I had hoped that your brother was only slightly wounded, but have since learned different, I think Josiah was wounded in the head, after Josiah fell we were driven back about a half a mile, leaving our wounded in their possession, but only for a short time, on Wednesday evening a sergeant from the ambulance corps (that had been over the river with a flag of truce to take care of our wounded and bury our dead) brought Josiah's diary stating that he got it from a Rebel Lieutenant, the Lieutenant said the book was handed to him by a dying soldier at the Battle of Salem Church with the request that he should send it to his sister, as the sergeant was over there the Lieutenant gave it to him, the Captain has got it in charge and talks of getting a leave of absence in a few days, and will take it with him, or else it will be taken when we return home as that will be soon, it was thought best not to send it by mail, for fear you would not get it, Edwin Lloyd, George Hullings and several others from our company are still missing, but we still have hopes for them, I am indeed sorry that your brother died on the battle field as our time was growing so short, but that is the way with this horrid war, when will it be over, my dear friend I can truly

287

simpathise with you in your bereavement. If there is any information that I can possibly give you I will gladly do it, as my time is somewhat limited I must close. Please excuse bad writing and mistakes.

Respectfully yours,

George W Sharp

To Mary Crispin
Company H, 23rd regt NJ Vol
P.S. please write for any information that I can give you.

Sharp read the letter over, made a few corrections, and walked over to Chaplain Abbott's tent. "Excuse me, Reverend, could I talk to you for a minute?"

"Ah, George, how are you this evening?" smiled the Chaplain.

"I am feeling low, sir. I got a letter from Josie Crispin's sister today. She asked for information about him, and I have a letter here telling what I know."

Abbott read the letter carefully and said, "That's very nice of you to answer so quickly."

"Well, sir, I don't have any stamps, and I heard a chaplain could write a note where the stamp goes and the mail would carry it."

"That's so. I'll be happy to do that. Give it here." George handed the letter to Abbott and watched as the minister wrote "W.S. Abbott, Chaplain, 23rd NJ" in the upper right corner of the envelope and then "In Haste" on the left edge. "That should do it."

"Thank you, sir," mumbled George, and turned to walk away.

Abbott looked after him. "George?"

Sharp stopped and turned.

"Are you all right?"

Sharp just shook his head no. "Reverend, Crispin and Lloyd and Hullings deviled the daylights out of me and Terhune all of the time. I never realized how much fun we had." He sobbed, "God, I miss them."

May 25, 1863 - Camp White Oak Church, Virginia

Grubb was working at his desk when Captain Risdon reported. "Sir, can I see you for a minute, please?"

"Sure, Henry, come in and sit down."

"Sir, we got more Copperhead trouble back home."

"Now what?" asked Grubb in exasperation. It seemed like something was causing trouble back home every week, and it was constantly bothering the men.

"My wife wrote that some are saying Joe Ridgway was shot in the back by his own men because they didn't like him."

Grubb was not a man who swore often, but this one caught him off guard. "That's bullshit."

"Orderly!" he bellowed.

The orderly sprinted into the tent. If Grubb was swearing, there was a big problem, and the lowly orderly didn't want to be a part of it. "Yes, sir."

"Officers' call, right now. I don't care what they are doing, get them here."

"Yes sir."

The officers came on the run. Grubb asked Risdon to tell them what was going on, and the news was greeted with outrage. Woody Kirkbride was especially angry, "For Christ's sake, I was standing right in next to him. I saw him get shot. It hit him in the forehead, and he was facing the Rebs."

"This is slanderous, Colonel," muttered Parmentier. "This slanders the name of our regiment and Ridgway, and makes G Company out to be murderers. What are you going to do?"

"I need to talk to brigade headquarters about this. My feeling is this requires an official Army response from us here in the regiment. Would you men sign a letter to the New Jersey Mirror?"

All said they would. They started writing the letter while Grubb went of to the brigade. Brigade didn't want to dignify the rumor with an official Army response, but they encouraged Burd to let the men set the record straight. Word was out that Copperhead activities like this were happening all over New Jersey.

By the time Grubb got back, the word had spread throughout the regiment and G Company was outraged. Every single man wanted to sign the letter. The letter was mailed on May 27th.

The Late Capt Jos R Ridgway
Camp near White Oak Church, VA
May 27th, 1863

Mr. Editor – Around the home circles, since the great battle of Fredericksburg, fought on the 13th of December last, reports have been circulated detrimental to us as a Company. Some malicious, traitorous hearted wretch has said that Captain Jos. R. Ridgway, of our company, who fell upon the alter of his country while gallantly leading his men into action, was killed by his own men – they being dissatisfied with him, deliberately shot him, as though he had been a traitor.

We, the members of his company, take this opportunity of denouncing said report, it being without the slightest foundation. As a Captain, he was beloved by all his men; and with the greatest confidence we followed him into battle willing to stand by him, obeying the commands of our young and noble Captain, satisfied that we were following an earnest patriot, and a fearless leader.

No Captain of our Regiment was more esteemed than was Captain Ridgway, and when the destroyer came and demanded his life; the Company lost an affectionate leader and an earnest friend.

We were greatly attached to our Captain and when we saw him defend so proudly our rights, sealing the defense with his blood, our attachment grew stronger than before, and his memory shall ever be cherished by us.

"Long live the name of Capt. Jos. R. Ridgway," and each member of Company G, says Amen.

Our sympathy for his bereaved parents and sisters is most heartfelt, and God forbid that any act or word of ours should add one single pang to their deep and just grief for his loss.

Andrew J Morgan	*Edwin Layton*
Wm H Garwood	*John W Boyle*
Richard S Adams	*Sergt Henry V Fenimore*
Sergt D W Clevenger	*Samuel R Stockton*
Benjamin F Stacey	*Corp Charles H Deacon*
Thomas F Cain	*Ezra Budd Stevenson*
Thaddeus W Lippincott	*Sergt Jno W Bright*
George S Vansciver	*George P Gillis*
Albert Seeds	*Jocob Severs*
Job Bell	*John W Letts*
George E Bridger	*James Allison*
John L Hubbs	*Charles P Lippincott*
William A Austin	*E S Parezo*
Amos B Deacon	*Sergt John S Ashton*

Charles T Southard	Mahion G Kesler
Ezra R Hewlings	Benj Frank Perkins
Spafford W Atkinson	Richard Horner
S Haines Bishop	Hezekiall Williamson
Jesse B Unsworth	John W Fenimore, Jr
Allen Hubbs	B H Vansciver
Thomas McHenry	William Dunn
William Hornby	Richard F Jordan
Joseph Zeiber	William S Powell
Franklin Adams	Corp E K Donaldson
Wallace Lloyd	James McMullen
Frederick Bechtel	William H McMullen
George W Southwick	Michael Davis
John W Anderson	B F Scott
Moses H Kiple	Lawrence A Bird
George Wilmerton	Watson Prickitt
John H Adams	Albert Vansciver
Charles E Warner	George W Vansciver
Paul Wilmerton	Sanford Murphy
Henry Collins	William Cheesman
Charles Gillis	William H Simpson

We, the undersigned, desire to add our testimony to the foregoing. Captain Jos. R Ridgway, was greatly esteemed by his brother officers, for the kindness and sociability which marked his character, and we were impressed with the apparent and we believe genuine good feeling which existed between the Captain and his Company. We regret that any such report as the above should gain credence, and we can but believe the author to be a base slanderer and the truth not in him.

William T Abbott, Chaplain, 23rd NJV
J P Barnett, Captain Company I
Henry C Risdon, Capt Co G
John F McKee, 1st Lieutenant Co G
R M Ekings, 1st Lieut Co I
E I Dobbins, 2nd Lieut. Co. I
Samuel Brown Jr, Lieut and Acting Adjutant
D G Hetzell, 1st Assistant Surgeon
Robert W Elmer, Assistant Surgeon
S E Branin, Lieut. Co R
F L Taylor, Lieut. Co H
S H Ashly 1st Lieut Co K

JAMES G. BUCK

A A Meseroll, Acting Lieut Co A
A F Smith, Acting Lieut Co D

I take pleasure in adding my testimony as to the falsity of the charge concerning Capt. Joseph R. Ridgway. I saw him on the battlefield, of the 13th of December, about five minutes before he fell. He was bravely rallying his Company. His last words were with sword, waving over his head, "Follow me, Company G!" as he went to the front of his Company and led them toward the enemy

W J Parmentier
Major 23rd Regiment NJV

It is a gratification to me to add my testimony to corroborate the statement of Major W J Parmentier. I was within four feet of Capt. Jos R Ridgeway when he fell. His face was towards the foe, and he in the very advance, - the wound being in his forehead, it could not possibly have come from any one, but the enemy. He was highly esteemed by us all, both officers and men.

E H Kirdbridge, Capt Co B

The Colonel and Lieut. Colonel in command the day of Capt J R Ridgway's death, and many of the line officers then in the Companies, are now absent, but all present promptly and gladly sign it.
Never was a more groundless falsehood circulated, and may shame and confusion follow its originator. He was known among us only to be loved, by both men and officers.

A H Nichols
Regimental Quartermaster

June 3, 1863 - Camp White Oak Church, Virginia

Grubb and the Sergeant Major, Scattergood, worked with the ambulance drivers who had gone to Salem Church. They pieced together what happened to some of their missing. Dennis Green from E Company was captured and was probably in a prison in Richmond. Of the seventeen enlisted men reported killed in action on the 9th, eight had straggled back into camp. Ed Lloyd was among them. Vann, Fox, Reed, Malsbury, Budden, Jones and Hullings were dead.

The Rebs found Henry Locke, Reading Havens, Reuben Goff and F Company's 1st Sergeant Smith severely wounded. Reb doctors took over Salem Church and used it for a hospital. Goff died there late on May 3rd followed by Locke on the 4th, Smith on the 9th, and Havens on the 10th.

Most of the thirty-one men reported missing made it back to the unit, but Cliver, Crispin and Atkinson were dead. Bakeley, Lannigan, Vansciver and Wright did not recover from their wounds. Doc said three more would probably die. Hankins and Haines were still unaccounted for. The regiment lost eighteen dead, fifty-eight wounded with two missing and one POW. The world didn't stop because the battle was lost. Disease claimed two men left at the division hospital while the regiment was away.

The men were proud of the way they behaved in the fight, but they, along with the rest of the Army of the Potomac, were in a foul mood. Once again they were mourning lost friends and relatives. Each had to deal with horrible memories of the battle. They were tired of losing, and felt their lives were being wasted by generals who didn't know how to win. Many were rankled by the announcement that their nine-month term of service started on September 13th instead of the day they joined their companies.

The regiment returned from three days on the picket line around noon. There were only ten days left in their enlistment. Everyone was sure they would be heading for Beverly any minute. So, the news that they were to draw and cook three days' rations and head back across the Rappahannock was greeted first with disbelief, and then outrage.

The Yahoos believed some General was about to pick a fight simply because he would lose a sizable portion of the army when the enlistments were up in a few days. They were not about to go out and risk their lives again when they had been handled so poorly in the past. Within an hour, tempers flared, and officers reported the men were nearly mutinous. They refused to get ready to march, and Grubb could no longer ignore the situation. He ordered the officers to assemble the men without arms. The very angry troops assembled in a hollow square.

Grubb entered the square and gazed around the companies. "I understand you have a problem with our orders." Muttering came from all around him.

"You men have earned a great reputation in the last nine months. You came into the brigade in October, a bunch of raw recruits who couldn't beat each other, let alone the Rebs. In two short months you trained well enough to give a respectable accounting of yourselves at Deep Run. I was there, I saw it. Together, you made it through the winter and did every job that was asked of you. You put up with disease. You stood guard and picket in the snow and rain. You hauled your guts out in the Mud March. Your behavior in the fight at Salem Church will go down in history as one of the finest actions a nine-month regiment ever fought."

Every man in the regiment was looking at the Colonel. He had their undivided attention.

"The 23rd has established itself as a solid fighting regiment. Many other regiments in this army have nowhere near that claim to fame. You earned it with your blood, and some of your friends paid for it with their lives. It is my duty to care for and keep that reputation untarnished."

He continued in a firm, even voice, "So, I ask you. How am I supposed to explain your behavior this afternoon to your sweethearts and wives, and the Sunday School Army who collected their pennies to buy your flag?" He paused, "What am I to tell the families of our comrades who died, or the men who were crippled by your side? What do I say to Joe Ridgway's family, or that Copperhead you H Company men wrote to back in Moorestown?"

Feet started to shuffle, and men started looking at each other out of the corners of their eyes.

"What am I supposed to say?" His voice rose in anger. "A hooting rabble was twice beaten by the Rebs, and the third time was afraid to meet them?"

That hurt their pride. Men frowned and looked at the ground in shame. Mumbling started in the ranks, and a few seconds later someone yelled, "We will go." Others started yelling, "We are not afraid." And still others were hollering, "Three cheers for Colonel Grubb."

In the middle of the hip-hip, Grubb shut them off. "Let's all get something straight. I did not come out here to be cheered and hurrahed. I am here to remind you of your duty to this regiment and this country, most importantly, your duty to each other, your solemn duty to watch out for and care for each other. You are bonded to each other more tightly than brothers."

"I have orders to prepare to meet the enemy. I am marching out to do that in the morning. If we get into a fight, I hope we can win a great victory that will remove the sour taste of defeat from our mouths forever, and bring new honor to this command."

"Tomorrow morning, the regiment, and those of you who refuse to obey orders, and are still alive... will march at daylight."

He turned and walked out of the square. It took several minutes for the officers and men to realize he wasn't coming back. The men were dismissed. They slowly made their way back to camp, drew their rations, and prepared to march.

June 10, 1863 - Fredericksburg, Virginia

The work on the enemy side of the Rappahannock was anticlimactic. The regiment approached the river on the 4th, and crossed the pontoon bridge on the night of the 5th. They formed a line of battle on the plateau west of Marye's Heights while sappers and engineers built a solid line of breast works behind them.

The Rebs opened fire on them as soon as daylight made them visible, but the fire had no effect.

Soon, the new works were strengthened with sand-bagged gun positions for several very big guns. Yahoo attitudes were markedly more relaxed after the Grubb speech. It marked a turning point in the men's relationship to the Army. Before, they considered themselves individuals just passing through the Army experience. After, they realized the Army experience was part of who they would be for the rest of their lives.

The long-awaited journey home started at 7 AM. They laughed and cheered as they crossed the pontoon bridge for the last time. They marched directly to Falmouth Station and caught the 10:30 train to Aquia Creek.* By 2:30 PM, they were on the mail boat to Washington.

June 11th, 1863 - Cooper Shop Refreshment Saloon, Otsego Street, Philadelphia

It took a while, but the regiment got on a train out of Washington. The train chugged past Forts Lincoln, Saratoga and Bunker Hill. It crossed over the white-washed bridges they had passed eight months before. It stopped at the broad Susquehanna, and the boys crossed it on the ferry Maryland. Then they boarded another train and traveled all night through Maryland, Delaware and Pennsylvania. They finally got to the Philadelphia, Wilmington and Baltimore Railroad Station at the corner of Broad and Washington Street just after dawn.

*Elmer Diary and Baquet pg 278 say Aquia Creek. Foster, pg. 512, says Belle Plaines Landing, Foster.

As if drawn by a magnet, they formed up and marched back to the Cooper Shop Refreshment Saloon. Coffee and breakfast was waiting. The veterans were much more subdued than they had been on their first visit. More then a hundred ghosts left along the march hovered over their meal. Sharp and Terhune celebrated their return, but in the back of their minds was a deep, unspoken sadness. Memories of Josie and Lloyd teasing them about this place weighed heavy.

The 23rd was escorted onto the steamers by the 25th N. J. Infantry Band. Large numbers of friends came to ride with them on the last leg of their journey home. They set sail on the steamboat up the Delaware to the Beverly Wharf. The boats arrived at 6 PM, and the Yahoos marched up Broad Street through a cheering crowd to Camp Cadwalader. The men living closest to camp received furloughs and went home. Bob Elmer hitched a ride to Bridgeton to meet his new daughter. Forrester Taylor went home to meet Sallee and his new son.

June 17, 1863 - Camp Cadwalader, Beverly, N.J.

June 13th came and went without mustering out. The men did not seem overly upset about it, as long as they could go home on furlough. Grubb took the train to Trenton to talk with Governor Parker, to see if the process could be sped up.

He met with the Governor and General Stockton. They agreed to take immediate steps to close out the enlistments. General Stockton invited Grubb to his home for lunch. They were having a pleasant meal with the general's family when an orderly came rushing to the house with a telegram.

Stockton opened the telegram and read it. "Oh, good God, Grubb.

Lee has invaded Pennsylvania again and is moving on Harrisburg. Governor Curtin is asking us to send every man we've got. Will your men go?"

"Yes, sir," answered Grubb. He hoped he was right.

The officers excused themselves and rushed to the capitol to find Governor Parker. While Parker was reading the telegram, Stockton commandeered a locomotive and telegraphed Beverly to round up the troops. He came in just as Parker asked Grubb if his men would go. Again, Grubb answered yes. It wasn't until he was on the train headed south that it dawned on him what an awesome responsibility he had taken upon himself.*

*Grubb's account of the events of the afternoon can be found in Baquet, pg 278.

An hour later, Governor Parker, followed by General Stockton and Grubb, hurried onto the parade ground to find the 23rd and two other nine-month regiments formed up and waiting. Grubb rushed to the front of his regiment.

Parker removed his hat and started pacing in a small area in front of the men. He made an impassioned speech, thanking them for their service, and praising them for their sacrifice. He told them that neither the country nor the state had any claim on them, but the capital of Pennsylvania was in danger of a Rebel invasion. He read Governor Curtain's telegram and pleaded with them to go to the aid of their sister state.

He concluded his remarks by saying, "Now, every man who will go to Harrisburg, take three steps forward. The entire 23rd took three steps. Not a man in the other two units moved a muscle.

Grubb looked at Sergeant Major Scattergood. Scattergood winked. Grubb grinned, "Well, I'll be damned. Had to almost shoot them to get them to stay two weeks ago, and now we can't make them go away."

Scattergood grinned back. "The honor of the regiment is at stake. The regiment's honor is their honor. You made them understand. You made them grow up, Sir."

Grubb led his troops off the steamer at Philadelphia's Washington Street Wharf late in the evening. He thought they were the first regiment to move toward Harrisburg, but soon heard different.

The 7th New York was ahead of them and celebrating at the Cooper Shop Refreshment Saloon. There is only 77 of them.*

Burd wanted his men to get credit for being the first regiment to Harrisburg. The regiment formed and marched up Chestnut Street to get ahead of the New Yorkers. The race was on. Since they were first to the station, they would be first to embark. They spent the night at the Odd Fellows Hall in West Philadelphia. The New Yorkers were angry, but none of the Yahoos cared.

June 18th, 1863 – Harrisburg, Pennsylvania
The 23rd arrived in Harrisburg around 3 PM on a train of coal cars, and they were the first organized regiment to arrive. They had their

*Recorded in the **History of the Cooper Shop Volunteer Refreshment Saloon**.

knapsacks, the worthless 1842 converted Springfields, and a mere twenty rounds of old round ball ammunition per man. There were 369 men present. Kirkbride caught up with them with another twenty-five who wandered into Beverly from furlough. A militia company from Mount Holly named the American Blues, under Captain Laumaster, joined them.

Grubb reported to General Darius Couch. Couch directed the regiment to build earthworks at Harris Park to defend a ford across the Susquehanna River. Every single man pitched in to build the position, including Grubb. A fence masked the work from the river, so there would be an element of surprise when the Rebs came. The walls of all of the houses in the neighborhood were loopholed, so they could be used as forts. Couch remembered his lessons from Fredericksburg. There would be plenty of dug-in sharpshooters defending the ford.

However, it appeared the Rebs weren't coming right away.

That afternoon, General Stockton was at his desk when a messenger brought a sealed letter from Grubb. He opened it, and read:

Sir:
I leave in a few minutes for Harrisburg. The transportation was delayed last evening until 8 o'clock and the New York 7th passed me. But, while they were in the Cooper Saloon, I marched up Chestnut Street and Jersey has the credit for being ahead. My men have only volunteered to go to Harrisburg <u>and I am pledged to bring them back by the end of the week</u>. It was the only <u>way that I got them to go at all</u>. Allow me to request that you interest yourself in this matter for the credit of the state. It will not do to force the men. If attempted, a disgraceful scene will certainly result, and considering the peculiar circumstances under which the men have gone, and that the crisis in Pennsylvania has ceased to exist, I think there will be no need for their services longer than Friday night. The credit of the state is saved. The regiment has the éclat of being <u>first</u>. Why ruin all. If an attempt is made to coerce them a mutiny is the sure result.

Very respectfully,
E. Burd Grubb
Col. 23rd N.J.V.

Stockton thought for a moment. Under normal circumstances, a letter like this would bring the wrath of God upon the commander who wrote it. But, these weren't normal circumstances. Grubb was right, the emergency was over. The Yahoos had only been paid twice during their nine-month enlistment. They had never been given the equipment they needed to go into winter quarters, and still, the men had volunteered to go *after* their enlistments expired. Since there was no impending battle, it was only right they should come home as soon as practical. He wired Couch to cut them loose as soon as he could.

June 20th, 1863 – Harrisburg, Pennsylvania

The regiment spent two days finishing the earthwork at Harris Park. It was hard work, but once the men knew they weren't going into battle, they relaxed. They were with their friends, getting paid and nearly out of the Army. They spent their off-duty hours harassing Copperheads, and Harrisburg had a lot of them. There were so many that Grubb and the officers had to step in to keep some overzealous Yahoos from harming them.

The regimental band serenaded Generals Couch and Milroy. The Generals responded with glowing words for the Jerseymen who were first to come to the defense of Harrisburg. In the end, General Couch put the Yahoos on a train for Philadelphia at 4 on Saturday afternoon. They arrived late in the evening and boarded the steamer Burlington for the Beverly Wharf.

June 27, 1863 – Camp Cadwalader, Beverly, N. J.

The regiment had spent a week preparing to muster out. This involved cleaning equipment and turning it in to the quartermaster. It also meant filling out paperwork to account for missing and worn-out items. Every piece of equipment had to be accounted for before the Quartermaster could receive his discharge. Sometimes, this involved convening a board of officers to examine equipment, and certify it was worn out. Equipment lost in battle or in circumstances that were beyond a soldier's control could be written off with a sworn affidavit. The cost of equipment lost through the fault of a soldier was deducted from his final pay. A lot of affidavits were written.

Each company checked and rechecked its muster roles and service records. All of the company records, morning reports and order books had to be examined and signed for before the officers were permitted to leave the army.

When all was ready, Major Newton of the 2nd U.S. Cavalry arrived to pay them and muster them out. It took all day on June 27, 1863.

299

When all was completed, the books were piled on the Camp Cadwalader parade ground. Unfortunately, no one was detailed to guard them. Books were a valuable commodity. Most of them disappeared before the end of the day. Along with them went the detailed records of the regiment.

The Yahoos moved on with their lives. Over the years, they came to understand the value of the service they had given the United States. They missed the company of those with whom they had endured so many trials and tribulations. Eventually, they formed the Reunion Society of the 23rd New Jersey Volunteers. They raised a beautiful monument at Salem Church to commemorate the battle, and in time, befriended the brave Alabama boys who had been their foe. They held numerous reunions and wrote the *History of the 23rd New Jersey Reunion Society*, but they were never able to reconstruct the story they lost on their last day in the Army, when their books disappeared.

Epilogue

One week after the Yahoos mustered out, July 2, around 5:30 in the afternoon, Lieutenant Rufus C. Jones and the 9th Alabama were fighting near a little Pennsylvania town named Gettysburg. They were attacking a place called Cemetery Ridge with Wilcox's Brigade and Longstreet's Corp. They were near the top of the ridge when the Union counterattack came. The 1ST Minnesota surrounded a good part of the Alabama unit and captured a lot of men, including Jones and most of its officers.

Over the next few days, Jones and the Confederate officers were moved by train and the steamship *Susquehanna* to the POW camp at Fort Delaware, south of Wilmington. On July 18th, he and a number of Alabama officers were moved to Johnson's Island Prisoner of War Camp at Sandusky, Ohio. They traveled by train to Philadelphia and then through Harrisburg on to Ohio. They arrived at Sandusky near dusk on the 20th, and were taken to the prison within an hour.

Mary Crispin wrote Jones a letter on October 1st. Somehow, it traveled through the Union and Confederate lines to what was left of the 9th Alabama. Someone forwarded her letter to Jones at Johnson's Island. He received it on October 13th.

He wrote to Mary the same day.

October 13, 1863—Johnson's Island

I received your letter of the first and hasten to give you all the information in my power concerning your brother, J.B. Crispin. On Sunday the 3rd of last May the battle of Salem Church was fought. After the battle was over I was passing over the ground which was held a few minutes before by the Union forces, when my attention was attracted by a groan from a man I had thought was dead. I went to him and turned him over (he was lying on his face) and found he was still alive. I drew my flask from my pocket and I poured some of the contents down his throat. When he soon revived and asked me in a weak voice if I was going to kill him. I spoke to him kindly and asked him if I could do anything more for him by opening his coat. I saw that he was mortally wounded and would soon die as a Minie ball had pierced his left breast, just below the nipple, in the region of the heart. As soon as he came to himself and saw that I was not going to hurt him, he asked me to move him in the shade (as the sun was shining and very warm where he fell) which I did. I spread down a blanket and fixed his knapsack under his head, so as to give him temporary ease from his pain. I filled his canteen with water from my own and started to leave him for the purpose of sending our ambulance corps to have him sent up to our hospital. When he called me back and looking up in my face remarked that this war was a cruel, cruel, thing. I saw that he was sinking very fast and I raised his head upon my knee and gave him a strong drink of brandy and water. He thanked me very kindly and with tears coursing down his bloody cheek exclaimed, "My dear sister, Mary, I will never see you again and you will wait in vain for my return. Oh my god! Why did I leave my happy home? I know that death has laid his heavy hands upon me, but I am thankful that I am not afraid to go." He then put his hand into his breast pocket and took out his diary handing it to me saying, "Take this, my kind friend, and read it if you choose. It is the idle thought of a poor soldier while far away from those he loved and then send it to my sister Mary. You will find her address on the inside of this poor diary of mine. Give me your hand. And may God bless you for the kindness you have shown to an enemy. My sweet sister Mary." He fell back as the last words fell from his lips and expired. I raised his head, but his soul had taken its flight from this battlefield to where all is peace and the clash of arms are never heard. I have passed through much and witnessed many sad scenes, but none have left such an impression upon my memory as the death of this brave soldier. I had him buried with several others in the immediate vicinity of the stately old church, Salem Church (whose name will grace the pages of our country's history for future generations to come). A small and rude pen of rails marks his last resting place. If in recalling his last words to my memory I have caused you pain, I hope you will excuse me for I assure you it was not my intention. When I am exchanged (which God grant may not be far off as I am in rather a forlorn condition, not having relatives or friends North to whom I might apply to for assistance in time of need) I will return to my regiment near Fredericksburg and anything I can do for you, to his grave, or body, will cheerfully be done. Please to let me know when you receive this. Hoping you may find comfort and consolation for the loss of your brother.

From him who never turned his back on those who seek Him, I remain

Very Respectfully your observant servant,

Rufus C Jones, 1st Lieutenant
Company H, 9th Alabama Regiment
Wilcox Brigade, Longstreet's Corps
Army, Northern Virginia

History does not tell us if Mary ever contacted Jones again. She certainly was unable to arrange a parole. By the end of 1864, Jones had had his fill of prison life. On January 5 at 9 A.M., Jones, dressed as a Union private, followed the Union guards out the prison gate after morning roll call. The guards did not spot him.

Johnson Island is a fairly big island, so a man dressed as a Union soldier near a Union army post in a Union state would not draw much attention. At some point, Jones discarded his Union uniform, which he had worn over civilian clothes, and blended in with the population.

It had been bitterly cold for several weeks prior to the escape, so Jones walked 3 miles across frozen Lake Erie to the main land and headed south. His absence was not noticed until late in the afternoon when roll call was completed. That was about 4 PM. By that time, he had at least a six-hour head start, and it was almost dark. Colonel Charles Hill, the Johnson Island Camp Commander, was furious. He immediately offered a $100 reward for Jones' apprehension, and placed a certain Lieutenant Smith in close confinement for impersonating another prisoner during roll call.

Rufus avoided capture. Confederate muster rolls show that he was back in Dixie possibly as early as February 10th. A muster slip from Sanders' Old Brigade, Mahone's Division of the 3rd Corps, Army of Northern Virginia of that date shows he had been promoted to Captain during his captivity. It also claims he was from Harney's unit.

On March 11, the register of Receiving and Wayside Hospital Number 9 in Richmond shows he was moved to Stuart Hospital.

The records of Stuart Hospital show he was admitted with a diagnosis of debilitis. Debilitis is defined as an abnormal weakness of the body. Under normal circumstances, Jones would not be considered a well man. He had just survived 17 months in a prison camp with poor food, close quarters and plenty of exposure to contagious diseases.

Previously, in 1862, he was diagnosed with syphilis, which was sweeping through the south. Colonel Hill, upon his escape from Johnson Island, described him as having a scrofulous sore on his neck. The term scrofulous is generally applied to a form of tuberculosis. It is possible the sore could have been a syphilitic infection of a lymph node, but it is also possible he suffered from both afflictions

The war was coming to a close at that time, and no one really knew how the reconstruction would be handled. Jones' status as an escaped prisoner would play against him if he were captured again. It is unknown if Jones tried to return to 9th Alabama or simply went home to Limestone County, Alabama. Stuart hospital records say he deserted on March 15th.

The 1870 census shows a Rufus C. Jones living in Limestone County. He was married and his wife had two children.

William "Bully" Brooks, the 1st Division Commander, never did catch Cadmus Wilcox. Bully went on to command the 1st Division, XVIII Corps at Cold Harbor and Petersburg. He resigned due to poor health in 1864, and died in 1870 on his farm near Huntsville, Alabama.

Burd Grubb, the 23rd's last Colonel, returned to Burlington and worked in his family's foundry business. He returned to the army in 1864 to command the 37th New Jersey Volunteers. He was promoted to Brigadier General in 1865. Many Yahoo reunions were held at his home on the Delaware River, until his death in 1913.

Chaplain Frank Hall, the man who used his horse to rescue wounded soldiers of the 16th NY at Salem Church, was awarded the Congressional Medal of Honor for his heroism. His letters to his wife provide wonderful reading and can be found at http://www.kellscraft.com/civilwarcontent.html.

Herman Haupt, the railroad genius, played an important role in upgrading a decrepit spur line to Gettysburg, Pennsylvania, during the battle. His efforts supplied the army, and greatly aided in the evacuation of the wounded. After the war, he invented drilling equipment and proved oil could be transported in pipelines. He lost most of his fortune trying to complete the Hoosac railroad tunnel in New England.

Jonathan Letterman, Medical Director of the Army of the Potomac, continued his efforts to improve battlefield medicine. His

304

system of ambulances and forward field hospitals was so successful, it was officially established by Act of Congress in March of 1864. The Letterman Army Hospital at the Presidio of San Francisco is named after him.

Professor Thaddeus Lowe, the aeronaut, moved to California after the army abandoned his observation balloons. He invented and patented a process for making hydrogen gas from coal and steam, along with several patents for making ice. He made a fortune, but lost it in an attempt to build the Pasedena and Mount Wilson Railroad. Mount Lowe is named after him.

Marion Montieth, the owner of the farm occupied by Camp White Oak Church, filed a claim for $2,025 for the value of his lost fences, timber and horse. His sister, Jenny married a Union soldier named Willoughby. Willoughby died before the end of the war. It is believed the claim was paid because of this family tie to the North. The Montieth farmhouse that was Torbert's headquarters is much changed, but still stands on Caisson Road.

Gabe Paul, the General who served the court martial papers to Colonel Cox, was severely wounded at the Battle of Gettysburg. A musket ball struck him in the right temple and exited through his left eye. Mistaken for dead, he survived many hours without care before being found by a grave-digging detail. He was blinded and suffered brain damage that led to severe headaches and epilepsy. Congress awarded him permanent pay and allowances of a Brigadier General in 1870. He survived in poor health until 1886.

Henry Ogden Ryerson was wounded in the head by a sharpshooter while leading his 10th New Jersey in battle near Wilderness Tavern on May 6, 1864. The Rebels found him unconscious and took him to a hospital at Locust Grove, Virginia. He died there on May 12th without regaining consciousness. His body was recovered after the war, and is buried in New Jersey.

John Sedgwick, the VI Corps Commander, was shot and killed by a sniper near Spotsylvania Court House on May 9, 1864. Sedgwick was revered by his men. They had a statue of him cast from the VI Corps cannons and placed on the northwest corner of the parade ground at West Point. It is said that cadets in full dress uniform who spin the statue's spurs at midnight will pass their exams.

Forrestor L. Taylor, Crispin's company commander, was awarded the Congressional Medal of Honor for rescuing Wilson and Wainwright during the Battle of Salem Church. He re-entered the army in the fall of 1863 and commanded H Company, 34th New Jersey

Volunteers. Lieutenant Wilson never said thank you for the rescue. Wainwright did.

Alfred Torbert, commander of the New Jersey Brigade, left the brigade late in 1863 to command a Cavalry Division. He left the Army after the war as a Major General and entered the diplomatic service. His political enemies continued to hound him, and eventually pressured the government to remove him from his consular position. He drowned when the *City of Vera Cruz* sank in a hurricane off Cape Canaveral in 1880.

Cadmus Wilcox, the Confederate Brigadier General at Salem Church, watched the decimation of his Alabama Brigade at Gettysburg. He was promoted to Major General, became a division commander and saw heavy fighting from Spotsylvania to Appomatox. He went to Mexico after the war. Eventually, he grew homesick and crossed the border at El Paso. The first person he met upon his return was Brooks' former aide, Daniel Wheeler. Wheeler welcomed him home and the account of their meeting is on page 251 of Baquet's History of the 1st New Jersey Brigade.

Lieutenant Daniel Wheeler, General Brook's aide, received the Medal of Honor for his heroism at Salem Church. He stayed in the Army and was stationed in El Paso, Texas, after the war. One day he was approached by a poor man who said he was "the last of the ditchers" and wanted to come home. Ditchers were Confederate soldiers who fled to Mexico after the war. The man was Cadmus Wilcox. They became friends and spent long hours reliving their experiences. Wheeler retired from the army as a Brigadier General.

Lieutenant Edward Williston, whose double shots of canister figured so prominently in repelling the Confederate counter-attack at Salem Church, found himself in a similar situation a year later at Trevilian Station. Once again, his battery used double shots of canister to repel a Rebel attack. He was awarded the Medal of Honor for his actions and went on to become a brevet brigadier general.

Private Josiah Crispin was buried by Rufus Jones at Salem Church, but his grave has never been identified. Over the years, the U. S. government disinterred the bodies of as many soldiers as it could find from the various camp cemeteries and the Fredericksburg and Salem Church battlefields. They were reburied at the Fredericksburg National Cemetery on Marye's Hill. Josie could still be at Salem Church, or he may be among the 12,000 buried at the National Cemetery whose names are known only to God.

Bibliography

Alexander, Edward Porter. Military Memoirs of a Confederate. New York: Scribner's Sons, 1907.

Ambrose, Kevin. (Henry, Dan & Weiss, Andy) Washington Weather: The Weather Sourcebook for the D.C. Area. Fairfax, VA: Historical Enterprises, 2002.

Anderson, R. Instructions for Field Artillery. New York: D. Van Nostrand, 1864. Reprint copyright Bracken, John M. New Market, VA: New Market Battlefield Military Museum. 1994.

Baquet, Camille. History of the First Brigade New Jersey Volunteers.: McCrelish and Quigley, 1910.

Barrett, John G. Yankee Rebel, The Civil War Journals of Edmund DeWitt Patterson. Knoxville, TN: The University of Tennessee Press, 2004.

Baxter, D.W. The Volunteer's Manual. Philadelphia, PA: King and Baird, 1861. Reprint copyright Morgantown, PA: Sullivan Press, 1996.

Bilby, Joseph G. Three Rousing Cheers – History of the 15th New Jersey from Flemington to Appomatox. Hightstown, NJ: Longstreet House, 2001.

Bilby, Joseph G. & Coble, William "Remember You are Jerseymen". Hightstown, NJ: Longstreet House, 1998.

Beyer, W. F. and O. F. Keydel, ed. Deeds of Valor: How America's Civil War Heroes Won the Congressional Medal of Honor. Reprint. Longmeadow, 1994.

Carter, John C. Welcome the Hour of Conflict, William Cowan McClellan and the 9th Alabama. Tuscaloosa, AL: The University of Alabama Press, 2007.

Casey, ____. Infantry Tactics.: Van Nostrand, 1862.

Chadwick, Henry. Beadle's Dime Baseball Player. New York: Irwin P. Beadle & Company, 1860. Reprint copyright Morgantown, PA: Sullivan Press, 1996.

Crowell, Joseph E. The Young Volunteer.: Dillingham , 1906.

Debelius, Maggie. Echoes of Glory – Civil War Battle Atlas. Alexandria, VA: Time Life-Books, 1996.

Drury, Ian & Gibbons, Tony. The Civil War Military Machine, Weapons and Tactics of the Union and Confederate Forces. New York: Smithmark Publishers, 1993.

Esposito, Vincent. The West Point Atlas of American Wars. 2 Vols. New York:Frederick A Praeger,1959.

Foster, John Young. New Jersey and the Rebellion. Newark: Dennis & Co., 1868.

Freeman, Douglas Southall. Lee's Lieutenants. 3 vols. New York: Charles Scibner's Sons, 1942-1944.

Gabel, Dr. Christopher R. Railroad Generalship: Foundations of Civil War Strategy. Leavenworth, KS: Command and General Staff College, 1997.

Glazier, Willard. Three Years in the Federal Cavalry. New York: R. H. Ferguson & Company, 1874.

Goodwin, Doris Kearns. Team of Rivals. New York: Simon and Schuster, 2005.

Hall, Fanny and Frank. Spared to Each Other: The Civil War Correspondence of Fanny and Frank Hall. Plattsburgh, NY: The Kent-Delord House Museum. 2001. Found at http://www.kellscraft.com/civilwarcontent.html.

Henderson, George F. R. The Campaign of Fredericksburg. London: Gale and Polden, 1891.

History of the Reunion Society of the 23rd New Jersey Volunteers. Philadelphia, PA: Keystone Printing Company, 1890.

History of the 118th Pennsylvania Volunteers (Corn Exchange Regiment). Philadelphia, PA: J.L. Smith, 1888.

History of the 121st Regiment Pennsylvania Volunteers. Philadelphia, PA: Burke and McFetridge, 1893.

Hungerford,. The Story of the B&O Railroad. New York: G. P. Putnam, 1928.

Kirkland, Frazier. The Pictorial Book of Anecdotes and Incidents of the War of the Rebellion. Hartford, CN: Hartford Publishing Company, 1866.

Lanier, Robert S. The Photographic History of the Civil War. 10 vols. New York: The Review of Reviews Company, 1912.

Le Grande, Louis. The Military Handbook and Soldiers Manual of Information. New York: Beadle and Company, 1861. Reprint copyright Topeka, KA: Kansas State Historical Society, 1996.

Miller, Alice E. <u>Cecil County Maryland - A Study in Local History</u>. Elkton, MD: C. & L. Printing and Specialty Company, 1949.

Mitchell, Joseph B. <u>The Badge of Gallantry: Recollections of Civil War Congressional Medal of Honor Winners</u>. New York: McMillan, 1968.

Moore, James. <u>History of the Cooper Shop Volunteer Refreshment Saloon</u>. Philadelphia, PA: James B Rodgers, 1866.

Morton, Joseph W. <u>Sparks from the Campfire or Tales of the Old Veterans</u>. Philadelphia, PA: Keystone Publishing Company, 1892.

Olsen, Judith Lamb. <u>Pemberton, An Historic Look At a Village on the Rancocas</u>. New Orleans: Polyanthos, 1976.

O'Reilly, Francis A. <u>The Fredericksburg Campaign – Winter War on the Rappahannock</u>. Baton Rouge: LA State University Press, 2003.

Schermerhorn, Edward. <u>History of Burlington New Jersey.   </u>: Enterprise, 1927.

Slade, A. D. <u>A. T. A. Torbert: Southern Gentleman in Union Blue</u>. Dayton, OH: Morningside House, Inc. 1992.

Stackpole Edward J. <u>Chancellorsville, Lee's Greatest Battle</u>. Harrisburg, PA: The Stackpole Company, 1958.

Stryker, William S. <u>Record of Officer and Men of New Jersey in the Civil War, 1861 – 1865</u>. Trenton: Adjutant General of the State of New Jersey, 1876.

Swinton, William. <u>Campaigns of the Army of the Potomac</u>. New York, Charles B. Richardson, 1866.

Taylor, Frank H. <u>Philadelphia in the Civil War.</u> Philadelphia, PA: Published by the City, 1913.

U.S. War Department, <u>A System of Target Practice for the Use of Troops when Armed with Musket, Riffle-musket, Rifle, or Carbine</u>. Washington, D.C.: U.S. Government Printing Office, 1862. Reprint copyright Morgantown, PA: Sullivan Press, 1999.

U.S. War Department, <u>Rules for the Management and Cleaning of the Rifle Musket, Model 1861</u>. Washington, D.C.: U.S. Government Printing Office, 1862. Reprint copyright Morgantown, PA: Sullivan Press, 2002.

U.S. War Department, <u>The War of the Rebellion: A Compilation of the Official Records of the Union and Confederate Armies</u>, 128 Vols. Washington, D.C.: U.S. Government Printing Office, 1880-1901.

Wilbur, C. Keith. <u>Civil War Medicine 1861 – 1865</u>. Guilford, CN: The Glode Pequot Press, 1998.

JAMES G. BUCK

Magazine Article Sources
Hoober, Richard T. Volunteer Refreshment Saloons, Numismatist, Vol.
  81, No. 2, February, 1968.
Horstman, James A. The Brief But Legendary Career of Confederate
  Colonel John Pehlam. Military History, March, 2007.
Ward, David A. Of Battlefields and Bitter Feuds (6th Pennsylvania
  Volunteer Infantry). Civil War Regiments, Volume 3, Number 3,
  1993. found at http://www.geocities.com/g96thpvi/cof.html.

Interviews
Newton, D.P. Personal Interview with Owner/Curator of the Camp
  White Oak Church Museum, June 22, 23 &24, 2007.
Newton, D.P. Personal Interview with Owner/Curator of the Camp
  White Oak Church Museum, January 5, 2008.

Maps
Sketch of the battles of Chancellorsville, Salem Church and
  Fredericksburg, May 2, 3 and 4 1863 / prepared by order of
  General R. E. Lee, by Jed. Hotchkiss, Topogl. Engr., 2d Corps, A.
  N. V., Library of Congress.
Upper Potomac from McCoy's Ferry to Conrad's Ferry and adjacent
  portions of Maryland and Virginia, Library of Congress.
New map of the seat of the war in Virginia and Maryland Drawn by J.
  G. Bruff. Lit of Lang and Cooper, New York, Library of
  Congress.
New railway guide containing all rail roads in Pennsylvania & N.
  Jersey with portions of New York, Ohio, Maryland and Virginia,
  Library of Congress.

Newspaper Sources
Magruder, Ted. Typhus, Typhoid Fever Were Deadly to Soldiers.
  Fredericksburg, VA: Free Lance Star, 9/30/2006. Found at
  http://www.fredericksburg.com/News/FLS/2006/092006/0930200
  6/225093.
Hunterdon Republican
NJ Mirror
NJ Dollar Newspaper
Southern Watchman

Personal Letters, Diaries Papers and Military Records
Carter, James 1Lt, Military Personnel Record
Cook, William Surgeon, Military Personnel Record

310

Cox, John Colonel, Military personnel Record
Crispin, Josiah, Diary
Crispin, Josiah, Military Personnel Records
Elmer, Robert, Diary
Falkenburgh, Hays Military Personnel Record
Grubb, E. Burd Letters and Papers
Jones, Rufus C, Letter
Jones, Rufus C, Military Personnel Records
Mount E. F, Letters
Ryerson, Henry Ogden, letters
Sharp, George, Letter
Taylor, Forrester L, Military Personnel Records

Websites
Anderson, Ken. Hardtack. Found at www.kenanderson.net/hardtack/.
Civil War Generals from West Point. Found at
    http://sunsite.utk.edu/civil-war/wpclasses.html. (List has been
    based on several works: Ezra Warner's Generals in Gray and
    Generals in Blue, Francis Heitman's Historical Register and
    Dictionary of the U.S. Army and John and David Eicher's Civil
    War High Commands.)
Civil War Interactive. Plasters, Poultices and Paregoric: The Civil War
    Medicinal Cookbook. (Cough syrup recipe) Found at
    http://www.civilwarinteractive.com/PoulticePlasterParegoric.htm.
Cohen, Robert. History of the Long Railroad Bridge Crossing Across
    the Potomac River. Copyright 2003. Found at
    http://www.dcnrhs.org/dc_rail_history_long_bridge.htm.
Cronkite, J. W. A Brief Historical Sketch of the 121st Volunteer
    Infantry as written in The Report of the Gettysburg Monument
    Committee of the 121st New York Volunteers. Found at
    http://www.rootsweb.com/~nyotsego/hist121.htm.
Definition of Civil War Terms. Found at
    www.civilwarhome.com/terms.htm Source: "Historical Times
    Illustrated Encyclopedia of the Civil War" edited by Patricia L.
    Faust and "The Civil War Dictionary" by Mark M. Boatner III.
National Park Service. Washington Defenses (Or search Washington
    Forts) Found at http://www.nps.gov/archive/rocr/ftcircle/.
Niepert, Robert. Civil War Pontoon Bridges. Found at
    http://floridareenactorsonline.com/pontoon.htm.
Stanage, Justin A. Use and Manufacture of Field Artillery in the
    Confederacy. Found at www.iusb.edu/~journal/2001/stanage.html
www.civilwarhome.com/ambulancecorps.htm

JAMES G. BUCK

www.civilwarhome.com/ambulanceor.htm
www.civilwarhome.com/ambulancewagons.htm
www.civilwarhome.com/civilwarmedicine.htm
www.civilwarhome.com/civilwarmedicineintro.htm
www.civilwarhome.com/civilwarmedicinehistory.htm
www.civilwarhome.com/sicktransportation.htm
www.civilwarweek.com

Printed in the United States
129913LV00005BA/9/P

9 781602 642102